LUKE

NCCS | New Covenant Commentary Series

The New Covenant Commentary Series (NCCS) is designed for ministers and students who require a commentary that interacts with the text and context of each New Testament book and pays specific attention to the impact of the text upon the faith and praxis of contemporary faith communities.

The NCCS has a number of distinguishing features. First, the contributors come from a diverse array of backgrounds in regards to their Christian denominations and countries of origin. Unlike many commentary series that tout themselves as international the NCCS can truly boast of a genuinely international cast of contributors with authors drawn from every continent of the world (except Antarctica) including countries such as the United States, Puerto Rico, Australia, the United Kingdom, Kenya, India, Singapore, and Korea. We intend the NCCS to engage in the task of biblical interpretation and theological reflection from the perspective of the global church. Second, the volumes in this series are not verse-by-verse commentaries, but they focus on larger units of text in order to explicate and interpret the story in the text as opposed to some often atomistic approaches. Third, a further aim of these volumes is to provide an occasion for authors to reflect on how the New Testament impacts the life, faith, ministry, and witness of the New Covenant Community today. This occurs periodically under the heading of "Fusing the Horizons and Forming the Community." Here authors provide windows into community formation (how the text shapes the mission and character of the believing community) and ministerial formation (how the text shapes the ministry of Christian leaders).

It is our hope that these volumes will represent serious engagements with the New Testament writings, done in the context of faith, in service of the church, and for the glorification of God.

Series Editors:
Michael F. Bird (Ridley College, Melbourne, Australia)
Craig Keener (Asbury Theological Seminary, Wilmore, KY, USA)

Titles in this series:
Romans Craig Keener
Ephesians Lynn Cohick
Colossians and Philemon Michael F. Bird
Revelation Gordon Fee
John Jey Kanagaraj
1 Timothy Aída Besançon Spencer
2 Timothy and Titus Aída Besançon Spencer
Mark Kim Huat Tan
2 Peter and Jude Andrew Mbuvi
Luke Diane Chen

Forthcoming titles:
James Pablo Jimenez
1–3 John Sam Ngewa
Acts Youngmo Cho and Hyung Dae Park
Matthew Jason Hood
1 Peter Eric Greaux
Philippians Linda Belleville
Hebrews Cynthia Westfall
Galatians Brian Vickers
1 Corinthians B. J. Oropeza
2 Corinthians David deSilva

LUKE
A New Covenant Commentary

Diane G. Chen

CASCADE *Books* • Eugene, Oregon

LUKE
A New Covenant Commentary

New Covenant Commentary Series

Copyright © 2017 Diane G. Chen. All rights reserved. Except for brief quotations in critical publications or reviews, no part of this book may be reproduced in any manner without prior written permission from the publisher. Write: Permissions, Wipf and Stock Publishers, 199 W. 8th Ave., Suite 3, Eugene, OR 97401.

Cascade Books
An Imprint of Wipf and Stock Publishers
199 W. 8th Ave., Suite 3
Eugene, OR 97401

www.wipfandstock.com

paperback ISBN: 978-1-62032-439-4
hardcover ISBN: 978-1-4982-4605-7
ebook ISBN: 978-1-4982-4604-0

Cataloguing-in-Publication data:

Names: Chen, Diane G.

Title: Luke : a new covenant commentary / Diane G. Chen.

Description: Eugene, OR: Cascade Books, 2017 | Series: New Covenant Commentary Series | Includes bibliographical references and index.

Identifiers: ISBN 978-1-62032-439-4 (paperback) | ISBN 978-1-4982-4605-7 (hardcover) | ISBN 978-1-4982-4604-0 (ebook)

Subjects: LCSH: 1. Bible. Luke—Commentaries. | I. Title. | II. Series.

Classification: BS2595.53 C4 2017 (print) | BS2595.53 (ebook)

Manufactured in the U.S.A.   01/02/18

To my three sisters:
Agnes, Lucy, and Irene

Contents

Outline of Luke ix
Acknowledgments xv
Abbreviations xvi

Introduction   1

Luke 1   12

Luke 2   30
  Excursus: Quirinius's Census   31

Luke 3   47

Luke 4   57

Luke 5   68
  Fusing the Horizons: Human Effort versus Divine Help   70

Luke 6   81

Luke 7   92

Luke 8   108
  Fusing the Horizons: Faith, the Antidote to Fear   121

Luke 9   123
  Fusing the Horizons: Radical Discipleship   143

Luke 10   145

Luke 11   159

Luke 12   176
  Fusing the Horizons: Wealth and Security   184

Luke 13   190

Luke 14   201
  Fusing the Horizons: Honoring the Sabbath   203

Luke 15   213

Luke 16   221

Luke 17   231
Luke 18   239
Luke 19   250
Luke 20   260
Luke 21   270
Luke 22   275
   Fusing the Horizons: Countercultural Greatness 281
Luke 23   292
Luke 24   305

Bibliography 315
Scripture Index 321
Ancient Sources Index 349
Author Index 355

Outline of Luke

Introduction / 1

Infancy Narratives / 12
    Prologue (1:1–4) / 12
    Annunciation of John's Birth (1:5–25) / 14
    Annunciation of Jesus' Birth (1:26–38) / 19
    Song of Mary (1:39–56) / 22
    Song of Zechariah (1:57–80) / 25

    Birth of Jesus (2:1–20) / 30
    Dedication of Jesus at the Temple (2:21–40) / 38
    Jesus at Twelve (2:41–52) / 42

Time of Preparation / 47
    Baptism of John (3:1–20) / 47
    Baptism and Commissioning of Jesus (3:21–22) / 53
    Genealogy of Jesus (3:23–38) / 55

    Testing of Jesus (4:1–13) / 57

Ministry in Galilee / 60
    Sermon at Nazareth (4:14–30) / 60
    Early Ministry in Galilee (4:31–44) / 65

    Calling of Simon Peter (5:1–11) / 68
    Controversy over Purity Law (5:12–39) / 71
        Cleansing a Leper (5:12–16) / 73
        Healing a Paralytic (5:17–26) / 75
        Calling of Levi (5:27–35) / 77
        Old versus New (5:36–39) / 79

    Controversy over Sabbath Law (6:1–11) / 81

        Plucking Grains on the Sabbath (6:1–5) / 82
        Healing a Man with a Withered Hand (6:6–11) / 83
    Naming the Twelve (6:12–16) / 84
    Sermon on the Plain (6:17–49) / 86
        The Crowd Flocks to Jesus (6:17–19) / 87
        Blessings and Woes (6:20–26) / 87
        Loving One's Enemies (6:27–36) / 88
        Warning Against Judging Others (6:37–45) / 90
        Wise and Foolish Builders (6:46–49) / 91

    A Centurion's Slave and a Widow's Son (7:1–17) / 92
        Healing a Centurion's Slave (7:1–10) / 92
        Raising a Widow's Son (7:11–17) / 95
    John and Jesus (7:18–35) / 98
        The One Who Is to Come (7:18–23) / 98
        Praise for John (7:24–30) / 99
        Two Roles, One Mission (7:31–35) / 100
    A Sinner and a Pharisee (7:36–50) / 102

    Faithful Women (8:1–3) / 108
    Hearing and Doing (8:4–21) / 109
    Faith and Fear (8:22–56) / 112
        Calming the Sea (8:22–25) / 113
        The Gerasene Demoniac (8:26–39) / 114
        Jairus's Daughter (8:40–56) / 117

Preparation of the Disciples and the Identity of Jesus / 123
    Sending the Twelve (9:1–10a) / 123
    Feeding the Five Thousand (9:10b–17) / 125
    Following the Suffering Messiah (9:18–27) / 127
    Transfiguration (9:28–36) / 131
    Faithlessness and Self-Importance (9:37–50) / 134
        Healing a Demon-Possessed Boy (9:37–43) / 134
        Passion Prediction (9:44–45) / 135
        The Greatest versus the Least (9:46–50) / 136

Journey to Jerusalem: the Way of Discipleship / 138
    Cost of Discipleship (9:51–62) / 138
        Rejection in Samaria (9:51–56) / 138

Self-Denial and Discipleship (9:57–62) / 140

Sending the Seventy-Two (10:1–16) / 144
Return of the Seventy-Two (10:17–24) / 147
Doing Mercy (10:25–37) / 150
    A Lawyer's Question (10:25–29) / 150
    A Good Samaritan (10:30–37) / 152
Martha and Mary (10:38–42) / 156

Teachings on Prayer (11:1–13) / 159
    The Lord's Prayer (11:1–4) / 159
    A Friend at Midnight (11:5–8) / 162
    Sayings on Prayer (11:9–13) / 165
Signs of Unbelief (11:14–32) / 167
    The Beelzebul Controversy (11:14–26) / 167
    The Sign of Jonah (11:27–32) / 169
Integrity and Hypocrisy (11:33–54) / 170
    The Lamp of the Body (11:33–36) / 170
    Woes to Pharisees and Scribes (11:37–54) / 171

Facing Persecution (12:1–12) / 176
Wealth and Worries (12:13–34) / 179
    A Rich Fool (12:13–21) / 179
    Freedom from Anxiety (12:22–34) / 182
Watchfulness in Uncertain Times (12:35–59) /185
    Be Vigilant (12:35–48) / 186
    Recognizing Crisis (12:49–59) / 188

Call to Repentance (13:1–9) / 190
    All Must Repent (13:1–5) / 190
    A Fruitless Fig Tree (13:6–9) / 191
Healing a Bent Woman (13:10–17) / 192
The Kingdom of God (13:18–30) / 195
The City that Kills the Prophets (13:31–35) / 198

Healing a Man with Dropsy (14:1–6) / 201
Honor in God's Kingdom (14:7–24) / 204
    Honor and Humility (14:7–11) / 205
    Undermining Balanced Reciprocity (14:12–14) / 206

A Great Banquet (14:15–24) / 207
Cost of Discipleship (14:25–35) / 209

Three Lost Parables (15:1–32) / 213
    Criticism and Defense (15:1–3) / 213
    One Lost Sheep (15:4–7) / 214
    One Lost Coin (15:8–10) / 215
    Two Lost Sons (15:11–32) / 216

A Dishonest Manager (16:1–13) / 221
The Place of the Law (16:14–18) / 225
A Rich Man and a Poor Beggar (16:19–31) / 228

Leaders of the People, Servants of God (17:1–10) / 230
Healing Ten Lepers (17:11–19) / 233
The Day of the Son of Man (17:20–37) / 235

A Widow and an Unjust Judge (18:1–8) / 239
A Pharisee and a Tax Collector (18:9–17) / 242
A Rich Ruler (18:18–30) / 245
Obtuseness and Insight (18:31–43) / 247

Zacchaeus the Tax Collector (19:1–10) / 250
The Slaves and Their Minas (19:11–27) / 253

Ministry in Jerusalem / 255
    Entry into Jerusalem (19:28–40) / 255
    Indictment of Jerusalem and Its Temple (19:41–48) / 258

Challenge and Riposte (20:1–20:44) / 260
    Jesus' Authority (20:1–8) / 260
    Some Wicked Tenants (20:9–19) / 262
    Paying Taxes to Caesar (20:20–26) / 264
    Interpreting Moses on Resurrection (20:27–40) / 266
    David's Son as David's Lord (20:41–44) / 267
Warnings Against the Scribes (20:45—21:4) / 268

Apocalyptic Discourse (21:5–38) / 271
    Fall of Jerusalem (21:5–24) / 271

The Parousia of the Son of Man (21:25–38) / 273

Passion and Resurrection of Jesus / 275
  Betrayal of Jesus (22:1–6) / 275
  Jesus Hosts the Passover Meal (22:7–23) / 276
    Preparation for the Meal (22:7–13) / 276
    The Last Supper (22:14–23) / 277
  Servanthood, Faithfulness, Preparedness (22:24–38) / 280
  Jesus' Arrest and Peter's Denial (22:39–65) / 285
    Prayer at the Mount of Olives (22:39–46) / 285
    The Arrest (22:47–53) / 287
    Peter's Denial (22:54–65) / 288
  Before the Sanhedrin (22:66–71) / 289

  Before Pilate and Herod (23:1–12) / 292
  Pilate's Verdict (23:13–25) / 294
  Crucifixion (23:26–43) / 296
  Death and Burial (23:44–56) / 300

  Resurrection (24:1–49) / 305
    An Empty Tomb (24:1–12) / 305
    To Emmaus and Back (24:13–35) / 307
    Commissioning the Twelve (24:36–49) / 310
  Ascension into Heaven (24:50–53) / 312

Acknowledgments

I would like to thank the editors of the New Covenant Commentary Series, Craig Keener and Michael Bird, for the opportunity to write this mid-level commentary on my favorite Gospel for my favorite target audience—seminarians, pastors, Bible study leaders, and the curious laypersons in the pews. I could not have asked for more patient and gracious editors than Craig and Mike, especially when administrative duties and my father's passing delayed my progress considerably at some points.

I am grateful for my students at the Palmer Theological Seminary of Eastern University and the members of the Narberth Presbyterian Church, whose eagerness to study Scripture to nurture their faith and deepen their Christian walk has been a source of delight and encouragement. They make it necessary for me to explain the complexities of a biblical text in accessible ways without dumbing it down, and their questions hold me accountable in my own discipleship.

I thank the trustees of Eastern University for granting me a sabbatical leave in 2015, during which a sizable portion of this commentary was written. Special thanks go to Jeron Ashford for her expeditious and careful editing, and to Chris Spinks, Mary Roth, and Ian Creeger of Cascade Books at Wipf and Stock Publishers for shepherding this project throughout the production process.

This work is dedicated to my three older sisters, Agnes, Lucy, and Irene, whose diligent study of Scripture, service to God, and ministry to the local and global church have been an example to me throughout my life. Now they can stop asking me to explain a passage, at least, from this particular New Testament document.

Abbreviations

AB	Anchor Bible
ASV	American Standard Version
BBR	*Bulletin for Biblical Research*
BCE	Before the Common Era
BECNT	Baker Exegetical Commentary on the New Testament
BibInt	*Biblical Interpretation*
BSac	*Bibliotheca Sacra*
BTB	*Biblical Theology Bulletin*
CBQ	*Catholic Biblical Quarterly*
CE	Common Era
CEB	Common English Bible
Colloq	*Colloquium*
CTJ	*Calvin Theological Journal*
CTR	*Criswell Theological Review*
DJG	*Dictionary of Jesus and the Gospels*, edited by Joel B. Green, Jeannine K. Brown, and Nicholas Perrin, 2nd ed. (Downers Grove, IL: InterVarsity, 2013)
DNTB	*Dictionary of New Testament Background*, edited by Craig A. Evans and Stanley E. Porter (Downers Grove, IL: InterVarsity, 2000)
ESV	English Standard Version
ETSMS	Evangelical Theological Society Monograph Series
ExAud	*Ex Auditu*

ExpTim	*Expository Times*
HTR	Harvard Theological Review
Int	*Interpretation*
JBL	*Journal of Biblical Literature*
JETS	*Journal of the Evangelical Theological Society*
JSNT	*Journal for the Study of the New Testament*
JSNTSup	Journal for the Study of the New Testament Supplement Series
JTS	*Journal of Theological Studies*
LCL	Loeb Classical Library
LXX	Septuagint
NASB	New American Standard Bible
NICNT	New International Commentary on the New Testament
NIGTC	New International Greek Testament Commentary
NIV	New International Version
NKJV	New King James Version
NLT	New Living Translation
NovT	*Novum Testamentum*
NRSV	New Revised Standard Version
NT	New Testament
NTL	New Testament Library
NTS	*New Testament Studies*
OT	Old Testament
PNTC	The Pillar New Testament Commentary
PRSt	*Perspectives in Religious Studies*
RevExp	*Review and Expositor*
RSV	Revised Standard Version

ScEs	*Science et esprit*
SNTSMS	Society for New Testament Studies Monograph Series
StBibLit	Studies in Biblical Literature (Lang)
TJ	*Trinity Journal*
TS	*Theological Studies*
TynBul	*Tyndale Bulletin*
WBC	Word Biblical Commentary
WTJ	*Westminster Theological Journal*
WUNT	Wissenschaftliche Untersuchungen zum Neuen Testament
ZNW	*Zeitschrift für die neutestamentliche Wissenschaft und die Kunde der* älteren *Kirche*

Ancient Sources

Jewish Sources

Apocrypha

Bar	Baruch
Sir	Sirach/Ecclesiasticus
Tob	Tobit
Wis	Wisdom of Solomon

Dead Sea Scrolls

1QM	War Scroll
1QSa	Rule of the Congregation (appendix a to 1QS)
4Q174	Eschatological Midrash
4Q252	Commentary on Genesis A, formerly Patriarchal Blessings or Pesher Genesis
4Q285	Sefer Hamilḥamah

4Q521	Messianic Apocalypse
11QMelch	Melchizedek

Josephus

Ag. Ap.	*Against Apion*
Ant.	*Jewish Antiquities*
J.W.	*Jewish War*
Life	*The Life*

Philo of Alexandria

Abraham	*On the Life of Abraham*
Embassy	*On the Embassy to Gaius*
Moses	*On the Life of Moses*

Pseudepigrapha

2 Bar.	*2 Baruch (Syriac Apocalypse)*
1 En.	*1 Enoch (Ethiopic Apocalypse)*
2 En.	*2 Enoch (Slavonic Apocalypse)*
3 En.	*3 Enoch (Hebrew Apocalypse)*
Jub.	*Jubilees*
Pss. Sol.	*Psalms of Solomon*
Sib. Or.	*Sibylline Oracles*
T. Dan	*Testament of Dan*
T. Jud.	*Testament of Judah*
T. Levi	*Testament of Levi*
T. Mos.	*Testament of Moses*

Rabbinic Literature

ʿAbod. Zar.	Avodah Zarah
ʾAbot	Avot
b.	Babylonian Talmud
B. Bat.	Bava Batra
B. Meṣ.	Bava Metziʿa
B. Qam.	Bava Qamma
Ber.	Berakhot
ʿErub.	Eruvin
Ḥag	Hagigah
Ketub.	Ketubbot
m.	Mishnah
Meg.	Megillah
Nid.	Niddah
Qidd.	Qiddushin
Šabb.	Shabbat
Sanh.	Sanhedrin
Šeb.	Sheviʾit
Šeqal.	Sheqalim
y.	Jerusalem Talmud
Yad.	Yadayim

Early Christian Sources

Clement of Alexandria

Strom.	Miscellanies

Eusebius

Hist. eccl.   *Ecclesiastical History*

Irenaeus

Haer.   *Against Heresies*

Jerome

Vir. ill.   *De viris illustribus*

Tertullian

Marc.   *Against Marcion*

Other Greco-Roman Sources

OGIS   *Orientis Graeci Inscriptiones Selectae*, edited by Wilhelm Dittenberger, 2 vols. (Leipzig: Hirzel, 1903–1905)

Dio Chrysostom

Or.   *Orations*

Euripides

Herc. fur.   *Madness of Hercules*

Herodotus

Hist.   *Histories*

Homer

Il.   *Iliad*

Od.   *Odyssey*

Ovid

Fast.   *Fasti*

Philostratus

Vit. Apoll.   *Vita Apollonii*

Pliny the Elder

Nat.   *Natural History*

Plutarch

Alex.   *Alexander*

Seneca

Ep.   *Epistulae morales*

Marc.   *Ad Marciam de consolatione*

Stobaeus

Flor.   *Florilegium*

Tacitus

Ann.   *Annales*

Hist.   *Historiae*

Introduction

Since many have undertaken to write a commentary on the Gospel of Luke, I too decided, after accepting an invitation from the editors of the New Covenant Commentary Series, to write an accessible explanation of this narrative on the life of Jesus for you, my dear readers. I hope this journey of discovery will be as enjoyable and edifying for you as it has been for me.

Alongside the authors of Matthew, Mark, and John, the third evangelist paints his distinctive portrait of Jesus while offering the added bonus of a sequel. The Acts of the Apostles carries the narrative beyond Jesus' ascension into the burgeoning mission of the early church. It is useful to refer to the two documents, Luke and Acts, as Luke-Acts, despite their separation in the canonical ordering by the Gospel of John. Not only do Luke and Acts share the same author and identify Theophilus as the dedicatee (Luke 1:3; Acts 1:1), the mission of Jesus in the Gospel is continued by the apostles and the early church in its sequel. Many echoes of Luke are found in Acts. For example, the range of healings performed by Jesus is mirrored in the miracles of Peter and Paul. The motif of journeying is prominent in both books, with Jesus' journey from Galilee to Jerusalem in Luke, and Paul's many missionary journeys as well as his final voyage to Rome in Acts. Even though this commentary covers only the Gospel of Luke, it is helpful to maintain a forward glance to Acts when reading the Lukan narrative, knowing that the larger story extends beyond Luke 24, and, for that matter, even beyond Acts 28 to the many generations of Christians that follow.

This introduction briefly addresses items "behind" the narrative, such as matters of authorship, dating, place of writing, intended audience, genre, purpose, thematic elements, and the like. While some may find these discussions tedious and speculative, they remind us that this narrative, which Christians embrace as holy Scripture and inspired word of God, is a historical document written by a human author for an actual audience in a language and setting very different from our modern context. It behooves us therefore to exercise intellectual humility and prudence in our interpretation of these ancient words even as we believe that God continues to speak powerfully through them to us today. There are many ways to engage a scriptural text, but the strategy employed in this commentary emphasizes a historical and literary reading as a helpful starting point for interpretation.

Authorship

It may come as a surprise to some readers that the original autographs of the four Gospels no longer exist. All the ancient manuscripts and fragments thereof that we have of Matthew, Mark, Luke, and John are copies. In the earliest of these manuscripts the author is not explicitly named, rendering the four Gospels anonymous documents. The designations found in our English Bibles, "the Gospel of Luke" or "the Gospel according to Luke," reflect traditional attributions. In many of the writings of the early church fathers, dated to the first few centuries CE, we find references to a person named Luke as the author of this account of the life of Jesus. Because this information does not come from within the narrative itself, we call these references "external evidence."

One of the earliest manuscripts of the Gospel of Luke written on papyrus has a postscript that reads, "Gospel according to Luke."[1] Among the patristic writings of the early church fathers, we find attestations to a person named Luke as the author of this Gospel, who was a fellow-laborer and companion of Paul, a physician from Syrian Antioch, and the author of the Acts of the Apostles as well.[2] In addition, the anonymous Anti-Marcionite Prologue for Luke states that the author was unmarried, had no children, and died in Boeotia at the age of eighty-four.[3] Three Pauline letters in the NT mention a man named Luke, known to Paul's readers as "the beloved physician" (Col 4:14), a companion of Paul (2 Tim 4:11), and a coworker of Paul (Phlm 24). In the book of Acts, there are segments in which the narrative switches to the use of the first person plural pronoun, suggesting that the author was with Paul when those events occurred (Acts 16:10–17; 20:5–15; 21:1–18; 27:1—28:16).

---

1. P75, dated to 200 CE.

2. See Clement of Alexandria (second century) *Strom.* 5.12; Irenaeus (second century) *Haer.* 3.1.1; 3.14.1; Tertullian (second/third century) *Marc.* 4.2.2; 4.2.5; 4.5.3; Eusebius (third/fourth century) *Hist. eccl.* 3.4.6; Jerome (fourth/fifth century) *Vir. ill.* 7.1.

3. The Prologue to Luke within the Anti-Marcionite Prologues is dated to the second half of the second century (Koester 1992: 335).

Some interpreters view these so-called "we-passages" as evidence of the author's knowledge of Paul, hence his ability to write extensively about Paul's ministry in Acts.[4] While it is possible that an initial erroneous attribution of the authorship to Luke was passed down from one generation of Christians to another, it seems more likely that the broad agreement of Lukan authorship across a wide range of ancient documents other than the NT has to do with the veracity of that attribution. Given that Luke-Acts constitutes a rather substantial piece of writing, it is unlikely that nobody in the early Christian movement knew who wrote it. Anonymous does not mean unknown.

It is not easy to determine whether Luke the physician was a Jew or a gentile. Even though one may deduce from Col 4:11 that the Luke mentioned in Col 4:14 could be a gentile, there is no indication in the writings of the patristic fathers to confirm it. Can the internal evidence, drawn from the Gospel itself, shed light on the ethnicity of the author whom we assume to be Luke the physician? From the prologue we note that the author was not an eyewitness to the ministries of Jesus (1:2). The sophistication of the Greek prose of Luke-Acts points to a highly educated individual, who was simultaneously at home in Greco-Roman culture and philosophy and well-versed in the Septuagint, the Greek translation of the Hebrew Scriptures. This information, however, is not sufficient to draw firm conclusions about Luke's ethnicity. He could have been a Jewish Christian of the Diaspora, a gentile who converted from paganism to the Christian faith, or a gentile God-fearer who had spent time exploring Judaism and its Scriptures before becoming a Christian (cf. Acts 10:35; 13:16, 26). A well-educated man in any of these categories could fit the profile. Even the universal outlook in Luke-Acts does not necessitate that the author be gentile.

In spite of the widely-accepted opinion that Luke the physician authored this Gospel, our inability to draw a definitive conclusion about the author begs the question of the importance of an irrefutable answer for understanding the book's message. Put differently, does not knowing more about Luke beyond some general tidbits change our reading of the narrative as a credible presentation and sound interpretation of Jesus? The answer is, "No, not as far as the key theological message about God's plan of salvation is concerned." We believe that the transmitters of the Jesus traditions, from whom Luke gathered his materials, as well as Luke

4. Hagner 2012: 246; Edwards 2015: 6.

himself, remained faithful in passing on the teachings and actions of Jesus as truthfully and accurately as they knew how. Some uncertainty on the issue of authorship notwithstanding, the text of the Gospel of Luke, as we now have it, is trustworthy for faith and discipleship.

Reading the Gospel as Scripture is at its core a matter of trust. The reader has to trust Luke the historian, biographer, theologian, and Christ-follower. More importantly, the reader has to trust God's intervention in the writing, transmission, and reading of this Gospel. The process by which the Holy Spirit connects the author, the text, and the reader for the latter's formation and edification remains a mystery of faith. In this commentary, I will refer to the author as Luke, with the understanding that this identification, albeit an educated guess, comes with a considerable amount of credible circumstantial evidence.

Recipients, Dating, and Place of Writing

Ideally, information on Luke's original readers and their situation would shed light on the impetus behind Luke's writing and the interpretation of his message. Among the four evangelists, Luke was already the most specific in naming the person for whom he crafted his narrative—one "most excellent Theophilus" (1:3), a man of considerable standing in his community. Beyond the fact that Theophilus is a Greek name, hardly anything else is known of this person; his location, profession, and the reason for his elevated status remain opaque to us. Also, we cannot assume that Luke was located where Theophilus and his community of faith were at the time of writing. Guesses among scholars on the location of the author and his original audience cover a wide geographical area, from Syrian Antioch, Ephesus, Philippi, Corinth, to Rome.[5] From the letters of Paul, we note that these are all cities where Christian communities were operational in the first century CE.

Even though there is only one specifically named dedicatee, Luke's narrative would have been read by more than Theophilus alone. A wider circle of followers of Jesus, perhaps the faith community of which Theophilus was part, would have listened to a public reading of Jesus' story. Given the content of Luke-Acts, the sophisticated Greek prose, and the direction in which the gospel was spread from Palestine to the larger Greco-Roman world in the first few decades of the early church, one may

---

5. Marshall 1978: 35; Edwards 2015: 12–13.

surmise that Luke's audience consisted mainly of urban gentile Christians, though Christian communities across the Roman Empire would have had a mix of Jewish and gentile believers in differing proportions.

The challenge of dating the Gospel of Luke is bound up with at least three considerations: the dating of the Gospel of Mark, the dating of the Acts of the Apostles, and the interpretation of the description of the fall of Jerusalem within the narrative. First, since Mark is widely accepted to be one of Luke's sources, Luke must post-date Mark. Second, since the opening line in Acts refers to the Gospel of Luke as "the first book" (Acts 1:1), Luke must predate Acts, whether by a little or a lot. Third, the description of Jesus' judgment on Jerusalem (19:43–44; 21:20–24; cf. 13:34–35) seems very similar to how Jerusalem was conquered by the Romans in the First Jewish Revolt. One wonders if what actually happened was written back into the predictions of Jesus. If so, the Gospel of Luke would have had to be composed after 70 CE. Given that there is no mention of the fall of Jerusalem in Acts, and that Acts concludes not with the death of Paul but with his house arrest in Rome, some scholars place the dating of Luke to the early 60s. Most are content with situating the Gospel of Luke within the two decades after the fall of Jerusalem, somewhere between 70 and 90 CE.[6] The outer edges of scholarly guesses put the Gospel as early as the 60s and as late as the first part of the second century.[7] It is difficult to be precise with the when and where of writing because so little information is available on either Luke or Theophilus.

Genre

Understanding the genre of a piece of writing allows us to read it co-operatively and intelligently. How we read a letter is different from a newspaper editorial or, for that matter, a tabloid we pick up while waiting in a supermarket check-out line. At first glance, the Gospel of Luke is a narrative, within which specific portions are given to other genres such as prologue, poetry, genealogy, and parable, just to name a few. Narrative, however, is still too broad a genre. Fable and fiction are narrative in form, but neither fits what we read in Luke. "Gospel" is not in and of itself a genre, at least not among secular Greco-Roman writings of the time. The word "gospel," which means "good news" in the Greek (*euangelion*),

---

6. Marshall 1978: 34–35; Edwards 2015: 11–12.
7. Carroll 2012: 4.

describes the content of the narrative rather than its literary form. The good news is about Jesus Christ, the Son of God.[8] Subsequently, this particular message of salvation comes to be known as "the gospel," lending a more technical meaning to the word *euangelion* in Christian parlance.[9]

How, then, do we classify the genre of the third Gospel? Comparing Luke to other ancient writings in form and content, the most relevant correspondence is that of ancient historiography.[10] Since the focus of the narrative is on the life of Jesus, it may be more fitting to call it biography than historiography.

Some characteristics of ancient biographies, such as Plutarch's *Lives* or Suetonius's *The Twelve Caesars*, may be found in the Gospel of Luke. For example, ancient biographies tend to be less concerned about chronological exactitude, something to which modern biographies are held accountable. In Luke's Gospel, the general chronology of Jesus' life is rather non-negotiable: for example, the infancy narrative must come before Jesus' adult baptism and temptations, followed by his Galilean ministry. At some point Jesus heads for Jerusalem where he is crucified, buried, raised, and then he ascends into heaven. This overall framework of Jesus' chronology, including major milestones of Jesus' life, is fixed. But in between key events, the author has some freedom in the detailed ordering of the accounts of Jesus' teachings and healings. Given how the traditions of Jesus were passed down in bits and pieces in oral and written forms through multiple channels over a span of decades, it would be unrealistic to expect Luke to present the sequence of events in exact chronological order. Using the order of Mark's story as a point of departure,[11] Luke sometimes steps out of Mark's ordering, rearranges it for a better narrative flow and inserts materials from other sources. This redactional freedom does not make Luke a more credible or less credible historian than Mark. Furthermore, this editorial necessity was not unique to Luke, as Matthew, Mark, and John faced similar challenges.

---

8. In the Septuagint, the Greek translation of the Hebrew Scriptures, the verb *euangelizō* is found in contexts that speak of God's salvation, e.g., Pss 11:1; 95:2; Isa 49:2; 52:7; Joel 3:5.

9. E.g., Matt 4:23; Mark 1:14; Rom 1:1; Rev 14:6. This term is used in Acts (15:7; 20:24) but not in Luke.

10. Green 1997: 2–6; Carroll 2012: 5–6.

11. E.g., Mark 1:14—3:19//Luke 4:14—6:16; Mark 11:27—13:32//Luke 20:1—21:33.

Another similarity between ancient biography and the Gospel of Luke is a heavy focus on the subject's ideas, words, deeds, and the way in which the person dies, especially in the case of a heroic death. Much of Luke's story contains Jesus' teachings, miracles, healings, and exorcisms. Through Jesus' encounters with the crowd, his disciples, his family, and his enemies, the storytelling discloses the identity and mission of Jesus. In particular, the death of Jesus and its significance receive much emphasis. The passion narrative, from Jesus' entry into Jerusalem to his resurrection and ascension, covers twenty percent of the entire book.

Aside from Luke being a historian qua biographer, the interpretive lens through which he filters his historical account about Jesus is first and foremost theological. As stated in the prologue, Luke writes in order that Theophilus might "know the truth concerning the things about which [he had] been instructed" (1:4), a truth embedded in "the events that had been fulfilled among [them]" (1:1). This truth is about God and God's actions in human history, which leads us to the following section on several prominent themes found in the Gospel that reflect the author's purpose and agenda.

Purpose and Themes

In the opening prologue of his long narrative, Luke does not denigrate the contributions of his predecessors as inadequate or inaccurate. His goal is not to improve on others' stories about Jesus, nor to generate new converts, but to bring edification and spiritual nurture to his readers who are already Christians. Even though anyone may be led to faith in Jesus from reading the Gospel of Luke, this work is not an evangelistic tract but a means to strengthen the faith of Theophilus and his community.

Without knowing with precision the date and place of writing of the Gospel of Luke, we could only take an educated guess at the challenges faced by Christians living in urban areas across the Roman Empire in the first century, and how Luke-Acts would be an encouragement to them. At that time, Jewish and gentile Christians alike would feel pressure coming externally from unbelieving Jews and unbelieving gentiles, as well as internally from fellow Christians as they struggled to cross racial-ethnic barriers to live peaceably with one another in their shared reality as equal members of God's household. In light of these points of tension, Luke's presentation of Jesus' salvific mission as the fulfillment of God's promises to Israel would connect the Christian movement to its Jewish roots. His universal outlook, noticeable already in the Gospel but further developed in Acts, would maintain that God's plan of salvation is ultimately for the whole world even if it came first to the Jews. Luke thus uses his narrative to assure Theophilus and his community, wherever they might be, that what they have learned about Jesus is true and trustworthy, and that they must stay firm in their bold witness and faithful discipleship in spite of persecution and rejection.

What then is characteristic of Luke's Gospel, given that it shares quite a bit of common traditions with at least two of the three other Gospels?[12] We find materials that are peculiar to Luke but not found in Matthew and Mark especially helpful in identifying a Lukan distinctiveness. While space does not permit an exhaustive treatment of Luke's emphases in this short introduction, it is helpful to consider the following themes that can be traced from the Gospel of Luke all the way into the Acts of the Apostles.

First, the story of Jesus is the centerpiece of the plan of salvation ordained by the sovereign God, a plan that began with Israel but is intended for the nations. The Gospel opens with Gabriel's appearance to Zechariah at the temple in Jerusalem and concludes with the disciples worshiping at the same temple. Between these bookends, Jesus carries out his mission among the Jewish people with occasional forays into gentile territory. Yet hints of the universality of this divine plan may be detected early in Luke's narrative. Holding Jesus in his arms, Simeon refers to the infant as God's salvation, "a light for revelation *to the gentiles* and for glory to [God's] people Israel" (2:32). Citing from Isaiah, the author then identifies John the Baptist as the voice crying out in the wilderness to prepare the way of the Lord, so that "*all flesh* shall see the salvation of God" (3:4–6). While Acts also opens with the disciples waiting in Jerusalem for the outpouring of Holy Spirit, by the end of Acts, we find Paul under house arrest in Rome. Throughout the book, the apostles bear witness to the gospel, according to Jesus' charge, "from Jerusalem, Judea, Samaria, to the ends

---

12. With the majority of NT scholars, I subscribe to both Markan priority and the four-document hypothesis to account for the literary relationship between the Synoptic Gospels (Matthew, Mark, and Luke). First, Mark is the earliest of the four canonical Gospels. Second, both Matthew and Luke used Mark and Q as their sources. Q, a hypothetical source, contains the sayings of Jesus common to both Matthew and Luke. Third, all remaining materials found only in Matthew is attributed to the M source, and those found only in Luke, to the L source. In short, these four documents (Mark, Q, M, and L), together explain how Matthew, Mark, and Luke can have overlapping materials but are not identical in order and detail.

of the earth" (Acts 1:8). Because everything that happened to Jesus, even his suffering and death, is part of God's sovereign plan (Acts 2:23; 4:38), Theophilus and his community, as well as later generations of Christians, can read the Gospel of Luke with hope.

Second is Luke's realized eschatology, his message that in Jesus' coming God's future salvation has impinged upon the present. Those who believe in Jesus experience the relationships and ethics of the kingdom of God now even as its final consummation lies in the future. Eternal salvation is not effected only through the death, resurrection, and exaltation of Jesus. Even during his earthly ministry, Jesus brings release from bondage and reversal of conditions to those who repent and humbly receive the gift of salvation. Jesus' direct ministry to those around him is salvific in the eschatological sense, as the poor receive the good news of God's kingdom, the captives and the oppressed are set free, the blind see, the lame walk, the deaf hear, the lepers are cleansed, and even the dead are raised (4:18–19; 7:22). Because Jesus embodies the saving power of God both in life and in death, the theological use of the word "today (*sēmeron*)" in Luke connotes both the immediacy of God's salvation through Jesus and the urgency of its proclamation (2:11; 4:21; 19:9; 23:43).

Third, and consonant with the theme of reversal, the Lukan narrative puts a heavy emphasis on the faith and humility of those with low status in their openness to the good news of Jesus. Tax collectors, sinners, gentiles, Samaritans, women, children, the sick, the handicapped, and the demon-possessed are recipients of Jesus' healing touch and acceptance.[13] By contrast, the religious leaders who criticize Jesus for breaking Sabbath and purity laws while bringing people to wholeness are indicted for their self-righteousness (5:31–32; 11:42). This emphasis on lifting up the lowly and putting the proud in their place is also apparent among the many parables of Jesus found only in Luke. These include stories such as the two debtors (7:41–43), the good Samaritan (10:25–37), the lost sons (15:11–32), the rich man and Lazarus (16:19–31), the widow and the unjust judge (18:1–8), and the Pharisee and the tax collector (18:9–14). It is no wonder that this Gospel is deeply embraced by liberationist theologians and communities that identify with the oppressed and the underdogs in various times and places.

Fourth, a journey motif cuts across Luke-Acts. The saving plan of God is always in motion, seen in the lives and proclamation of Jesus'

---

13. E.g., 4:33–35; 5:17–26, 29–32; 7:11–15, 36–50; 17:11–19; 18:15–17, 35–43.

disciples. From the very beginning, Mary travels south to visit Elizabeth. The two women, both with child, confirm that God is about to fulfill his promise to Israel (1:39–45). Nine months later, Joseph and Mary travel from Nazareth to Judea. Even though the couple embark on that journey to comply with the edict of Caesar, the emperor's oppressive act of census-taking becomes an unwitting instrument to situate the Messiah's birthplace in Bethlehem in fulfillment of the words of the prophet Micah (2:1–7; cf. Mic 5:2). Throughout the narrative, Jesus conducts an itinerant ministry around Galilee, moving from one town to another to preach the good news (4:14–15, 43–44). Twice, he sends his disciples to do likewise (9:1–6; 10:1–12). Most distinctively, however, is the large section from 9:51—19:27, commonly known as the "travel narrative," which begins with Jesus setting his face toward Jerusalem and ends right before his entry into the city. On the one hand, these chapters cover a physical journey, as Jesus and his entourage make their way from Galilee to Judea where Jesus will meet his destiny.[14] On the other hand, this section is replete with teaching materials concerning the path of discipleship, addressing topics from prayer and money to repentance and judgment. After the death and resurrection of Jesus, the final chapter of Luke contains one more important journey to and from Emmaus. On this journey two disciples leave Jerusalem in despair and return with great joy and insight, having traveled and shared table with the risen Christ (24:13–33). The twin themes of the dynamic movement of the gospel and the notion of journey as discipleship continue into Luke's second volume. Known as "the Way,"[15] the early Christian movement is shown in Acts to take the good news of salvation out of Jerusalem and Judea into Samaria, Phoenicia, Syria, Cyprus, Asia Minor, Macedonia, Achaia (Greece), and Rome.

Beyond these key themes, others, such as God's fatherhood, Luke's prophetic portrayal of Jesus, the importance of prayer, the proper use of wealth, and the call for perseverance are also worthy of attention when reading the Lukan narrative. The more familiar we are with the individual vignettes and how they contribute to the overall flow of this long book, the better equipped we are in finding those delightful nuggets of rhetorical and theological truths that the author has artfully woven into the narrative. As we invest time and energy into the meaning of the text,

---

14. Even so, the name places in these stories, if plotted out on a map, show a rather meandering itinerary. The point is not to track Jesus' geographical progress from town to town but to show a deliberate movement toward the climax of his mission.

15. E.g., Acts 9:2; 18:25–26; 19:9, 23; 22:4; 24:14, 22.

may we also sit with prayerful hearts ready to receive the instruction and convictions of the Holy Spirit. Welcome aboard this journey through the Gospel of Luke.

Luke 1

Prologue (1:1–4)

Prologues appear in a wide range of ancient Greco-Roman writings, from histories and biographies to rhetorical and scientific treatises. Generally they identify the author and the person to whom the work is dedicated, vouch for the importance of the subject matter, evaluate prior work of a similar nature that might warrant comparison or critique, and comment on the methodology that support the research and composition.[1]

The first four verses of Luke's Gospel contain the classic components of a prologue. These verses comprise a single, elegant Greek sentence, its vocabulary and structure indicating a highly educated author. Luke is quick to admit that his project is not an original idea (1:1a). Yet even as he aligns himself with his predecessors he also distinguishes his work from theirs. It is not as though he found terrible fault with others' narratives about Jesus. Rather, he gleans from available written sources, adds other traditions to which he has access, and creates an integrated piece to deepen his audience's understanding of Jesus' story.

Without mentioning Jesus by name just yet, Luke highlights the significance of his subject matter as pertaining to "events that have been fulfilled (*peplērophorēmenōn*) among us" (1:1b). The passive voice and perfect tense of the participle *peplērophorēmenōn* indicate that these events constitute a culmination of a plan or a promise that has its beginning far back in time. The passive here signifies a divine passive; God is bringing to fruition the plan that he has promised and put in motion. The perfect tense denotes a past event with ongoing present effects. The historical events that Luke is about to narrate belong to a larger framework, as their effects continue beyond the narrative time to the present.

---

1. Cf. Josephus *Ag. Ap.* 1.1–5; Polybius 2.37; Diodorus Siculus 1.3. Alexander (1986: 48–74) notes similarities with prefaces in scientific works, and Moles (2011: 1–82) with those found in Greek decrees.

Luke is not an eyewitness, but having obtained his materials from eyewitnesses, he meets the standard of credibility expected of an ancient historian.[2] His sources were there from the beginning of Jesus' ministry, and, after Jesus' departure have since become "servants of the word" (1:2). "The word" refers to the message of salvation embodied in the life and mission of Jesus (Acts 4:4; 8:4). At the time of writing, some eyewitnesses might still be alive to recall and verify the sayings and deeds of Jesus. But even if some traditions came to him as second- or third-hand transmission, they could still be traced back to original eyewitnesses and thus deemed trustworthy.

Since the Jesus traditions were highly valued and used in teaching in the early church, maintaining accuracy in transmission was a high priority. A conscientious historian, Luke verifies his sources by "investigating everything carefully from the very first" (1:3a). Although the adverb *anōthen* can mean "for a long time" or "from the very first," the latter translation is preferred. "From the very first" echoes verse 2 where it describes the eyewitnesses as "from the beginning."

All this preparatory work culminates in an "orderly (*kathexēs*) account" for Theophilus to "know the certainty[3] concerning the things about which [he has] been instructed" (1:4). Normally, *kathexēs* ("orderly") implies a sequential arrangement, putting one thing after the other, as linearity is necessitated by a narrative genre. Having received some traditions in snippets and others in a more organized form, Luke would not have all the temporal information to lay out in exact chronological order when Jesus said and did all these things. His notion of an orderly account must be interpreted realistically as an order that makes the best sense in view of his ultimate goal. Luke's aim is to assure his readers that what they have been taught is eminently trustworthy. Surely Luke's checking for the veracity of these historical events is an essential part of the work of a careful historian, but as a writer he also has the prerogative to tell stories in a way that serves his theological agenda. Luke wants his readers to subscribe to his interpretation of Jesus' significance in light of God's

---

2. For the value placed on eyewitnesses in ancient historical writing, see Josephus *Ag. Ap.* 1.53–56; Eusebius *Hist. eccl.* 3.39. See Bauckham 2006: 21–30 on eyewitnesses as a "living and surviving voice." The work should be useful, instructive, important, and truthful.

3. The Greek word *asphaleia* may be translated as "certainty," "surety," or "assurance." "Truth" (NRSV) is less specific but communicates credibility and theological significance. Strelan (2007: 163–71) adds "soundness in argumentation," the ability to stand up to challenges.

overarching plan of salvation. The orderliness of the narrative serves his persuasive intention.

Theophilus, which means "friend of God," was a common name among both Jews and Greeks, attested in writings as far back as the third century BCE. While Theophilus may function as a stand-in for any God-loving reader, symbolic dedication was uncommon in ancient prologues. Theophilus was likely a person of standing, worthy to be addressed as "your Excellency" (1:3b), an honorific title befitting of a Roman official (Acts 24:3; 26:25). The assumption that he funded the writing of the Gospel is speculative. A literary patron could facilitate the dissemination of the book through influence and access to educated friends without supporting the author financially.[4] With Luke's level of education, the author might have been a man of means himself. The identity of Theophilus remains a mystery beyond the fact that he was a first century Christian of recognizable stature in the community. We can safely assume that he was not the sole reader, but others in his circle of believers would also have benefited from the public reading of this Gospel.

Annunciation of John's Birth (1:5–25)

Without warning, the style, tone, and vocabulary of the polished, literary, and secular-sounding prologue give way to an account that sounds as though it were taken straight out of the OT with its Semitic and pietistic flavor. Bringing the readers to the world of first century Palestine, Luke reaches back to the promises of God in the OT and points forward to the next phase of God's salvific plan for Israel and the nations.

Luke begins with an important time stamp: "In the days of King Herod of Judea" (1:5),[5] which hints at the religious, social, and political tensions in the Jewish world at the time of John's and Jesus' birth.[6] Herod the Great was ruler over Judea, Samaria, Galilee, parts of Idumea, and parts of Perea from 37 to 4 BCE. Of Idumean origin, he came into power by election of the Roman Senate. A pro-Roman vassal king, he was known for his paranoia and cruelty, killing off rivals, and executing even his wife Mariamne. He also embarked in massive building projects, establishing towns and monuments. His most impressive achievement

---

4. Green 1997: 44.
5. Cf. the time formula, "In the days of King 'X'" (Isa 1:1; Jer 1:2; Amos 1:1).
6. Ford (1984: 1–12) describes first-century Palestine as a "seething cauldron."

was the restoration of the temple in Jerusalem, which gave him control over the priestly families and strengthened his clout with Rome.[7] Under Roman rule, the yearning for God's salvation and the anticipation of the promised Messiah continued to percolate in the Jewish consciousness when the curtains of the Lukan narrative were drawn.

The opening scene features Zechariah and Elizabeth, a couple struggling with a tension of their own. Zechariah is a priest of pure Aaronic pedigree. His ancestors, from the family of Abijah, constitute the eighth of twenty-four divisions of priests named after Aaron's descendants. These divisions were reconstituted upon the Jews' return from exile in Babylon.[8] Zechariah's wife, Elizabeth, is also notably a daughter of Aaron. Priests may marry any Israelite virgin, but to take a wife within the priestly family is preferable to maintain the purity of the blood line (Lev 21:14). This couple represents the purest of priestly stock, which underscores the high standard of piety maintained on both sides of the family for many generations.

Zechariah and Elizabeth live up to their pedigree. "Both of them were righteous (*dikaioi*) before God, living blamelessly according to all the commandments and regulations of the Lord" (1:6a). Luke applies the descriptor "righteous" (*dikaios*) to the likes of Simeon, Jesus, and Cornelius (2:25; 23:47; Acts 10:22). In the OT, righteousness (*dikaiosyne*) means more than moral uprightness; it connotes a right relationship with God.[9] Zechariah and Elizabeth are exemplary in their obedience. Their consistent fidelity to God is a way of life.

All should be well for these good priestly folks, but it is not. Elizabeth has been unable to have children, and both are now old and beyond childbearing age (1:7, 18). In today's world, we tend not to attribute infertility to moral failure or divine retribution. Empathy, rather than ostracism, is the typical response. In the biblical world, however, barrenness was viewed as a curse from God.[10] After all, God gave creation the mandate to be fruitful and multiply (Gen 1:28; 8:17). If having children was considered a sign of blessing, then the natural explanation for God to close the womb would be a well-deserved punishment. Imagine the gossips and side glances between neighbors, the pretense of cordial

---

7. Bond 2013: 380.
8. 1 Chr 24:6–19; Neh 12:1–7; Josephus *Ant.* 7.363–66.
9. Gen 15:6; Ps 17:15; Isa 32:17.
10. Gen 20:18; Lev 20:21.

interaction, and the ostracism so poorly disguised. Imagine the shame that Zechariah and Elizabeth have to endure decade after decade. Without children there will be no one to support them in their old age or bury them at death. Yet the two continue to carry themselves before God in dignity and faithful service. Unless God intervenes, theirs is a socially lonely and economically precarious existence.

For readers familiar with the OT, Zechariah and Elizabeth are in good company. Rachel, Hannah, and Manoah's wife were all once barren, but God opened their wombs and they gave birth to Joseph, Samuel, and Samson.[11] A wisp of hope hovers in the background. As we read on, it is the story of Abraham and Sarah—another righteous and barren couple whose advanced age makes conception a biological impossibility—that emerges as the type after which Luke patterns the announcement of John's birth. In Genesis, the birth of Isaac involved an angelic visitation (Gen 17:1), a promise of a son named by God (Gen 17:16, 19), a response of incredulity from the barren couple (Gen 15:8; 17:17; 18:11–13), a confirmation of the conception (Gen 21:2), and a vindication from shame (Gen 21:5). Similar elements are found in John's birth narrative.

The stage is set for a theophany. According to Jewish customs, daily sacrifices at the Jerusalem temple were made in the morning and in the evening, accompanied by the offering of incense in the sanctuary. Temple duties were distributed among the twenty-four orders on a rotational basis, a week at a time, twice a year for each order. Given the large number of priests, the responsibility of offering incense at the altar was assigned by lot. For Zechariah, it is a once-in-a-lifetime opportunity to have the lot fall on him. By God's choosing, what is in store for Zechariah and Israel will far exceed the honor of the ritualistic task.

During the evening service, while the worshipers are praying outside, Zechariah goes alone into the sanctuary, puts the incense on the altar, and prostrates himself in prayer.[12] Given that the altar is situated immediately in front of the curtain behind which is the holy of holies, Zechariah is standing at the most sacred location inside the temple that a priest of his rank will ever find himself (Exod 30:1–6). This is holy and dangerous ground.

A visit from an angel is terrifying. Zechariah is in the midst of performing a very sacred task in the second most holy part of the temple,

---

11. Gen 29:31—30:23 (Rachel); 1 Sam 1:1–20 (Hannah); Judg 13:2–24 (Manoah and his wife).

12. Exod 29:38–42; 30:7–8; *m. Tamid* 5:1—7:3. So Hamm 2003: 220–21.

so any misstep may result in God sending an angel to destroy him. The angel, though, appears on the right side of the altar, which is both the authoritative and the favorable side.[13] Still, Luke thrice emphasizes Zechariah's fear: "he was terrified; and fear overwhelmed him" (1:12). Without introducing himself, the angel opens with an assurance that he comes not with judgment but with favor: "Do not be afraid" (1:13a).[14]

At first glance, the angel's message seems to affect only Zechariah's and Elizabeth's private lives. He declares that Zechariah's prayer has been heard and that Elizabeth will bear him a son to whom the name John, which means "God has been gracious," will be given (1:13b). Yet John's life will have an effect stretching far beyond his immediate family to the people of God. The joy he brings will be of national proportion, for beginning with his mission God will set in motion God's salvation promised through the prophets of old (1:14–17). John's greatness will reside in his divine commission and the high esteem in which he will be held (7:24–28).

Specific instructions are given as to how John will conduct himself and what his life's work will entail. First, set apart to be God's servant, John will be filled with the Holy Spirit even in his mother's womb and must never drink wine or any alcoholic beverage (1:15). According to the OT, priests also did not drink alcohol when serving at the temple (Lev 10:9). It is not necessary to label John as a Nazirite (Num 6:1–8), but asceticism is indicative of a life dedicated to God's service (Mark 1:6).

Second, John will be endowed with the spirit and power of Elijah (1:16–17). This promise recalls the words of Malachi: at the end of the age God will send a messenger to prepare the way before his coming (Mal 3:1). Malachi subsequently identifies this messenger as Elijah, who will "turn the hearts of parents to their children and the hearts of children to their parents, so that [God] will not come and strike the land with a curse" (Mal 4:5–6; cf. Sir 48:10). Although the wording in Luke 1:16–17 is not identical to that in Malachi, common to both are the themes of repentance and familial reconciliation, so that Israel will be prepared for the return of YHWH. John is to assume the role of this eschatological Elijah, calling Israel to repentance in advance of the arrival of the Lord, who, as we shall see, will come in the person of Jesus the Messiah.[15]

---

13. Fitzmyer 1981: 324–25.

14. Gen 21:17; Judg 6:23; Luke 1:30; 2:10.

15. In Luke John is identified with the eschatological Elijah of Mal 3, whereas the depiction of Jesus frequently contain allusions to the historical Elijah of 1–2 Kgs (e.g.,

Is the angel referring to Zechariah's personal prayer for a child or the prayer he prays on behalf of Israel as their priest? If the former, given the couple's old age and the hopelessness of their conceiving a child, the prayer that God has heard may have been a distant memory by now. If the latter, what Zechariah prays for inside the sanctuary concurs with those of the people outside, petitioning God to bring about the restoration of Israel (cf. 2:25, 37–38).

Zechariah's response fixes on the first part of the message, rather than on John's role in God's plan. His question, "How will I know that this is so?" (1:18), asks for a sign to assure him that the angel is telling the truth. Had he and Elizabeth still been praying for a son far into their advanced years, one would expect Zechariah to burst out in excitement: "This is unbelievable! Thank you, Lord, for answering our prayer for a son, the prayer that we pray every day, all the time!" Instead, Zechariah is doubtful that a prayer uttered long ago is still in effect. Unbelief sets in. It is not the first time that God opened the womb of a barren woman, so why should he doubt? His lapse of judgment earns him a divine reprimand.

The angel identifies himself and asserts his authority (1:19). In Jewish literature, Gabriel ("man of God") is highly regarded as God's personal servant and emissary.[16] Zechariah's unbelief is no small offense. He will indeed receive a sign, says the angel, and a punishment to boot (1:20). Zechariah is immediately struck mute until after the birth of the child. Since he is unable to speak, the good news that will bring joy to all Israel will remain an untold secret until the appropriate time of disclosure.

With Zechariah's delay inside the sanctuary, the people outside wonder if something has gone awry. When he finally emerges they conclude from his gestures that he must have seen some vision rendering him unable to speak (1:21–22). If Zechariah cannot even pronounce the benediction at the end of the Tamid service (Num 6:24–26), he may as well return home and wait out the months of silence until the birth of his son (1:23).

This section closes with the confirmation that Elizabeth becomes pregnant soon after (1:24). Her words express gratitude to God for showering favor upon her and vindicating her from the shame she has experienced (1:25). In spite of Zechariah's moment of distrust, Elizabeth joins him in preserving this secret until the baby's development becomes

---

4:24–26; 7:11–17; 9:52–55). See Miller 2007: 1–16.

16. 1 *En.* 20:1–7; 40:1–10; *T. Levi* 3:5–8.

apparent to all. The five months of solitude may also explain Mary's ignorance of Elizabeth's change of circumstances until Elizabeth is in her sixth month (1:36).

Two final notes are worth mentioning. First, the strong allusion to the story of Abraham and Sarah reminds the reader of God's overarching plan of salvation. God declared that the nations would be blessed through Abraham's offspring (Gen 12:1–2). The miraculous birth of Isaac was a gift after all human means had been exhausted. The same God who did the impossible for Abraham and Sarah is now doing the impossible for Zechariah and Elizabeth as part of the blessing for Israel and the nations. Second, as God responds to the yearning of Israel for deliverance, he weaves into that grand solution an answer to the personal need of righteous Zechariah and Elizabeth. The God of the big picture does not miss the fine details. In this regard, Zechariah's name fittingly describes his conviction and his experience, that indeed "YHWH remembers."

Annunciation of Jesus' Birth (1:26–38)

Six months have gone by since Gabriel's appearance to Zechariah. Elizabeth has reemerged from seclusion as her pregnancy is now visible to all. The scene changes dramatically, moving from the holy place of Jerusalem to the humble family home of a young woman in the nondescript village of Nazareth.[17] The sharp contrasts in status—from the holiness of the temple to the simplicity of a village abode, and from a respected male priest to a lowly female teenager—continue the theme of reversal that permeates the entire narrative. The reversal of Elizabeth's predicament from shameful barrenness to blessed conception is but the foretaste of a much more significant reversal in this pericope as Gabriel reveals to Mary her role as the mother of Israel's Messiah.

Unlike the detailed description of Zechariah's and Elizabeth's pedigree, Mary's family of origin is not even mentioned. Instead, repeatedly noted are that Mary is a virgin (1:27 [2x], 34), and Joseph, to whom she is betrothed, is of Davidic descent (1:27; 2:4). According to ancient Jewish marriage custom, a marital arrangement could be made for a young Jewish woman at the age of twelve or thirteen. After the bride price had exchanged hands, the woman became the wife of her husband, even though the couple would not yet be living together. The betrothed remained

---

17. Sitting in the shadow of nearby Sepphoris, the capital of Galilee, Nazareth was small and poor. Cf. John 1:46.

in her father's house for another year until she moved to her husband's house.[18] When Mary appears on the narrative stage, she is already legally bound to Joseph, even though she is still a virgin living in her childhood home. Although they have not consummated their marriage, her being the wife of a Davidide will legitimize Jesus as a descendant of that royal line. When Jesus is born, Joseph will become his adoptive father, as he carries no biological role in Jesus' conception (3:23; 4:22).

Gabriel's opening greeting is simultaneously affirming and shocking: "Rejoice (*Chaire*), highly favored one (*kecharitōmenē*)! The Lord is with you!" (1:28). Although *Chaire* is normally rendered as "Greetings!" (NRSV, NIV, ESV), hearing the words *Chaire* and *kecharitōmenē* in quick succession makes translating *Chaire* as "Rejoice!" a rhetorically attractive option. Being favored by God is surely a cause for rejoicing. In fact, the birth narratives of Luke are shot through with the theme of joy (1:14, 44, 47, 58; 2:10). Even before Mary knows of her assignment, she is assured of God's abiding presence. By her own admission, her lowly status makes it inconceivable that she should be the recipient of God's favor (1:48): "Who, me? Are you sure?" In reply, the angel points to her blessed state again: "Do not be afraid, Mary, for you have found favor (*charin*) with God" (1:30).

Gabriel first explains the "what" of Mary's favored status (1:31–33), followed by the "how" of its accomplishment (1:35–37). Mary is going to be the mother of the Davidic Messiah. The staccato in the string of future tenses—"You *will* conceive . . . you *will* name . . . he *will* be great . . . he *will* be called . . . the Lord God *will* give to him . . . he *will* reign . . . his kingdom *will* be"—injects a sense of certainty characteristic of a divine mandate. God's plan will come to pass, and Mary is called upon to bring the Davidic Messiah into the world. Verses 31 to 33 are pregnant with explicit messianic allusions taken from the OT. The name Jesus (*Iesous*), meaning "God saves," is the Greek form of the Aramaic name *Yeshu'a*, a variant of *Yehoshu'a* (Joshua). While John will be "great before the Lord" (1:15), Jesus will be great—without qualification (Deut 10:17). The titles, "Son of the Most High" and "Son of God," are identical in meaning and force (1:32, 35).

Although in many ancient cultures the ruler was thought to be the son of a deity, in Luke, the concept of divine sonship is derived from

---

18. Matt 1:18; *m. Ketub.* 4:5; Brown 1993: 123–24. Ancient betrothal was not analogous to the modern notion of engagement, it served an economic function for the two families to finalize the dowry (Hanson 2008: 31, 34–35).

the OT. The people of Israel had always understood themselves to be God's children by divine election. They prayed to God as "Our Father" and cherished their unique relationship with YHWH that set them apart from the nations.[19] In particular, Israel's king was vested with the honorific role as God's son. He represented the people of Israel before God and ruled over them on God's behalf. In the book of 2 Samuel, God did not allow David to build a temple for him, but instead gave him an even better promise. Not only would David's son build a house for God, but God would establish the throne of David's kingdom forever: "I will be a father to him, and he shall be a son to me" (2 Sam 7:14). The psalm sung at coronation ceremonies of a king's accession likewise reflected the same understanding of the privileged status of Israel's king: "[The LORD] said to me, 'You are my son, today I have begotten you. Ask of me, and I will make the nations your heritage, and the ends of the earth your possession'" (Ps 2:7-8; cf. Ps 89:26-29). God's promise to David became the basis of the dominant strand in Jewish messianic expectations that the Messiah would be a king descended from David.[20]

Given this background, the implication of Gabriel's words to Mary is obvious. Betrothed to Joseph the Davidide, Mary will carry in her womb the Davidic Messiah. Mary has not misheard the angel's message, but her concern is logical and practical: "How can this be, since I am a virgin?"(1:34). Mary expects this conception to occur at once or at least in the near future, not when she finally has sexual relations with her husband.[21] Her question is different from that of Zechariah (1:18). Zechariah wanted proof that his old and barren wife would really bear a son. To Mary, if Joseph has no part in her impregnation, what other option can there be? Puzzlement, not doubt, lies behind her response (cf. 1:45).

Mary's pregnancy will happen through the power of the Most High (1:35a). The verbs, "will come upon you" (*epeleusetai*) and "will overshadow you" (*episkiasei*), are mutually interpretive. Neither carries a sexual connotation. In the wilderness, God's presence overshadowed the tabernacle (Exod 40:35). In this mysterious yet divinely empowered conception, the Holy Spirit will create the baby in Mary's womb. The exact mechanism is not revealed, but the creative role of the Spirit in human

19. Exod 4:22; Isa 63:16; 64:8; Jer 31:20.
20. Isa 9:6-7; 11:1-10; Jer 23:5; 33:15; Ezek 34:23-24; 37:24-25; Amos 9:11; Mic 5:2; Zech 6:12-13; 9:9-10; 4Q174 3 I, 11; 4Q252 V, 3-4; 4Q285 V, 2-4; 4 *Ezra* 12:32; *Pss. Sol.* 17-18.
21. Landry 1995: 72-76.

life is foundational to Jewish thought (Job 33:4; Ps 104:30; Eccl 11:5). As divine Son of God, Jesus is holy because he is born of the Holy Spirit (1:35b). At the same time, Jesus the human Messiah is holy in that he is set apart for a life dedicated to God's service.

In contrast to Zechariah asking for a sign (1:20), Gabriel offers Mary a sign without being asked. Elizabeth's miraculous pregnancy, now progressing well and visible to all, signifies that God's power defies human limitation (1:36-37). The repeated mention of "the sixth month" ties the story of Mary's conception to that of Elizabeth (1:26, 36). The two mothers are kinswomen of each other. This fact, not disclosed until now, makes the double miracle all the more notable. Translated in the NRSV as "nothing will be impossible with God," the Greek actually reads "the word (*rhēma*) of God will not be disabled" (1:37). This is reminiscent of God's response to a laughing Sarah upon hearing that she would bear a child, "Is anything too wonderful for the LORD?" (Gen 18:14). If God's word came to fruition in Sarah and Elizabeth, so it will in Mary. The pericope closes with a calm, submissive consent of Mary to the will of God, "Here I am, the servant of the Lord; let it be with me according to your word (*rhēma*)" (1:38). With that note of deference on Mary's part, the angel departs.

There are many literary features tying the two annunciations together. The parallelism in form, down to specific wording, is remarkable. The same angel appears to both Zechariah and Mary (1:19, 26). Gabriel tells both of them not to be afraid (1:13, 30). Both respond to the message with a question (1:18, 34), and both are given a sign to prove the veracity of the angel's word (1:20, 36). Both births are miraculous, and both infants have clearly delineated roles in God's purposes. At every turn, the parallelism also shows a step up from John to Jesus. As miraculous as it is for God to open the womb of Elizabeth for John's conception, the way in which Mary becomes pregnant has no human precedent. The kingly status of Jesus also surpasses that of John, who even with the spirit and power of Elijah is at best the forerunner of the Messiah. Jesus is point-by-point superior to John even as both participate in the same saving mission of the one sovereign God.

Song of Mary (1:39-56)

Having received a sign from Gabriel, Mary embarks on a journey from Nazareth of Galilee to the hill country of Judah, near Jerusalem, to pay

Elizabeth a visit (1:39–40). The Greek words *meta spoudēs* can be translated as "hastily" or "eagerly." Either would fit Mary's disposition, given the situation. One might wonder how a young teenager could make that journey of seventy to eighty miles, over a course of three to four days, safely or readily, as ancient travel could be slow and dangerous. Perhaps she joins a caravan or she has a chaperone. The author does not elaborate, except that the next scene places her in the home of Elizabeth. At the least, this visit reflects Mary's faith in Gabriel's words, for she would not have been privy to Elizabeth's pregnancy since her relative has sequestered herself from public view (1:24).

Upon Mary's arrival, both Elizabeth and her unborn child respond with divinely inspired expressions of joy. Elizabeth is filled with the Holy Spirit, and Gabriel has already pronounced the same concerning her child "even before his birth" (1:15). The repetitions between verses 39 and 45 underscore the intensity of the emotions: Mary's greeting (1:41, 44), the leaping of the child in Elizabeth's womb (1:41, 44), and the blessing of Mary are all mentioned twice (1:42, 45).[22] The sense of joy, implicit in Elizabeth's loud cry and John's leaping, is carried from the anticipation of John's birth to that of Jesus (1:14, 44). More rejoicing will take place when each baby arrives (1:58; 2:10).

Whether it is Elizabeth blessing Mary or John greeting Jesus with his joyful jolt, the elder is acknowledging the younger. Mary has yet to tell Elizabeth the purpose of her visit, let alone the angel's message, but the latter is already blessing "the fruit of [her] womb" (1:42; cf. Deut 28:4). We suppose the filling of the Holy Spirit has resulted in Elizabeth's prophetic utterances. Elizabeth blesses Mary, not only for her role as the mother of Israel's Messiah, but especially for her trust in God's fulfillment of everything the angel has said about her and the destiny of her child (1:45). Noteworthy is Elizabeth's humility. Being much older and married, her social status is higher than that of Mary, a teenager living under her father's roof. Yet Elizabeth deems herself unworthy to receive a visit from "the mother of [her] Lord" (1:43). Even before his birth, Jesus is called "Lord,"[23] a title used of God himself in the OT. By addressing Jesus

---

22. The Greek words *eulogēmenē* (1:42) and *makaria* (1:45) are both translated as "blessed" in the NRSV. Although *eulogeō* usually means "to give thanks," it can denote blessedness (Mark 11:10).

23. In Luke, Jesus is called "Lord" by those who exhibit faith in him (5:8; 7:6; 9:54; 10:17, 40; 11:1; 12:41; 13:23; 18:41; 22:33, 38, 49). This may reflect the postresurrection perspective of the author and his audience.

with an elevated title, Elizabeth trades places with Mary, lifting the latter's status above her own.

Mary appropriately attributes the honor bestowed upon her to God's benevolence. The Song of Mary is poetic in form with its requisite parallelism and chiasm. While Moses, Miriam, Deborah, and Asaph all sang of God's mighty deeds,[24] in content Mary's Song is more reminiscent of that of Hannah, who praised God for answering her prayer for a child (1 Sam 2:1–10). This song is a collage of themes and phrases found in various Psalms and other OT passages, which articulate Israel's experience and understanding of YHWH as mighty savior and promise keeper.

Although Mary begins the song with her personal blessedness (1:46–49), in the second half she expands the recipients of God's goodness to all Israel (1:50–55). She testifies to the favor that God has bestowed upon her, not for self-elevation but to declare what God has done and will do for his people as he has for her. God is the main actor in this song and the subject of the active verbs: "he has looked . . . has done . . . has shown strength . . . has scattered the proud . . . has brought down the powerful . . . [has] lifted up the lowly . . . has filled the hungry . . . [has] sent the rich away . . . has helped" (1:48, 49, 51–54). God saves by enabling a reversal of conditions, for God is merciful, God remembers, and God is powerful.

First, God is merciful toward those who fear and revere him. Given the covenantal relationship between Israel and the almighty God, this fear engenders respect and faithfulness on Israel's part. Second, because God remembers his promise to Israel's ancestors, his mercy is a sustaining grace that stretches from generation to generation. Despite Israel's sufferings and faithlessness then and now, the people continue to trust that YHWH remembers them and his promises to them (1:54–55). Third, God has the power to save. The exodus is the paradigmatic event of God's deliverance of his people. Through the time of the judges, the kings, the exile, and the post-exilic period, Israel continued to experience God's help when their enemies came upon them. Israel was lowly, oppressed, afflicted, and weak, but God always came through. God's past acts of deliverance form the basis of Israel's hope for future salvation.

Mary depicts God as the divine warrior who shows strength with his arm (1:49, 51), exercising justice as he extends mercy (Exod 6:6; cf. Deut 4:34; Ps 77:15). He liberates those who need deliverance and punishes those who deserve condemnation. On the one hand, the lowly, the poor,

---

24. Exod 15:1–21 (Moses and Miriam); Judg 5:1–31 (Deborah); 1 Chr 16:7–36 (Asaph).

the oppressed, and the underprivileged are lifted up. On the other hand, the proud, the rich, the arrogant, and the powerful are brought down.[25] The reversal levels the playing field. While the historical backdrop of the song comprised actual wars that God fought for Israel, Mary is expressing a hope that transcends nationalism and militarism (1:51–52). She envisions a subversion of socio-economic power structures toward mutuality and equality, as expressed in the chiastic arrangement of verses 52 and 53:

> He has brought down the powerful from their thrones,
>   and lifted up the lowly;
> He has filled the hungry with good things,
>   and sent the rich away empty.

But that is not all. The polarities between power and lowliness, hungry and rich, and so on, have a spiritual dimension. The lowly ones who earnestly seek after God will enter the kingdom, and those with power and an inflated sense of self-righteousness will be denied (cf. 5:29–32; 6:20–25; 18:9–14). The theme of reversal will continue to play out in the mission, teaching, death, and resurrection of Jesus. Mary and Elizabeth are poised at the cusp of change. Their supernatural conceptions testify that God is setting in motion his final act of salvation by sending the Davidic Messiah and his forerunner. Not only does this song provide assurance, it engenders hope that defies even the uncontested power of Rome.

The scene ends with a statement that moves the timeline toward the next important event, the birth of John. If Mary remains with Elizabeth for another three months, it is possible that she stays long enough to be present at the next scene (1:56a). Then Mary returns to her father's house (1:56b), still a virgin betrothed to Joseph, bearing the Son of God in her womb. How heavy a responsibility that is for a young maiden to carry!

Song of Zechariah (1:57–80)

The announcement of John's birth takes us back to Gabriel's appearance to Zechariah (1:57–58). Gabriel's prophecy that Elizabeth "will bear a son" (*gennēsei huion*, 1:13) is now fulfilled. Luke uses near-identical language here: "she bore a son" (*egennēsen huion*, 1:57). Gabriel predicted that Zechariah "will have joy (*chara*) and gladness, and many will rejoice (*charēsontai*) at [his son's] birth" (1:14), and here the neighbors

---

25. Deut 10:17–18; Prov 3:34; Isa 2:11–12.

and relatives "rejoiced (*synechairon*) with her" (1:58). The theme of joy, already echoed in John's leaping in his mother's womb (1:44), will appear in the birth of Jesus as well (2:10). But for now, Zechariah will have more to say about the future role of his son, which sets the stage for the coming of the Messiah.

Customarily, Jewish male babies were circumcised on the eighth day (Gen 21:4; Acts 7:8). The rite of circumcision was a sign of the covenant between God and Abraham, and stood at the core of Jewish identity and self-understanding as God's chosen people (Gen 17:9–14; Lev 12:3). Naming a child at circumcision was a departure from traditional practices.[26] Traditionally, a child was given a name at birth (Gen 25:25–26). Greeks, however, named their children seven to ten days after birth. That John is named on the day of his circumcision may reflect an adoption of a popular Hellenistic practice in first-century Palestine.

At this joyous occasion, neighbors and relatives function as well-wishers and witnesses to the parents' obedience to the law. When a dispute arises over the naming of the child, the spectators turn from being witnesses to challengers. Their expectation that the baby be named after Zechariah does not stem from any specific custom that must be followed, though naming a boy after his father or grandfather was not uncommon in that culture (1:59).[27] In their enthusiasm and presumptuousness, the bystanders overstep their boundaries and begin to deliberate over what to call the child. The flurry of opinions has created a tense moment in an otherwise celebratory occasion.

But Elizabeth holds her ground: "No, he is to be called John" (1:60). The naming of a child by the mother was not an issue even in that patriarchal society.[28] Perhaps Elizabeth has not divulged that God has already named the child (1:13). Her words fail to satisfy the relatives, whose objection that the name "John" is not used elsewhere in the family seems arbitrary (1:61). Unconvinced, they gesture to the one who is yet unable to speak to overrule his wife. Unfazed by the commotion, Zechariah puts an end to the dispute. He writes on a wax-coated wooden tablet: "His name is John" (1:63). The phrasing has a definitive ring to it. The name "John" is a constant reminder that "YHWH has shown favor" to Elizabeth, Mary,

---

26. Evidence of such a practice is found in later Jewish literature (Nolland 1989: 79).

27. *Jub.* 11:15; Josephus *J.W.* 5.534; Josephus *Ant.* 14.10; 20.197.

28. Seth, Moab, Reuben, Simeon, Levi, Judah, Onan, and Shelah were all named by their mothers (Gen 4:25; 19:26–37; 29:32–35; 38:4–5).

and all Israel. Immediately his tongue is loosened and his punishment is over (1:20, 64).

The people are amazed, and the news spreads like wildfire (1:65). Even though a clear picture will not emerge for another few decades, the people's wonderment concerning the destiny of this newborn child invites another song (1:66), in which Zechariah picks up where Mary leaves off and offers an interpretation of these evolving events. Filled with the Holy Spirit, Zechariah pronounces a blessing on God's saving provision for Israel and a prophecy of his son's future role in it (1:67). Poetic in form, what follows connects thematically with Mary's song, circling back to the themes of remembrance, Abrahamic covenant, divine mercy, promise of salvation, etc., and at the same time moves the audience further in their anticipation of the future mission of John as the Messiah's forerunner.

The Song of Zechariah opens with a familiar blessing: "Blessed be the Lord God of Israel" (1:68; cf. Pss 41:13; 72:18). First, Zechariah blesses God for having fulfilled the promise given to Israel through the prophets by sending a messianic redeemer (1:69-71). This divine deliverance has a political or nationalistic dimension. The descendant of David is expected to rule over Israel, teach God's people, and exercise justice, but above all he is to be a warrior king or "a mighty savior" who can lead Israel to military victory against her enemies.[29] Behind the translation "a mighty savior" in the NRSV is the Greek phrase *keras sōtērias*, "a horn of salvation." An animal fights with its horn, making it an effective symbol of power and strength. While David calls God "the horn of [his] salvation" (2 Sam 22:3; Ps 18:2), another psalmist applies the metaphor directly to the royal Messiah: "I will cause a horn to sprout for David; I have prepared a lamp for my anointed one. His enemies I will clothe with disgrace, but on him his crown will gleam" (Ps 132:17-18). As such, the Davidic Messiah will assume a role attributed to God; he will become Israel's horn of salvation.

Second, God saves in order for Israel "to serve (*latreuein*) him without fear in holiness and righteousness" (1:74-75). When God sent Moses to Pharaoh, the rationale was the same: "Let my people go, so that they may serve (*latreusē*) me in the wilderness" (Exod 7:16). Since the verb *latreuō* encompasses the ideas of both worship and service, divine rescue is not only from imprisonment to freedom but also from malicious domination to beneficent lordship. All this has little to do with what

29. See p. 21, n. 20.

Israel can offer but everything to do with God's grace, mercy, election, and faithfulness as he remembers his covenant with Abraham (1:72–73). A God who remembers, acts. Since God has decreed that Abraham's numerous descendants will bless the nations (Gen 12:2–3; 22:16–18), every time the existence of Israel is threatened, God must stretch out his hand of deliverance to make good on his promise (Exod 2:24–25; Ps 105:8–9).

Third, serving as prophet of the Most High, John will awaken God's people to be ready for their mighty savior (1:17a, 76). The task of preparation for the Messiah's coming hearkens back to the words of the prophets: "A voice cries out: 'In the wilderness prepare the way of the LORD, make straight in the desert a highway for our God'" (Isa 40:3); "See, I am sending a messenger to prepare the way before me, and the Lord whom you seek will suddenly come to his temple" (Mal 3:1a). In these passages, the coming one is God himself. But the uniqueness of Jesus as the agent of salvation and Son of God conceived by the Holy Spirit makes it fitting to identify him as "the lord/Lord" of these passages. The role of the forerunner remains unchanged. John is the eschatological messenger who "will go before the Lord—[Jesus]—to prepare his ways" (1:76b; cf. 3:4; 7:27). John's mission is reconciliatory, for he will turn many in Israel back to God (1:16), which is what the eschatological Elijah will do when he appears (Mal 4:5–6). Turning is an image of repentance, used by the prophets to persuade Israel to turn from their evil ways (Isa 31:6; Jer 18:11). Now John will again urge Israel to repent. He is to "give knowledge of salvation to [God's] people by the forgiveness of their sins" (1:77; cf. 3:3). Israel's preparation is not military but spiritual. The Messiah will be greeted not by an army thirsty for bloodshed, but by a lowly people, humble in heart and grateful for God's mercy. Redemption here is rescue not from the Romans but from sin (Ps 130:7–8).

Fourth, God's redemption results in peace and life for all Israel (1:78–79). The English translation, "By the tender mercy (*dia splanchna eleous*) of our God, the dawn (*anatolē*) from on high will break upon (*epeskepsato*) us" (1:78 NRSV), obscures the richness of the images that are loaded with messianic significance. God's *splanchna* refers to God's "heart" or "gut" in anthropomorphic terms. They are the "inner organs" in which God's deepest emotions reside. God's saving actions are motivated by his most tender, loving, and sympathetic compassion for his own (cf. 7:13; 10:33; 15:20). The dawn or sunrise is only one meaning of *anatolē* (cf. Isa 60:1; Mal 4:2), which fits well with its goal "to give light to those who sit in darkness and in the shadow of death" (1:79a). Light is a common metaphor to denote God's presence (Exod 13:21; Ps 27:1). Salvation is described as moving from darkness into light (Isa 9:2; 42:7). Another meaning of *anatolē* is shoot, sprout, or branch, which reminds us of depictions of the Davidic Messiah as "a righteous Branch" (Jer 23:5), "[God's] servant the Branch" (Zech 3:8), "a man whose name is Branch" (Zech 6:12), "a shoot [that comes] out of the stump of Jesse" (Isa 11:1), and "the root of Jesse" (Isa 11:10). All these layers of meaning for *anatolē* converge at the Davidic Messiah who leads God's people into "the way of peace" (1:79b; cf. Isa 9:6–7; 59:8).[30] It is noteworthy that the glorified Jesus in the book of Revelation makes this claim: "I am the root and the descendant of David, the bright morning star" (Rev 22:16; cf. Num 24:17)![31]

The last verse of chapter 1 fast-forwards through the childhood and youth of John with a summary of his physical and spiritual maturity (1:80). This statement is reminiscent of similar ones said of Samson (Judg 13:24–25) and Samuel (1 Sam 2:26; 3:19). Both, like John, were born of mothers who were once barren until God opened their wombs and were dedicated by those mothers to God's service.

---

30. Gathercole (2005: 471–85) suggests that 1:78 further emphasizes the heavenly origin of the Davidic Messiah, who is traditionally expected to be a human figure.

31. Strauss 1995: 103–8.

Luke 2

Birth of Jesus (2:1–20)

When Gabriel announced the supernatural births of John and Jesus, Jesus' superiority over John was already evident in the description of each child's status and role.[1] The same pattern is found in the account of each birth. For instance, the author locates John's birth "in the days of King Herod of Judea" (1:5), but places Jesus' birth on a much wider religio-political platform during the reign of Augustus Caesar and the governorship of Quirinius (2:1). Whereas friends and relatives spread the miraculous happenings surrounding John's birth through the human grapevine (1:65), an angel announces the birth of Jesus (2:9). Over and above the Spirit-filled Zechariah who interprets the significance of John's birth and prophesies over his newborn son (1:67–79), angelic hosts now declare the heavenly and earthly implications of the coming of God's Son (1:13–14). Luke clearly elevates the status of Jesus above that of John. He includes details of Jesus' dedication at the temple and the child's return twelve years later. While John and Jesus are both key players in God's plan of salvation, there is no mistaking the lesser as the greater, or confusing the forerunner with the long-awaited Messiah.[2]

Augustus Caesar, born Gaius Octavian, was the first of twelve Caesars in the Roman Empire of the first century. He was the grandnephew of Julius Caesar, who adopted him and made him his heir. After the assassination of Julius Caesar in 44 BCE, the Roman Republic crumbled until Octavian persevered over his rivals, unified the empire in 31 BCE, and inaugurated the golden era of the *Pax Romana* ("Roman Peace"). In 27 BCE, the Roman Senate conferred upon him the honorific title of Augustus, which not only meant eminent and majestic, but was suggestive of something numinous.[3] After the posthumous deification of Julius

---

1. See p. 22.
2. See Kuhn 2001: 38–49.
3. Ferguson 2003: 26–30.

Caesar, Augustus assumed the title *Divi Filius* ("son of the divine" or "son of a god"), paving the way for his own veneration in the imperial cult. Augustus died in 14 CE and was succeeded by his stepson Tiberius.[4]

Setting the birth of Israel's king against the backdrop of Augustus's reign, Luke makes a bold theological and political statement. There are ample literary, numismatic, archaeological, and inscriptional records to show that the titles "Savior," "Ruler" ("Imperator"), "Son of God," and "Father of the Fatherland" had all been used of Augustus.[5] For us modern readers, when the angel refers to Jesus as "Savior" and "Lord" (2:11), we are reminded of God as "Savior" and "Lord" in the OT. But in the first century, every proclamation of Jesus in royal and divine terms could be construed as an act of sedition against the Roman emperor.

Excursus: Quirinius's Census

The account of Jesus' birth begins with Joseph and Mary traveling to Bethlehem as required by a census under the decree of Augustus (2:1–5). The reference to this census has presented a number of challenges. Although the Romans were known for keeping good historical records, scholars have yet to unearth any evidence of an empire-wide census ordered by Augustus within the time frame in question. In Matthew, Jesus was born before the death of Herod the Great in 4 BCE. The census in Luke, however, would have placed the birth of Jesus no earlier than 6 or 7 CE, within a small window of time during which Quirinius served as governor of Syria. Surely Jesus could not have been born *both* before 4 BCE *and* after 6 CE! Even if we assume Luke's date to be erroneous, so that the census was actually conducted earlier under the kingship of Herod the Great and not the governorship of Quirinius, to what extent would Roman practices have influenced the administration of Judea, which at the time of Herod was still a client kingdom not yet annexed into the Roman Empire? Could Quirinius have had a wider realm of authority before his appointment in Syria, so that an earlier Herodian census could have been associated with his office? Could Herod have offended Augustus so that a Roman census was imposed on

---

4. Grant 1975: 52–80.

5. An example of a Myrian inscription: "Divine Augustus Caesar, Son of a God, Imperator of land and sea, the Benefactor and Savior of the whole world" (Green 1997: 125).

Herod's territory to assert Roman dominance? Coming at it from a textual-grammatical point of view, could the adjective *prōtē* in 2:2 be understood, not as "the *first* registration [that] was taken while Quirinius was governor of Syria," as in first among several censuses, but that "the registration [was] taken *before* Quirinius was governor of Syria" a few years earlier? The second translational option for *prōtē*, "*before* Quirinius," might resolve the awkward presence of that ten-year stretch between 4 BCE and 6 CE in which Jesus could not have been born, but the question still remains as to whether or not Quirinius administered that census that coincided with the birth of Jesus.

The problem goes beyond a matter of dating to the actual practice of census-taking. The Romans counted people based on principal residency rather than ancestral origin. Could a Herodian census be conducted differently from a Roman census? Did regional customs come into play? That Joseph has to be registered in person in Bethlehem rather than in Nazareth may imply that he owns property in his ancestral town, necessitating his going back there to be counted as head of the household. Even so, is Mary's presence mandatory? Her accompaniment on the journey may mean that the betrothal period is over, and they are traveling as a married pair. And if not, then being with Joseph may still be preferable to enduring the gossips alone in Nazareth as her pregnancy becomes visible.

Questions abound, and each hypothesis comes with assumptions.[6] Due to gaps in historical knowledge, it is doubtful that an airtight reconstruction of the timing of Jesus' birth that perfectly reconciles the accounts in both Matthew and Luke is possible. The historical questions are interesting, but there must be a more constructive way to honor Luke's aim at presenting a narrative that proclaims the truth about Jesus without writing him off as an incompetent historian!

Whereas historical questions at this point are difficult to resolve, considering Luke's storytelling from a theological point of view casts a different light on the account. The census, a negative symbol and painful reminder of subjugation, is mentioned four times in the first five verses.

---

6. Brown (1993: 412–18) provides a thorough discussion of the historical problem. Rist (2005: 489–91) postulates that Luke confused Quirinius with Quintilius Varus. A reference to the latter would have set the date of Jesus' birth around 6 BCE, in line with the Matthean account given that Herod died in 4 BCE.

When Augustus became emperor, he reinstituted the census system as part of an empire-wide administrative reform to formalize taxation and military service. While the Jews were exempt from serving in the Roman army, they were not excused from taxes. The decree in 2:1 might refer to an overarching imperial order, so that Roman officials could use Augustus's edict to justify their regional or provincial censuses.

Although it cannot be ascertained if the census that affected Joseph and Mary was the one Quirinius conducted in 6 CE, that census was especially infamous as *the* census of shame and coerced loyalty. It marked the turning point at which Judea fell under the direct control of Rome without the buffer of a Jewish client kingdom. The Herodian monarchs were cruel, corrupt, and pro-Rome, but they were still not Romans. Paying taxes to Herod stung less than paying taxes to Caesar. But with the deposition of Herod Archelaus, Quirinius's census signaled the definitive defeat of the Jews, putting an end to any lingering vestige of Jewish autonomy. This was a difficult pill to swallow.[7]

Precisely because Augustus and Quirinius represented Israel's subjugation under Roman hegemony, their naming in Jesus' birth narrative (2:1–2) is central to Luke's daring literary strategy. Mary is pregnant as she embarks on this journey to Judea (2:5–6). The couple returns to Joseph's city of origin, "the city of David called Bethlehem" (2:4). Luke's interest in David and Joseph lies primarily in their blood ties (1:27). Bethlehem, about five miles south of Jerusalem, is "the city of David" insofar as it is where David was born and where Samuel anointed him as king (1 Sam 16:1–13; 17:12, 58).[8] Through Joseph, Jesus can legitimately be considered a *Davidic* Messiah, a king born and anointed in the city of David (1:32; 2:11; cf. 3:23, 31). As perfect timing and location converge, even powerful Augustus becomes an unwitting instrument of the divine plan. The census that signifies oppression serves to locate the mother of Jesus in the right city at the right time, so that Jesus' birth in Bethlehem fulfills the prophecy of Micah: "But you, O Bethlehem of Ephrathah, . . . from you shall come forth for me one who is to rule in Israel" (Mic 5:2; cf. Matt 1:6).

After a journey of about three days, Mary and Joseph arrive in Bethlehem. At this point the typical scene in a modern-day Christmas pageant of one heartless innkeeper after another turning away a desperate Joseph

---

7. Garland 2012: 117–19.

8. "The city of David" can also point to Jerusalem (or Mount Zion), the capital from which King David ruled (2 Sam 5:7; 2 Chr 5:2).

with a wife in labor in the thick of night requires a major re-envisioning. A close reading of Luke reveals a scene that is less chaotic and a point that has more to do with status reversal than with inhospitality and rejection.

Mary goes into labor (2:6), but "there was no place for them in the inn (*katalyma*)" (2:7c NRSV). The translation of *katalyma* as "inn" is misleading, for the word has a wider range of meaning, from an inn to a guest room of a house. Since Bethlehem is not located on any main travel thoroughfare, that small town may not even have a commercial lodging place. Later in the narrative Jesus sends his disciples to a guest room (*katalyma*) to make preparations for the Passover meal (22:11). But a different word, *pandocheion*, is used to denote an inn with an innkeeper (*pandocheus*) with whom the Samaritan in Jesus' parable leaves the injured man (10:34–35). It seems likely that Joseph and Mary have found shelter at the home of a relative, not that they have been going from inn to inn looking for vacancy.[9]

Modest peasant homes in the ancient world consisted of one large room for living and sleeping, with an adjacent area at a lower level under the same roof where animals were kept when brought in for the night. A cave could also be used to shelter animals. Perhaps, due to overcrowding, the host family has run out of guest quarters and the only place the relatives can offer Mary and Joseph is space with the animals (2:7c). The couple is not turned away—as implied in many Christmas plays—but is shown hospitality in spite of the humble circumstances. A manger (*phatnē*), or more crudely, a feeding trough, is improvised as a crib for the baby Jesus. Mary wraps her infant in long strips of bandages to keep his arms and legs from moving and to provide a sense of warmth and security (Wis 7:4). While a baby bound in swaddling cloth is a common sight, one sleeping in a manger is not. This unusual combination makes an effective sign for the shepherds to recognize the Messiah (2:7b, 12, 16).

The child is Mary's firstborn son (2:7a). This particularity signifies birth order as well as responsibility and status. The law stipulates that the firstborn of human beings and animals are to be dedicated to God (2:23; cf. Exod 13:2, 12; 34:19–20). The firstborn son is also entitled to a double portion of his father's inheritance (Deut 21:15–17). Similarly, Israel is identified as God's firstborn on the basis of their election (Exod 4:22; Jer 31:9; Sir 36:17). Therefore, it is fitting for Mary's firstborn, the Son of God

---

9. Green 1997: 129; Marshall 1978: 107.

and Davidic Messiah, to rule over and represent Israel, God's firstborn, with all its privileges and obligations.

From one humble situation to another, the author moves the spotlight from the manger to the open fields where some shepherds are "keeping watch over their flock by night" (2:8). Shepherding was a despised profession in the ancient world. Shepherds were often poor peasants who hired themselves out to earn supplemental income to support their families.[10] They worked in teams and took turns keeping watch at night, being on the lookout for wolves and thieves. The angel's appearance to these shepherds echoes the theme of status reversal already sounded in Mary's song (1:48, 52). The first to hear of Jesus' birth will not be the religious and political powerbrokers in Jerusalem, but a group of forgotten and lowly hired hands in the lonely fields of a small town.

It may be worth noting that David started off as a shepherd caring for his father's sheep in Bethlehem (1 Sam 16:19; 17:15; Ps 78:70–71). In the OT, shepherd is a metaphor for describing God's care and oversight of his people (Pss 23:1; 80:1; Ezek 34:12–16; Mic 7:14). Furthermore, Israel's kings and religious leaders were also tasked to shepherd God's flock. Since many failed to do so properly (Jer 23:2; Ezek 34:8), God said he would remove the bad shepherds and send a replacement shepherd, that is, the Messiah, to rule over Israel on his behalf (Ezek 34:23; 37:24). These connections make the announcement to shepherds, rather than farmers, day laborers, or other forms of peasantry, especially poignant. The proclamation that these shepherds are about to hear pertains to God's eschatological shepherd, a king from the line of David, who may also be found, like themselves, in a humble state, lying in a manger in a peasant home.[11]

Dazzling brightness signifies the presence of God's glory when an angel appears before the shepherds (2:9). The scene enacts the conclusion of Zechariah's hymn, literally and spiritually: "The dawn from on high will break upon us, to give light to those who sit in darkness" (1:78–79). When light pierces through darkness, it is sudden, illuminating, and terrifying. The shepherds' frightened response is expected as the angel greets them with the same words spoken to Zechariah and Mary: "Do not be afraid" (2:10a; cf. 1:12–13, 29–30). Then he continues, "For behold, I am bringing you good news (*euangelizomai*) of great joy for all the people"

---

10. Harris 2012: 18–20.
11. Ibid., 27–30.

(2:10b). The same verb, *euangelizō*, is used in Isaiah to denote the good news of God's salvation (Isa 52:7; cf. 40:9; 61:1–2). The phrase, "for all the people," foreshadows the expansion of God's saving horizon from the Jews to the gentiles (2:30–32; 3:6; Acts 1:8). Israel's good news is destined to be good news for the whole world.

The content of the good news is focused on one figure: "to you is born this day in the city of David a Savior, who is the Messiah, the Lord" (2:11). The wait is over. God's promise to Israel's ancestors has come to fulfillment with the arrival of the Davidic Messiah. Savior, Messiah, and Lord—these three titles encapsulate the function and status of Jesus. He is the "horn of salvation" in Zechariah's hymn (1:69–71); he shares the title "Savior" and "Lord" with YHWH;[12] he is also the Messiah, the anointed king born in "the city of David" who belongs to the house of David and will sit on the throne of David forever (1:32–33, 69). Luke's readers already know this Messiah is God's divine Son. Paradoxically, the sign that verifies the truth of the angel's words is "a child wrapped in bands of cloth and lying in a manger" (2:12). Instead of a heaven-sent warrior on horseback, ready to annihilate the Romans, the Savior-Messiah-Lord enters the human stage as an infant gurgling in an animal feeder.

To the bright light we now add the collective voices of the attendants of God in a heavenly chorus. The angel is joined by "a multitude of the heavenly host (*stratias*) praising God" (2:13). The Greek word *stratia*, often translated as "host," also means "army." YHWH is a mighty warrior (1:51–52; cf. 10:18), thus the sending of the Davidic Messiah is both good news and the battle cry of God's salvation.[13] The angels sing of the effects of the Messiah's birth, that God in heaven is glorified and exalted, and people on earth experience true peace (2:14). Recalling Zechariah's prophecy, this Savior will guide "our feet into the way of peace" (1:79). This peace does not mean cessation or absence of war and strife, but reconciliation between God and those who receive by faith his gracious gift of salvation through Jesus. God's peace will have its ultimate expression when God's reign is manifested in the eschaton, so that life in that blessed eternity will be characterized by perfect security, harmony, abundance, and health. The coming of the Messiah is the beginning of a journey with eternal peace as its destination.

---

12. The title *Kyrios* ("Lord") is applied to YHWH in 1:6, 9, 11, 15–16, 25, 28, 32, 38, 45–46, 58, 68, and to Jesus in 1:17, 43, 76. The title *Sotēr* ("Savior") is applied to YHWH in 1:47, and to Jesus in 1:69 and 2:11.

13. Verbrugge 2008: 301–11.

The Greek phrase, *en anthrōpois eudokias*, introduces some ambiguity (2:14b). Translated word for word, it reads "among men of goodwill (or favor)." Whose goodwill or whose favor is in view? On the one hand, human beings are blessed only because God bestows his favor upon them, as Elizabeth and Mary have testified (1:25, 48). On the other hand, the recipients of God's blessings have to demonstrate an attitude of goodwill to be ready to receive God's benign intervention (1:17, 77). In the end, God's initiative meets human response to actualize eternal peace between both parties. Because God's initiative always comes first, human responsiveness presupposes divine favor. Therefore, 2:14b is better rendered as "peace on earth among the people whom God has favored."[14]

The angel departs, leaving the shepherds to decide what to do with what they have just seen and heard (2:15). Like Mary, they proceed with haste to follow the sign (2:12, 16; cf. 1:36, 39). When they find Mary, Joseph, and the infant, they relate everything that has been told to them, which Mary treasures and ponders in her heart (2:17, 19–20). The three-stepped pattern of hearing, seeing, and repeating the message becomes the means of bearing witness to the good news, from the shepherds to Mary and Joseph, and to others who are present.

Hearing or reading the story of Jesus' birth, Theophilus and his community would probably notice subtle similarities with common inscriptions or writings concerning Augustus. For example, below is an inscription concerning Augustus's birthday (italics mine):

> Since Providence which has ordered all things and is deeply interested in our life, has set in most perfect order by giving us Augustus, whom she filled with virtue that he might benefit humankind, sending him as a *savior*, both for us and for our descendants, that he might end war and arrange all things, and since he, Caesar, by his appearance, surpassing all previous benefactors, and not even leaving to posterity any hope of surpassing what he has done, and since *the birthday of the god Augustus was the beginning of the good news for the world* that came by reason of him . . .[15]

---

14. The translation in the NKJV, "goodwill toward men," reflects a textual variant that has *eudokia* (a nominative) instead of *eudokias* (a genitive). The genitive has stronger textual support among the more reliable manuscripts.

15. Priene Inscription (*OGIS* 458), cited in Evans 2005: 313. See also Porter 2000: 533.

Worldwide salvation, benefaction, and peace are attributed to Augustus, a suprahuman-like emperor sent by Providence as a gift to humankind. Is Luke's description of Jesus' birth intentionally polemical against the laudatory praise of Augustus? How will Jesus, Israel's Savior-Messiah-Lord, compare with Rome's Savior-God? Will Jesus' kingdom be set on a collision course with Caesar's empire? Luke's readers are invited to contemplate such possibilities by holding in tension the welcome of Israel's Savior on the one hand, and his rejection on the other.

Dedication of Jesus at the Temple (2:21–40)

A male child would normally be named before his circumcision on the eighth day, but Luke reports the two as a single event both with John and with Jesus (1:59; 2:21). "[The child] was called Jesus, the name given by the angel before he was conceived in the womb" (2:21). God the Father, not Jesus' earthly parents, names his Son "Jesus," as implied by the passive voice of the verb. The name, meaning "YHWH saves," is exactly what Jesus will come to embody and actualize.

A woman remains ceremonially unclean for seven days after giving birth to a boy (Lev 12:2). On the eighth day the infant is circumcised (Gen 17:12; Lev 12:3). His mother's state of purification continues for thirty-three days, during which she may neither enter the temple nor come in contact with holy things. At the end of her purification period, she offers a lamb for a burnt offering and a pigeon or turtledove for a sin offering. For the poor, another turtledove or pigeons may take the place of the lamb (Lev 5:11; 12:1–8). In general, Luke's account reflects closely the stipulations of the law except for two minor details (2:22–24). Only Mary, the mother, is in need of purification, but Luke speaks of "their purification," perhaps because both she and Joseph are present. Also, the couple brings Jesus to the temple on the eighth day for his circumcision, but the sacrifice is supposed to be made weeks later upon the completion of Mary's days of purification. It is not clear if the deviation from Leviticus stems from the author's storytelling or changes to traditional practices in the first century. But one thing is clear: Jesus' parents are law-abiding Jews even though they have modest means.

Every Israelite firstborn, whether human or animal, is consecrated to God (Exod 13:2; Neh 10:35–36). The notion of redeeming the firstborn is not in view here, as nothing is said of Jesus' parents paying the priest any redemption price (Num 18:15–16). Rather, the presentation of Jesus at the temple parallels Hannah's dedication of Samuel to the service of the Lord when she brought him to Eli the priest (1 Sam 1:24–28). While Jesus is not offered for lifelong priestly service, God has already laid claim on his life. Luke's reference to the law, "Every firstborn male shall be designated as holy to the Lord" (2:23), recalls Gabriel's words to Mary, "the child to be born will be holy" (1:35), for indeed Jesus is conceived by the Holy Spirit and set apart for God's service.

The next two scenes are complementary (2:25–38). Like Zechariah and Mary, Simeon and Anna form a male-female pairing to bear witness to the purposes of God.[16] Both are depicted as pious and steadfast before God. While Simeon is explicitly stated as having the Holy Spirit resting on him (2:25–27), the work of the Spirit on Anna is implied, since she is a prophetess (2:36). Simeon is righteous and devout (2:25), and Anna, throughout her widowhood, "never left the temple but worshiped there with fasting and prayer night and day" (2:37). Both of them hold fast to the promises of God by aligning themselves with those who are waiting patiently for the consolation of Israel and the redemption of Jerusalem (2:25, 38; cf. 23:51; Isa 52:9; 66:13).

The meeting between Simeon and Jesus' family is orchestrated by the Holy Spirit (2:27), the fulfillment of a revelation from the Spirit to Simeon that he will see the Lord's Messiah during his lifetime (2:26, 29).[17] Holding Jesus in his arms, Simeon praises God and expresses his readiness to die, for God's salvation, embodied in the person of the Messiah, has finally arrived (2:28–29). The verb *apoluō*, which means "to dismiss" or "to release," is a double-entendre. On the one hand, it is a euphemism for death. God can now release Simon and let him die in peace. On the other hand, God the master is dismissing Simeon because the servant's task of waiting for God's salvation is now accomplished (2:29).

The vocabulary and themes in the next three verses are drawn heavily from Isaiah 40–66. Looking at the baby Jesus, Simeon declares, "My eyes have seen your salvation" (2:30; cf. Isa 51:5–8; 52:10; 56:1). Jesus is not merely the bringer or agent of God's salvation; he is God's salvation personified. He will embody God's saving actions in his person—in life and in death, in word and in action.

---

16. See p. 66, n. 12.

17. The Greek participle *kechrēmatismenon* (2:26) carries a sense of command. Simeon is ordered by the Holy Spirit to recognize Jesus as the embodiment of God's salvation. His role is to recognize and bear witness to Jesus. See Soards 1990: 403.

Even as faithful Jews are waiting for Israel's Messiah, ultimately God's salvation has been "prepared in the presence of *all peoples*" (2:31; cf. 2:10; 3:6). For the gentiles, the Savior will be a light that illumes the darkness, the spiritual blindness, in which those who do not know God find themselves (2:32a; Isa 42:6–7). Israel was supposed to be a light to the nations, so that through Israel's witness the nations might come to know YHWH and be saved (Isa 49:6). Israel, however, failed to live up to this role, which will be fulfilled completely and perfectly by Jesus. Yet there is still a sense that salvation will go to the gentiles through the agency of Israel. The gospel will be preached to those outside of Israel by Jesus' followers who are themselves Jews, from Jerusalem to Judea, Samaria, and to the ends of the earth (Acts 1:8).

There is a hint of irony for the gentiles to be mentioned before the Jews (2:32b). Be that as it may, the people of Israel already know God, so the coming of the Messiah is not so much for their illumination as it is for their glory (Isa 46:13). Glory connotes the sense of honor and revelation. Israel will share in the Messiah's glory, a glory that will only be fully appropriated with the inclusion of the gentiles, something that faithful Israel must learn to do (Acts 9:15; 10:45; 11:18).

Mary and Joseph are amazed by Simeon's words, which necessitate further pondering (2:33; cf. 2:19, 50–51). Simeon's pronouncement about Jesus provides the lens through which Jesus' life must be interpreted, but full understanding lies yet in the future. Then, addressing Mary in particular, Simeon portends future conflict that leaves her, and the readers, with a sense of foreboding. Opposition will come from within God's people: "This child is destined for the falling and the rising of many of Israel, and to be a sign that will be opposed" (2:34). Signs point beyond themselves and are made to be followed, so to oppose a sign defeats the purpose of having a sign in the first place. The Messiah will point the way forward for Israel, but he will receive a mixed reception. Some will heed the sign and rise while others will refuse to follow and stumble (Isa 8:14–15). Those who reject God will fall, and their inner thoughts and hypocrisy will be exposed. In the end, it will become clear who will be judged and who will be blessed (2:35a; cf. 3:17).

The last thing that a mother would want to hear is that her firstborn child will encounter hostility, even to the point of death, as implied in Simeon's last phrase, "and a sword will pierce your own soul too" (2:35b). Indeed, Mary will outlive Jesus and experience the deep anguish of a mother witnessing the death of her son. But this is the same Mary who responded to Gabriel, "Here I am, the servant of the Lord; let it be with me according to your word" (1:38). As she dedicates Jesus to God, is she able to relinquish her son's life into God's hand in total trust? As with the rest of Israel, the inner thoughts of Mary's heart will undergo severe testing.

With Simeon's words still hanging in the air, in comes Anna the prophetess. She is from the tribe of Asher, where Elijah the prophet preached (1 Kgs 17–18). Her father's name, Phanuel, is the Greek form of the Hebrew Peniel/Penuel ("face of God"), which is the name Jacob gave to the place where he wrestled with the angel to commemorate his having "seen God face to face" (Gen 32:30–31). All these biographical details, together with the explicit identification of Anna as a prophetess, situate her squarely among the recipients of God's revelation. By her piety she bears witness to this special heritage and identity.[18]

Although Luke does not record Anna's exact words (2:38), we may assume that her praise to God is congruent with those of Mary, Zechariah, and Simeon. While the description of Anna's constant presence at the temple may be a bit of an exaggeration in the literal sense, it is not in Luke's estimation of her faithfulness and credibility. This is brought out in the detailed description of her old age and personal circumstances (2:36–37). The Greek here suggests that Anna is either eighty-four years old, or that she has been a widow for eighty-four years after seven years of marriage, which puts her at a ripe old age of 105 if she married at the age of fourteen![19] Regardless of whether she is eighty-four or 105, Anna the prophetess has a lifelong track record of devotion to God that earns her a rightful place in the narrative.[20] Together with Zechariah, Elizabeth, and Mary, Simeon and Anna complete the chorus of faithful voices in Israel, and their convictions about God's faithfulness and promises place the story of Jesus at an exciting edge of anticipation.

This section closes with an affirmation, for the fifth time, of Mary's and Joseph's adherence to the law (2:39; cf. 2:22, 23, 24, 27). The family returns to Galilee and settles in Nazareth, where Joseph has already made a home (2:39; cf. 2:4). The first summary statement of Jesus' physical, mental, and spiritual growth functions as a bridge between infancy to late

---

18. See García-Serrano 2014: 468–69 and Thurston 2001: 49–50.

19. If there is symbolism in the number 84, García-Serrano (2014: 470) notes that Anna "lived a perfect married life (seven years) and an even more perfect widowhood (seven times twelve years)."

20. Thurston 2001: 50–52.

childhood (2:40). It will be followed by another enhanced statement after the account of the twelve-year-old Jesus at the temple (2:52). One might consider 2:40 and 2:52 as forming an *inclusio* around the next pericope, but it seems fitting to close this section with verse 40, "the favor of God was upon him," in light of the heavy emphasis of God's favor upon the faithful ones of Israel thus far in the narrative.

Jesus at Twelve (2:41–52)

Childhood stories of heroes are not uncommon in ancient literature. Authors and biographers believed that the paths and attendant traits that made certain characters great in adulthood were already latent in their youth. For example, Josephus, the Jewish historian, claimed that Samuel began to prophesy at the age of twelve (*Ant.* 5.348) and that Josiah began instituting reforms in Israel when he was twelve (*Ant.* 10.50). Elsewhere in Greco-Roman writings, famous figures like Alexander the Great, Epicurus, Apollonius of Tyana, and Cyrus were all seen as child prodigies who had the acumen and prowess that made them productive and powerful later in life.[21] Listening to an account of Jesus as a child, Luke's readers are primed to look for clues that will help them imagine what Jesus will be like as an adult.

Jesus' parents have a habit of making an annual trip to Jerusalem to observe the Passover, so this year is no different (2:41–42). Jewish men were required to attend three annual pilgrimage feasts, namely, Passover, Pentecost, and Tabernacles (Exod 23:14–17).[22] For many Jews, going to Jerusalem three times a year would pose a hardship. Still, the feasts were well attended. These pilgrimages soon became a family affair as women and children went up to Jerusalem as well.[23] Traveling with other families as a group reduced costs and provided protection from robbers along

---

21. Philostratus *Vit. Apoll.* 1.7 (Apollonius of Tyana); Plutarch *Alex.* 4.4—5.5 (Alexander); Diogenes Laertius 10.14 (Epicurus); Herodotus *Hist.* 1.114–16 (Cyrus). Billings (2009: 70–89) thinks that Luke's inclusion of the childhood story of Jesus anticipates the presentation of the adult Jesus as superior to Augustus.

22. In Deut 16:16 these feasts are referred to as Unleavened Bread, Weeks, and Booths, respectively. Passover was immediately followed by the Feast of Unleavened Bread, which lasted a week (Lev 23:5–6; Deut 16:1–4). By the time of Jesus, the names of these two feasts were used interchangeably. See Ferguson 2003: 557–59.

23. Hannah went up to Jerusalem "year by year" with her husband Elkanah (1 Sam 1:3, 7, 21; 2:19), although the text does not specific which feast.

the way (2:44).²⁴ There is no indication that this is Jesus' first return to Jerusalem since his presentation as an infant. We assume that Mary and Joseph have been bringing him with them for some time already.²⁵ At twelve, Jesus is a year shy of entering the religious community officially but old enough to appreciate the significance of Passover.

Nothing unusual occurred during the feast. It is afterwards that Mary and Joseph lose track of Jesus. The text never addresses why Jesus does not tell his parents his whereabouts. Neither is it necessary to charge the couple with negligence. Since Jesus is no longer a toddler and should be fully capable of keeping up with the group traveling together, it seems reasonable for Mary and Joseph to assume that he is within the proximity of the moving caravan, playing with other children among the relatives. In this manner they travel for an entire day northward, covering about twenty miles. Perhaps they finally notice his absence by evening when the group settles down for the night. Letting the caravan continue on its way the next day, Mary and Joseph retrace their steps and hurry back to Jerusalem. Imagine the difficulty of going "against traffic," trying to move toward Jerusalem when hordes of pilgrims are coming out of the city. Added to the exhaustion of travel for the couple from a small village is the anxiety of trying to find their firstborn son in a large city. We can appreciate Mary's and Joseph's frame of mind, a mixture of exasperation and relief, when on the third day since their original departure from Jerusalem they finally locate their son in the temple (2:43–46a).

At this point, the reader may be tempted to dive into the interchange between Mary and Jesus. Instead, the author focuses first on what Jesus is doing, to make sure that an important point is not overshadowed by the emotions of the reunion. Jesus is engaged in active conversation with a group of teachers, listening to them and asking questions in return (2:46b). They are probably discussing the fine points of the law. Even at twelve, Jesus impresses the teachers with his acumen and depth of understanding (cf. 2:40). The teachers of the law do not know that Jesus is the Son of God and Israel's Messiah, but the readers do. Isaiah speaks of the shoot from the stump of Jesse as being imbued with God's Spirit of wisdom, understanding, counsel, and knowledge (Isa 11:1–4).²⁶ While

---

24. Keener 2014: 186.

25. According to the School of Hallel, younger children were permitted to attend the three pilgrimage feasts as long as they could hold their father's hand and walk from Jerusalem up to the Temple Mount (*m. Ḥag.* 1:1).

26. See also *Pss. Sol.* 17:37; 1 *En.* 49:1–4.

these teachers may find this precocious young man delightful, next time Jesus is shown to be in discussion with other learned elites at the temple, those teachers will not be amused (19:47—21:38).

An astute reader may wonder how Jesus managed for two days on his own. Was he allowed to stay at the temple? Did someone take him in for the night? Did he think about his family? Was he scared? These questions may very well have crossed Mary's and Joseph's minds while searching for Jesus. But when they are finally reunited with him, the first thing that comes out of his mother's mouth is a note of rebuke: "Child, why have you treated us like this? Look, your father and I have been searching for you in great anxiety!" (2:48).[27] It is Mary who speaks on behalf of both of them. Luke continues to de-emphasize Joseph's role even though he is acknowledged to be Mary's husband and Jesus' adoptive earthly father.

Jesus' response addresses the issue of who his father is and to whom he owes primary allegiance. His first counter-question, "Why were you searching for me?" (2:49a), may be heard as an expression of genuine surprise or a tinge of gentle reproach. Without the tone of his voice, it is difficult to tell if the young Jesus is really that oblivious of Mary's and Joseph's parental concern.

The second counter-question is more telling, "Did you not know that I must be *en tois tou patros mou*" (2:49b)? The word-for-word translation of *en tois tou patros mou* is "in/among/about the [something] of my father." Both the preposition *en* and the dative article *tois* are grammatically ambiguous, especially when the noun that follows the article is not provided. There are three options. First, most English versions use "in my Father's house" because Jesus is physically found in the temple precincts.[28] The temple is where God's presence resides, hence the house of God (Ps 11:4; Hab 2:20). Jesus is asking his parents a rhetorical question: "Isn't it obvious that of all the places in Jerusalem I ought to be right here in the temple?" Jesus' answer states the obvious but does not explain why he did what he did. The second option, "I must be about the affairs of my Father,"[29] implies that the discussion with the teachers of the law is part and parcel of Jesus being involved in God's work and mission. This rendering enhances the first option without contradicting it. Jesus is in the temple engaged in conversations about God's law with the of-

---

27. The language implies a sense of betrayal. Cf. Gen 12:18; 29:25; Exod 14:11; Num 23:11; Judg 15:11.

28. ESV, NASB, NIV, NRSV.

29. Or "my Father's business" (NKJV).

ficers of the temple. This makes sense because as Israel's Messiah he will be embodying God's salvation and interpreting the precepts of God to God's people. There is yet a third possibility: "I must be among those who belong to my Father." While this translation is grammatically acceptable, the meaning is too vague to be useful.

I suggest we take advantage of the grammatical ambiguity and allow for a nuanced interpretation of Jesus' answer that combines the first two options. On one level, Jesus has to be found in the temple because this is where he is doing God's work, engaging the teachers in the matters of the law. On another level, Jesus is compelled to align himself with the affairs and purposes of his heavenly Father, even at the cost of causing emotional upheaval for his earthly parents. The Greek verb, *dei* ("it is necessary"), is frequently used in Luke's Gospel to denote a divine necessity that something must happen as God's plan unfolds.[30]

Their knowledge of Jesus' true origin notwithstanding, Mary and Joseph still have a hard time grasping the implications of their son's words and actions (2:50). This incident marks a needed demarcation of Jesus' loyalties. Priority must go to God the Father through whose Spirit Jesus was conceived in Mary's womb. In light of God's fatherhood, the place of Mary and Joseph must be relativized. Lest Jesus be misinterpreted as a smart-alecky and insubordinate young man, in the very next verse Luke assures his readers that Jesus returns to Nazareth with his parents and remains obedient to them (2:51a). Nevertheless, Mary continues her ruminations on all these matters, first the words of Simeon about the fate of her child (2:34–35), and now Jesus' own assertion of God's preeminent role as his Father, over and above that of her husband Joseph (2:51b).

One final summary statement brings the infancy narrative to a close. Similar to the earlier statement in 2:40, Jesus is said to grow in wisdom and in *hēlikia*, which can be translated either as "age" or "stature" (2:52).[31] The former coheres with the increase in wisdom along the lines of his becoming "older and wiser," whereas the latter echoes verse 40, "The child grew and became strong." Either way, the resulting picture is the same. Jesus matures in body and in mind, and enjoys favor with God and with people. This trajectory will continue for almost two decades as

---

30. 4:43; 9:22; 13:33; 17:25; 19:5; 21:9; 22:37; 24:7, 44.

31. Both senses are found in Luke. Worrying will not extend one's age or lifespan (12:25) and Zacchaeus is short in stature (19:3).

the readers turn the page to chapter 3. John, now an adult, reappears on stage as the forerunner of the Messiah.

Luke 3

Baptism of John (3:1-20)

The narrative is fast-forwarded by several decades as John, the prophet of the Most High, reenters the narrative stage. Among the prophetic books of the OT, God's prophets are often introduced by a formulaic statement, "the word of the LORD came to [Prophet A] during the reign of [King B]."[1] Identifying the sitting monarch allows the reader to situate the proclamation of the prophet within the history of Israel and the people's spiritual condition in that period. Luke reflects this convention in 3:1–2 by listing seven names that belong to the powers that be. Collectively these figures of authority contribute to the tension-filled picture of the religio-political landscape in the Jewish milieu of John and Jesus.

Tiberius succeeded Augustus as Roman emperor in 14 CE, so the fifteenth year of his reign would be 29 CE when John began his baptizing activities.[2] After the death of Herod the Great in 4 BCE, his territory was divided between his sons. Both Herod Antipas and his half-brother Herod Philip II were minor princes carrying the title of tetrarch. Antipas ruled over Galilee until 39 CE and Philip over Trachonitis and Iturea until 34 CE. One of Antipas's claims to infamy was his beheading of John (3:19; cf. Josephus *Ant.* 18:116–19).[3] Lysanius controlled Abilene. Herod Archelaus, another son of Herod the Great, was ethnarch of Judea for ten years until he was deposed in 6 CE. After that Rome sent procurators to oversee the region, among whom was Pontius Pilate, who became governor or prefect of Judea in 26 CE. In extrabiblical Jewish and Roman writ-

---

1. Jer 1:1–3; Ezek 1:1–3; Mic 1:1; Hag 1:1; Zech 1:1.
2. Tiberius co-ruled with Augustus starting 11/12 CE, so John could have begun his ministry as early as 26/27 CE (Garland 2011: 151). On Tiberius, see Grant 1975: 83–107.
3. Jesus calls Herod Antipas a fox (13:32). Antipas disrespected Jewish sensitivities, built the city of Tiberius on a graveyard (Josephus *Ant.* 18.36–38), and installed pagan images in public places (Josephus *Life* 65–66).

ings of the time, Pilate was described as greedy, unjust, hot-tempered, and oblivious to Jewish sensitivities. He was finally recalled to Rome in 36 CE.[4] On the religious front, Luke's mention of "the high priesthood of Annas and Caiaphas" (3:2; cf. Acts 4:6) requires some clarification, for at any given time there could only be one high priest. Caiaphas held this office from 18 to 37 CE, but his father-in-law, Annas, who was high priest from 6 to 15 CE, continued to exert tremendous influence after leaving office.

Together these seven names represent the political, religious, social, and economic setting in which the remainder of the narrative is situated. Palestine was an insignificant outpost at the far reaches of the Roman Empire. Those invested with political and religious responsibilities were marked by cruelty and incompetence on the one hand, and manipulation and self-interest on the other. The temple leadership and pro-Roman Jewish vassal kings colluded with the Romans to maintain a delicate symbiotic relationship of mutual benefit. In spite of the piety exhibited by Zechariah, Elizabeth, Mary, Joseph, Simeon, and Anna in the first two chapters, we must not be naïve about the negotiations and compromises behind the scenes. The families of Annas and Caiaphas must have exhibited a high level of political prowess to stay in power for three decades, holding the Romans at bay while solidifying their dynastic base among the Jews. The power struggle at the top resulted in oppression of those at the bottom. Such was the world of suffering and tension that John encountered as he emerged from his years of seclusion to begin proclaiming "a baptism of repentance for the forgiveness of sins" in the region near the Jordan (1:80; 3:3).

Luke identifies the voice crying in the wilderness in Isaiah with John who "[prepares] the way of the LORD" (3:4; Isa 40:3). In the context of Isaiah, "the LORD" refers to YHWH, for Israel is expecting God to return to Zion. Luke transfers the reference onto Jesus, as John is the forerunner of the Messiah. Whereas the Isaianic quotation ends with 40:3 in Mark 1:3 and Matt 3:3, Luke includes two more verses, culminating in the declaration that "all flesh shall see the salvation of God" (3:5–6; Isa 40:4–5). This extended citation brings out Luke's universalism and echoes Simeon's prayer that God's salvation is for Israel and the nations (2:31–32; cf. Acts 1:8).

---

4. On Pilate, see Philo *Embassy* 299–305; Josephus *Ant.* 18.35, 55–62, 85–89; Tacitus *Ann.* 15.44.

The substance of John's proclamation implies that Israel is far from ready to receive the Messiah. This prophet must issue an urgent call to repentance like his predecessors of old.[5] Presenting oneself to be baptized constitutes a public admission of sinfulness, a humiliating thing to do in a status-conscious society that elevates honor and denigrates shame. A penitent person would assume this posture of humbleness and receptivity to be baptized by John.

The purpose of baptism is explicitly stated, but how baptism is a fitting ritual to signify repentance and forgiveness of sins is less obvious. The notion of baptism is related to washing and cleansing. In the OT, washing signifies repentance (Isa 1:16–17; Jer 3:14) as well as God's cleansing of a person from sin (Ps 51:5; Ezek 36:25, 33). The Jews practice cleansing for purification (Lev 14–15), but these rites are performed repeatedly whereas John's baptism seems to be a one-time event. John himself cannot dispense forgiveness, since it is a divine prerogative, but he can at least prepare those who are willing to receive God's forgiveness and salvation when the Messiah comes.

As the crowds flock to John in droves, the prophet confronts them with a two-pronged challenge. To those who will not repent, John warns of impending judgment. To those who do, he gives practical exhortations on what it means to "bear fruit worthy of repentance" (3:8a). John pulls no punches when it comes to those who rely on their Abrahamic ancestry for absolution of guilt (3:7, 8b). Calling the Jews "a brood of vipers" is highly inflammatory as far as invectives go. We think fearfully of vipers because they are poisonous, hence the metaphor gives an impression of danger, evil, and threat.[6] Ancient Greeks and Romans believed that vipers killed their mother when they were born, rendering the offspring of vipers especially contemptible.[7] If the coming of God or his Messiah signals the day of judgment to those who do not repent,[8] and these vipers think they can slither away unscathed by virtue of their Abrahamic ancestry, then they are deceiving themselves. If God so chooses, even the inanimate stones strewn all over the wilderness can be raised up to take their place as Abraham's children and God's elect. Their status as

---

5. Cf. Isa 31:6; Jer 15:19; Ezek 14:6; 18:30.
6. See Job 20:16; Isa 14:29; 59:5.
7. Keener 2005: 6–7.
8. See Zeph 1:14–15; 2:1–2; Mal 3:2–3.

Abraham's offspring gives them no immunity when it comes to the need for repentance (cf. John 8:33–39).

The analogy of the fruit tree drives home the points of urgency and judgment (3:9). Healthy trees naturally bear good fruit, and those that do not are cut down and burned.[9] Similarly, genuine repentance should produce behavior that befits one's claim to be a bona fide child of God. Otherwise, destruction by fiery judgment is imminent and inescapable, as depicted by the picture of an ax ready to strike at the bottom of a dead tree.[10] The fact that the unproductive tree has not yet been cut down offers a glimmer of hope at the eleventh hour. There is still time to repent, even for "the brood of vipers."

In response to the crowd's request for specific instructions, John lays out practical examples of fruit-bearing (3:8, 10). Justice, charity, and honesty must characterize communal life. In spite of sparse resources, people must care for one another with a spirit of generosity, sharing clothing and food (3:11). God has always instructed the Jews to care for the poor and needy among them, and they should continue to do so.[11]

More unexpected is the willingness of tax collectors and soldiers, people marked by their exploitative behaviors, to respond positively to John's call (3:12, 14). In those days, there were two types of taxes, direct and indirect taxes. Direct taxes (head and land taxes) were collected by the Jewish authorities. The collection of indirect taxes (for customs, tolls, and duties) were farmed out to local tax collectors. Whoever had the highest bid would advance the money to the Romans to earn the right to assess the value of goods and determine how much to tax. Not only did a tax collector have to collect enough from his fellow Jews to recoup the outlay, he would also demand extra to cover his expenses and make a profit.[12] A fine line lay between legal taxation and unjust practice. Operating with Roman authority, a greedy Jewish tax collector could line his pockets living off the backs of the common folks. Needless to say, tax collectors were hated and despised as unclean and traitorous because of their dealings with the Romans and their exploitation of their own people.[13] John does not order the tax collectors to change their profession,

---

9. Cf. Ps 1:1–3; Jer 17:7–8; Luke 6:43–44.

10. The image of a tree being cut down denotes divine judgment. See Isa 10:33–34; Ezek 31:10–12; Dan 4:14.

11. E.g., Isa 58:7; Ezek 18:7; Tob 1:17. Cf. Acts 4:34–35.

12. Corbin-Reuschling 2009: 71–72.

13. Tax collectors are often mentioned together with sinners (5:27–30; 7:29, 34;

but he challenges them to "collect no more than the amount prescribed" (3:12–13). After all, Rome will still demand taxation, but reformed tax collectors can effectively penetrate a corrupt system with justice and integrity, until the idea of an honest tax collector is no longer an oxymoron.

To soldiers John directs an exhortation not to "extort money . . . by threats and false accusations, and be satisfied with [their] wages" (3:14). Although it is unclear what type of soldiers these are, those paid meagerly may be tempted to bully others to get what they want.[14] Again, honesty and contentment are expected of a life oriented toward God, especially when it is so easy for a soldier to intimidate others with their strength and weapon.

John must have left quite an impression on his hearers, for messianic speculation quickly surrounds him (3:15). While many Jews expected the Messiah to be of royal Davidic pedigree (1:32–33; 2:10–11),[15] others envisioned a Messiah to be a prophetic figure like Moses or Elijah.[16] John's denial redirects the crowd's focus on the real Messiah who is to come (3:16–17). First, John highlights the power differential between him and the Messiah in the most emphatic of terms. He construes his relationship to the Messiah as that of a slave before his master. By claiming that he is unworthy to untie the thong of the latter's sandals, John places himself lower than the lowest, for this demeaning task is normally left to gentile slaves (*b. Qidd.* 22b). That which Luke implies in the step-parallel pattern of the birth narratives, that the Son of the Most High is far greater than the prophet of the Most High, is now made explicit in John's admission.[17]

Second, John's baptism pales in comparison to the Messiah's baptism. While this is not meant to devalue the significance of John's baptism, it anticipates the greater impact of Jesus' baptism with the Holy Spirit and fire (3:16). An outpouring of the Spirit upon God's people is a sign of the

---

15:1; 18:10–14; 19:1–10). Next to murderers and thieves, tax collectors represent the class that all Jews, even those of low status, would write off as disgraceful, unclean, and irredeemable. See Edwards 2015: 111–12.

14. Guesses include Jewish soldiers tasked to protect tax collectors or Herod Antipas (Nolland 1989: 150; Marshall 1978: 143), or non-Jewish troops from Syria working for the Romans (Keener 2014: 188).

15. See p. 21, n. 20.

16. Deut 18:18–19 (a prophet like Moses); Mal 3:1–3; 4:5–6 (an eschatological Elijah). See Collins 2010: 128–31.

17. See p. 22.

last days.[18] In the Greek, there is only one preposition governing both nouns, *en pneumati hagiō kai puri* ("*with* the Holy Spirit and fire"), so one single baptism is in view. But is this a baptism of judgment or of blessing?

The theme of judgment looms large in the immediate context, as fruitless trees and chaff are about to be burned (3:9, 17). Since the Greek word for Spirit, *pneuma*, also means wind, the combination of Spirit, wind, and fire recalls Isaiah's description of God's judgment as a fiery wind (Isa 29:5–6). Whoever refuses water baptism for forgiveness of sins will have to face the Messiah's baptism of judgment (12:49–53). Although the Holy Spirit judges the wicked, it also blesses the righteous through purification, refinement, and empowerment.[19] For Luke, receiving the Holy Spirit is a gift from God (11:13; 24:49). From this angle, the baptism of the Holy Spirit and fire anticipates the outpouring of the Spirit in tongues of fire on the day of Pentecost, interpreted by Peter as a sign of the last days (Acts 1:5; 2:1–21).[20]

Perhaps it is best to let both positive and negative images of the Messiah's baptism with the Holy Spirit and fire stand without privileging one over the other. According to Simeon, Jesus is "destined for the falling and the rising of many in Israel" (2:34). There will be a mixed reception. For those who welcome the Messiah, the baptism of Spirit and fire will be a guarantee of the Spirit's empowerment now and an assurance of salvation in eternity. But for those who reject him, final destruction is their end.[21]

Third, using yet another farming analogy, John stresses the judging function of the Messiah (3:7–9, 17). John pictures a scene after the wheat harvest. Threshing is the process by which bunches of wheat are beaten with a flail so that the grains fall off the stems. Then a winnowing fork is used to toss the grains into the air, separating out the light, dry, but inedible chaff. The grains are then collected into the granary and the useless chaff is burned. Winnowing is a common image found in the OT for judgment.[22] As God's emissary, the Messiah will be the one to separate the righteous from the wicked, and the saved from the doomed. John's

---

18. Isa 32:15; 44:3; Ezek 36:27; 37:14; Joel 2:28–29.

19. Isa 1:25; Zech 13:9; Mal 3:2–3.

20. Klassen-Wiebe (1994: 398) distinguishes between John's traditional understanding of the outpouring of the Holy Spirit and fire as an event at the end of time (Isa 4:4), and Luke's interpretation that this eschatological event has been fulfilled when the Spirit is given at Pentecost (Acts 2:1–4).

21. Dunn 1972: 86.

22. Prov 20:8, 26; Isa 41:16; Jer 15:7; 51:2.

message is clear: "This fire is unquenchable; it portends eternal torment. Repent before it is too late."[23]

The section on John's baptizing ministry closes with a fleeting mention of Herod Antipas's imprisonment of John (3:19–20). Luke makes a cryptic reference to John rebuking the king concerning his brother's wife Herodias. In brief, Herod did not appreciate John's criticism of his adulterous actions in taking Herodias from his brother and marrying her (Mark 6:17–29).[24] Although the ordering of events seems awkward, that Luke should speak of Herod throwing John into prison *prior to* his account of Jesus' baptism *by John*, this inverted order allows the author to "remove" John from the narrative stage and shine the spotlight exclusively on Jesus in the next scene.

Baptism and Commissioning of Jesus (3:21–22)

In recounting the baptism of Jesus, Luke is more interested in the supernatural events that follow than the baptism itself. John's baptizing of Jesus is not even described, but simply implied, to make way for this revelatory moment: "The heaven was opened, . . . the Holy Spirit descended" (3:21–22a). The reason why Jesus needs to go through a baptism that denotes repentance is not provided.[25] Noting that "all the people were baptized" before adding that "Jesus also had been baptized" (3:21a), Luke situates Jesus' baptism as the climax of John's ministry.

Of the four Gospels, only Luke shows Jesus to be in prayer when the heavens open (3:21b). Aside from his baptism, prayer is also highlighted at various pivotal moments of Jesus' life: before calling the Twelve (6:12), at the transfiguration (9:28), at the garden before his arrest (22:41–42),

---

23. Webb (1991: 103–11) argues that the Greek noun *ptuon* refers to a winnowing shovel and not a winnowing fork (*thrinax*). The specific farming action in 3:17 is not winnowing (the separating of the grain from the chaff) but the clearing of the threshing floor afterwards. Even though the end result is the same, that the wheat will still go into the barn (salvation) and the chaff will be burned (destruction), this shift from a winnowing fork to a winnowing shovel makes Jesus the sweeper of the threshing floor and John the winnower of the grains. In my opinion, Webb is splitting hairs. Both the ministries of John and Jesus serve to separate the penitent from the impenitent. It is not necessary to insist that one holds the fork and the other the shovel.

24. Josephus claims that Herod imprisoned John to preempt a political unrest among John's followers (*Ant.* 18.118).

25. Matt 3:13–15 implies that Jesus goes to John for baptism "to fulfill all righteousness," as an act of solidarity with the penitent among Israel.

and on the cross (23:34, 46). For Luke, prayer is a key indicator for understanding the Father-Son relationship between God and Jesus.

The opening of the heavens is associated with visions of God or special revelations from God.[26] The descent of the Holy Spirit upon Jesus "in bodily form like a dove" (3:22a) signifies Jesus' empowerment and equipping for everything else Jesus will do from this point onwards (4:1, 14, 18; cf. Acts 10:38). Although Luke stresses the material nature of the Spirit's anointing, we need not assume that the Holy Spirit appears literally in the shape of a dove. Regardless of its form, the Spirit's presence upon Jesus is unmistakable.

The voice from heaven declares, "You are my Son, the beloved; with you I am well pleased" (3:22b). This is the Father's commissioning of the Son of God and Messiah to his redemptive mission, endowing him with the authority and power of the Holy Spirit as the Father's representative *par excellence* and agent of salvation. The declaration itself comprises a juxtaposition of Ps 2:7, Isa 42:1, and echoes of Gen 22:2, yielding rich layers of meaning that explain Jesus' identity and mission.

The wording, *su ei ho huios mou* ("you are my Son"), in 3:22 is essentially the same as *huios mou ei su* ("my son you are") in Ps 2:7 in the Septuagint, the Greek translation of the OT. Since this psalm is recited at the coronation of a new monarch, the use of the father-son metaphor to describe the relationship between God and Israel's king hearkens back to the Davidic covenant. In 2 Samuel, God promised David that a king from his line will always sit on Israel's throne, and that God will be a father to the king and the king a son to God (2 Sam 7:14). As son of God (metaphorically), Israel's monarch is responsible for leading the people, the children of God, to serve and obey their Father in heaven.

When applied to Jesus, Ps 2:7 takes on a double meaning. As we already know from the infancy narrative, not only is Jesus the messianic king from the line of David, he is also the divine Son by virtue of his conception by the Holy Spirit (1:32–35). The modifying phrase in 3:22, *ho agapētos* ("the beloved"), is reminiscent of Isaac's description as Abraham's beloved son (Gen 22:2). Given that Abraham factors prominently in Luke 1, this echo lingers in the background. Isaac was Abraham's beloved son, yet Abraham was willing to sacrifice him in obedience to God (Gen 22:9–13). Might there be a hint of YHWH commissioning his Son

---

26. Ezek 1:1; Acts 7:56; 10:11.

to a saving mission knowing that it will culminate in the death of his beloved?

The last part of the heavenly declaration, *en soi eudokēsa* ("in you I am well pleased"), recalls the language that describes the servant of the LORD in Isaiah: "Here is my servant, whom I uphold, my chosen, in whom my soul delights" (Isa 42:1a). The verb in Isaiah is *prosdechomai* ("to receive" or "to welcome"), not *eudokeō* ("to be well pleased"). Even though the verbs are different, both texts convey divine joy and approval. Moreover, the rest of the verse, "I have put my Spirit upon him; he will bring forth justice to the nations" (Isa 42:1b) fits the occasion of Jesus' baptism, with the Holy Spirit descending upon the Son of God, who is commissioned to a kingly role to judge not only Israel but the nations as well.

Genealogy of Jesus (3:23–38)

Jesus is about thirty years old at this point of the narrative (3:23a). Joseph was thirty when he became Pharaoh's second-in-command (Gen 41:46), and David was thirty when he began his reign as king in Hebron (2 Sam 5:4). This is the age of a fully grown man, appropriate for public service (Num 4:3, 23). Here Luke provides another validation of Jesus' identity and status with an unusually formatted genealogy (3:23b–38). Typically, genealogies trace the lineage of families and legitimize the status of individuals or the kinship group as a whole. When social status is at stake, genealogies tend to put the family's best foot forward by removing questionable members from the listing of generations.

Luke's genealogy of Jesus reads very differently from the one in Matthew (Matt 1:1–17). The less problematic issue is the way in which Luke's genealogy begins with Jesus and works its way up the generations, even though this is an unconventional format among biblical genealogies.[27] More perplexing is any attempt to reconcile the details in Luke's genealogy with those in Matthew's. For starters, Luke has seventy-eight names compared to Matthew's forty-two, because he includes names from Adam to Abraham as well. There is considerable overlap between the names listed from Abraham to David.[28] While both genealogies pass

---

27. The format of the Matthean genealogy, which starts from the ancestor going down the generations, is more common. Cf. Gen 5:1–32; 11:10–26; 1 Chr 1:1–42.

28. These names appear in both genealogies between Abraham and David: Isaac, Jacob, Perez, Hezron, Arni/Aram, Amminadab, Narshon, Sala/Salmon, Boaz, Obed, and Jesse.

through David, Luke identifies Nathan as a son of David (3:31), but Matthew has David as the father of Solomon (Matt 1:6). Beyond that, the names between David and Jesus are almost entirely different, so much so that Luke identifies Joseph's father as Heli against Matthew's Jacob (3:23; Matt 1:16). The majority of names in Luke's genealogy are not mentioned elsewhere in the OT, making it impossible to verify the existence of these ancestors and their place in the family tree. Scholars have put forth various hypotheses to explain the differences, ranging from each genealogy representing the family line of Joseph and Mary respectively, to an appeal to levirate marriage as justification for moving through a different branch in the family tree. None appears satisfactory and free of conjecture.[29]

Historical conundrum aside, several observations point to the theological impulse behind Luke's presentation of Jesus' genealogy in this unusual manner. First, drawing from God's affirmation of Jesus as the divine Son, the genealogy culminates, after a string of seventy-odd names, in a crescendo to hail Jesus as "son of Adam, [who is] son of God" (3:38). Second, the parenthetical note at the beginning of the list, that Jesus was "the son (*as was thought*) of Joseph" (3:23), makes a distinction between the reader's knowledge of Jesus' divine conception and the ignorance of many in the narrative (4:22). It is as though the author was winking at his readers, saying, "That's what people think, but you know who Jesus' *real* Father is!" Third, on the human level, in spite of the many unrecognizable names in Luke's genealogy, the naming of Abraham and David supports both Jesus' Jewish identity and his royal pedigree (3:31, 34). Finally, by taking the names beyond Abraham all the way back to Adam (3:38), Luke situates Jesus in the family of Israel within all humanity. This speaks to Luke's universalism, that Jesus is Messiah of Israel and Savior of the world.

---

29. Brown 1993: 84–94.

Luke 4

Testing of Jesus (4:1–13)

We are accustomed to viewing Jesus' encounters with the devil as temptations. It is as appropriate to consider them as tests. Whereas Luke presents three incidents in which Jesus is tempted by the devil, the broader interpretive canvas is the preparation of the Messiah (3:21—4:13). By placing the accounts of Jesus' baptism, genealogy, and testing one after the other, Luke attends to the identity, legitimacy, empowerment, and training of the Son of God before his public ministry begins in earnest. The Greek verb *peirazō* can mean "to test" or "to tempt," leaving room for competing perspectives. Accordingly, the noun *peirasmos* can be translated as "test," "trial," or "temptation." God puts his Son's fidelity and obedience to the test by allowing the devil to present these tests as temptations.

In the OT, tempting and testing appear in various shades of meaning, depending on the context. God tested the faith and obedience of his people, as with Abraham in the command to sacrifice his son Isaac (Gen 22:1–19). He tested the Israelites through their need for sustenance while sojourning in the wilderness (Exod 16:4; 20:20). On the flip side, the Israelites were chided for testing God by not trusting in his provision (Exod 17:2; Ps 95:8–10). Then there was the serpent who tempted Adam and Eve to eat the forbidden fruit (Gen 3:1–19). Unequivocally, tests and trials from God are seen as positive and instructive, whereas temptations from the devil or from human beings are suspect.

Taken out of the narrative context of Luke 3–4, one might suggest that these three vignettes present Jesus' response as a model for fending off temptations, as though citing choice Bible verses would send the devil running. A deep knowledge of Scripture is certainly helpful in the face of temptations of any sort, but this interpretation is superficial. Jesus is engaged in a serious battle with the devil, not a Scripture-quoting contest. Seeing this account only as Jesus' identification with believers who face temptation in daily life misses the key themes in Luke's theological ruminations surrounding Jesus' divine sonship and messianic kingship. Now that Jesus has been filled with the Holy Spirit and commissioned as Israel's Messiah (3:21–22), he must demonstrate his unwavering fidelity to his Father's purposes, to make good on his claim that he must be about his Father's business (2:49).

The setting of the first test/temptation is replete with allusions to the exodus. First, Jesus is the Son of God, but so is Israel in a metaphorical sense (Exod 4:22–23; Hos 11:1). The father-son relationship expects fidelity from Jesus and Israel alike. Second, just as the Israelites were led by God in the wilderness for their humbling and testing (Deut 8:2), Jesus, "full of the Holy Spirit," is "led (ēgeto) by the Holy Spirit in the wilderness" (4:1). The double mention of the Holy Spirit underscores Jesus' empowerment and access to divine help. The passive imperfect verb, ēgeto, conveys a continual sense of the Spirit's presence, leading and guiding Jesus throughout this time, rather than simply bringing him to the place of testing and leaving him there to fend for himself. Third, Jesus' forty days in the wilderness parallel Israel's forty years of wandering (Neh 9:21; Amos 2:10). Fourth, the nature of all three tests/temptations and Jesus' responses take us back to specific experiences of Israel in their desert wanderings. Where Israel failed, Jesus prevails and shows himself worthy of the dual roles as the faithful representative of God before Israel and the obedient leader of Israel before God.

The first temptation involves the exploitation of privileges that come with divine sonship. Jesus has not eaten for forty days (4:2). Fasting and prayer put a person in an open posture before God, but by the end of this period Jesus is very hungry and the devil finds an opportunity to exploit this point of weakness. His opening bid, "if you are the Son of God" (4:3; also 4:9), does not express doubt but challenge. Neither Jesus nor the devil disputes the reality of Jesus' divine sonship. Based on this status, the devil asks, "*Since* you are the Son of God, why don't you take advantage of your authority and command this stone to become a loaf of bread? Come on, you are hungry, and your Father has given you the ability to solve this simple problem. What are you waiting for?"

Jesus' reply hearkens back to Israel's experience in the wilderness when the people were hungry and pining for the delicacies of Egypt (Exod 16:3). Jesus rejects Israel's distrustful attitude with a retort, "One does not live by bread alone" (4:4). This quotation, taken from Deuteronomy 8, addresses not only why God allowed hunger to set in but where true sustenance must come from: "He humbled you by letting you hunger, then by feeding you with manna, ... in order to make you understand that one does not live by bread alone, but by every word that comes from the mouth of the LORD" (Deut 8:3). The backdrop of the wilderness wanderings underscores the humility required of Israel, and now of Jesus, to trust that God is dependable and will feed his children (cf. 11:3; 12:22–24). The Son of God will not assuage the desires of his belly by his own means even if he has the power to do so. He chooses to depend on his Father's provision, given by God's initiative and in God's timing.

The devil next shows Jesus a bird's-eye view of "all the kingdoms of the world" (4:5). While no such place actually exists to provide a panoramic vista of this extent, the picture signifies the culmination of all earthly power and authority. The devil purports that he has been given authority over the entire world, therefore he has the right to give it away as he pleases. On that basis he demands homage in exchange for glory and power (4:6–7). Is the devil lying or does he, being the prince of darkness, really hold sway over the affairs of this world?

Jesus' rebuttal gets at the heart of the matter: "Worship the Lord your God, and serve only him" (4:8; cf. Deut 6:13). In the OT, Israel repeatedly failed to worship YHWH alone, beginning with the wilderness generation that worshiped the golden calf to subsequent generations drawn to the gods of the Canaanites.[1] Yet Jesus' citation comes at the heels of the Shema, commanding Israel to love YHWH, the only God, with all its heart, soul, and might (Deut 6:4–5). God's people must never bow down before other gods (Exod 20:2–3; Deut 6:13–14). The devil's temptation strikes at this fundamental loyalty concerning what it means to be the people of God and, above all, the Son of God. Moreover, in Psalm 2, after the affirmation, "You are my Son," (Ps 2:7; cf. Luke 3:22), God continues, "Ask of me, and I will make the nations your heritage, and the ends of the earth your possession" (Ps 2:8). Jesus' status as the divine Son already entitles him to have authority over all powers, given to him as his inheritance. He does not have to resort to inferior means to grasp that which is rightfully his.

The final temptation takes place at the highest point of the temple in Jerusalem (4:9). The devil uses Ps 91:11–12 to goad Jesus to make God prove his protective care. Jumping from the pinnacle of the temple will create a life-threatening spectacle. Attempting to sow a seed of doubt in Jesus, the devil says, "See if God will really keep his word and rescue

---

1. E.g., Exod 32:1–8; Judg 2:11–13; 2 Chr 28:1–4; Jer 9:13–14; Hos 11:1–2.

you. Make him prove it." Once more, Jesus replies, "Do not put the Lord your God to the test" (4:12; cf. Deut 6:16a). His answer deftly combats this temptation, but also recalls the sad history of how the Israelites did indeed put God to the test at Massah when they had no water to drink (Deut 6:16b; cf. Exod 17:1–7).

All three temptations take aim at Jesus' trust in God and fidelity to God. The devil strikes at Jesus' understanding of his divine sonship, but with every victory Jesus also redeems Israel's past failure as recalcitrant children of God. The devil temporarily concedes his failure and withdraws "until an opportune time" (4:13). That time will present itself in the passion narrative when the power of darkness will attack in full force (22:3, 31, 53; 23:44–46). Just as the Holy Spirit continues to empower Jesus throughout his ministry, the devil will keep obstructing Jesus by oppressing people with unclean spirits and crippling diseases.[2] By resisting these temptations, Jesus has also passed three tests and demonstrated total allegiance to and dependence on his Father. The Messiah is now ready for action.

Sermon at Nazareth (4:14–30)

With the completion of the time of preparation, Jesus returns to Galilee "in the power of the Spirit" (4:14; cf. 1:35; 3:23; 4:1). As Jesus begins his mission, his teaching activities in the synagogues place him in good repute throughout Galilee (4:14–15). Despite the people's positive opinions of Jesus, they are far from understanding his status and the substance of his teachings. The general acclaim in this summative statement will contrast sharply with the rejection Jesus will face. The words that Simeon spoke to Mary when Jesus was presented at the temple, that "[her] child is . . . to be a sign that will be opposed" (2:34–35), will soon materialize.

Nazareth of Galilee was a poor, insignificant village with an estimated population of barely a few hundred. Nothing much was found in its excavations—no public building, no fine pottery, no paved street, no inscription—that might justify a different impression.[3] In the first century, the Jews would gather for prayer and Scripture reading on the Sabbath in a synagogue. If the village was too small to have its own synagogue, a home was used. A typical service would begin with the recitation of the

---

2. 4:33–37; 8:28–30; 9:38–42; 10:17–19; 11:14–23; 13:11–16.
3. Walker 2006: 31–33; Garland 2011: 195.

Shema (Deut 6:4–9) and other set prayers, followed by readings from the Torah and the Prophets, a sermon, and a prayer to close.[4]

Jesus, the son of law-abiding parents (2:22–23, 39, 41), has the habit of going to the synagogue on the Sabbath (4:16). As he is about to read Scripture, the narrative time is slowed down considerably. The chiastic structure of the ensuing verses describing Jesus' actions moves the reader toward the quotation from Isaiah, and then all the way back until Jesus sits down (4:16–20):

> Jesus stood up to read (16c)
>> The scroll was given to him (17a)
>>> He unrolled the scroll (17b)
>>>> He read from Isaiah (18–19)
>>> He rolled up the scroll (20a)
>> He gave the scroll back to the attendant (20b)
> He sat down (20c)

The quotation from Isaiah, handpicked by Jesus to read, sits at the focal point of the chiasm (4:18–19). Segments of Isa 61:1–2 and 58:6 may be found in the composite quotation in 4:18–19. Aside from the glaring omission of the phrase, "the day of vengeance of our God" (Isa 61:2b), Jesus' reading captures the positive manifestations of "the year of the LORD's favor." It is not that God's final judgment is taken lightly, but the emphasis here is on the good news for "the poor" who are willing to receive it. In Luke "the poor" are not limited to those who are economically poor, such as peasants, slaves, beggars, and day laborers. Others viewed by their contemporaries as having low status are also considered to be "poor"—children, barren women, widows, gentiles, tax collectors, sinners, the demon possessed, and those with physical deformities and diseases. Some are relegated to a low status because of their age, gender, ethnicity, and socio-economic status; others due to moral and ritual impurity. In verse 19 the captives, the blind, and the oppressed constitute "the poor" to whom Jesus brings the good news of the kingdom of God.

The news is good because "the poor" will experience a reversal of conditions: the captives will be released, the blind will see, the oppressed will go free (4:18). This list is illustrative, not exhaustive. Jesus' reading of Isaiah puts the spotlight on the theme of reversal already introduced in Mary's song (1:51–53). This note will be repeatedly sounded as the

---

4. Marshall 1978: 181–82; Nolland 1989: 194.

narrative proceeds (6:20–26; 7:21–22; 16:19–31). Behind the quotations from Isaiah lies the OT concept of Jubilee. Every fifty years, Israel was to "proclaim liberty throughout the land to all its inhabitants" (Lev 25:10–17). In the year of Jubilee, the Jews were to leave the land fallow, set their slaves free, and forgive all debts. Although the Israelites never properly observed the year of the Jubilee, this image is evoked in later Jewish writings to describe the ideal conditions at the time of God's final salvation.[5]

But Jesus is more than a social reformer; his ability to reverse a person's situation goes far beyond writing off a debt or manumitting a slave. In conjunction with release and reversal on the physical and socio-economic level, Jesus effects spiritual renewal that reconciles the penitent to God through the forgiveness of sins (cf. 5:17–26; 7:36–50). Those who claim high social status by human standards can still find themselves in spiritual poverty, rendering them in dire need of salvation like everyone else (cf. 3:7–9).

Where does Jesus see himself in this depiction of the eschatological Jubilee? In Isa 61:1, the one anointed by the Spirit is God's prophet and servant. Reading the passage alone does not necessarily draw an immediate link between this figure in Isaiah, his message, and Jesus. But when Jesus sits down, assuming the posture of a teacher, he declares, "Today (*sēmeron*) this Scripture has been fulfilled in your hearing" (4:20–21). He claims that the future hope of the Jews is now present reality. The identification of Jesus with the Isaianic prophet may not be immediately apparent to those sitting in the synagogue at Nazareth, but the same Spirit who descended upon Jesus at his baptism (3:22) and led him through the tests in the wilderness (4:1, 14) now anoints Jesus as God's end-time prophet that inaugurates God's eschatological Jubilee here and now. The Greek word, *sēmeron* ("today") is more than a reference to that particular day in Nazareth (4:21). It is a catchword in Luke to denote the immediacy of God's salvation (2:11; 5:26; 19:9; 23:43). Jesus is making a bold claim that the salvation hoped for by generations of Israelites has arrived and he is the Spirit-anointed agent through whom all forms of oppression will be lifted.

At first "all spoke well of him" (4:22a), but by the end of the pericope, "all were filled with rage" (4:28). What causes the crowd's response to swing from one side of the pendulum to the other? Initially, the villagers

---

5. See 4Q521 2 II, 5–8. For the Qumran community, only insiders receive eschatological benefits. In Luke, Jesus' offer of salvation is universal, including both insiders and outsiders.

are impressed and receive Jesus' words as words of grace. They hear the message as spoken for them, that they are the beneficiaries of God's redemption. Without the tone, it is difficult to determine the attitude behind the ensuing question, "Isn't this Joseph's son?" (4:22b; cf. 3:23). Does this question ride on the momentum of the people's amazement or is it a sign of doubt? On the one hand, Jesus enjoyed divine and human favor while growing up (2:52), so his reputation must have been quite good. It is possible to interpret the question as a sense of hometown pride: "Isn't this Joseph's son? Look how well he has turned out!" On the other hand, the question may betray a tinge of contempt. According to Mark, not only do they claim to know Jesus' father, but also his mother and siblings, "and they took offense at him" (Mark 6:2–3). Are they mumbling to themselves, "Who does he think he is? How dare he make such a claim?" Some ambiguity remains as to when the shift in the public sentiment toward Jesus begins. Regardless of whether Jesus' familial background is used as a basis for parochial pride or a reason for skepticism, what he says next is bound to ignite a negative reaction from those who have yet to embrace his mission.

Having read their minds, Jesus reveals what the villagers were thinking, "Doctor, cure yourself! . . . Do here also in your hometown the things we have heard you did in Capernaum" (4:23). One might read the idiom as a challenge to walk one's talk: "If you are telling us what to do then you should do so yourself." A different take on the proverb reflects a provincial mindset: "If you have any benefit to offer, start with your own kinsfolk." The latter sense fits the current context better, given the reference to the deeds that Jesus has already performed in nearby Capernaum. Coupled with their view that Jesus is merely Joseph's son, they may be seeking a sign, at least implicitly, to validate his prophetic utterance.

Only at this point does Jesus identify himself with the Isaianic figure: "No prophet is accepted in the prophet's hometown" (4:24; cf. Mark 6:4; Matt 13:57). Because Israel had a track record of rejecting God's prophets, Jesus is comparing his contemporaries with their forebears and indicting them for their hardness of heart. In the rest of the narrative, Luke will continue to present Jesus as a rejected prophet whose message of salvation will fall on deaf ears again and again (11:47–50; 13:33–34; 20:9–19).

Specifically, Jesus alludes to Elijah and Elisha to illustrate that God's mercy is broad enough to embrace outsiders (4:25–27). At the time of King Ahab and his wife Jezebel, severe drought struck the land when

God punished Israel for its idolatry and wickedness. Elijah was sent to Zarephath to the home of a Sidonian widow and her son. Through God's miraculous provision, Elijah, the woman, and her son survived because their meal and oil never ran out. When the widow's son died, Elijah prayed and brought him back to life (1 Kgs 17:8-24). Elisha ordered Naaman the commander of the King of Aram to wash seven times in the Jordan to cleanse his flesh from leprosy (2 Kgs 5:1-14). Common to Elijah's and Elisha's stories was their mission to those despised by reason of their gender (woman), marital status (widowed), gentile origin (Sidonian and Syrian), and physical deformity (leper). It was not as though Elijah and Elisha did not help their fellow Israelites, but Jesus emphasizes that even with the needy among Israel, God chose to send his prophets to those of even lower status—a gentile widow and a gentile leper. Indeed, God's grace extends beyond the boundaries of Israel, a lesson so difficult for Jesus' compatriots to learn.

Because Jesus is their homegrown son, the people of Nazareth expect him to privilege them over others, especially their neighbors in Capernaum.[6] Is this too much to ask? Isn't Nazareth a poor village that needs relief from oppression? Shouldn't Jesus' relatives and friends be first in line to receive God's blessings? If the people interpret Jesus as casting his sights on unclean and lowly outsiders instead of on them, no wonder they are deeply offended. Their self-serving mindset sees Jesus bypassing his in-group and giving the benefits to undeserving outsiders. What a reprehensible way to repay one's kin! The dynamics quickly shift from goodwill to anger, and the earlier acclaim deteriorates into murderous fury, so that "all in the synagogue were filled with rage" (4:28). Their attempt to throw Jesus off the cliff (4:29), if successful, would have been followed by hurling stones down the steep drop to finish him off. Although some may justify the mob action as the stoning of a false prophet (Deut 13:1-11), it is not a legal execution, and certainly not on the Sabbath! Jesus cuts through the crowd and leaves the scene of rejection (4:30). Manipulation and hostility will not distract Jesus from his central mission, and he will continue to do what he is commissioned to do.[7]

---

6. See pp. 65-66.

7. Longenecker (2012: 42-50) links the verb, *eporeueto* ("[he] went on his way," 4:30b) with other uses of *poreuomai* ("to go") in Luke that highlight Jesus' movements on his fateful journey toward Jerusalem where he will be killed (9:51, 57; 10:38; 13:33; 17:11; 19:28, 36). Jesus' death will not take place in Nazareth but in Jerusalem. But even from the start of his ministry, Jesus' "going" is aligned with the purpose for which

Early Ministry in Galilee (4:31–44)

This section parallels more or less the narrative framework of Mark 1:21–39. While Mark has Jesus calling his first four disciples before relating his ministry at Capernaum (Mark 1:16–20), Luke recounts the call story in greater detail (5:1–11) after this series of vignettes. This rearrangement makes better narrative sense by explaining the fishermen's knowledge of Jesus prior to their decision to follow him. An exorcism is followed by a healing (4:31–39), showing how Jesus brings "release to the captives . . . [and] let the oppressed go free" (4:18). These two miracles lead to many other similar actions that Luke simply notes in summary (4:40–41). The section closes with Jesus' declaration that his mission is to go to all the cities and proclaim the good news of God's kingdom (4:42–44).

The cosmic battle between God and evil is played out on the human stage, with Jesus as God's agent and the demon as Satan's minion holding a man hostage. The first of Jesus' many miracles that Luke presents is an exorcism on the Sabbath at a synagogue in Capernaum (4:31–37). Although more populated and prosperous than Nazareth, Capernaum was still a poor fishing village at the time of Jesus. Excavations uncovered little sign of wealth in the form of fine pottery and expensive frescoes.[8] From Matthew and Mark we learn that Jesus made his home in Capernaum at some point (Matt 4:13; Mark 2:1). Luke never alludes to this fact, even though he locates Jesus in Capernaum on multiple occasions in his narrative (4:23, 31; 7:1).

Many in Capernaum are drawn to Jesus even though they are not fully aware of his identity and mission. His authority is already widely acknowledged among the populace (4:32). On this occasion, a man with an unclean spirit[9] disrupts the service at the synagogue (4:33). The demon is no match against Jesus, but he puts up a loud and rambling protest (4:34). The Greek interjection, *ea*, is more than an exclamation of surprise. It implies resistance, which some English translations express as "Let us alone!" (NRSV, NKJV) or "Go away!" (NLT).[10] The question that

---

he is sent—to preach the kingdom of God (4:43) until the mission culminates in his ultimate sacrifice.

8. Garland (2011: 214) estimates the population of Capernaum at the time of Jesus to be about 600 to 1500, and Nazareth about 400.

9. The "uncleanness" of demons has to do with purity laws, which separate the clean from the unclear, and the pure from the impure. See pp. 72–73.

10. Jesus rebukes the demon directly in the second person singular in v. 35. But when the man screams at Jesus in v. 34, he speaks in the first person plural, joined with

follows, *ti hēmin kai soi* (literally, "What to us and to you?"), is idiomatic, connoting suspicion and rejection: "What have you to do with us?" or "What have we to do with you?" (cf. Judg 11:12; 2 Sam 16:10). According to ancient magical practices, calling an enemy by name in an incantation was a power play.[11] This demon not only recognizes Jesus as "Jesus of Nazareth" but "the Holy One of God" as well (cf. 1:35). In vain he tries to claim superiority by naming Jesus, yet his pretense is futile. In the end, his question, "Have you come to destroy us?" becomes a self-fulfilling prophecy.

Jesus does not need any lengthy incantation, for his word is authoritative enough to drive out the demon: "Be silent and come out of him!" (4:35). Even though the unclean spirit knows who Jesus is, this must not be proclaimed by an enemy of God. Immediately the demon's power is subdued and it departs with a whimper, throwing the man down on the floor without doing him further harm. The eyewitnesses are now impressed by Jesus' exorcising power in addition to his teachings (4:36–37). The news spreads like wildfire, but the people have yet to figure out what this is all about.

Moving from the public to the private sphere, Jesus leaves the synagogue and enters the house of Simon, whose mother-in-law is suffering from a high fever (4:38). Consistent with Luke's penchant to pair a story of a man with that of a woman,[12] the recipient of Jesus' saving act also moves from a demon-possessed man to a sick woman. There are interesting similarities in the description of the exorcism and this healing. Jesus "rebuked (*epetimēsen*) the fever" (4:39) just as he "rebuked (*epetimēsen*) [the demon]" (4:35; cf. 4:41). Then the fever "left her" (4:39) just as the demon "came out of him" (4:37). Just as the man was released from the bondage of an evil spirit, Simon's mother-in-law is now freed from the oppression of grave sickness. That she is able to get up and wait upon Jesus and his companions further proves the efficacy of Jesus' healing power and her response of gratitude.

The summary statement of 4:40–41 gives the readers an idea of Jesus' impact thus far. By the end of the Sabbath, crowds flock to Jesus, bringing with them many who are afflicted by disease and demons, and

---

the demon within him.

11. Garland 2011: 215.

12. E.g., Zechariah and Mary (ch. 1); Simeon and Anna (ch. 2); a centurion and a widow (ch. 7); Jairus and a hemorrhaging woman (ch. 8); a bent woman and a man with dropsy (chs. 13–14).

all are cured. More demons are cast out and silenced by Jesus because they know his true identity as Son of God and Messiah. The battle line is drawn, but with whom the people of Capernaum will align themselves is yet to be seen.

The next morning Jesus withdraws to a deserted place, presumably to pray (4:42a; cf. Mark 1:35), but the crowd catches up with him soon enough. Like the villagers of Nazareth, the people of Capernaum also want to keep Jesus for themselves, but are again told that his mission includes other cities as well (4:42b–43). The verb *apestalēn* ("I was sent") is passive, which denotes agency. Jesus is sent by God, not only to Nazareth or Capernaum, but throughout the region and beyond. Implicit in the verb *dei*[13] ("it is necessary;" "I must") is a divine necessity; Jesus is under God's compulsion to proclaim the good news, which is spread through Jesus' words as well as his actions.

The final verse of this section, "so [Jesus] continued proclaiming the message in the synagogues of Judea" (4:44), hearkens back to 4:14–15, reminding the readers that while Jesus' acts of wonder are impressive and effective, teaching remains central to his mission. Teaching and healing go hand in hand in Jesus' encounters with "the poor" everywhere. The reference to Judea here should be understood as "the land of the Jews," a general term for the whole of Palestine, including Galilee, and not only the region surrounding Jerusalem.[14]

Different responses to Jesus are emerging; the crowds are awestruck, and the demons are defiant. Neither exhibits a model response. Only Simon's mother-in-law is shown to express her gratitude in the form of service. In her we catch a glimpse of what constitutes a proper response to Jesus. In the next chapter, we trace Simon's movement from observer to follower as Luke returns to the account of Jesus calling his first disciples.

---

13. See p. 45, n. 30.
14. Luke 6:17; 7:17; Acts 10:37; 26:20.

Luke 5

Calling of Simon Peter (5:1–11)

Luke's account of how Jesus calls his first disciples is quite different from Mark's, but the two are by no means contradictory. Reading Mark, one may wonder why four seasoned fishermen would drop everything to follow a stranger simply on the basis of the words, "Follow me" (Mark 1:16–20). Luke's decision to relocate the call story in his narrative, from before the exorcism at the synagogue to after the healing of Simon's mother-in-law, implies that Simon has already witnessed Jesus' power up close by the time Jesus calls him. Luke's redaction makes better sense and improves the flow of the narrative.

Jesus' popularity continues to grow as we now find him teaching by the Lake of Gennesaret, also known as the Sea of Galilee (5:1). The crowds are pressing in on him so that he is getting closer and closer to the water. The part of the lake near Capernaum is shaped like a bowl, giving rise to a natural amphitheater of sorts. Jesus borrows Simon's boat to use as a floating pulpit, from which he can take advantage of the topography's acoustics and teach from a short distance offshore (5:3–4).[1] Luke's main interest is in what transpires afterwards. He drops a hint in verse 2, noting that Jesus notices some fishermen washing their nets next to their boats.

Simon and his business partners, James and John, are not the poorest class of fishermen who cast nets by the shore, as they own boats (5:7, 10). A set of trammel nets could be stretched out between two boats to round up large amounts of fish as the boats were repositioned. This method was used at night when the fish could not see the net. The night before, however, Simon and his crew were unsuccessful; they caught nothing even though they worked long and hard (5:5a). When Jesus saw them that morning, they were probably tired and dejected. They had nothing to bring to the market and still had to clean the debris off the nets (5:2).

---

1. Garland 2011: 226.

Imagine Simon's response when Jesus asks him to take the boat out again to deep water and let down the nets (5:4): "You, a carpenter and itinerant teacher, want me, an experienced fisherman, to take my crew out again to where we know there is no fish? Besides, the timing is bad. It's broad daylight. The fish will see the net and swim away. What if we return empty-handed again? I will become a laughingstock!" It is not difficult to feel skeptical. Yet Simon replies, "If you say so, I will let down the nets" (5:5b). His tone does not appear disrespectful, having seen Jesus heal his mother-in-law (4:38–39). With his nascent faith edging out his personal misgivings, Simon summons his crew to take the boats out and cast the net into the deep again.

What a yield from that half-hearted act of obedience! The size of the catch is beyond anyone's imagination, so much so that the nets are about to break. Even with the help of James and John, the two boats are so full of fish that they can barely stay afloat (5:6–7). Not only does the miracle demonstrate Jesus' abundant provision, it reveals a profound truth about Jesus' identity, which Simon recognizes immediately.

Instead of exuberant joy, Simon Peter[2] falls down before Jesus and says, "Go away from me, Lord, for I am a sinful man!" (5:8). Instead of "Master" (5:5) he now calls Jesus "Lord."[3] Simon recognizes a theophany in the holy encounter and becomes keenly aware of the distance between him and Jesus. His response reminds us of Isaiah's confession when the prophet saw the vision of the throne of God: "Woe is me! I am lost, for I am a man of unclean lips, and I live among a people of unclean lips" (Isa 6:5). When human sinfulness meets divine holiness, it is not repulsion but a sense of unworthiness that prompts Simon to ask Jesus to leave. Unlike the people of Capernaum and Nazareth who want to claim Jesus for themselves (4:23, 28–29, 42–43), Simon draws back in reverent fear.

Jesus gives the same words of assurance to Simon as did the angels to Zechariah, Mary, and the shepherds: "Do not be afraid" (5:10a; cf. 1:13, 30; 2:10). In addition, he pronounces Simon's future mission that "[he] will be catching people" (5:10b). Catching people is an apt image for these fishermen who have just caught two boatloads of fish. The metaphor, however, comes not from fishing but from hunting and warring. People are captured alive as prisoners of war and subsequently tortured

---

2. Jesus does not give Simon the name "Peter" until 6:14.

3. See p. 23, n. 23.

or killed.[4] But people-catching for Jesus leads not to death but to life. Simon's catch of people will be as fruitful as the large catch of fish before his eyes (Acts 2:41; 4:4). A self-identified sinner who repents and follows Jesus, Simon paves the way for all other sinners who receive God's gift of salvation. The story closes with Simon, James, and John leaving everything to follow Jesus (5:11; 18:28). Yet there are others who do not think they are sinners. By their own volition they bar themselves from the kingdom of God. We meet them in the next section.

Fusing the Horizons: Human Effort versus Divine Help

Simon Peter and his partners worked all night long and returned empty-handed. Imagine the tone of this seasoned fisherman when he told Jesus that they caught nothing. Was there a note of resentment, disappointment, or embarrassment? After all, effort should yield proportionate result; so says my Chinese upbringing. According to my cultural work ethic, diligence can compensate to a large degree for the lack of genius. Even Albert Einstein concurred that genius is one percent inspiration but ninety-nine percent perspiration.

When things do not go the way we expect, we look for a logical explanation. Did I miss something in the planning? Did I lack know-how? What should I have done instead? Peter did not appear to be guilty of any of these. His perceived failure was not because of sloth or ineptitude. Returning empty-handed after a night of fishing was more than an inconvenience. Not only was there no income from selling fish that day, Peter also may have taken additional loss from owing his crew their wages. Given Peter's frame of mind, Jesus' suggestion to drop the net again in deep water was like rubbing salt into a wound. Thankfully, Jesus was not asking for wholehearted enthusiasm on Peter's part but simply a crack of openness. Although Jesus' suggestion seemed to go against wise fishing practice and recent objective data, and Peter had to risk seeing a repeat of the previous night's failure, his consent—reservations notwithstanding—led to a theophany and a catch that covered his economic loss and some!

The availability of divine help is not a license for idleness, as though we should simply sit back, fold our arms, and watch God do all the work. More often, however, it is not our inaction but impatience that gets in the

---

4. Garland 2011: 230; Green 1997: 234.

way. We forge ahead with our ideas and plans, and when things do not go our way we frantically try one thing after another in the hope of turning failure into success. When we fail to wait for the green light from the Holy Spirit and take the lead from our own hunches or ambitions, we miss out on the unexpected blessing to witness God at work.

The miraculous catch of fish went beyond bounty provisions to a changed life. It all began with an ambivalent consent, "If you say so, Master." At that time, Peter had barely met Jesus. There was no deep faith of which to speak as yet. He was an ordinary fisherman with just enough willingness to override his resistance, and that was enough for Jesus to begin his good work in this disciple. Likewise, God will take our tentative and hesitant "Yes" and turn it into a surprising adventure. Is that too difficult a step to take—a small step of obedience in the right direction?

Controversy over Purity Laws (5:12–39)

After expounding on the account of the calling of Peter, James, and John (5:1–11), Luke resumes Mark's ordering of events until the Sermon on the Plain in 6:17–49. The spotlight now focuses on the religious elites who find fault with Jesus despite the high praises he receives from the people.

Simply labeling the scribes and the Pharisees as legalistic hypocrites does not adequately explain their disagreements with Jesus. Why do learned and well-respected religious leaders fail to see God's truth and saving actions through Jesus? If they love the law and revere God, how is it that their appropriation of the commandments differs so drastically from that of Jesus? If both sides claim fidelity to God, who holds the correct interpretation of God's will? In order to address these questions, we need to first consider the understanding of the law, as well as larger issues of Jewish identity and praxis under the socio-political conditions of first-century Palestine.

For centuries leading up to the time of Jesus, Israel repeatedly fell into the hands of foreign rulers—the Assyrians, the Babylonians, the Persians, the Greeks, the Ptolemies, the Syrians, and now the Romans. The Jews were determined to preserve their unique identity as God's chosen people even though their pagan overlords attempted to wipe out their national self-understanding through exile, introduction of foreign gods, culture, education, and prohibition of Jewish practices. At times God's people were scattered from their homeland. At other times their temple lay in ruins. Even after the Jews had rebuilt the temple, the second one was desecrated by the pagans. Yet throughout the precariousness of Israel's national existence, the Jews always had Moses's law. The law was God's gift and instruction to his elect. In the post-exilic period, the study and interpretation of the law became increasingly crucial for maintaining Jewish identity. The teachers and experts of the law were committed to "[making] a fence around the law" (*m. 'Abot* 1:1). Their deliberations on the application of the law in every aspect of life were passed down as a set of oral traditions deemed equally binding as the law itself.

Commandments surrounding circumcision, purity, food, and the Sabbath were of particular importance as key identity markers that distinguished the Jews from the gentiles. After all, God said to Israel, "You shall be holy, for I the LORD your God am holy" (Lev 19:2). Holiness demanded separation from everything profane—clean from unclean, pure from impure, moral from immoral. Piety and fidelity were measured by adherence to the law and the oral traditions of the rabbis. Not only would disobedience call down divine judgment upon the individual, it would jeopardize the fate of the entire nation.

The opponents of Jesus often appear in groups. The Pharisees are paired with either lawyers (*nomikoi*, 7:30; 14:3), scribes (*grammateis*, 5:21; 6:7; 15:2), or teachers of the law (*nomodidaskaloi*, 5:17). Lawyers, scribes, and teachers are the legal experts of the temple establishment, not to be confused with Pharisees, who are members of the laity. All of them share the same concern over the proper and meticulous adherence to the law. They form a united front in their disapproval of Jesus' observance of purity, food, and Sabbath laws.

The sect of the Pharisees was known for its separatist attitude toward all that was ritually and morally unclean. The Pharisees held themselves to strict standards of purity and operated within a very tight circle of hospitality to avoid contamination from outsiders. They were held in high esteem for their meticulous practiced the law. Even though they were not temple personnel, they garnered the respect of the people and enjoyed high social status among the Jews.[5]

---

5. Mason 2000: 782–87.

Were the Pharisees "legalists" then? They were, in the sense that they followed the letter of the law to the utmost detail. So did the scribes and the teachers of the law. This should not necessarily imply a negative motive on their part. To live out one's fidelity to God by subsuming all of life under God's law was a commitment to be admired. Most people were not as knowledgeable about the law or as diligent about its observance. In their zealousness to abide by the law, however, the Pharisees and the scribes had the tendency to overlook the compassion of God. Hence they must be brought back to the true intentions of the law, given by God to engender life and not to stifle it. The tension between Jesus and the religious elite revolved around this sort of corrective.

Of particular relevance to the Lukan narrative are the purity laws and the Sabbath laws. More will be said about the Sabbath laws in chapter 6. Purity laws contain a moral as well as a ritual dimension. While ritual impurity in and of itself is not sinful, it renders the unclean person ineligible for communion with God and God's people. Impurity can be reversed by ritual cleansing, but the list of things that can render a person unclean is long—coming into contact with gentiles, having a physical handicap (paralysis, blindness, etc.), displaying open sores and skin lesions, being possessed by a demon ("an unclean spirit"), exhibiting a flow of blood, touching a dead body, just to name a few. Food laws constitute a type of purity law that have to do with eating clean foods with clean vessels in the company of clean people.

Because impurity can be transmitted through contact, it becomes all the more important for the scribes and the Pharisees to censure those with whom they keep company and share a table. Much to the chagrin of the religious leaders, Jesus is found among many who are unclean ritually, morally, and in some cases, even perpetually. Imagine the tension that arises when, on the one hand, Jesus' teaching and healing are attributed to divine empowerment, yet on the other hand, respected religious leaders disapprove of his words and actions. Who speaks for God and models the salvific will of God for Israel?

Cleansing a Leper (5:12–16)

This story features a leper in an unspecified town somewhere in Galilee (5:12). Leprosy in the Bible was not the same as what we moderns understand to be Hansen's disease. It covered a spectrum of skin diseases from mild to severe, as identified by sores, lesions, discoloration, disfiguration, and other abnormalities of the skin. Some forms were more curable than others. More damaging than the physical impact of biblical leprosy were its social and spiritual implications. The leprous condition was thought to be a smiting from God for serious sin.[6] Lepers had to announce their approach by crying out, "Unclean! Unclean!" (Lev 13:45–46). "Put out of the camp" of Israel (Num 5:2–3), they were shunned, ostracized, and forbidden to stay within the city boundaries, lest they spread their uncleanness to those whom they came into contact.

Given the stigma surrounding leprosy, the leper who approaches Jesus exhibits great faith. His condition is serious; he is "*covered* with leprosy" (5:12a). Yet knowingly crossing permissible social boundaries, he enters the city, seeks out Jesus, and pleads with him, "Lord, if you choose, you can make me clean" (5:12b). The use of cleansing language, as opposed to healing or restoring, signifies the connection between leprosy and impurity. Like Peter, the leper falls down before Jesus and calls him "Lord" (5:8). Like Peter, he recognizes the numinous in Jesus, yet dares not presume upon his generosity. In response, Jesus stretches out his hand, touches the leper, and speaks to both parts of his petition with the affirmative, "I do choose. Be made clean" (5:13). In the OT, God redeemed Israel "with an outstretched arm" (Exod 6:6). Now Jesus reaches out to touch a leper nobody dares to touch, and in doing so violates the law of purity and contracts the man's uncleanness. While Jesus' words immediately effect the physical healing, his touch communicates an invitation back into the community of God's people. Even the untouchable has dignity in the sight of God.

Jesus instructs the leper not to tell anyone of his cleansing but to first show himself to the priest as required by the law of Moses (5:14). The priest would pronounce the ritual uncleanness of a person stricken with leprosy, as well as monitor the disease as it progressed. If the disease receded, the priest would examine the invalid and verify the completeness of the physical cleansing. He would then oversee the sacrificial offerings to render the person—clothes, house and all—ritually cleansed before an official clean bill of health could be issued (Lev 13:1—14:57).

The summative statement of this story echoes prior statements affirming much of the same, that Jesus' fame continues to spread as people flock to him for his teaching and healing (5:15; cf. 4:37, 40). But Jesus is

---

6. Num 12:1–15 (Miriam); 2 Kgs 5:20–27 (Gehazi); 2 Kgs 15:5 (Azariah).

not taken by the attention. Instead, he withdraws to lonely places to pray to draw strength for his messianic mission (5:16; cf. 4:42).

Healing a Paralytic (5:17–26)

This episode takes place in an unnamed town.[7] There is no mention of the Sabbath. Instead of the synagogue, Jesus is teaching at someone's house, and the place is filled to capacity. The phrase, "the power of the Lord was with him to heal" (5:17; cf. 4:18–19), reminds the readers that Jesus' teaching and healing ministries are inextricably related. Every healing is an object lesson; and every teaching has its restorative effect on his listeners.

Sitting in the audience are some Pharisees and teachers of the law who have come from all over, even as far as Jerusalem, to hear Jesus (5:17). Nothing is said of their motive. They may be drawn by curiosity or genuine interest in what Jesus has to say. But their attitudes will soon be revealed from their response to Jesus' handling of an unexpected situation.

Jesus is interrupted by the arrival of a paralytic, carried by four men, coming not through the door of the house but from above, through the roof (5:19). The paralytic's four friends refuse to let a crowd hinder his access to Jesus. Like the leper who had the audacity to enter the town to find Jesus (5:12), these four friends barge in, not only uninvited but also by creating their own "door." It is unlikely that they have asked for permission. Luke's description of a tiled roof may strike some as odd, for houses in Galilean villages were much more modest, with roofs made of reeds, branches, and dried mud.[8] That aside, the focus is on the faith of the four friends, which does not escape Jesus' notice (5:20a). Imagine the people in the house, hearing the sound from above, realizing what is going on, stepping back to avoid being hit by falling debris, and making way for the mat to be lowered right in front of Jesus.

Instead of asking what the five want or curing the paralytic right away, Jesus addresses the man on the mat, "Friend, your sins are forgiven you" (5:20b). This is not a strange thing to say, for in the ancient world sickness and disease were often thought to result from divine

---

7. Mark 2:1 identifies the locale as Capernaum.
8. Garland 2011: 242.

punishment.[9] What is unacceptable to the Pharisees and the teachers of the law is Jesus' perceived infringement on God's unique right to forgive sins, and in doing so committing blasphemy (5:21).

The Pharisees and the legal experts are not incorrect. Only God can forgive sins, and there are proper channels in the cultic practices of Israel by which one can ask God for forgiveness. In their view, Jesus is usurping divine prerogative and is deserving of death by stoning (Lev 24:14–16). They refuse to believe that the Son of Man has been given the power from God to forgive sins (5:24). Even when Jesus has the authority, he does not flaunt it. Instead of telling the paralytic, "I forgive you," Jesus says, "Your sins are forgiven you." The passive voice insists that God is still the subject of the action as the one who forgives sinners.

The bottom line is that the man needs both physical and spiritual healing. The connection between the two forms of restoration is drawn in Jesus' challenge to his opponents (5:22). At first glance, Jesus' question is unanswerable: "Which is easier, to say, 'Your sins are forgiven you,' or to say, 'Stand up and walk?'" (5:23). Being forgiven by God is more important than being healed, yet it seems easier to pronounce forgiveness than to make a lame man walk. Whether the man is truly forgiven or not cannot be proven, but the effectiveness of a miracle is immediately apparent. Ultimately, forgiveness and physical healing are two sides of the same coin. If the paralytic walks, it confirms that God has empowered Jesus' healing and has also forgiven the man. If the man remains paralyzed, his sins remain and Jesus is exposed as a blasphemous charlatan. One does not happen without the other.

By ordering the man to "stand up and take [his] bed and go to [his] home," Jesus shows the skeptics "that the Son of Man has authority on earth to forgive sins" (5:24).[10] Through Jesus, the messianic Son of Man, God's eschatological forgiveness and means of reconciliation have been brought forward into the present, here on earth (2:14). This is a very bold claim that dovetails John's "baptism of repentance for the forgiveness of sins" (3:3). Prior rituals of forgiveness are relativized by Jesus who

---

9. Zechariah was struck dumb because of unbelief (1:20). See Deut 28:15, 27–28; Ps 107:17; John 5:14; 9:2.

10. According to Bock (1991: 119–21), by calling himself Son of Man Jesus is claiming to be a unique man, a human representative of God who may exercise the divine prerogative of forgiving sins. The claim is legitimized by the successful healing of the paralytic. If the man walks, Jesus is uniquely related to God. If the man does not, Jesus blasphemes.

directly pronounces God's forgiveness. The longstanding cultic system of bringing a sin offering to the temple has been supplanted by a better means of atonement. For those who do not believe that Jesus has such authority, his declaration of forgiveness is way out of line. The onlookers may exclaim that they have seen strange things (*paradoxa*), but for those who embrace Jesus by faith, these "paradoxes" signify the good news of God's salvation, which is no longer a future hope but a present reality, displayed today (*sēmeron*, 4:21; 5:26), before their very eyes.

Calling of Levi and Table Fellowship with Sinners (5:27–35)

From a leper and a paralytic, both unemployable and poor, Jesus next comes across a tax collector. While rich enough to throw a banquet and invite a lot of guests, as a tax collector Levi is despised by all but his business partners. His uncleanness follows him on account of his ill-gotten gains and traitorous interactions with the Romans.[11] He is seen as unclean in every way, being morally, spiritually, and socially suspect. Despite his wealth, he numbers among "the poor" to whom Jesus is sent with the good news of salvation (4:18).

Levi is sitting at his tax station, assessing higher-than-appropriate tariffs, when Jesus summons him (5:27). This is indeed a startling invitation from a rabbi to a thief and traitor. Equally incredible is Levi's response. Without hesitation, he arises from his workstation, leaves everything, and follows Jesus (5:28), mirroring what Simon, James, and John did when they brought their boats to shore after the miraculous catch of fish (5:11).

A new allegiance and a transformed life call for celebration. Levi hosts a banquet with Jesus as the guest of honor. Jesus' disciples and many tax collectors are among the invited guests. Banqueting is an important Lukan motif. First, it marks a joyous occasion. Levi's turning to Jesus anticipates the parables of the lost sheep, the lost coin, and the lost sons in chapter 15, where there is celebration and joy in heaven when a sinner repents. Second, it demonstrates the social significance of table fellowship.[12] According to ancient social norms, eating with those from one's in-group was an expression of kinship and camaraderie, trust and intimacy, shared values and social status. That Jesus and his disciples are

---

11. See p. 50, n. 13.
12. See pp. 204–5.

eating with not just Levi but a large crowd of tax collectors is sending a signal that puts Jesus' reputation under jeopardy (cf. 7:34; 15:1–2). Why does a respected teacher keep such disreputable company?

Ancient banquets were rather public events, and a meal was often followed by some teaching, discussion, or entertainment. Onlookers were permitted to wander in and out. It is unlikely that the Pharisees and scribes are among the invited guests at Levi's banquet, though it does not take much for this event to gain notoriety as the talk of the town: "Guess what! Jesus is at the home of you-know-who and his cronies!" Instead of challenging Jesus directly, the Pharisees and the scribes voice their disapproval to his disciples, "Why do you eat and drink with tax collectors and sinners?" (5:30).[13] This question is an indictment that Jesus is keeping filthy company, transgressing purity laws by eating the food of sinners with the vessels and utensils of unclean people. By honoring shameful people, his brings dishonor upon himself. In the eyes of his critics, the whole scenario casts doubt on Jesus' integrity and respectability.

Jesus addresses the criticism with a proverb: "Those who are well have no need of a physician, but those who are sick; I have come to call not the righteous but sinners to repentance" (5:31–32). This saying is reminiscent of the healing of the paralytic in which physical restoration and forgiveness of sins are closely related (5:23). Clearly Jesus identifies himself with the physician, but who the well (righteous) and the sick (sinners) are is open to evaluation. The Pharisees and the scribes believe that they are well and do not need a physician. They are the righteous, the tax collectors are the sinners, and the boundary between the two must never be crossed. Jesus does not disagree with his critics' assessment of the tax collectors, but is there anyone who is completely righteous and in no need of repentance? Those who do not acknowledge their spiritual impoverishment remain mired in self-deception.

Jesus does not save from a distance. In order to reach sinners, he comes in their midst, eats at their table, and risks being misunderstood by "the righteous party." The carefully guarded boundaries of honor versus shame, in-group versus out-group, and friend versus foe are demolished in Jesus' company. This physician makes house calls by extending grace and acceptance, so that sinners are "loved into" the kingdom of God.

---

13. "Sinner" in Luke, as in ancient Judaism, is a moral category. A person who transgresses the law of God is under the wrath of God and in need of repentance. Luke emphasizes the sinner's need for repentance more so than the person's rebellious actions against God. See Adams 2010: 23–67, 181–96.

Still hovering around the topic of eating and drinking, the Pharisees and scribes accuse Jesus' disciples of impiety because they do not fast and pray like their own disciples or John's disciples (5:33). Fasting has always been an important discipline for the Jews to signify penitence, mourning, humility, petition, or preparation for divine instruction.[14] Given that the Pharisees fast twice a week (cf. 18:12), Jesus' disciples strike them as revelers by comparison. And since the behavior of the disciples is a reflection on their teacher, the finger is pointed at Jesus.

Jesus answers the criticism with another metaphor: "You cannot make wedding guests fast while the bridegroom is with them, can you?" (5:34). Of course not! Levi's banquet has morphed into a wedding banquet, and Jesus, Levi's guest of honor, is now the bridegroom and the host. As long as the bridegroom is present, feasting is the proper response. The role of the guests *is* to eat, drink, and celebrate with gusto. After all, the coming of Jesus is "good news of great joy for all the people" (2:10). There will come a time when "the bridegroom will be taken away" (5:35), and mourning and fasting will be appropriate and necessary (23:27, 48). While the foreshadowing of Jesus' death injects an ominous note to an otherwise delightful picture, that time has yet to come.

The Pharisees and scribes have a hard time reconciling Jesus' words and actions to what they perceive as God's will for God's people. Trapped by the strictures of the purity laws and the social hierarchies that promote self-protection and separatism, they are horrified that Jesus blurs their carefully constructed lines of demarcation and challenges their sense of status and space, all the while claiming divine sanction. The final two illustrations of this chapter summarize the dissonance that arises when old meets new.

Old versus New (5:36–39)

Both images are taken from situations in everyday life that appeal to the common sense of the hearers. First, an old garment has a rip and needs to be repaired. It would be silly to cut a piece from a brand new garment and sew the patch on the old garment. The old one will have an odd piece of new fabric on it that does not match, and the new one will have a big hole in it. The result is two ruined garments, each undesirable in its own way (5:36).

---

14. See 2 Sam 1:12; Ezra 8:21; Esth 4:16; Joel 1:14; Jonah 3:5.

Second, new wine increases in volume in the fermenting process. When poured into a fresh wineskin, the new skin is stretchable to absorb the stress exerted by the expanding wine (5:38). But an old wineskin has already been stretched. If new wine is poured into an old wineskin, the new wine will expand, but the old wineskin is no longer flexible and will split apart. At a result, the new wine is spilled and the old wineskin is broken (5:37).

Both pictures speak to the incompatibility between old and new. The Pharisees and scribes cling to the old ways of Judaism, privileging the laws of purity above all else and excluding all those who fall short of their standard. Jesus' new way is welcoming and inclusive. He crosses boundaries to reach those in need of deliverance regardless of purity standards. On the one hand, there is obvious discontinuity between old and new. One cannot simultaneously include and exclude. The two are incompatible, just like a new patch on an old garment or new wine in an old wineskin. On the other hand, the Pharisees' program and Jesus' program both have their roots in Israel's Scriptures. There is continuity between the two, and Jesus does not represent a break from the faith of Israel's forebears.

Metaphors have their limits, so these illustrations cannot be pressed too far, as though the old should be discarded and only the new should be retained. God authorizes Jesus to do a new thing that expands the limited horizons of the old program. Jesus has not abandoned the law; he embodies in word and deed its true meaning and renews its appropriation in life-giving ways. The new, however, cannot exercise its life-changing effects unless one is willing to loosen one's grip on the old. Jesus' closing statement is a sad commentary: "No one after drinking old wine desires new wine, but says, 'The old is good'" (5:39). Most people prefer aged wine to new wine. Likewise, the Pharisees and the scribes will continue to cling stubbornly to the old and familiar and will never fully understand the breadth and depth of God's generosity and mercy because they refuse the new wine that Jesus offers.

Luke 6

Controversy over Sabbath Law (6:1–11)

In addition to the controversies concerning purity in the previous chapter, Jesus' adherence to the Sabbath law also comes under scrutiny. The rules about keeping the Sabbath were derived from the fourth commandment of the Decalogue: "Remember the Sabbath day, and keep it holy" (Exod 20:8–11; Deut 5:12–15). At the end of creation, God rested on the seventh day and made it holy (Gen 2:2–3). Refraining from work on the Sabbath was a gift from God as well as an imitation of God. Because the holiness of the Sabbath reflected God's own holiness, failure to observe the Sabbath was a serious infraction punishable by death (Exod 31:12–17). At the time of Jesus, Sabbath observance set the Jews apart from the gentiles who worked seven days a week. It served as an important identity marker for a people striving to maintain their fidelity to God while living under foreign domination.

The prohibition to work on the Sabbath in the OT did not come with specific details. In the post-exilic period, Israel's teachers debated among themselves and came up with thirty-nine classes of work that were later codified in the Mishnah (*m. Šabb.* 7:2). Among them were activities like reaping, threshing, grinding, sifting, kneading, baking, spinning, tying, sewing two stitches, writing two letters, kindling fire, carrying from one location to another, just to name a few. Together they covered all aspects of daily life. Although the rabbis admitted that "the rules about the Sabbath, festal offerings, and sacrilege are as mountains hanging by a hair, for Scripture is scanty and the rules many" (*m. Ḥag.* 1:8), these practical injunctions were needed to protect Israel from assimilation to the culture of their pagan overlords. Observing the law strengthened Jewish self-understanding and identity. Therefore, before we dismiss these details as an obsession with minutiae and trivialize them, we must remember that the specific prohibitions, as well as the details concerning purity and food laws, all grew out of Israel's desire to subsume all of life under God's law.[1]

Plucking Grains on the Sabbath (6:1–5)

While passing through some grain fields on a Sabbath day, Jesus' disciples pluck some heads of grain, rub them in their hands to get rid of the chaff, and eat the kernels (6:1a). Because farmers are instructed by Moses not to reap all the way to the edges of their fields during harvest time and save some for the poor to glean (Lev 19:9; Deut 23:25; Ruth 2:2–3), the disciples are not stealing. The Pharisees, however, charge them with breaking the Sabbath law (6:1b), if plucking the grains is equated with reaping and rubbing the heads with threshing. Even the thirty-nine classes of work are subject to further interpretation.

Jesus is responsible for his disciples' actions as well as their defense. Rather than arguing with the Pharisees on the definition of work, he illustrates his point with a story. When David was on the run from Saul, he came to Nob and asked the priest Ahimelech for bread. All Ahimelech had was the bread of the Presence reserved for priests to eat, which David took anyway for himself and his men (1 Sam 21:1–6; Luke 6:3–4).[2] Jesus then draws a comparison between David and himself. David's incident did not take place on the Sabbath, so Jesus is addressing a principle broader than Sabbath observance alone. Strictly speaking, both of them broke the letter of the law. Their actions involved the alleviation of hunger and spoke to God's merciful provision for those in need. If the Pharisees view Jesus as a lawbreaker by condoning his disciples' behavior, to be consistent they ought to condemn David as well. The assumption is that the Pharisees disapprove of Jesus but not of David because in their view David was God's anointed but not Jesus. Employing the Jewish technique of argumentation from the lesser to the greater, Jesus asserts that if David, the king of Israel, could sidestep the law to preserve his life and his men's lives, how much more can Jesus, Son of God and Davidic Messiah, do the same? Therefore, the Son of Man is Lord of the Sabbath (6:5), and his authority surpasses even that of David (cf. 20:41–44)![3]

---

1. Nolland 2013: 820–23.

2. Mark identifies Abiathar as the high priest (Mark 2:26). It should be Ahimelech according to 1 Sam 21; Abiathar is the son of Ahimelech (1 Sam 22:20). Luke omits the name altogether.

3. Marshall 1978: 232. For "Son of Man" as a title of authority, see pp. 127–28.

Jesus is not suggesting that one should ignore the Sabbath law with impunity. Instead, he brings out the true meaning of the Sabbath as a stipulation that is designed for the benefit of God's people. The Sabbath should not be a measuring stick of one's faithfulness, even though the seriousness with which the Pharisees take the Sabbath law is commendable. The issue is not whether Jesus' disciples should have skipped a meal and waited till after the Sabbath to eat, since they are not dying of hunger. The Sabbath law, in all its importance, must not stand in the way of God's grace. How ironic it would be to defeat the purpose of the Sabbath in the name of observing the Sabbath! Accused of violating the Sabbath, Jesus is in fact living out the true significance of Sabbath rest and has the authority to make that determination.

Healing a Man with a Withered Hand (6:6–11)

On another Sabbath, Jesus is teaching in a synagogue and a man with a withered right hand is in the audience (6:6). In the OT, to will someone's right hand or arm to be withered was a curse to invoke divine judgment (Ps 137:5; Zech 11:17). King Jeroboam was punished in this manner when he rejected the words of a prophet (1 Kgs 13:1–6). Here the subject of this man's sin is not broached, so we should not assume a cause-and-effect relationship between his guilt and his handicap. In any case, the stigma remains on him.

Present as well are some Pharisees and teachers of the law who are looking for violation of the Sabbath law on Jesus' part (6:7). Knowing their motive, Jesus brings the man to the front for an open confrontation (6:8). Instead of waiting for his opponents to strike first, Jesus goes on the offensive and asks, "Is it lawful to do good or to do harm on the Sabbath, to save life or to destroy it?" (6:9). The ensuing silence shows the reluctance of Jesus' opponents to give him any leeway at all. The oral traditions of the rabbis included provisions for breaking the Sabbath under extenuating circumstances. Circumcision (*m. Šabb.* 19:2) and midwifery (*m. Šabb.* 18:3) were permissible work on the Sabbath, as was action taken to save someone from dying (*m. Yoma* 8:6). Therefore, the real answer to Jesus' question is, "It depends," but his opponents are not willing to say as much. If the man's withered hand is not life-threatening, Jesus should wait till after the Sabbath to heal him. Why violate the Sabbath law on account of a few hours? This is like asking why Jesus' disciples could not have waited till after the Sabbath to pluck grains if they were not dying of starvation (6:1–2).

Two good things are in competition—obeying the Sabbath law and exercising God's saving grace. The Pharisees and the teachers privilege the law whereas Jesus privileges the needy person. To Jesus, a few more hours to the end of the Sabbath are a few more hours in which this man has to suffer his handicap. Doing nothing is tantamount to doing harm and destroying life.[4] Although the man can surely survive with a withered hand for a little while longer, it is the principle behind what Jesus is doing that is communicated in hyperbole. God's salvation is available today, right now, immediately, so Jesus' work of restoration must not be hampered or delayed, even on the Sabbath.

To confirm God's validation of his doing good on the Sabbath, Jesus commands the man to stretch out his hand (6:10). Being healed requires faith. Just as the paralytic had to believe that if he stood up his legs would not give way (5:24–26), this man has to trust that those shriveled fingers will move when he stretches out his hand. As he obeys, his hand is completely restored. But the Pharisees and the teachers of the law remain unmoved. They reject Jesus' authority, his interpretation of the Sabbath law, and his shaming of them in a setting where they enjoy high regard. What they consider as "righteous anger" will soon turn into malicious intent (6:11).

Luke has painted a clear picture of the conflict between Jesus and the religious elites of his day. More controversies are still to come. Who speaks for God? Who appropriates the true intentions of the law? The mercy that permeates Jesus' healings, exorcisms, and table fellowship with outcasts will set the standard for those who follow him, beginning with the Twelve.

Naming the Twelve (6:12–16)

The crowds have been flocking to Jesus for quite some time, and now Jesus chooses a specific group of twelve whom he calls "apostles" (*apostolous*, 6:13). While Luke uses the term "disciples" (*mathētai*) to refer to these twelve in particular (8:9, 22; 9:14, 40; 11:1) and others who display a serious commitment to follow Jesus (6:4; 14:26–27), the designation "apostles" is reserved for these twelve alone (9:10; 17:5; 22:14; 24:10).

---

4. Marshall 1978: 235; Carroll 2012: 140.

Together they are sometimes referred to as "the Twelve" (8:1; 9:1, 12; 18:31).[5] The author's careful choice of terminology respects the distinctive meaning of *apostolos*. An apostle is one who is sent, recalling the Jewish idea of an agent who is given the authority to act on behalf of the sender. Before the Twelve can be sent, they are to be "with Jesus" (7:11; 8:1; 9:10; 22:11). Their task is twofold—to bear witness to Jesus' words and deeds and to spread the good news through their own ministry of preaching and healing (9:1-6; cf. Mark 3:14). Choosing the Twelve is therefore an important undertaking, hence Jesus spent the whole night on the mountain in prayer, seeking guidance from God (6:12).

Matthew and Mark also record that Jesus calls twelve disciples (Matt 10:1-4; Mark 3:13-19), but there are discrepancies between their lists and this one in Luke (6:12-16). A person might have been known by more than one name,[6] and variations might have cropped up when stories about Jesus were being circulated. More significant is their collective referent as "the Twelve," an identification used by all four evangelists.[7] There are twelve tribes of Israel, and now there are twelve apostles. As Jesus reconstitutes the people of Israel under his messiahship, he installs a new leadership. One day the Twelve will judge the twelve tribes of Israel (22:30).

Among the names in Luke's listing, Simon Peter, James, and John have already been introduced (5:1-11). Peter (*Petros*), which means "rock," is a name given by Jesus to mark a new life or relationship (6:14).[8] In the rest of the narrative, Peter, James, and John will appear as an inner circle within the larger group (8:51; 9:28). Judas will betray Jesus (22:3, 47-48), and Philip is featured in Acts 8. Beyond that, there is no specific mention of the other apostles except for a near-identical list in Acts 1:13, minus Judas Iscariot.

Whenever there are two persons by the same name, Luke adds an identifier to tell them apart: James the son of Alphaeus, Simon the Zealot, Judas the son of James, and Judas Iscariot. A zealot can mean a zealous person (Acts 21:20; 22:3), or Luke may have used the term anachronously

---

5. In Acts, Luke mostly uses the term "apostles" (1:2; 2:37; 4:33) and refers to them as "the Twelve" only once (6:2).

6. Nathanael (John 1:45-49; 21:2) is not found in any of the lists in the Synoptic Gospels. Could he have gone by a different name? See Bauckham 2006: 96-101.

7. E.g., Matt 26:14, 20; Mark 4:10; 14:17; Luke 8:1; 18:31; John 6:67; 20:24.

8. Matthew explains the significance of the name: "On this rock I will build my church" (16:18).

to emphasize Simon's political bias. The Zealots, who were revolutionaries in Judea involved in the rebellion against the Romans, were not formalized as a group until the mid-60s CE.[9] "Iscariot" may indicate that Judas is not from Galilee, but a "man of Kerioth." Others surmise that Iscariot may be derived from an Aramaic word that means "the false one."[10] Tag lines such as, "the one who betrayed him," or "the traitor," follow Judas in all four Gospels,[11] as he will forever be remembered by his infamy.

Finally, in Luke, Levi is the tax collector who left his booth to follow Jesus (5:27; so Mark 2:14). In Matthew, the tax collector's name is Matthew (Matt 9:9; 10:3). In all three lists in the Synoptic Gospels, however, Matthew is named but Levi is not. On what basis are we to assume Levi is Matthew? To complicate matters, James the son of Alphaeus appears in all three lists, yet Mark also identifies Levi the tax collector as the son of Alphaeus! Is Levi then not Matthew but James, or has Alphaeus fathered two sons, Levi and James, who both follow Jesus? There is not enough information to solve the puzzle. In the final analysis, the important thing to remember is the number twelve.

Sermon on the Plain (6:17–49)

There is considerable overlap between the materials in Luke's "Sermon on the Plain" and Matthew's "Sermon on the Mount" (Matt 5:1—7:29), though some teachings in Matthew's sermon are found elsewhere in a different setting in Luke. Both authors appear to have drawn from similar traditions, but each takes his authorial liberty to insert these materials where most appropriate in their respective narratives. It is possible that Jesus taught similar things on multiple occasions. Through these teachings, Jesus makes known the values of God's kingdom that turn the world's norm on its head. Cultural systems of interpersonal engagement, such as honor and shame, balanced reciprocity, and patron-client relationships are scrutinized, challenged, and reframed by God's ethos of generosity, mercy, and integrity.

---

9. Skarsaune 2002: 126–29.
10. Marshall 1978: 240–41.
11. Matt 10:4; 27:3; Mark 3:19; Luke 6:16; John 6:71; 12:4; 18:2, 5.

The Crowd Flocks to Jesus (6:17–19)

Having assembled the Twelve, Jesus returns with them to the public arena. Once again, disciples and onlookers alike come to Jesus from all over Palestine, from Jerusalem to the gentile regions of Tyre and Sidon (6:17). Jesus' teachings will challenge his listeners to love their enemies (6:27–36). As with previous summary statements of Jesus' teaching, healing, and exorcising activities, no one is turned away and everyone is healed (6:18–19).

Blessings and Woes (6:20–26)

Blessings and woes describe opposite states of being, delineating the respective consequences for those who welcome the good news that Jesus brings and those who remain stubborn, haughty, and self-reliant. The four blessings match the four woes in content. Together they accentuate Luke's emphasis on the release from bondage and the reversal of conditions as manifestations of God's salvation, bringing to mind Mary's song (1:51–53) and Jesus' sermon at Nazareth (4:18–19).

The first three blessings of those who are poor, those who are hungry, and those who weep are different ways of expressing the same thing (6:20–21). The poor in Luke encompasses a broad definition. Poverty is experienced economically, emotionally, communally, and spiritually. The poor includes peasants who can barely survive on a subsistence level, the sick plagued with demon possession and debilitating handicaps that render them unclean, tax collectors and sinners despised for their moral infractions, and others of low status who are kept there by the hierarchical society in which they live.[12] Whether they are poor, hungry, or weeping, their humbled state and shared neediness make them receptive to help from above. They trust that God's heart is inclined toward the afflicted and that he hears the cries of the weak (Pss 10:17–18; 68:5–6; Ezek 34:16). As they rely on God for his deliverance and provision, their hunger will be assuaged, and their tears will turn into laughter. Although the reversal of condition lies yet in the future, their place in God's kingdom is assured even now. On that final day of salvation, there will be no more mourning (Jer 31:13; Isa 35:10; 60:20) but only overflowing abundance at God's banqueting table (Isa 49:10; Jer 31:12; Ezek 34:29).

---

12. See p. 61.

The fourth blessing addresses the conflict that will arise when allegiance to Jesus competes with allegiance to the world (6:22–23). The rapid chain of verbs, "hate you, . . . exclude you, revile you, and defame you," describes ostracism against the disciples' person and reputation on account of their commitment to the Son of Man. Persecution is to be expected, but may the disciples not lose heart, for heavenly reward and eternal joy await them. The way of the prophets, of Jesus, and now of his followers, is marked with sufferings, but God will vindicate his faithful ones.

The reversal of condition works in both directions. While some are lifted from lowliness to exaltation, others will plunge from the pinnacle of pride to the pit of humiliation. Four inverse formulations address the short-sightedness of the rich, the full, the laughing, and the popular (6:24–26). The consolation of the rich is the sum total of the benefits they have amassed with their own resources, namely, wealth, power, fame, and status. In God's economy, none of these worldly achievements will last (cf. 12:15–21; 16:19–31). The woes may not strike immediately, but judgment will come. Deprivation will befall those who now have plenty to eat. Mourning and weeping will overcome those who wallow in ungodly revelry. And false prophets, then and now, who never ruffle a feather and only say what people want to hear will be exposed and destroyed (cf. Jer 5:12–13; 23:16–18). In the end, their so-called reputation will amount to nothing.

Loving One's Enemies (6:27–36)

Jesus' opening admonition to love one's enemies may strike his audience as counterintuitive and difficult (6:27a).[13] In the ancient world of clear social boundaries, those who did not belong to one's kinship group were treated as outsiders and enemies. There would not be any business dealing, table fellowship, or communal worship with one's enemies. To love one's enemies was a total contradiction in terms.

Further elaborations on what it means to love one's enemies bring clarity but do not make things any easier: "Do good to those who hate you; bless those who curse you; pray for those who abuse you" (6:27b). Not

---

13. See Nolland 1989: 294–95. The call to love one's enemies can be found in ancient Jewish and Greco-Roman ethical and philosophical writings as well. The motivation to do so ranges from a sense of moral superiority to the imitation of the gods. Still, most people would rather not blur the line between friend and foe.

repaying evil with evil is a given. Over and beyond that, Jesus demands that his disciples not only counter the negative treatment they receive by non-retaliation, but that they also infuse it with a life-giving overture. The hard part is to genuinely and ungrudgingly wish for the wellbeing of an enemy. Love is not sentimentalism, but a decisive action that runs counter to the natural vindictive response of fallen human nature.

Jesus gives two illustrations from daily life. The first has to do with turning the other cheek (6:29a). Luke omits Matthew's mention of the blow on the right cheek (Matt 5:39), which is especially insulting to Jews because it implies a back-handed slap (*m. B. Qam.* 8:6). To offer the other cheek for a second blow communicates not only non-retaliation, but also one's openness to the action of the aggressor, who may choose to stop hitting or deal another blow. The second example presents a scenario in which a robber takes one's outer garment by force, and Jesus exhorts his followers to be ready to let go of their inner tunic as well (6:29b). Surely Jesus is not advocating a doormat mentality, allowing his disciples to be taken advantage of. Quite to the contrary, doing an enemy good requires internal strength that neutralizes the force of the assailant's attack. It cultivates a spirit of generosity that does not keep score between two people (6:30). Essentially, Jesus invokes the golden rule: "Do to others as you would have them do to you" (6:31). Even though loving one's enemies is a tall order that does not guarantee friendly reciprocity, the benefit exceeds the cost by a grand margin.

One can imagine the protest: "Do you have any idea how I have been mistreated? Why do I have to go beyond the call of duty for someone so undeserving?" But Jesus has a ready answer: "You are not like them; you are my disciples and I expect more from you." Even among sinners, the lowest common denominator is the principle of balanced reciprocity (6:32–34). Sinners love, do good, and lend to one another in their in-group, in order to get back in equal amount that which has been given. If the expectation is that minimal, such that even sinners can abide by it, what makes association with Jesus and following Jesus' ethos an alternative vision to life that pleases God?

Jesus further grounds his injunction to love one's enemies in the imitation of God.[14] The adage, "like father, like son," or, "the apple doesn't fall far from the tree," ought to apply here. The children of the Most High

---

14. Topel (1998: 475–85) argues that the golden rule has more to do with one's first action rather than one's response to another person's action. He explains the golden rule not in terms of reciprocity but the imitation of God's radical love and benevolence.

should take on their Father's merciful character. While the people of the world operate on the basis of liability and credit, Jesus and his disciples live by the mercy of a God who chooses to be kind even to "the ungrateful and the wicked" (6:35; cf. Exod 33:19; 34:6). Therefore, those who have experienced God's mercy must extend the same mercy to others and be like their Father in heaven (6:36; cf. 11:4; 23:34).

Warning against Judging Others (6:37–45)

A merciful attitude toward others is only possible in the absence of a judgmental spirit. The Greek verbs in verses 37 and 38, *mē krinete* ("do not keep judging"), *mē katadikazete* ("do not keep condemning"), *apoluete* ("keep forgiving"), and *didote* ("keep giving"), are in the present tense, signifying ongoing action. Jesus is not abolishing all God's standards and withholding all evaluations and correctives. He is speaking against finding fault with a spirit of censoriousness and superiority. By the same token, deeds and attitudes of generosity will not go unnoticed. God gives to those who give, and he forgives those who forgive. In fact, God's generosity compensates far more than what has been given and forgiven. Pictured here is a generous merchant measuring grain, spice, or corn, whatever that is sold, before pouring it into the fold of the customer's garment. He shakes the measuring vessel to remove excess air, packs the grain, fills it to overflowing, and does whatever it takes to transfer as much as possible to the recipient (6:38). Likewise, God's reward will always be greater than the sacrifice of those who trust in his goodness.

Two short images illustrate condemnatory judgment at work. First, the disciples must pick the right teacher. It is proverbial that a blind person leading another blind person will only result in disaster, as incompetence cannot be trusted to guide incompetence (6:39). Hence a student needs a good teacher to help him or her grow to the level of that teacher (6:40). Now Jesus is the competent teacher who will teach his students well, and they will emerge from their apprenticeship proven and insightful. But if they follow the Pharisees and the scribes, they and their blind guides will end up in a pit, mired in darkness and making no progress.

Second, the ridiculous image of a person with a log in the eye trying to remove a speck in the eye of another exposes a lack of self-awareness (6:41–42). It is hypocritical to quibble with someone else's small imperfection while remaining oblivious to one's own glaring error. Jesus is not talking about the hierarchy of sins. Rather, self-examination and repentance must precede any attempt to fix the wrongs of a neighbor. The Greek noun *hypokritēs* ("hypocrite") originates from the theatrical domain. A hypocrite engages in play-acting, pretending to be one thing on the outside but is actually something else on the inside. A judgmental person may not even be aware of his or her hypocrisy. Self-deception and self-righteousness often go hand in hand.

With a twist of a pun, Luke moves from speck (*karphos*) to fruit (*karpos*) to address the integrity of the heart. The flip side of being hypocritical is having integrity, when the external consistently reflects the internal. The agricultural illustration is self-explanatory (6:43–45). The fruit of a tree is the undisputed product of the tree, both in quality and type. A good tree will not yield bad fruit, nor can a bad tree produce good fruit in spite of itself. Figs must come from fig trees and grapes from grapevines. The law of nature governs this consistency. Likewise, the heart, whether good or evil, controls a person's words and deeds. A person of good character does not have an evil heart, and vice versa. A hypocrite can only pretend for so long before the truth is revealed.

Wise and Foolish Builders (6:46–49)

The integrity of the heart is now applied to the challenge of discipleship as Jesus brings the Sermon on the Plain to a close. True disciples of Jesus hear his word and do it, unlike those who pay him lip service with the honorific title "Lord" but do not follow through with acts of obedience (6:46; cf. 8:21). Jesus likens the journey of discipleship to the building of houses. The first builder sets his house on a foundation that digs deep into the bedrock, solid enough to withstand the floodwaters of the river (6:47–48). The second builder is a failure. Foundationless, the house topples as soon as the river hits against it (6:49).

While Luke's version of Jesus' parable focuses on the foundation and Matthew's on the ferocity of the storm (Matt 7:24–27), the result is the same. Wisdom and obedience keep the house standing. To the contrary, a house built on foolishness and disobedience is bound to collapse. Since building a house takes time, commitment, consistency, diligence, and care, this is a fitting metaphor for the life of discipleship. Calling Jesus "Lord" will inevitably lead to "floods," be they persecution, calamities, or trials of life. Will Jesus' disciples hold up under pressure?

Luke 7

A Centurion's Slave and a Widow's Son (7:1–17)

In this chapter, the prophetic identity of Jesus is highlighted, making explicit the earlier comparison between him and Elijah and Elisha (4:24–27). Jesus' healing of the centurion's slave from a distance is reminiscent of the cleansing of Naaman from leprosy by Elisha, also from a distance (2 Kgs 5:1–14). The raising of the dead son of the widow in Nain bears uncanny similarities to the account of Elijah bringing back to life the child of the widow of Zeraphath (1 Kgs 17:8–24). For readers familiar with the OT, these allusions are hard to miss. Also instructive in the stories of Luke 7 is the interplay of social rules in ancient Jewish and Greco-Roman communities. The importance of purity laws for separating insiders from outsiders, the clean from the unclean, the interrelated dynamics of patronage and reciprocity, as well as the status-consciousness inevitable in a hierarchical society, provide the backdrop for understanding why the characters think and behave as they do, and how Jesus reframes their social expectations.

Healing a Centurion's Slave (7:1–10)

A centurion was a Roman officer who had command over a hundred men. It is unsure if Roman forces were present in Galilee before 44 CE and, if not, whether a centurion at the time of Jesus could be a non-Jewish soldier working for Herod Antipas.[1] At any rate, a centurion was a gentile who represented Rome's oppressive powers and would have been feared or hated by the Jews. The centurion in this story, however, breaks the stereotype. He is stationed in Capernaum, where Jesus often ministers (4:23, 31).[2] He is the main benefactor of the city; he loves the people and built their synagogue for them (7:5). Is he a friend or a foe, given that "gentile"

---

1. Marshall 1978: 279; Garland 2011: 294.
2. See p. 65.

and "benefactor" do not normally belong together in one breath? How are the dynamics between overlord and subject and between gentile and Jew to be navigated when the illness of the centurion's slave brings these awkward questions to the foreground?

The centurion's slave is near death, too ill to be brought to Jesus (7:2). The Greek word *doulos* can be rendered either as "slave" or "servant." In the ancient world, even though slavery meant the loss of freedom and full ownership by the master, slaves performed a wide variety of tasks in rural and urban settings. Some were relegated to menial labor, while more fortunate ones were given an education and assigned responsibilities to manage their master's affairs. Although not all masters treated their slaves humanely, many would be concerned about their well-being, at least to prolong their usefulness.[3] In this story, the slave is highly valued by his master, who goes out of his way to gain access to Jesus, whose healing power is well known in Capernaum.

At first, the centurion employs Jewish emissaries, being sensitive to Jewish prejudice against gentiles. Because the Jewish elders owe him a favor for his benefaction, they approach Jesus on his behalf, whether willingly or obligatorily. They present his acts of kindness as evidence of his worthiness of Jesus' attention (7:4).[4] A centurion, albeit a friendly one, is still a gentile. A generous reading of the elders may view them as eager and helpful, but a skeptical reading may conclude that they are manipulative, trying to coerce Jesus into helping the centurion as a repayment for the good deeds the latter has done for the town.[5] The elders' words betray their ethnocentricity: "He loves *our* people and it is he who built *our* synagogue for *us*" (7:5). They are concerned with maintaining a cordial relationship between the locals and their Roman superior. Yet none of their politically correct considerations seems to affect Jesus' response when he agrees to go with them to the centurion's house. If Jesus is willing sit at table with Levi and his fellow tax collectors (5:29–31), why will he not enter a gentile's house? Ritual contamination is not a deterrent.

The second set of emissaries, made up of the centurion's friends, reflects their sender's intentions more accurately (7:6–8). This time a verbatim message, in the centurion's own words, is given to Jesus. The

---

3. On slavery in the ancient world, see Harrill 2000: 1125–26; Jeffers 1999: 220–36.

4. Gagnon (1994: 130–37) surmises that Luke includes the Jewish elders' approval of the centurion to encourage Jewish approval of the mission to the gentiles in the evangelist's own context.

5. Green 1997: 287.

centurion employs the vocative "Lord" (*kyrie*, 7:6), which spells respect. While *kyrios* can also mean "lord" or "sir" in a non-religious sense, Luke tends to reserve this form of address for those who have faith in Jesus.[6] Contrary to the elders' opinion that he is very worthy, the centurion actually thinks he is unworthy to have Jesus come to his house. The elders attribute high status to the centurion because of his beneficence. But the centurion's assessment exhibits self-awareness and cultural sensitivity. Rather than summoning Jesus to his house to heal his slave, he knows his home is ritually unclean by Jewish standards. His sense of unworthiness is reminiscent of that of John, who did not consider himself adequate to untie the thongs of Jesus' sandals (3:16). Given that the Jew-gentile divide is part of the cultural dynamics behind this interchange, the centurion's humility is all the more remarkable because the Romans have the upper hand over the Jews. The centurion must think exceptionally highly of Jesus, as well as of his slave, to come down from his lofty political position to elevate the status of this Jewish healer above his own.[7]

Moreover, the centurion's appeal to authority is not manipulative like that of the Jewish elders, stuck in the system of patronage and power play. As a military veteran who receives and gives orders, the centurion lives by the absolutes of authority and obedience. He applies the same logic to what he understands to be Jesus' healing power. Jesus has not recommended that he heal the slave from afar to avoid contracting impurity. The centurion simply believes that Jesus can heal his slave by the sheer authority of a word without stepping foot in his house (7:7–8). This confidence takes faith and humility, for the centurion is a man of standing in the community and his honor is at stake. No wonder Jesus is impressed and commends him before the Jewish crowd, "Not even in Israel have I found such faith" (7:9). To end the story, the restoration of the slave from near death to good health is acknowledged to validate both Jesus' healing power and the centurion's spiritual insight (7:10).

Comparing this event to the healing of Naaman by Elisha, the image of Jesus as a prophet is strengthened by the obvious echoes (2 Kgs 5:1–14). Both Naaman and the centurion were gentile army officers. Even though Naaman, and not his slave, was healed, he himself was also referred to as a servant of the King of Aram (2 Kgs 5:6). Both Naaman and the centurion used a go-between. Naaman learned about Elisha through

---

6. See p. 23, n. 23.
7. Gagnon 1994: 141–42.

a Jewish slave girl, and the centurion sent two rounds of emissaries to Jesus. Neither Naaman nor the centurion's slave saw their healer in person; both miracles happened from a distance. By alluding to this Elisha story here and earlier in 4:27, Luke affirms that God's compassion is not limited to Israel. The faith of this centurion anticipates the meeting of Peter and Cornelius, another centurion and a God-fearer, in Acts 10.[8] The trajectory of a saving mission to the gentile world will continue well into Luke's second volume (Acts 1:8; 28:28).

While it is impressive that Jesus snatches a man from the jaws of death, the next pericope presents Jesus with a man who is already dead. The social dynamic changes once again. In stark contrast to a wealthy and highly regarded centurion, it is a destitute and lowly widow who is now blessed by the Messiah who shows no partiality.

Raising a Widow's Son (7:11–17)

The obscure village of Nain is twenty-five miles southwest of Capernaum and six miles southeast of Nazareth.[9] The setting is a funeral procession outside the town gate. In the warm climate of Palestine, burial immediately followed death before the body had time to decompose. The corpse was cleaned, anointed, wrapped, and carried on a bier or in a coffin to be buried outside the city in sand or salt if the family could not afford a tomb. It was important for the villagers to show solidarity with the grieving family by participating in the funeral procession.[10] The story begins where two large crowds meet. Jesus is heading toward Nain accompanied by a crowd made up of disciples and onlookers (7:11). Coming out of Nain is another crowd accompanying a bereaved mother whose son has just died. His body is being carried out to the burial site (7:12). Because of the size of the throng, what is about to happen will have many witnesses.

The situation is especially tragic. The mother is a widow and now her only son is dead. To lose an only child was especially painful because the surviving parents would have no one to carry on their name, take care of them in their old age, and bury them at death. With neither husband nor son, the social and economic consequence for this widow portends a fearful future with no means of support and utter vulnerability. The son's

---

8. See Gagnon 1994: 129 for many points of contact between Luke 7 and Acts 10.
9. Carroll 2012: 164.
10. Green 1997: 281; See Evans 2012: 114–17 for Jewish burial practices.

death effectively signals her demise. The OT is full of injunctions to care for and not to oppress widows because God's heart is especially inclined toward them.[11]

The sense of finality that death brings hangs in the air. No mention is made of the widow's faith and no one expects Jesus to do anything. The initiative comes from Jesus alone, fueled by divine compassion (7:13a). Various English translations read: "he had compassion" (NRSV), "his heart overflowed with compassion" (NLT), "he felt compassion" (NASB), and "his heart went out to her" (NIV). All of them rely on the nouns "compassion" and "heart" to express how Jesus feels about the situation, but they fail to bring out the poignancy in the Greek text, where a verb (*esplanchnisthē*), and not a noun, is used.[12] The noun *splanchnon* literally means "bowel" or "gut," but metaphorically it refers to the seat of one's tender emotions. Back in chapter 1, Zechariah attributes the arrival of "the dawn from on high" to *splanchna eleous theou hēmōn*, "the tender mercy of our God" (1:78 NRSV). Jesus' compassion for the widow and her plight is a verb; it is visceral, arising from his deepest innards. It also expresses the tender mercy of God himself toward one of his own who is in deep distress.

"Do not weep" (7:13b), Jesus says, recalling the word of grace he gave in the previous chapter: "Blessed are you who weep now, for you will laugh" (6:21). These are not just words of condolences, but a prelude to God's mighty action soon to follow. The eschatological reversal from sorrow to joy and death to life is about to become a present reality. Rendering himself ritually unclean on account of corpse impurity (Num 19:11–16; Ezek 44:25–27),[13] Jesus touches the bier and stops the funeral procession in its tracks. One can imagine a gasp, a pause, and then a flutter of murmurs rippling through the large crowd: "Oh my, what is he doing?"

With authority and power, Jesus commands the dead to life: "Young man, to you I say, rise (*egerthēti*)!" (7:14). Translating *egerthēti* in the active voice makes for smoother English: "Rise!" (NRSV), "Arise" (ESV, NASB), or "Get up!" (NIV, NLT). But the imperative verb *egerthēti* is actually a divine passive. It is God who raises the dead man, and Jesus is

---

11. E.g., Deut 26:12–13; Isa 1:17; Jer 7:5–7; Zech 7:10. On the plight of widows see p. 239 and Snodgrass 2008: 453.

12. Luke uses the verb form also to express the compassion of the Samaritan (10:33) and the father of the prodigal son (15:20).

13. See pp. 72–73.

God's agent through whom the gift of life is dispensed. Not only is Jesus calling the man to come back to life, he is ordering him to physically get up, as he did with the paralytic (5:24). Since the bier is a wooden plank, the dead body is in plain sight. Sitting up and speaking are clear signs of life, at which point Jesus gives the son back to his mother. His revivification in a sense also brings his mother back to life, for without his support, her livelihood, and even her own life, will be in jeopardy.

The two crowds have merged into one large chorus of fear and praise (7:16). The witnesses draw two conclusions. First, they interpret Jesus as a great prophet and that "God has looked favorably (*epeskepsato*) on his people." The same verb appears in Zechariah's prophecy to speak of God "[looking] favorably (*epeskepsato*) on his people and [redeeming] them" (1:68). God's care is not aloof; he comes to his people and enacts his benevolent mercy in their midst. The crowd recognizes God's visitation that day in the life of this young man and his widowed mother. But this recognition is short-lived, for later Jesus will lament that Jerusalem fails to "recognize the time of [its] visitation (*tēs episkopēs*) from God" (19:44).

To identify Jesus as a great prophet, the people draw from their memories of Elijah and Elisha (1 Kgs 17:8–24; 2 Kgs 4:18–37). Both prophets raised a boy from the dead. The Elisha allusion is secondary, as Luke has just compared Jesus with Elisha in the healing of the centurion's slave (7:1–10). Luke is clearly interested in comparing Jesus with Elijah, a connection already established a few chapters ago (4:26). He patterns this narrative after the story of Elijah's miracle in 1 Kings.[14] For instance, Elijah and Jesus both met the widow at the town gate. Both sons were young. Both dead bodies were carried, one by Elijah to his room and the other by the bier-bearers to the burial site. And both miracle workers were regarded as divine emissaries. Luke even uses a verbatim quotation, *kai edōken auton tē mētri autou* ("and he gave him to his mother," 7:15; 1 Kgs 17:23 LXX) to signal a connection between the two stories. There are also differences. While Elijah placed himself on the dead body three times and pleaded with God to bring the boy back to life, Jesus achieved the same with one command. Indeed, Jesus' greatness surpasses that of even the most revered of Israel's prophets.

---

14. Philostratus recounts a story of Apollonius of Tyana, an ascetic and itinerant teacher, who brought a young bride back to life (*Vit. Apoll.* 4.45). Like Jesus, Apollonius stopped at the bier, halted the funeral procession, and addressed the young woman. She came back to life and began to speak. Philostratus, however, doubts if this was merely a resuscitation and not a true revivification.

Because of the magnitude of this miracle, Jesus' reputation spreads in "Judea and all the surrounding country" (7:17). Increased impact attracts stronger opposition. More situations of tension are sure to follow, but this is a good place for Luke and his readers to pause and ponder the meaning of Jesus' activities. The question raised by John in the next section provides an occasion for Jesus to offer his own interpretation.

John and Jesus (7:18–35)

Since the beginning, the reception to Jesus' public ministry has been mixed. There are committed disciples, curious onlookers, and skeptical critics. Looking at the same actions and hearing the same words of Jesus, some charge him with blasphemy (5:21) while others hail him as the great prophet of God (5:24; 7:17). For Jesus' disciples, even his forerunner John, clarity comes in fits and starts. This segment, prompted by John's question, will confirm Jesus' messianic identity, yet it still needs to be discerned through the eyes of faith.

The One Who Is to Come (7:18–23)

Since his imprisonment by Herod Antipas (3:19–20), John has been hearing about Jesus from his disciples (7:18). He now sends two of them to ask about Jesus' identity. The question is so important that Luke has it asked twice, once on the lips of John and again on the lips of his messengers: "Are you the one who is to come (*ho erchomenos*), or are we to wait for another?" (7:19, 20; cf. 13:35; 19:38). *Erchomai* ("to come") is a common verb, but it carries messianic connotations in places where God's future salvation is referenced (Ps 118:26; Dan 7:13; Zech 9:9). It hearkens back to John's own preaching when he himself said of the Messiah, "The one more powerful than I, is coming (*erchetai*)" (3:16).

If John has been anticipating judgment alongside his call for repentance, Jesus' healings and exorcisms, including his eating with tax collectors and sinners, may not strike him as burning the chaff with unquenchable fire (3:7–9, 15–17). But to say that John's faith is shaken, or that he is sitting in prison riddled with unbelief, is also an overstatement. Whether it is a combination of doubt, hunch, curiosity, or ignorance, this question captures the crux of the matter. Is Jesus the coming one, the Messiah of Israel?

Between the question and Jesus' answer, Luke deftly inserts a summary statement. In one verse, he has Jesus cover the gamut of cures, from diseases, plagues, evil spirits, to many cases of blindness (7:21). Only after that display does Jesus ask John's disciples to relay back to John that which they have seen and heard (7:22). They came as two messengers from John but return as two witnesses, the requisite number for credible testimony (Deut 19:15).

The list Jesus gives encompasses the various types of healings recounted by Luke up to this point, and even anticipates some that have yet to be recounted: "the blind receive their sight (7:21; 18:42), the lame walk (5:25), the lepers are cleansed (5:13; 17:14), the deaf hear, the dead are raised (7:15; 8:55), and the poor have good news brought to them" (6:20; 7:22). Together they form a collage of God's saving activities as prescribed in Isaiah: "On that day the deaf shall hear . . . the eyes of the blind shall see" (Isa 29:18; cf. 35:5; 42:18; 43:8), and "the lame shall leap like a deer" (Isa 35:6). These acts of wonder bear witness to God's saving agenda, described in terms of release from oppression and reversal of condition. Earlier Jesus concluded his sermon at Nazareth with the pronouncement, "Today this scripture has been fulfilled in your hearing" (4:21). Now we have the evidence that indeed God's eschatological future has invaded the present.

In spite of the good news, unbelief lurks in the background. Hence Jesus closes his answer to John with an encouragement: "Blessed is anyone who takes no offense at me" (7:23). Already many, such as the Pharisees and the scribes, have taken offense at Jesus (4:28–29; 5:21, 30; 6:2, 7, 11). They have preconceived notions of what the Messiah should do and whom the Messiah should save, and they refuse to be shaped by Jesus' program of salvation.

Praise for John (7:24–30)

After the departure of John's disciples, Jesus continues to speak of John as a transitional figure standing on the threshold between the old era and the new, between the anticipation of God's salvation and its actualization. Thrice Jesus asks the crowd what they go out to the wilderness to see (7:24–26). Surely they are not out there for the swaying reeds. Neither will they catch a glimpse of royalty dressed in fine linens, for those reside in palaces. Instead, they find a prophet preaching a message of repentance and modeling that attitude with an ascetic lifestyle.

On the one hand, John is the precursor that prepares the way of the Messiah by announcing his coming (Mal 3:1). On the other hand, he leads Israel toward a posture of humility and penitence, so that they are ready to receive the Messiah when he arrives (Exod 23:20; Mal 4:5-6; Luke 1:16-17). Jesus clearly identifies John with the end-time Elijah prefigured in Malachi. It is in this eschatological sense that John is "more than a prophet" (7:26-27). Even as Jesus elevates John to a position above "those born of women," he immediately repositions him so that "the least in the kingdom of God is greater than he" (7:28). It is not as though Jesus had inconsistent opinions about John. Rather, the ethos of the kingdom of God will turn traditional and cultural expectations on their heads. Greatness will be redefined by the surprising dynamic of inversion, so that the strong will be brought low and the weak will be lifted up (1:50-53; 6:22-26). If God is inaugurating a new era of salvation with new garments and new wineskins (5:36-38), then having a place in the kingdom of God, no matter how insignificant, is better than staying entrenched in the old era (5:39).

Jesus and John conduct their ministries differently, but they receive similar responses from the same groups of people. Those who have been baptized by John, including tax collectors with sketchy track records (3:12-13), are among those who "justified God" (7:29). Now the thought that God is in need of "justification" may strike some as odd, not to speak of justification by the likes of tax collectors and sinners. In order to circumvent this conceptual difficulty, some English translations steer clear of the verbal form and go with something along the lines of acknowledging the justice of God (NRSV, NASB) or agreeing to the rightness of God's ways (NIV). On the contrary, the Pharisees and the lawyers reject John as baptizer just as they reject Jesus as physician (5:31-32). As a result, they disqualify themselves from the plan of God and do not even realize it (7:30).

Two Roles, One Mission (7:31-35)

To reiterate the point that Jesus and John share the same mission and receive the same treatment in spite of their differing roles, Jesus employs an image taken from child's play. In this game, the children divide themselves into two groups, callers and responders. The callers will initiate an action, to which the responders must answer in an appropriate manner. The two groups of children in Jesus' picture, however, are not playing well together. When the callers play the flute and make merry music, as one does in a wedding, the responders refuse to dance to the music. Then the callers switch scenes and pretend to be mourners wailing at a funeral, and still the responders will not cooperate by exhibiting corresponding expressions of grief (7:31–32). As a result, both sides are frustrated and the purpose of the game is derailed. The dialogue of verse 32 is the crosstalk between the two, with the callers charging the responders with ruining the game.

Who are the callers and who are the responders when it comes to Jesus, John, and their opponents, whom Jesus calls "the people of this generation" (7:31)? There are two viable options. The people of this generation are the callers, asking for behavior that fits conventional ways of being and relating both on social and religious terms, but Jesus and John fail to respond as expected.[15] If we switch the two sides, the image works as well. Jesus and John are the callers, but the people of this generation are not interested in aligning themselves with either one of them.[16]

Although both interpretations arrive at the same conclusion, that the conflict between the two groups results in the rejection of Jesus and John, the second one works better in context. The merrymaking with the flute playing may be likened to the joy of restoration that Jesus brings to the poor, the sick, the demon-possessed, the outcasts, and even the dead. His table fellowship has already been compared to a wedding feast with Jesus as the bridegroom (5:29–35). Yet the religious elites will not dance. They disapprove of Jesus' tablemates and brand the Son of Man as "a glutton and a drunkard, a friend of tax collectors and sinners" (7:34). Neither does John's approach appeal to them. His asceticism embodies his message of repentance and humility (1:15; Mark 1:6), and his preaching sounds like a funeral dirge. Not admitting their need for baptism, the Pharisees and the scribes dismiss John as a man with a demon (7:30, 33). Both Jesus and John are God's emissaries who make the purposes of God known in different ways. But the "people of this generation" are unmoved. In spite of their meticulous obedience to the law, their tunnel vision prevents them from experiencing the expansive vision of God's grace-filled generosity.

In the end, Jesus pronounces the verdict in a summative statement: "Nevertheless, wisdom is justified (*edikaiōthē*) by her children" (7:35).

---

15. Green 1997: 303.
16. Nolland 1989: 344–46; Fitzmyer 1981: 678–79; Neale 1991: 137–40.

Wisdom in this context does not refer to human wisdom but is identified with God himself.[17] In Jewish wisdom literature, the concept of personified wisdom is used to denote God and God's activities (Prov 8:1–9:6; Sir 1:1–30; 24:1–34). The verb *dikaioō*, which means "to justify or to pronounce right," takes us back to verse 29, where the people who embrace John's baptism are said to have "justified (*edikaiōsan*) God." Both verses make the same claim, that it is those who respond positively to Jesus and John who are the true children of God because they prove that God's way is right. Yet Jesus has not given up on "the people of this generation," for in the very next pericope he accepts an invitation to dine in the home of Simon the Pharisee. No one is beyond the reach of God's saving purposes if they are open to Jesus. Will Simon the Pharisee exhibit a change of heart, or will he cling onto the old wine in the old wineskin (5:39)?

A Sinner and a Pharisee (7:36–50)

The story of Jesus being anointed with perfume by a woman appears in all four Gospels.[18] Upon close comparison, the four accounts are as different as they are similar. Luke is the only author that situates the story within the Galilean ministry of Jesus, in the context of a dinner banquet in the house of a Pharisee. The other three place the anointing story in the passion narrative, where it serves as a foreshadowing of the death of Jesus.[19] Other differences include the name of the host, the part of Jesus' body that is anointed, the response of the bystanders, Jesus' interpretation of the woman's action, and various other descriptive details. It is impossible to harmonize these four accounts. We may continue to wonder if Jesus was anointed more than once, and if not, when it really happened. More instructive is to ask how Luke uses the story to press his theological agenda to support the unfolding picture of Jesus' identity and mission.

Jesus has accepted an invitation to a banquet at the home of a Pharisee, the first of three such invitations in this Gospel (7:36; 11:37; 14:1).

---

17. Contra Phillips (2008: 385–96), who understands wisdom as referring to human wisdom discussed in Greco-Roman philosophy, according to which a wise person drinks with moderation. Since John does not drink enough and Jesus drinks too much, verse 35 is an indictment on John and Jesus as being unwise.

18. Matt 26:1–13; Mark 14:3–9; Luke 7:36–50; John 12:1–8.

19. The Johannine Jesus identifies the act of anointing explicitly with his burial (John 12:7). In Matthew, Mark, and John, Jesus defends the woman's use of extravagant ointment by saying that the poor they will always have with them, but not him, alluding to his departure and death.

The way in which Luke describes these dinners is reminiscent of a Greco-Roman symposium, where the meal is followed by a conversation or a debate of some sort. Because these are rather public events, they provide opportunities for Jesus to meet his dinner companions where they are at, opening up possibilities for transformation.

We do not learn of the name of Jesus' host until later into the story (7:40), after Simon has been called a Pharisee four times (7:36 [2x], 37, 39). The repetition reminds the reader of Simon's concerns—ritual purity, separation of outsiders from insiders, and adherence to legal minutiae. His motive for inviting Jesus is not stated, but can be deduced from his thoughts, dialogue, and behavior, to which we will return. Suffice it to say that Simon's invitation is not prompted by close friendship, but by a tentative respect with an intention to evaluate Jesus for himself.[20]

Soon after Jesus' arrival, an intruder, "a woman in the city who was a sinner" (7:37), enters the scene with an alabaster jar of perfume in her hand. Though unnamed, she is not unknown. Her notoriety follows her wherever she goes, even into the home of a Pharisee for whom ritual purity is paramount. Some surmise that she is a prostitute, a courtesan, or someone who sells sexual favors for a living.[21] The sin that identifies her as a "sinner" is not specified but the insinuation is strong based on how the rest of the story plays out.[22] Imagine the moment she walks into the room. Conversations stop at mid-sentence. Raised eyebrows and knowing glances fuel the whispers: "What is she doing here? Who let her in? What contamination!" Her ability to gain access to the dinner party is not surprising, as in ancient banquets the doors were left open so that people could come in and listen in on the intellectual exchanges around the table. Infuriating, though, is that she scandalizes the owner of the house with her presence by bringing uncleanness into the Pharisee's guarded domain.

The woman comes with a purpose. Seen but not heard, she heads straight for Jesus. Since diners recline around a U-shaped low table, leaning on their left side, with their feet stretched out behind them, the

---

20. Green 1997: 307; Garland 2011: 324.

21. Many infer from the phrase "a woman of the city" (7:37) that she is a prostitute (Nolland 1989: 353; Marshall 1978: 308). Cosgrove (2005: 687) widens the range of possibility, claiming that her sin could be adultery or something else.

22. Kilgallen (1998: 106) argues that the stress is not that she is a sinner but the people in the city thinks that she is. Jesus has already forgiven her prior to this encounter, but the community fails to acknowledge it and continues to brand her as a sinner.

woman has access to Jesus' feet without disturbing the proceedings. Luke then describes her actions in one action-packed sentence. Weeping, her tears fall onto his feet, which she wipes dry with her hair. Meanwhile, she kisses his feet repeatedly and anoints them with perfume (7:38), even though normally it is the head that is anointed. Everyone is staring and no one is talking. The silence is deafening.

Not knowing her intentions, those present are likely to pick up all the wrong signals of sexual innuendo. In that culture, wearing head coverings was standard for women. Any respectable woman would not be seen in public with her hair let down, let alone touching a man and kissing his feet.[23] Her weeping is overshadowed by her seemingly erotic expression of affection for Jesus. Some interpreters try to tone down the offensiveness of her actions, claiming that it was culturally acceptable for a grieving woman to weep with her hair unbound as a sign of deep sorrow.[24] Others suggest that the woman has not planned on creating a scene. She is overwhelmed by emotions and has no choice but to use her hair as a towel to salvage the embarrassing situation.[25] Luke's point, however, is not whether the woman's plan has gone awry, or if a different interpretation of her actions will ease the tension. In fact, Luke is not interested in having Simon and his guests give her a more generous assessment. Precisely because of her reputation in the city as a "sinner," it is natural for anyone around that table, even Luke's readers before they get to the end of the story, to assume that her actions carry sexual connotations.

Simon's soliloquy[26] betrays his misunderstanding of both the woman and Jesus. He labels her "a sinner" and "[that] kind of woman." In polite company, it is below him to say out loud what kind of woman she is. Imagine him murmuring in disgust: "She is doing what people have always known her to do, spreading her uncleanness wherever she goes. But to do that in my house, what nerve!" His evaluation of Jesus is no better: "If this man were a prophet, he would have known who and what kind

---

23. Married women in antiquity normally wore their hair long and had it tied up in a braid, and unbound hair often did send signals of sexual availability. But there was evidence in Greco-Roman literature that in some settings unbound hair could indicate gratitude, veneration, and religious devotion (Cosgrove 2005: 678–81). Green (1997: 310) paints a provocative picture with words like "temptress," "sex object," "erotic," "fondling," and "sexual favors."

24. Cosgrove (2005: 677–78, 82–84) cites stories in which a woman's disheveled hair is a public expression of grief.

25. Marshall 1978: 308; Nolland 1989: 354.

26. See p. 180, n. 9.

of woman this is who is touching him" (7:39). Simon does not believe for a second that Jesus is a prophet. Perhaps he expects Jesus to put a stop to the nonsense, reprimand her, and send her away. Jesus' seeming ignorance of someone so morally despicable reflects a questionable ethic as well as a lack of clairvoyance. In Simon's view, all this disqualifies him from being a prophet. He invites Jesus to dinner to see for himself if the man matches his reputation. This incident, offensive as it is, has provided the answer. Nevertheless, being the host, some sense of decorum must be maintained. At best, Simon will call Jesus "Teacher" as an equal (7:40), but no more than that.[27]

Simon's conclusion that Jesus is a false prophet is ironic, especially when Jesus knows what Simon is thinking. The point of the parable of the two debtors is obvious. The larger debt of five hundred denarii amounts to over a year's worth of wages for a day laborer, whereas the smaller debt of fifty denarii is shy of two months' pay (7:41). Inability to repay a creditor could land a debtor in prison or in slavery. So when both debts have been cancelled, one would expect the debtor who owes more to be more grateful. Therefore, Jesus' question as to which debtor would love the creditor more has only one possible answer (7:42), and Simon's reluctant identification of the one with the greater debt is correct (7:43). Jesus is making a connection between the cancellation of debt and the forgiveness of sins, with God as the benevolent creditor and the woman as the debtor with a large debt. But the parable implicates Simon as well. While Jesus does not identify Simon directly as the debtor with the small debt, he does imply that by Simon's estimation the woman's debt is far greater than his. Since the creditor has canceled both debts regardless of their size, Simon should reconsider his judgment of the woman's worthiness of God's forgiveness, and in doing so admit that he, too, is a debtor.

To bring Simon to the place of self-examination, Jesus compares his behavior with that of the woman. One by one, Jesus names where Simon has fallen short as a host (7:44–46).[28] He has not provided water for Jesus to wash his dusty feet, but the woman washes them with her tears. He has not given him a towel, but she uses her hair to dry his feet. He has not greeted him with a kiss on the cheek, but she kisses his feet, the part of the body deemed unsightly and dirty. And, he has not anointed his head with olive oil to refresh his face, but she has lavished his feet with

27. "Teacher" is the title by which Jesus is addressed in Luke by those who are not his disciples or followers, e.g., 8:49; 9:38; 10:25; 11:45; 12:13; 19:39; 20:21, 39.

28. Bailey 2008: 242–43.

perfume. The two are polar opposites in their treatment of Jesus. The woman's act of love is extraordinary, but so is Simon's negligence. Jesus has effectively handed Simon's role of host to the woman, whose genuine and extravagant hospitality far exceeds his token expression of minimal politeness. This is a hard pill to swallow, given the social distance between a highly respected, law-abiding leader of the community and a sinful woman whom everyone despises.

Finally, Jesus gets to the crux of the matter and explains his view of the woman's action. Behind her loving gestures is a deep gratitude for the forgiveness of her sins. He says, "Therefore, I tell you, her sins, which were many, have been forgiven; hence (*hoti*) she has shown great love" (7:47 NRSV). Her love is not a prerequisite in order for her to be forgiven, but a manifestation of her transformed life. The Greek conjunction *hoti* can also mean "because," which is how the NIV puts it: "her many sins have been forgiven—for she loved much." The rendering in the NIV is problematic because it sounds as though she had to demonstrate enough love or enough faith in order for God to be willing to forgive her. More likely, there is a back story to this incident. The woman has had some prior interaction with Jesus that is not recorded in Luke, in which she repented and received the gift of forgiveness.[29] Upon learning that Jesus is dining at the house of Simon the Pharisee, she comes to show gratitude. Her tears are tears of gratitude, not of remorse or guilt. Therefore, Jesus' statement to Simon, "Her sins, which were many, have been forgiven" (*apheōntai*, 7:47), as well as his direct address to her, "Your sins have been forgiven" (*apheōntai*, 7:48), are not initial declarations of forgiveness but confirm a release of conscience. The word *apheōntai* is a perfect passive indicative verb that says two things. First, it is a divine passive; God is the subject of the action. God has forgiven her those sins. Second, the perfect tense in the Greek denotes a past action with effects that continue into the present. She had already been forgiven prior to this and she continues to be forgiven, even now. Jesus acknowledges her checkered history, but more importantly her present status: she is saved, forgiven, and renewed.

While God has given the woman a clean slate, the community has not. She is still stigmatized by her past reputation. That is why Jesus twice states that she has been forgiven (7:47–48). Those words are more for Simon and the others to hear, so that they may recognize her new status,

---

29. Kilgallen 1998: 108–11.

not unlike the way in which a priest declares a leper cleansed (5:14; 17:14). The goal is for her to be restored, spiritually as well as socially.

Those in attendance seem not to hear Jesus at all. Their focus moves from the woman's sins to Jesus' usurping of divine prerogative: "Who is this who even forgives sins?" (7:49). This is hardly a new charge leveled against Jesus, as other Pharisees and teachers of the law have exhibited the same indignation when Jesus healed the paralytic (5:21). But Jesus' focus remains on the woman as he says to her, "Your faith has saved (*sesōken*) you; go in peace" (7:50; cf. 8:48; 18:42). As with the declaration of forgiveness, the acknowledgement of the woman's salvation, *sesōken*, is also in the perfect tense. She was saved and continues to be saved. With this assurance, even the customary Jewish farewell, "Go in peace," takes on a richer meaning.

Both the woman and the centurion are commended by Jesus for their faith (7:9, 50). Her past sins and his gentile status are barriers to their inclusion in the community. Yet Jesus is not bound by the world's standards. He operates according to the inverted ethos of God's kingdom, where the poor, the outcast, and the lowly are embraced by God's mercy. Their faith, born out of desperation, exhibits an insight absent from those well ensconced in the religious establishment of the day. In the end, self-righteousness may turn out to be the most impenetrable barrier between a person and God's salvation. One does not have to be a Pharisee to possess a holier-than-thou attitude. Simon's lesson may well be ours.

Luke 8

In the previous chapter, the centurion and the sinful woman were commended for their faith (7:9, 50). The theme of faith is further developed in this chapter: first, the contributions of some faithful women are acknowledged (8:1-3); second, authentic faith calls the believer into persevering action (8:4-21); and third, fear can derail faith, hence the importance of trust (8:22-56).

Faithful Women (8:1-3)

At first glance, the first three verses seem perfunctory, reiterating how Jesus preaches the good news from city to city accompanied by his twelve disciples (8:1). Striking, though, is the mention of a group of women who are with them. Given women's restricted mobility at that time, their "going on the road" with a rabbi and his male disciples can easily be seen as scandalous (8:2-3).[1]

Mary Magdalene, Joanna the wife of Chuza, and Susanna receive special mention. Later, Mary and Joanna will also be named among the women at the empty tomb (24:10; cf. 23:55). They are exemplary disciples, as credible as their male counterparts in bearing witness to Jesus' ministry. Mary is from Magdala, a town about three miles north of Tiberias on the west coast of the Sea of Galilee.[2] Joanna is the wife of Chuza, the steward of Herod Antipas. She is a woman of means with considerable social standing, at least in particular political circles.[3] Nothing else is known about Susanna in the NT. Common among them, and others in the traveling group, is the experience of being healed by Jesus. Luke identifies Mary Magdalene as the one from whom Jesus cast out seven demons, a condition of severe bondage. Using their own resources, these women express their gratitude by supporting Jesus' itinerant ministry,

---

1. Witherington 1979: 244-45.
2. Marshall 1978: 316.
3. Given Herod Antipas's notoriety and cruelty, Joanna's connection with his court may cause her to be shunned by commoners. See de Boer 2004: 146.

Hearing and Doing (8:4–21)

As Jesus' reputation grows, so does the size of the crowd around him, forming an eager audience to his teaching (8:4). The setting of the parable of the sower should be familiar to Jesus' audience, many of whom are peasants and farmers. In ancient Palestine, farming methods varied with local customs and weather conditions. Sometimes the land was tilled before sowing, and at other times the order was reversed.[4] The techniques are irrelevant to the point of the parable. A sower sow seeds with liberality and exuberance. Some seeds are expected to land on unfavorable ground and others on rich soil. The sower is not incompetent or careless just because some seeds land on unproductive places. He sows and sows and sows some more. There is confidence that enough will take hold to yield an abundant harvest.

Four types of soils are mentioned, but nothing in the parable suggests that they are evenly distributed over the farmer's property. It is not as though only a quarter of the land was worth planting, making it an inefficient and undesirable undertaking. Any field will have some unevenness in quality. A sower could only hope that most of his field is made up of good soil, but the strip by the side of the footpath is bound to be harder, and rocky and thorny patches are expected to crop up here and there.

Jesus' focus rests on what happens after the seeds have been sown. First, the seeds that fall by the path will not stand a chance. The ground is so hardened that the seeds cannot penetrate the soil at all. They are either stepped on by people or picked off by birds (8:5). The seeds in the next two types of soil manage to sprout but never reach full harvest. The lack of moisture in the rocky soil prevents the root system to develop properly and sustain growth (8:6). The seeds that grow in thorny soils cannot compete with the thorns for nutrients (8:7). Despite the disappointing outcomes of the first three scenarios, Jesus saves the best for last. The seeds in the rich, fertile soil grow downward and upward, yielding a

---

4. Snodgrass 2008: 166–67.

bumper crop (8:8a). The fecundity of the good soil is more than enough to compensate for the losses in the first three types of soil.[5]

Jesus closes his parable with an exhortation, "Let anyone with ears to hear, listen!" (8:8b). The question is not "What kind of soil are you?" or "Will you try to become good soil?" After all, soil is a passive image; it cannot improve its fertility on its own. Yet the fruitfulness of the seed depends on the soil in which it germinates. Rather, Jesus' point has to do with the result when seed and soil come together. As we shall see from Jesus' explanation below, the parable describes the mixed responses to his proclamation, and prescribes the sort of response that can lead to the best outcome.

Although the message of God's kingdom is veiled in mystery, it is meant to be revealed (8:9–10). The difference lies in the timing of its revelation and its reception by the hearers.[6] Hearing and seeing alone do not guarantee comprehension. The crowds hear Jesus' teachings and witness his miracles, but on their own they are unable to grasp the connections between Jesus' words, actions, identity, and mission.

"To you it has been given to know the secrets of the kingdom of God, but to others, I speak in parables" (8:10a). Having left everything to be with Jesus (5:11, 28; 18:28), the Twelve are committed to Jesus, unlike the casual onlookers who are curious but whose interest in Jesus is fleeting. Ultimately, God conceals or reveals[7] the secrets of his kingdom. God will benefit those who are open to receiving the good news with humble hearts and teachable spirits. To those who harbor a hardness of heart, the parables will remain obscure in meaning (8:10b; cf. Isa 6:9–10). Because they refuse to look carefully and listen well, their spiritual blindness and deafness deny them access to God's mystery. Initial skepticism grows into stubborn unbelief. At first, it may seem as though all who were not believers were set up for failure, if the main purpose of parables was to keep them in the dark. The *hina* ("so that") clause in verse 10, however, indicates result rather than purpose. Jesus is stating the inevitable outcome of

---

5. Luke's contrast between no yield and a hundredfold yield (8:8) is more dramatic than Mark's gradation of increasing yield, from 30, 60, to 100. The yield is realistic (Gen 26:12). See Snodgrass (2008: 155) for estimates of farming yields in the ancient world.

6. As a metaphor for the kingdom of God, the parable of the sower is about mystery and faith and not productivity and predictability. See Foster and Shiell 1997: 259–67.

7. "It has been given to know (*dedotai*)" is a divine passive (8:10). The revelation of God does not depend on the hearer's intelligence.

persistent stubbornness. For those who do not hear him well, the veiled messages embedded in his parables will remain enigmatic, and as a result these people will neither perceive nor understand the plan of God. The division between insiders and outsiders has nothing to do with access to Jesus' words and deeds, but everything to do with how one responds to them.[8]

With that in mind, the meaning of the parable becomes clear. Jesus is the sower and the seed is the word of God (8:11). The soils and the growth of the seeds in them reflect the different responses to Jesus' ministry. First, the seeds on the hardened soil by the footpath will never germinate. In direct opposition to the aim of God, the devil reaches into the heart of the hearer and snatches away the word of God, as fast as the birds swooping down from the sky to grab the seeds on the ground (8:12). Satan will do anything to sabotage faith. Next we have the rootless growth of a quick germination that results in a dry, withered plant. The enthusiasm toward God's word is temporary and temperamental. In times of testing, only firmly grounded faith will stay rooted (8:13). This picture reminds us of another parable in which a house without a foundation will collapse as soon as the river bursts against it (6:49). If Jesus is subject to testing (4:1–13), so will his disciples be; the latter will face persecution, doubt, temptation, and other ordeals in life (22:31–34, 40, 46). The seeds in the third type of soil also falter midway, choked by the thorns growing alongside them. Thorns are aggressive competitors for nutrients, space, sun, and air, stunting the growth of the plant. Likewise, the preoccupations of life, from worries to riches, become distractions that overtake a person's desire for God (8:14; cf. 12:22–31; 16:13). To go the distance in the life of discipleship, a single-minded devotion is non-negotiable.

In spite of the losses along the way, the word of God continues to spread with extraordinary fruitfulness, like seeds in fertile soil. Two qualities undergird a successful discipleship: "an honest and good heart, and . . . patient endurance" (8:15). Since trials and temptations are inevitable, a disciple who is truly committed must exhibit perseverance and steadfastness. Those who fall away forfeit the salvation that could be theirs. But those who remain faithful will receive their reward in due time (18:29–30; 22:28–30).

---

8. Just as Isaiah spoke to rebellious Israel in the past, Jesus now confronts the same in his day. Unbelief is a vicious cycle that yields its own punishment. See McComiskey 2008: 59–60, 83–85.

The refrain that is repeatedly sounded is hearing *and* doing. True disciples are like an oil lamp on a lampstand, giving light to those who enter the room (8:16). Light is a common biblical metaphor for God's salvation (1:78–79; cf. Ps 27:1; Isa 9:2; Acts 13:47). It does not make sense to suppress the light by putting it under a vessel or a bed; the lamp must do what it is supposed to do. Similarly, the integrity of one's hearing is proven in one's doing, like how a tree is judged by the fruit it bears (6:43–45).

The next saying also uses light as a metaphor, as in the idiom, "coming to light" (8:17). The idiom itself carries a sense of disclosure, that something is about to be revealed. This verse loops back to the thought of the mysterious nature of the kingdom of God alluded to in verse 9. From the postresurrection perspective of Luke, God's plan of salvation, including Jesus' identity as Messiah, will be clarified in due time. In the meantime, the quasi-hiddenness of God's plan is necessary. The road ahead presents many challenges, hence Jesus sounds a note of encouragement and of warning: "To those who have, more will be given; and from those who do not have, even what they seem to have will be taken away" (8:18). This is not the time to be indecisive. The further one is willing to go with Jesus, the more God will deepen one's understanding of divine mysteries. But for those who turn a blind eye and a deaf ear to Jesus, their self-deception will cloud their judgment, and they will lose all understanding, including whatever little they have to begin with.

At this point, Jesus is told that his family members are unable to reach him because of the size of the crowd (8:19–20). Taking the concept of human family and applying it to the budding spiritual family established around him, Jesus declares that "[his] mother and his brothers are those who hear the word of God and do it" (8:21). This is neither a negative judgment on Jesus' earthly family nor the negation of family bonds. Family represents shared identity, allegiance, values, and vision. By changing the criterion of the membership in Jesus' family, Jesus privileges spiritual kinship above physical kinship. It is no longer blood ties, not even Abrahamic ancestry, that determine one's sense of belonging (3:8). Faith in Jesus is the new determinant.

Faith and Fear (8:22–56)

Jesus teaches that faith must go beyond a cerebral consent to become an embodied participation in the good news of salvation. Hindrances to faith and fruitfulness, however, will present themselves, and Jesus' disciples should not be naïve about them. In the following episodes, Luke hones in on the triggers of fear and how to combat fear with trust.

Calming the Sea (8:22–25)

It is Jesus' idea to cross the lake (8:22), which suggests that neither the storm nor his encounter with a gentile demoniac on the other side is accidental. The Sea of Galilee is a freshwater lake 680 feet below sea level. It is surrounded by hills, and the ones to the east are especially steep, some rising up to 2,000 feet high. Most of the time, the lake and its harbors are well protected, except when the wind changes direction. Cold air from the high mountains descends rapidly toward the valleys and meets the warm, moist air above the surface of the lake. Because the lake is at most 200 feet deep, the energy of the wind cannot be absorbed fast enough, resulting in dangerously strong squalls and high waves.[9]

This natural phenomenon is familiar to those who fish regularly in the lake, so a sudden storm is not unexpected. The ferocity of it, nevertheless, takes even seasoned fishermen by surprise. Coupled with the popular belief that the sea symbolizes primeval chaos and threatens life, fear sets in and the disciples think they are going to die. They wake Jesus up with urgent cries, "Master, Master, we are perishing!" (8:24). Their panic stands in sharp contrast to Jesus' tranquility, which is uncanny, given the situation. Jesus has been sleeping while the boat is taking in water, being tossed about by the waves (8:23). Does he already know what he is about to do, or is he resting in the knowledge that God will sustain him under all circumstances (cf. Pss 3:5; 4:8)?

Just as Jesus rebuked demons (*epetimēsen*, 4:35; *epitimōn*, 4:41) and the fever of Simon's mother-in-law (*epetimēsen*, 4:39), he now rebukes the wind and the waves (*epetimēsen*, 8:24). By the sheer authority of his word, he commands the storm to be still. According to the psalmist: "They cried to the LORD in their trouble, and he brought them out of their distress; he made the storm be still, and the waves of the sea were hushed" (Ps 107:28–29). Jesus has just done what God did. Immediately there is calm. Jesus' question, "Where is your faith?" (8:25), presupposes that the disciples are not entirely void of faith. Their embryonic faith may not envision that Jesus can command the forces of nature, but if Jesus can

---

9. Walker 2006: 66.

raise the dead and cast out demons (4:33–36; 7:11–17), surely he can do better than bailing water from a sinking boat!

The fear of the disciples has not subsided even when the storm is stilled. Their fear of death has morphed into a reverent fear (cf. 5:8–10). Their amazement at Jesus' authority notwithstanding, this miracle stands in a category of its own, for only God can subdue the power of nature.[10] No wonder they ask, "Who then is this that he commands even the winds and the water, and they obey him?" (8:25). In spite of their fear, their faith is deepening. They are beginning to engage the question of who Jesus is, not just what he does. The disciples may falter in times of weakness, but they are on the right track.

The Gerasene Demoniac (8:26–39)

On the opposite side of Galilee is the country of the Gerasenes (8:26), in the region of the Decapolis. The exact location is disputed. While Luke retains the location identified in Mark (Mark 5:1), Matthew changes the name to "Gadarenes" (Matt 8:28). Three similar sounding place names have been found in various manuscripts—Gerasa, Gadara, and Gergasa—but each one is problematic. "Gerasa" is attested in the best manuscripts, but that city was actually in Transjordan, thirty miles southeast of the Sea of Galilee. The region attached to that city extended for quite a distance but was not far enough to reach the shores of the lake. "Gadara" was closer, only five miles to the southeast, and the likelihood of its hinterland reaching the waters was higher. "Gergasa" was even closer to the water with nearby cliffs.[11] Whatever the historical location may be, by Jesus' initiative he and his disciples have ventured into unclean gentile territory by entering the Decapolis (8:22). Immediately they encounter a man possessed by an army of unclean spirits who lives among the tombs near where pigs are herded. The entire scene is soaked in impurity.

Even the narration has a confusing feel to it. In chronological time, Jesus would have come ashore, seen the demon-possessed man coming toward him, and ordered the demons to leave. The man would then have fallen down at Jesus' feet, at which time Jesus would have asked him his name. Luke, however, injects flashback into the narrative, so that the readers learn of the man's defiant response before they know that Jesus

---

10. Pss 65:7; 74:13; 77:16; 89:9.
11. Marshall 1978: 336–37; Nolland 1989: 406–7.

has commanded the unclean spirit to come out (8:28–29). Also, the man is introduced at the beginning of the encounter, but more information concerning his frightening behavior is not released until later. This jumbled order underscores the man's chaotic and maniacal existence and adds an element of suspense to the drama.

The word "inhuman" sadly summarizes the pitiable condition of the demoniac. For the longest time he has been ostracized by his community. He wears no clothes and lives among the tombs. He is violent and strong, letting out bloodcurdling screams that drive people away. No one can control him, not even with fetters, chains, and shackles. Everyone is afraid of him (8:27–29). If this is how he is treated by his fellow gentiles, imagine the reaction of the Jewish disciples who have arrived with Jesus. This man is unclean, even deemed beyond redemption, until he comes face to face with Jesus.

Jesus' command to the unclean[12] spirit to leave the man brings the demoniac to his knees (8:28–29a). This is by no means a gesture of reverence or deference, for in defiance the madman screams at the top of his lungs, "What have you to do with me, Jesus, Son of the Most High God? I beg you, do not torment me" (8:28). The man is shouting, but it is the demon doing the talking. First, the demon knows who Jesus is, like others that Jesus confronted before (4:34, 41). Second, he uses a distancing idiom, not wanting to have anything to do with Jesus.[13] Third, he knows he is at the mercy of Jesus' power.

Given the severity of this man's demonic state, there must be more than one demon.[14] When Jesus asks for his name,[15] behold, it is "Legion" (4:30). *Legiōn* is a Latin loanword; a legion in the Roman army consisted of anywhere from 5000 to 6000 men. The army of demons explains the man's Herculean strength, but it is strength for destruction and not for good. With so many demons tormenting him, his suffering is unimaginable. He may as well be dead.

Still trying to make a last-ditch effort for self-preservation, the demons beg Jesus not to send them into the abyss, but to let them enter a

---

12. By calling a demon an unclean spirit, Luke draws attention to purity concerns, see pp. 72–73.

13. See Luke 4:34; Judg 11:12; and 2 Chr 35:21.

14. While there are many demons inhabiting one host, Jesus addresses the legion as one unclean spirit, opposing God and wreaking havoc as one unit.

15. If an exorcist knows the name of the power that he is up against, it gives him leverage over that power (Twelftree 1993: 84).

large herd of swine feeding on a nearby hillside (8:31–32a). Demons are parasites; they need a host through whom to carry out their evil mischief (11:24–26). The abyss (*abyssos*), or the bottomless pit, is the place of final imprisonment and punishment for demons.[16] Since pigs are deemed unclean animals by the Jews (Lev 11:7; Deut 14:8), it almost seems fitting for the unclean spirits to inhabit them instead.

The thought that these demons are given room to negotiate with Jesus, and that Jesus actually grants them their request, is unsettling (8:32b–33). Surely Jesus cannot be capitulating to the enemy! A reader may complain that while the pigs are unclean in Jewish eyes, that large number of pigs, two thousand in all according to Mark 5:13, are nonetheless valuable to the swineherds and their gentile masters. To claim that one man is worth more than two thousand pigs is tenable from Jesus' point of view, but where is the compensation for the owner of the pigs, who suffers economic loss through no fault of his own? These questions Luke leaves unanswered.

More significant than counting the losses is the undeniable proof that the entire legion of demons has left the demoniac and taken residence in the pigs. First they drove the man to utter madness and sub-human existence; then they cause the pigs to stampede off a cliff and plunge to their death. With the new hosts destroyed, will the demons survive? Is the bottom of the lake analogous to the abyss, the bottomless pit? Again, the text offers no answer. For Luke, the restoration of the man is much more important than the fate of the demons and other collateral damage that comes with their destruction.

The disciples are eyewitnesses to the whole event, but so are the gentile swineherds who have to account for the loss of the pigs. Obviously terrified, if not also angry at what Jesus has done, they scurry off to report the incident, and the people of the city come out to assess the damage (8:34–35a, 36). They find the former demoniac in a total reversal of conditions. He had many demons; now they are gone. He was naked; now he is fully clothed. He challenged Jesus with loud cries; now he is seated at Jesus' feet like a student at the feet of a rabbi. He was out of control; now he is in his right mind (8:35b). All this should be cause for celebration—a man who was "dead" has been brought back to life. Instead, fear grips the people, and they ask Jesus to leave (8:37). It is unclear whether they are afraid that Jesus may cause them to suffer more economic loss or that his

---

16. So Rev 11:7; 17:8; 20:1–3. See also 1 *En.* 10:4–6; 18:11–16; *Jub.* 5:6–11.

supernatural power is too much to bear. They have no interest in Jesus' identity perhaps beyond anything more than a magician. By rejecting Jesus, the townspeople forfeit the salvation that could be theirs.

But this opportunity is not lost to the ex-demoniac. He begs to go with Jesus, but his request is denied. While this may seem harsh, Jesus proposes a better strategy, "Return to your home and declare how much God has done for you" (8:39a). Formerly the demons drove the man away from his home and his city; now Jesus sends him back. His social and communal restoration will complete his physical, mental, and spiritual healing. This man is the first missionary, sent by Jesus, to this gentile area. By "proclaiming throughout the city how much Jesus has done for him" (8:39b), he declares that the work of the Messiah is tantamount to the work of God.

Jairus's Daughter and the Hemorrhaging Woman (8:40–56)

These two accounts that link faith with fear are presented as an intercalation, a literary device that embeds one story within another. The account of the raising of Jairus's daughter from the dead (8:40–42; 49–55) is interrupted midstream by the healing of the hemorrhaging woman (8:43–48). This sandwich-like arrangement signifies that the two accounts are mutually interpretive. It heightens the suspense of the first story's denouement as the second story is being told.

Many details connect the two stories, already bound together by the story-within-a-story juxtaposition. Both invalids are female. The girl is twelve years old whereas the woman has been suffering for the same number of years. Both are in desperate need of healing; the girl is near death and the woman has exhausted all her resources to get well. Both are potential transmitters of ritual uncleanness, the woman by her constant flow of blood, and the girl should she die and someone touches her dead body. Yet touch is involved in Jesus' interaction with both of them, leading to immediate healing. Finally, both the girl's father and the woman fall on their knees before Jesus, and both are challenged to overcome fear with faith.[17] Narrative correspondences aside, the two stories also move toward a common crescendo. The faith of the bleeding woman serves as an encouragement to Jairus while his daughter's life hangs in the balance. He will need even stronger faith when he learns of her death. From the

---

17. Green 1997: 343.

healing of the woman to Jesus' revivification of the girl, there is a dramatic elevation of Jesus' power, not unlike the build-up from his healing of the centurion's slave at a distance to his raising the dead son of the widow in Nain (7:1–17).

Rejected by the people of Gerasa, Jesus returns to Galilee to a crowd full of anticipation and welcome (8:40). A man of considerable status appears and gets down on his knees in front of Jesus. This in itself is an unusual picture, but Jairus does not have time for formalities. As the synagogue ruler, Jairus is highly respected in his community. He is responsible for arranging worship services, presiding over public meetings, and conferring honors, among other things.[18] Unlike the Jewish delegate in Capernaum who tried to persuade Jesus to help the centurion by promoting the latter's benefactions (7:3–5), Jairus does not use his position to manipulate Jesus. Humble and desperate, he begs Jesus to come with him, for his only daughter, merely twelve years of age, is dying (8:41–42). The loss of an only child is especially painful for a parent (cf. 7:12; 9:38). At twelve, she has just reached a marriageable age. Her illness is casting an ominous shadow over an otherwise period of joyous anticipation for the family. How tragic if talks of betrothal had to give way to talks of burial. Without delay, Jesus sets off to Jairus's house with his disciples and the crowd in tow.

Right when the narrative is moving along at a good clip to mimic the urgency of Jairus's quandary, Luke slows it down to introduce an interloper. The status differential between Jairus and this unnamed woman is striking. He is known to all and she lives in self-imposed obscurity. Her illness, some form of uterine hemorrhage, renders her in a perpetual state of ritual impurity (Lev 15:25–27; Ezek 36:17). Her bed, or anything she sits on, is unclean. No man can have sexual relations with her without bringing the uncleanness upon himself. All this creates a tremendous barrier for any normal interaction with people in her community. In this condition, she is far from marriageable. In addition to her social and religious isolation, she is impoverished, having spent all her resources on doctors but to no avail (8:43).[19]

The woman's presence in the crowd is highly suspect. With people pressing in on Jesus and on one another, it is impossible for her to refrain from contaminating others. Her surreptitious approach is risky. If she

---

18. Garland 2011: 367.
19. Marshall 1978: 344; Carroll 2012: 198–99; Green 1997: 346.

is found out, she may be subject to even more stringent ostracism and severe reprimand, not least by Jairus the synagogue ruler! But the woman is at the end of her rope, and Jesus is her only hope. Coming from behind, she barely makes it far enough to touch the fringe[20] of Jesus' garment. "Immediately her hemorrhage stopped" (8:44).

So does Jesus. "Who touched me?" he asks. To Peter, Jesus is stating the obvious (8:45). On the one hand, the denial is valid. Everyone is touching Jesus by virtue of being in a crowd, jostling one against the other, but no one is touching him in particular. On the other hand, the woman's touch, however minimally obtrusive, has not gone undetected. Insisting that healing power has gone out of him, Jesus repeats the question, "Who touched me?" (8:47; cf. 6:19). He is not concerned about ritual purity (5:13; 7:14), nor is he ignorant about where his healing power has gone. But he is not going to continue until someone owns up to the action. One may ask, "If the woman has already been healed, why not let her slip out quietly, rather than embarrass her in public?" But this is precisely the point. Her healing has a public dimension to it, as with the leper, the paralytic, the man with the withered hand, the Gerasene demoniac, and many others that Jesus has healed. She is not merely made whole in the body; she needs to be restored to the religious and social life of the community as well. To call the woman to accountability is an act of validation, not shaming.

With trepidation the woman falls down at Jesus' feet. Imagine her trembling voice, mingled with fear, awe, and gratitude. "In the presence of all the people," she explains her motive for touching Jesus and testifies to her immediate healing (8:47). Now that her secret has been exposed, how will she be received? First, Jesus calls her "Daughter," a term of kinship that gives her a place in the family of faith, among those "who hear the word of God and do it" (8:21). He expects the community to embrace her as one of theirs again. Second, his parting blessing is exactly the same as that which he gave to the woman who anointed him at the house of Simon the Pharisee, "Your faith has saved[21] you; go in peace" (*hē pistis sou sesōken se; poreuou eis eirēnēn*, 7:50; 8:48). Once again, physical heal-

---

20. The Greek noun *kraspedon* means border, but also refers to the tassels on the four corners of the garments to remind an observant Jew of the Torah (Num 15:38–40; Deut 22:12).

21. It is unfortunate that the NRSV translates *sesōken se* as "has saved you" in 7:50 and "has made you well" in 8:48, for the impact of an identical wording in both places is lost as a result.

ing is inseparable from spiritual healing. Overcoming the obstacles of fear, marginalization, access, and physical weakness, the woman's belief in Jesus causes her to exercise her faith in such determination that calls forth the healing power of God. Her crossing of boundaries of purity and social propriety in search for wholeness is not that different from Jesus' violation of the same boundaries for the sake of another's salvation. When divine grace is met with human openness, restoration occurs.

All the while, Jairus stands watching and waiting. However long this interruption has lasted, it must have felt like eternity for this worried father. His daughter is dangerously close to death and there is no time to spare. We do not know whether he feels resentful toward the woman, is amazed at her healing, or is too riddled with anxiety to think anything at all. But there is no time to process what has just happened, for even before Jesus finishes talking to the woman, his worst fear materializes. Word is sent from his house to deliver the sad news that his daughter has died (8:49). The euphoria of the woman's healing gives way to the deep sorrow of a loving father.

Luke, though, keeps his focus on Jesus, who says, "Do not fear, only believe (*pisteuson*), and she will be saved (*sōthēsetai*)" (8:50). Comparing these words to what Jesus has just told the woman, "Your faith (*pistis*) has saved (*sesōken*) you" (8:48), the connection between faith and salvation cannot be missed. Neither twelve years of uterine hemorrhaging nor death is beyond the healing power of God. In the face of the seeming finality of death, Jairus has to stretch his faith to where it has never gone before. He may or may not know about the raising of the widow's son in Nain, but Luke's readers do and are rooting for Jairus to rise to the challenge.

Upon arrival at the house, there is yet another obstacle to faith. The commotion of the mourners' weeping and wailing erases any vestige of hope. Those who hear Jesus say that the girl is merely asleep laugh at him (8:52–53). They have seen the girl and she is dead as a doornail. Without faith, they miss the pun in Jesus' statement. Since sleep is a common euphemism for death,[22] Jesus is referring to what he is about to do. People think that she is "sleeping" (as in "dead"), but she is really sleeping (as in "dozing") because Jesus will bring her back to life.

Five people bear witness to this miracle: Jairus, his wife, Peter, James, and John. No one else is permitted inside the house (8:51). And,

---

22. See Dan 12:2; Acts 13:36; 1 Cor 11:30.

reminiscent of the raising of the widow's son in Nain, Jesus takes the girl by the hand and commands her back to life. To the widow's son, Jesus summons, "Young man, . . . be raised (*egerthēti*)!" (7:14); and to Jairus's daughter, "Child, arise (*egeire*)!" (8:54). It is the same command, the first in the passive imperative and the second in the active imperative. The results are the same. The girl gets up immediately and Jesus orders that she be given something to eat, which in itself is a proof of life (8:55).

Astonishment does not begin to describe the elation of the girl's parents. Yet the pericope ends with a rather strange directive from Jesus to them and his three disciples, that they tell no one about that which they have just witnessed (8:56). How could that even be carried out if the mourners outside are so certain that the child was dead before Jesus' arrival? The point is not whether Jesus is bent on deceiving people by concealing the truth. Rather, the command to silence may have to do with the general lack of faith among the crowd and the potential of their following him for the wrong reason.[23]

Fear threatens to be an impediment to faith for Jairus and the hemorrhaging woman. Both have good reasons to be afraid in the midst of hopeless and dire circumstances. Faith is challenging because the desired outcome is entirely dependent on God's power and mercy. The question that ties all four miracles in this section together is that of Jesus' identity. He is more than a teacher, more than an exorcist, more than a healer, and more than a prophet. Who, then, is he? In the next chapter, Jesus' disciples will finally become privy to things about Jesus that the readers have known all along.

Fusing the Horizons: Faith, the Antidote to Fear

In Luke 8, the author brings together four consecutive accounts, all of which are filled with fearful people. The disciples were afraid of drowning, caught in a ferocious storm in the middle of the sea. The people of Gerasa were first afraid of the demoniac and his uncontrollable strength, and later they were afraid of what other losses they would incur should Jesus stay any longer in their region. The woman whose hemorrhage was stopped by a touch of Jesus' cloak was afraid of being exposed for surreptitiously pen-

---

23. Green 1997: 351; Carroll 2012: 202.

etrating the crowd while ritually unclean. And Jairus was afraid of losing his only daughter to death.

In all these situations, faith in Jesus was key to their resolution, as seen through the responses of the various characters. The disciples should have exhibited more trust in Jesus; the woman's faith was affirmed as instrumental to her healing; the Gerasenes forfeited more salvific blessings by rejecting Jesus; and Jairus was told to keep believing and not be afraid. The object of faith called for in every case was the person of Jesus who, empowered by the Holy Spirit, exercised the divine prerogative to give life.

Fear continues to pervade our world in many dimensions of life. On a personal level, we may be anxious about our health, our jobs, our relationships, our parents, our children, and our future. On the societal and global level, there is the fear of war, the fear of global warming, the fear of economic instability, the fear of extremist terrorist groups, the fear of neighborhood violence, the fear of the influx of refugees and illegal immigrants, and the list goes on. We respond to these triggers of fear, sometimes in paralysis and at others in reactivity. We complain rather than pray, bear arms rather than talk peace, and point fingers rather than take responsibility. We operate out of our natural instincts, and faith tends not to be the first thing we reach for in times like these.

Indeed, exercising faith is not our strong suit, not even for those who profess to follow Jesus. But everyone starts somewhere in the journey of faith. Jairus' faith was a fearful trust, so also that of the hemorrhaging woman in her trepidation. At this point, the disciples asked who Jesus was that even the wind and the waves obeyed him, but one day they would confess that he was the Messiah of Israel. If even a demoniac who was completely out of his mind and as good as a walking dead could develop faith in Jesus, what is our excuse?

Luke 9

Sending the Twelve (9:1–10a)

Chapter 9 is a transitional chapter as the author wraps up Jesus' Galilean ministry and presents the Messiah as setting his face toward Jerusalem (9:51). In fact, Jesus and his disciples will not arrive in Jerusalem until chapter 19. Between 9:51 and 19:27 is a section commonly known as the "travel narrative." While a literal journey, it is especially poignant in its symbolic effect. In this large block of narrative space, Luke includes many teachings of Jesus on discipleship, wealth, prayer, humility, and the like. The Twelve undergo spiritual formation on the way of the cross, a journey of shame and suffering on which they may one day find themselves. Since being chosen to be apostles (6:12–16), they have been with Jesus. Now Jesus is about to send them on a mission to put what they have learned into practice. Again employing the literary device of intercalation,[1] Luke inserts Herod Antipas's musings on Jesus (9:7–9) in between the sending of the disciples and their return (9:1–6, 10a). As the message of the good news is spread, opposition rears its ugly head.

The Twelve are commissioned by Jesus to proclaim the message of the kingdom of God and to heal, and healing entails not only curing diseases but also exorcising demons (9:1–2). They are to do what Jesus himself has been doing in his saving mission. God sends Jesus, and now Jesus sends his disciples. Specific instructions are given. They are to travel light—so light that they are forced to rely on other people's hospitality wherever they go. They are to set out with no staff, no knapsack, no money, no bread, not even an extra tunic (9:3). This requirement goes beyond simply being unencumbered because of the urgency of the mission, or not being mistaken as one of those Hellenistic wandering preachers who go about charging people to listen to them.[2] Rather, Jesus is instilling in his

---

1. Note the intertwining of the story of Jairus and the hemorrhaging woman (8:41–56) on p. 117.
2. Nolland 1989: 427; Marshall 1978: 350.

disciples an attitude of total dependence on God for everything that they need, from food and shelter to even a change of clothes. It is not God's trustworthiness that is at stake, but the disciples' faith and faithfulness.

Sustenance will come from the hospitality of villages that welcome them (9:4). Jesus exhorts the Twelve to be content with whatever is provided for them, rather than to hop from house to house in search of more comfortable quarters. Once they enter a village, they should stay with the same household from beginning to end. The disciples, however, may not always encounter positive reception from a village. When that happens, Jesus instructs them to "shake the dust off [their] feet" as they leave a hostile town (9:5). What does this gesture signify? Usually, a Jewish person, having been in the land of foreigners, might shake the dust off his or her feet in order not to bring home gentile dirt and defilement.[3] But since Jesus' disciples will be preaching and ministering in Galilean villages, their rejection is all the more inexcusable. To treat these hostile Jews as though they were gentiles would indeed be a damning testimony against their unbelief.

The disciples spread themselves out among the villages of Galilee, "bringing the good news and curing diseases everywhere" (9:6). Upon their return, they report all that they have done (9:10a). It is not stated whether Herod Antipas has gotten wind of Jesus' preaching and healings, or that the activities of the Twelve are creating a stir among the populace. Herod may even have learned about Jesus through his steward Chuza, the husband of Susanna, one of Jesus' female disciples (8:3). Whatever his source of information, Herod is troubled by the rumors. Public opinion gravitates toward viewing Jesus as some sort of a prophet (9:7–8), ranging from John, to an ancient prophet who has risen from the dead, to the eschatological Elijah[4] mentioned in the book of Malachi (cf. 4:24–27; 7:16). While there is truth and relevance to a prophetic characterization of Jesus, in the end Jesus is much more than that.

Especially perplexing to Herod is the popular opinion that Jesus may be John *redivivus*. Without the benefit of the other Synoptic Gospels (Matt 14:3–12 // Mark 6:17–29), this is the first time Luke's readers hear of John's beheading. Herod's persecution of John (3:19–20) foreshadows

---

3. Green 1997: 360.

4. In Luke, John is clearly identified as the "eschatological Elijah" appearing before the day of the lord (Mal 3:1–2; 4:5–6; cf. Luke 1:16–17; 7:24–27). This is not to be confused with Luke's portrayal of Jesus that reminds the readers of the "historical Elijah" (4:25–26; 7:11–17).

his treatment of Jesus later on. In spite of their different styles, Jesus and John share the same mission of God's salvation (7:24–35). Herod's desire to see Jesus may be motivated by curiosity (9:9), but curiosity will eventually turn into malice (13:31; 23:7–11). John's death is a prophet's death, and so will Jesus' be. Even in the midst of a successful mission (9:1–6, 10a), the forces of evil lurk in the background.

Feeding the Five Thousand (9:10b–17)

Jesus and his disciples are about to have some time away from active ministry when the ubiquitous crowd catches up with them. Instead of sending the people away, Jesus extends hospitality by welcoming, teaching, and healing them (9:10b–11). Having recently benefited from much needed hospitality during their mission, the Twelve should be eager to show hospitality to others. But when this opportunity presents itself, they fail to rise to the occasion.

Bethsaida was a town in the tetrarchy of Herod Philip, to the east of Galilee just beyond the territory of his brother Herod Antipas. The town sits at the northern tip of the Sea of Galilee where the Jordan flows into the lake. It may seem odd that Luke introduces Bethsaida as "a city" (9:10), whereas the disciples call the place where Jesus is teaching the large crowd "a deserted place" (9:12). Perhaps naming the town simply approximates their location. The mention of Bethsaida anticipates Jesus' indictment of the town's unbelief in the next chapter (10:13–14).

After a day of preaching and healing, a practical concern comes to the fore as evening draws near. At first glance, the concern of the Twelve is logical and considerate. Soon it will be dark, and the people will need food and lodging, especially those who do not have a home in Bethsaida. It seems wise to disperse them now, so they can fend for themselves in nearby villages before it is too late (9:12). Jesus' response, however, puts the responsibility of hospitality back on their shoulders: "*You* give them something to eat" (9:13a). The disciples have already done the calculations. There are five thousand men, more if they count women and children, and only five loaves and two fish. Clearly there is neither food nor money to feed everyone (9:13b–14a). From the human point of view, the problem is too big and the reasonable solution is not to be hospitable.

Instead of chiding them for an attitude of inhospitality, and for not recalling God's gracious provision when they were in need, Jesus gives the Twelve an opportunity to practice hospitality. He has them sit the people down in manageable groups of fifty (9:14b–15). To their credit, the disciples obey and do not question his intentions. Soon Jesus will also have them distribute the food (9:16b), keeping them as participants, not just onlookers, of his ministry of hospitality.

With five loaves and two fish in hand, Jesus acknowledges God as the provider who feeds his people. Using these four verbs to denote Jesus' actions—take, bless, break, and give (9:16a)—Luke prepares his readers to hear them again in the account of the Last Supper, in which Jesus will take a loaf of bread, break it, and give it to his disciples (22:19). At the end of the Gospel, Jesus once again will take, bless, break, and give bread to the two disciples at table with him in Emmaus (24:30). While these are standard gestures at a meal, the fact that Luke repeats the sequence three times is not insignificant, especially when at Emmaus these are the very actions by which the two disciples recognize the risen Lord.[5] Besides, this feeding miracle is located at the point in the Lukan narrative where Jesus' identity and his pending death in Jerusalem are about to be revealed. The host who feeds the multitudes at this wilderness table will give his life to welcome believers at the messianic table.

The actual multiplication of the fish and loaves is not described, but the effect is emphatically stated: "All ate and were filled" (9:17a). Mary's song comes to mind, that God "has filled the hungry with good things" (1:53), as does Jesus' blessing that those "who are hungry now, . . . will be filled" (6:21). This is a meal of grand proportions, yet it undermines the very nature of meals as boundary delimiters. Strangers eat sitting side by side. Some are clean, others unclean. There is no water to perform the necessary rituals of cleansing and no means of determining if the fish and loaves are kosher.[6] The only operative word is abundance; there is plenty to share. The twelve baskets of leftovers underscore the generosity of God's provision. Each basket is an object lesson for each of the twelve disciples, reminding them of the importance of unwavering trust in Jesus and the wideness of divine hospitality.

This feeding recalls how Elisha fed a hundred people with twenty barley loaves and some ears of grain in spite of his servant Gehazi's skepticism (2 Kgs 4:42–44). A connection may also be made with God

---

5. The verbs vary due to the use of cognates and synonyms, but for the most part the same series of actions runs through all three occasions: *lambanō, eulogeō, kataklaō, didōmi* in 9:16; *lambanō, eucharisteō, klaō, didōmi* in 22:19; and *lambanō, eulogeō, klaō, epedidōmi* in 24:30.

6. Green 1997: 365.

providing the Israelites with manna in response to Moses' petition (Exod 16; cf. Ps 78:19–20). Since both Moses and Elisha were prophets, the characterization of Jesus as a prophet is affirmed again by these allusions (9:8, 19). But it will soon be made known that Jesus is more than a prophet through the event of his transfiguration (9:28–36).

Following the Suffering Messiah (9:18–27)

Marking a break in the narrative time line, Luke returns to the issue of Jesus' identity and its implication for discipleship. Jesus has been praying by himself before broaching this important subject even though the Twelve are with him (9:18a). As with the account of Jesus' baptism (3:21) and his choosing of the apostles (6:12), Luke's connection between prayer and special revelation is sounded again. Though not explicitly stated, the readers are led to attribute Peter's correct identification of Jesus as Messiah to Jesus' prayer (9:20; cf. Matt 16:15–17).

Jesus asks, "Who do the crowds say that I am?" (9:18b), echoing the musing of Herod Antipas (9:9). Similar answers derived from popular opinion are proffered—John the Baptist *redivivus*, the eschatological Elijah, or one of the ancient prophets (9:7–8, 19). These suggestions reflect some insight into Jesus' role as God's emissary, but they fall short of fully capturing the essence of Jesus' identity.[7] Then Jesus narrows the scope of the question, "But who do *you* say that I am?" (9:20a), to which Peter, the group's spokesman, replies, "The Messiah of God" (9:20b). Luke's readers have been waiting for the characters in the narrative to recognize that Jesus is more than a prophet, a rabbi, or a healer, but Israel's long-awaited Messiah. Given Jesus' immediate command to silence (9:21), the disciples are to hold back from proclaiming this truth, for they need to first understand the implications of Peter's answer.

Jesus' explanation resides in four passion predictions in Luke, the first of which is that "the Son of Man must suffer many things, and be rejected by the elders, chief priest, and scribes, and be killed, and on the third day be raised" (9:22; cf. 9:44; 17:25; 18:31–33). "Son of Man" is an idiom, which can simply refer to the speaker, as in "I." Added significance in Jesus' use of "Son of Man" may be deduced from a heavenly vision in the book of Daniel, in which "one like a son of man" is presented before God to receive glory, authority, and everlasting dominion (Dan 7:13–14).

---

7. See p. 17, n. 15 and p. 100.

The meaning of this passage is debated, but one option is to interpret the Danielic son of man as a corporate representative of faithful Israel, who receives vindication from God after having endured persecution.[8] Likewise, Jesus the Son of Man is the faithful messianic representative of God's people, whose suffering will be redeemed by God with glory and kingship.

Even though "Son of Man" is not a messianic title per se, it carries a messianic connotation in Luke, and is found in contexts that speak of Jesus' authority, suffering, and vindication.[9] Both ideas are present in this passion prediction. Like the son of man in Dan 7, the rejection of Jesus, this Son of Man, will culminate in his death, though ironically at the hands of the leaders of the Jews. The elders, chief priests, and scribes constitute the Sanhedrin, the Jewish ruling council of the day. In the Greek text, the three groups share one article, tying them together as one evil triad seeking the Messiah's demise (cf. 20:1; 22:66).[10] Yet God's salvation trumps human machination. To say that the Son of Man must (*dei*) undergo great suffering signals a divine necessity[11] that governs the four infinitives that follow: to suffer, to be rejected, to be killed, and to be raised (9:22). The suffering of God's emissary is to be expected, like the suffering servant of the Lord in Isa 52–53 or the righteous sufferer in wisdom literature.[12] Persecution of the Messiah, even to the point of his death, will not have the last word. Beyond the suffering of the Son of Man is his vindication. On the third day he will be raised from the dead by none other than God himself (Acts 2:23–24; 3:14–15). While counterintuitive, this is the way in which God's purpose will be fulfilled (13:33; 17:25; 24:7).

Does the thought of a persecuted Messiah even have a place in the paradigm of these men who have left everything to follow Jesus? When Peter confesses that Jesus is God's Messiah, is he thinking of a Davidic king who will defeat the Romans and return Israel to its former political and national glory (cf. Acts 1:6)? Can they hear the note of vindication, or has the sense of foreboding regarding Jesus' rejection and death

---

8. For background to the "Son of Man" as a messianic figure, see Collins 2010: 191–214. On Jesus' use of "Son of Man" as a self-designation, see Bock 2013: 896–98; Dunn 1996: 65–97.

9. On authority, see 5:24; 6:5; 12:8; on suffering, see 9:44; 24:7; on glory and vindication, see 9:26; 17:30; 22:69.

10. Nolland 1993a: 464.

11. See p. 45, n. 30.

12. Pss 22, 31, 69; Wis 2:10–20; 3:1–9.

clouded their judgment and shaken their faith? On this side of the resurrection, their ability to understand the path of a crucified Messiah is limited. Following Jesus implies walking in his footsteps. If the path of Jesus' vindication and glory must come by way of suffering and death, his followers should expect the same. What he requires of them is total trust and commitment.

Jesus uses several images to issue the same basic challenge. The first is that of self-denial and cross-bearing (9:23). In the ancient Greco-Roman world, crucifixion signified the epitome of shame, over and above its cruelty as a means of capital punishment. Criminals were crucified naked, tied or nailed to a horizontal cross beam, with barely a piece of wood on the vertical beam to support their feet and their entire body weight. Many died by asphyxiation, if not severe loss of blood. It was such a slow and disgraceful death that even the word crucifixion was not to be mentioned in polite company.[13] Cross-bearing as a requirement of discipleship means ostracism and death. Condemned to death by crucifixion, the victim had to carry the cross beam to the place of execution. "Taking up the cross" implies "a dead man (or woman) walking." Jesus requires all would-be followers to take up their cross *daily*, dying repeatedly, day by day. Jesus is not interested in any masochistic glorification of shame and humiliation. Self-denial means letting go of everything that stands in opposition to God. It requires that one's identity, priorities, attitudes, and actions be reshaped and reformed. It is the relinquishment of all worldly values, possessions, and habits that stand in the way of obedience and fidelity to Jesus. This level of commitment will invite ridicule, misunderstanding, and retaliation—hence a daily cross-bearing.

The next saying contrasts the consequence of self-protection with that of self-denial (9:24). Saving life and losing life, holding onto and letting go, are polarities. On the one hand, there is the fleeting earthly life with all its material goods and earthly structures. On the other hand, there is the life that Jesus offers that promises a future in God's eternal kingdom. Those who deny themselves take the long view. They give up what they have in the present life to save their life in eternity. By contrast, those who are obsessed with preserving what they now have will in the end lose everything, including life itself. Such is the paradox of discipleship.

---

13. See p. 295. Seneca *Marc.* 20.3; Josephus *J.W.* 5.451. See Carroll and Green 1997: 167–70; Hengel 1977: 22–38, 46–63.

Unless a disciple invests in the right kind of "life," temporary profit will result in permanent loss (9:25). Perceived loss in the present, however, will yield lasting gain. The third image comes from the sphere of commerce and finance, as one envisions a balance sheet of debit and credit, profit and loss. "To gain the whole world" refers to the totality of life on this side of eternity—money, power, fame, and status. Following Jesus is worth more than all these put together. It may not look that way right now, but the final accounting is at the last judgment, at which point it will be too late to change course. True disciples of Jesus must commit to a profitable investment now, both for this age and the age to come.

Those who shun the shame of discipleship as defined by the standards of this world refuse to be identified with Jesus and his mission. Their rejection will come back and haunt them on the day of reckoning, when the glorified Son of Man will in turn be ashamed of them (9:26). The vision of the coming of the Son of Man in all his resplendent glory reminds the reader of the vindication of the Danielic son of man (Dan 7:13–14).[14] In the Greek, the noun *doxa* ("glory") is modified by three genitival clauses: *autou* ("of him"), *tou patros* ("of the Father"), and *tōn hagiōn angelōn* ("of the holy angels").[15] Jesus will be crowned with heavenly glory, even the glory of God himself, with all its concomitant authority, dignity, and sovereignty. If the end goal of salvation is to be received by Jesus into this eternal realm of life and joy, then any amount of earthly shame, suffering, and even death is by comparison a small price to pay.

Jesus' final remark, that some among the Twelve "will not taste death before they see the kingdom of God" (9:27), sounds enigmatic. In Luke, the kingdom of God is not only a future reality (11:2; 13:29; 22:16, 18), but has already manifested itself in the present through the person and work of Jesus (10:9; 11:20; 17:21). God's kingdom in this statement encompasses all that Jesus has been doing to save, bring wholeness, and gather together God's loyal subjects. In spite of Roman hegemony, the reign of God is active, reordering the world for those who believe in Jesus. Being with Jesus, the Twelve have the privilege to see the unfolding of God's plan up close. They are experiencing the kingdom of God in this lifetime, as they come with eyes of faith and open hearts.

---

14. See pp. 127–28.

15. Some English translations add an extra "glory," hence "when he comes in his glory and in the glory of the Father and of the holy angels" (NIV, NRSV, cf. NLT, ESV). This extra "glory" gives the misleading impression that Jesus' glory is somehow different from the others', but it is not (Green 1997: 375).

Transfiguration (9:28–36)

The progressive understanding of who Jesus is, from the crowd's assessment that he is a prophet (9:7–8) to Peter's confession that he is God's Messiah (9:20), will culminate in God's declaration that Jesus is God's Son (9:35). Prophet and Messiah, as relevant as they are for understanding Jesus, are human figures. Divine sonship places Jesus in the realm of heavenly transcendence, surpassing all earthly categories. This spectacle is therefore one-of-a-kind, engendering fear, awe, and hopefully, a deeper faith in Peter, James, and John.[16]

Luke's account of the transfiguration contains a tapestry of allusions. The primary backdrop is that of Moses and the exodus. The mountain setting, the change in Jesus' countenance, the use of the word *exodos,* the mention of tents, the divine presence in a cloud, and the fear of the disciples all hearken back to different vignettes in Israel's journey through the wilderness.[17] While the appearance of Moses is not surprising, the reason for Elijah's presence is less obvious. Perhaps the figure of a glorified Elijah affirms the comparison between him and Jesus in the Lukan narrative (4:24–26; 7:14–15; cf. 9:54). Furthermore, the voice from heaven at the transfiguration must be read with a backward glance at Jesus' baptism (3:21–22).

About eight days after Peter's confession of Jesus as God's Messiah, Jesus goes up to an unnamed mountain to pray (9:28). Just as Moses ascended Mount Sinai with Aaron, Nadab, and Abihu to meet with God (Exod 24:1, 9), Jesus brings three disciples—Peter, James, and John—with him. They were also the only disciples allowed to follow Jesus into Jairus's house to witness the raising of his daughter (8:51).

Luke explicitly links prayer to Peter's confession (9:18) and now to Jesus' transfiguration. In the midst of prayer, Jesus' appearance changes (9:29). Although Luke does not explicitly describe Jesus' face as shining like Moses' after being in the presence of God (Exod 34:29–30), that assumption fits the dazzling whiteness of Jesus' clothing. In biblical scenes, heavenly figures are often dressed in white (Mark 16:5; Acts 1:10; Rev 4:4; 7:9). The transfiguration of Jesus in appearance and garb transports him to a supernatural domain. The mountain has become the staging ground

---

16. The point of the transfiguration is for the disciples to hear from God that Jesus is a heavenly figure and his impending death aligns with God's will (Puig i Tàrrech 2012: 170–72).

17. Miller 2010: 502–5.

of a heavenly vision, and the disciples are beholding the Son of Man in all his future glory (9:26)!

Suddenly, talking to Jesus are two other glorified heavenly figures, Moses and Elijah (9:30). Do they represent the law and the prophets, both of which Jesus later claims to have spoken of him (24:27, 44)? Do they play the role as Jesus' precursors, so that there is continuity as God's purposes are carried out through each of them? Or are they here to testify to Jesus as God's eschatological prophet?[18] Regardless of why Moses and Elijah appear with Jesus, the content of their conversation is illuminating and revelatory.

The three are talking about Jesus' *exodos*, "which he was about to accomplish in Jerusalem" (9:31). The basic meaning of *exodos* is "departure." *Exodos* refers to God's paradigmatic deliverance of his people from bondage in Egypt (Exod 19:2; Num 33:38; Heb 11:22), but it is also a euphemism for death (Wis 3:2; 7:6; 2 Pet 1:15). In this context, both meanings are present. Jesus' *exodos* refers to his destiny in Jerusalem, which encompasses his death, resurrection, and ascension into heaven (24:51).[19] Even though Jerusalem is the place of Jesus' execution, it is also the locus of God's salvation and judgment.

Peter, James, and John see the glorified trio, but their comprehension of the disclosure of Jesus' *exodos* is compromised by drowsiness (9:32). Seeing that Moses and Elijah are about to leave, Peter scrambles to find a way to prolong the experience. Perhaps three shelters, one for each dignitary, would make the prophets extend their visit (9:33). There is no need to read too much into Peter's idea, which lacks insight into the significance of this heavenly meeting. Even the author dismisses it as some foolish babble.

In contrast to Peter's bumbling remark, the gravitas of God's entry is thrice underscored by the appearance of a cloud, the voice that comes from it, and its overshadowing of the disciples (9:34). During the exodus, God proclaimed his name to Moses in a cloud (Exod 34:5–7). God led the Israelites with a pillar of cloud as they sojourned through the wilderness (Exod 13:21–22; 40:36–38; Num 9:18, 22). When the Israelites set up camp, the cloud hovered at the entrance of the tabernacle (Exod

---

18. Marshall 1978: 384; Nolland 1993a; 498; Green 1997: 381.

19. Garrett (1990: 666–70, 677–80) proposes that this chain of events reenacts the exodus motif. Just as Moses led the Israelites out of bondage to Pharaoh, now Jesus will lead those who believe in him out of bondage to Satan.

33:9–11). So when the cloud comes upon them while Peter is still thinking about tents, his jovial mood turns into fear.

The voice from the cloud marks a theophany: "*This is* my Son, my chosen; listen to him" (9:35). These words recall the same voice at Jesus' baptism: "*You are* my Son, the beloved, with you I am well pleased" (3:22). Whereas God spoke to Jesus at his baptism, now he speaks to Peter, James, and John to validate that Jesus is indeed God's Son. Although traditionally the king of Israel was seen as God's son in a metaphorical sense (2 Sam 7:14; Ps 2:7), Jesus' divine sonship is of a superior and different order, because he is conceived by the Holy Spirit (1:31–35). To call Jesus "Son of God" simultaneously acknowledges his divinity as well as his messianic status.[20]

"My chosen" is an allusion to Isa 42:1 that connects 9:35 to 3:22. Isa 42:1 reads: "Here is my servant, . . . *my chosen in whom my soul delights.*" The voice at Jesus' baptism picks up the phrase, "in whom I am well pleased," whereas here it refers to Jesus as "my chosen." Combining what the voice from heaven says on both occasions, Jesus, God's Messiah (9:20) and God's Son (9:35), is identified with the servant of YHWH (cf. 23:35). In Isaiah, the servant of YHWH represents Israel (42:1–4; 44:1–5; 49:7), commissioned to be a light to the gentiles. Jesus now takes on the role which Israel failed to fulfill (2:32), by bringing God's salvific purposes to fruition through his own suffering (cf. Isa 52–53).

Other than the servant of YHWH, David (Ps 89:19–20) and Moses (Ps 106:23) were also said to be chosen by God. The Davidic connection brings together "my Son" and "my chosen" in 9:35, whereas the allusion to Moses links "my chosen" with the command to the disciples, "Listen to him." God promised Moses that he would raise up a prophet like him to teach his people, and "[they] must listen to him" (Deut 18:18). Later on Peter and Stephen will also identify Jesus with this Moses-like prophet (Acts 3:22–23; 7:37).[21]

Moses, Elijah, David, and the servant of YHWH form the conceptual building blocks for understanding Jesus of Nazareth, whose identity as the holy and divine Son of God-Son of Man supersedes the combined weightiness of these figural comparisons. When the cloud clears, Moses and Elijah have disappeared, and the disciples are left with Jesus. If Jesus has already commanded his disciples not to tell anyone that he is God's

---

20. See p. 21, n. 20.
21. See Miller 2010: 512–17.

Messiah (9:21), these three know better than to say anything at all about the extraordinary spectacle they have just beheld (9:36).

The transfiguration provides a clarification of Jesus' divine status, a preview of his future glory, and a charting of the path of suffering that he will take in order to arrive at the place of vindication.[22] The disciples are beginning to realize that following Jesus entails both rejection and reward. Because death will precede glory, Peter, James, and John are given a glimpse of Jesus' transcendent glory at this time, lest they become too discouraged by the events that will unfold in Jerusalem. The three will not grasp the full significance of Jesus' transfiguration until after his ascension into heaven. But if their faith falters in the time of darkness between the crucifixion and the resurrection, the memory of this sacred moment will provide much needed reassurance and hope.

Faithlessness and Self-Importance (9:37–50)

Even with the most incredible mountain-top experience bar none, there is no guarantee of spiritual maturity.[23] Faithlessness, spiritual dullness, self-importance, and small-mindedness soon rear their ugly heads again as impediments on the uphill journey of faith.

Healing a Demon-Possessed Boy (9:37–43)

A large crowd is already waiting for Jesus as the group descends from the mountain. Immediate a father beseeches Jesus to help his only son (9:37–38). In the previous chapter, Jesus returned from the region of the Gerasenes and was likewise met by a waiting crowd when Jairus begged him to help his only daughter (8:40–41). Jairus's daughter was near death, and the condition of this man's son is serious. His symptoms include seizures, convulsions, and foaming at the mouth, which the text attributes to possession by an unclean spirit.[24] A powerful demon tortures the child relentlessly, mauling him and dashing him to the ground. Even the com-

---

22. Martin (2006: 16–24) stresses humiliation as an indispensable component of Jesus' glory to counter a eschatological triumphalist reading of the transfiguration.

23. Borgman (2006: 68–74) traces the disciples' obtuseness through the entire chapter, including their desire to dismiss the crowd (9:12) and Peter's suggestion to build three tents (9:33).

24. Nolland (1993a: 509) states that the boy has epilepsy, though Green (1997: 387) cautions against assuming modern diagnoses on ancient descriptions of ailments.

bined effort of nine disciples has failed to cast it out (9:39–40, 42a). The father is desperate; over and above the negative attention brought on the family in having a demon-possessed child and the purity concern that comes with it, if the boy dies, there will be no heir to carry on the family line.[25]

Aggravated, Jesus gives everyone a scolding, "You faithless and perverse generation, how much longer must I be with you and bear with you?" (9:41). The "faithless and perverse generation" includes his own disciples. Weren't they given "power and authority over all demons" when Jesus sent them into the villages of Galilee (9:1, 6)? Whether their ineffectiveness stems from overconfidence in themselves or lack of trust in God, the result is the same. The demon still has the upper hand.

Jesus rebukes[26] the unclean spirit and heals the boy. Just as he gave the only son of the widow at Nain back to his mother after raising him from the dead (7:15), Jesus now gives this only son back to his father (9:42). The people are amazed at God's greatness (9:43; cf. 5:26; 7:16; cf. 18:43), but whether these witnesses to Jesus' saving power will ever progress from mere astonishment to genuine faith is yet to be seen.

Passion Prediction (9:44–45)

While the onlookers are still mesmerized by the boy's cure, Jesus catches the attention of the Twelve with a solemn lead-in note, "Let these words sink into your ears" (9:44a; cf. 8:8; 14:35). What Jesus divulges next is not for the public to hear, that "the Son of Man is about to be handed over (*paradidosthai*) into human hands" (9:44b). The crowd may be oblivious of the hostile action against Jesus looming on the horizon, but his disciples have already been apprised of it (9:22). The Greek verb *paradidōmi* broadly means "to hand over," as in transmitting something from one to another. In a narrower sense, it means "to betray." Since *paradidosthai* ("to be handed over") is in the passive voice, who is responsible for that action? Some English versions render *paradidosthai* as "to be betrayed" (NRSV, NIV, NLT), claiming that Judas is in view (cf. 22:22, 48). Based on the notion of divine necessity[27] that undergirds the first passion

---

25. Garland 2011: 402.

26. The same Greek verb, *epitimaō*, is used here as in two other exorcisms (4:35, 41).

27. See p. 45, n. 30.

prediction that Jesus must suffer and be raised because *God* makes it necessary (9:22), perhaps two layers of meaning are intended.

Without the benefit of a postresurrection perspective, it is difficult for the disciples to wrap their minds around Jesus' talk of his own suffering and death as something endorsed by God. Their obtuseness is understandable (9:45a). But God is also responsible for their current incomprehension, for the meaning of Jesus' words "was concealed from them, so that they could not perceive it" (9:45b). Have the disciples, whom Jesus said have been "given to know the secrets of the kingdom of God," now become the "others" who look but may not perceive, and who listen but may not understand (8:9–10)? Has their fragile faith suffered a setback? Fear, the constant threat to faith, gets the better of the disciples. Instead of asking Jesus as they would in the past (9:45c; cf. 8:9), they shy away from what they do not want to hear. Consequently, their dullness persists.

The Greatest versus the Least (9:46–50)

In the highly stratified society of the ancient Greco-Roman world, interpersonal relationships were governed by a constant tussle of rank, position, privilege, and prestige. Within every class in the social hierarchy, honor was a coveted commodity. For a person to amass honor, someone else would suffer shame, leading to an unending competition to get ahead of one's neighbor. This vicious cycle was further exasperated by the code of reciprocity in patron-client relationships. In order to maintain one's honor on the social ladder, associations must be with someone in a comparable rank or above, but never with those below. Those of lower rank would not be able to reciprocate any favor extended to them. Not only that, they would even bring shame by association.

It is as though the disciples never heard what Jesus had told them about his suffering, for they are still consumed with status, jockeying among themselves for the top spot in greatness (9:46). Perceiving the inner machinations of their hearts, Jesus identifies a teaching moment to confront them, as he did with the Pharisees (9:47a; cf. 5:44; 7:39–40). To achieve the maximum effect, Jesus picks up the person with the lowest status, a child, in order to explain the meaning of true greatness.

The view of children in the ancient world was very different from modern attitudes. Although ancient parents loved their children, within the social structure children were at the very bottom in rank. That children were cute and innocent was beside the point. Little children had no intrinsic exploitable value—no status, no rights, no power, no position, not even the ability to give back what they have received. They were weak, vulnerable, needy, and dependent. From that point of view, little children were not worth much at all, and hence relegated to the bottom rung of the social ladder.[28]

Jesus puts the little boy beside him (9:47b), immediately elevating him to a position of honor next to the teacher. This gesture would have aroused some murmur of indignation from his disciples. In one sentence, Jesus draws a straight line from the child, through himself, to God: "Whoever welcomes this child in my name welcomes me, and whoever welcomes me welcomes the one who sent me" (9:48a). Hospitality is a key value in the communal dimension of faith and discipleship. Given the incomparable status of God and Jesus in the minds of the disciples, how can serving a lowly child be commensurate with serving God and Jesus? Welcoming children in the name of Jesus requires lowering oneself in more than one way. It disrupts the carefully navigated systems of balanced reciprocity and undermines the social acclaim of seeking honor. But that is precisely Jesus' point—"the least among all of you is the greatest" (9:48b)—in the economy of God's kingdom, greatness is measured by service and hidden in humility and lowliness.

No sooner has Jesus redefined true greatness as extending hospitality toward those without status or rank, John accuses an unnamed exorcist of casting out demons in Jesus' name. He even sounds self-congratulatory, reporting that he and the disciples "tried to stop him, because he does not follow with [them]" (9:49). It is not just John, but all twelve disciples, who think that they are the special ones through whom God has chosen to dispense his power. Perhaps the disciples think of themselves as the only "certified" representatives of Jesus, since they are the only ones called to be "apostles" (6:13). Are they jealous that someone else is casting out demons in Jesus' name when they have just failed to do so themselves (9:40)? Are they withholding honor from another because of their own sense of shame? Against the disciples' narrow-minded attitude, Jesus pronounces the final word, "Do not stop him; for whoever is not against you is for you" (9:50). The disciples' self-protective spirit runs counter to Jesus' generous hospitality that reaches out to the needy

---

28. At the top of the ladder of social status was the male head of the household, and at the bottom, the child, with the male child above the female child (Jeffers 1999: 190; Ferguson 2003: 80).

and to those eager to participate in his mission. Soon enough, Jesus will send another seventy into the field (10:2). Rather than evaluating other people's worthiness for the work of God's kingdom, the disciples should embrace those who join them in bringing liberation and wholeness to all.

The Twelve are not incorrigible, but these cultural values are so deeply entrenched that it will take many false starts for real progress to take root. Although it seems disappointing for Luke to conclude the Galilean ministry of Jesus on a note of the disciples' dismal track record, their unpreparedness for the trials ahead underscores the narrative need of a section devoted to the theme of discipleship.[29] In the travel narrative (9:51—19:27), Jesus will be teaching, shaping, and forming the Twelve, preparing them for the challenges ahead in Jerusalem.

Cost of Discipleship (9:51-62)

A new stage begins in the Lukan narrative as Jesus journeys to Jerusalem to fulfill God's purpose. The travel narrative begins on a rather ominous note. No sooner have Jesus and his disciples left Galilee they encounter rejection in Samaria. More opposition will follow. Jesus' determination to walk the path of suffering finds expression in the stringent demands he sets out for his followers. If they embark on this journey with him, God's mission must take priority, because the stakes are high and the time is short.

Rejection in Samaria (9:51–56)

The opening verse hearkens back to the transfiguration but also anticipates the end of Luke's narrative: "When the days drew near for his being taken up (*tēs analēmpseōs*), [Jesus] set his face to go to Jerusalem" (9:51). The last mention of Jerusalem was in 9:31, when Moses and Elijah "spoke of his departure (*tēn exodon*), which he was about to fulfill in Jerusalem." Read together, *tēs analēmpseōs* in 9:51 and *tēn exodon* in 9:31 are mutually interpretive. Jesus' "departure" (*exodos*) refers first to his death and then to his departure from this earth. In fact, "taking up" (*analēmpsis*) can also mean death in a figurative sense, but a more literal or spatial sense is intended here, that Jesus is physically taken up to heaven.[30] Together

---

29. Green 1997: 387.

30. Luke uses the cognate verb, *analambanō*, to speak of Jesus' ascension (Acts 1:2, 11, 22).

9:51 and 9:31 signify the chain of events that will occur in Jerusalem in fulfillment of God's saving agenda, from Jesus' death to his resurrection and finally his ascension into glory.[31] This climactic denouement of Jesus' earthly mission stands behind the strong resoluteness with which he sets his face toward his destination. The portent of death will not stop him, as vindication and glory lie beyond the suffering (9:22). His disciples, though, will require preparation for this confrontation in Jerusalem. The first test will present itself as they venture southward into Samaria.

For centuries leading up to the time of Jesus, there had been conflicts between the Samaritans and the Jews. Deep-seated prejudices ran in both directions. Some scholars who study the Samaritans at length doubt that the account in 2 Kgs 17:24–41, where the king of Assyria populated the area of Samaria with other conquered peoples, resulting in a mixed population with intermarriages between the Israelites and other foreigners, accurately accounted for the origin of the Samaritans.[32] Although the accounts concerning the Samaritans in the writings of Josephus may contain some historical inaccuracy and racial bias, they give a clear impression that Jews and Samaritans eyed each other with suspicion and hostility. The Samaritans worshiped on Mount Gerizim, had their own Samaritan Pentateuch, and refused to acknowledge any OT prophet other than Moses, on whom they modeled their messianic expectation. One time the Jews destroyed the Samaritans' temple, and another time the Samaritans desecrated theirs in retaliation. Other skirmishes had escalated into bloodshed and both sides were responsible for the violence.[33]

The historic bad blood between Jews and Samaritans allows us to appreciate the author's nuanced depiction of the Samaritans in Luke-Acts. While a Samaritan village may reject Jesus and his companions (9:52–56), Jesus will soon present a compassionate Samaritan as an exemplary figure in a parable (10:25–37) and praise the faith of a Samaritan leper (17:11–19). In Luke's second volume, Samaria is an intended mission field (Acts 1:8), and the Samaritans are shown to be responsive to the apostles' evangelistic efforts (Acts 8:5–25). Despite the lack of hospitality

---

31. Elijah was taken up into heaven (2 Kgs 2:10–11) and, according to Philo, so was Moses (*Moses* 2.291). It seems fitting for these two to be discussing Jesus' final departure in a similar manner. Besides, Elijah typology factors heavily in 9:52–56.

32. Williamson and Kartveit 2013: 832–36.

33. See p. 154, n. 24 as well as Green 1997: 405; Nolland 1993a: 535–36; Josephus *J.W.* 2.232–46; Josephus *Ant.* 18.29–30; 20.118–36.

of one Samaritan village toward Jesus and his disciples, Samaritans overall are not dismissed as unreachable for the gospel.

Instead of taking the circuitous route through Transjordan that avoids Samaria altogether, Jesus takes a direct route and heads right into Samaria. With a large traveling party, messengers are sent ahead to inquire about meals and accommodations (9:52). Practical concerns aside, Luke also has in mind how John prepared the way of the Messiah (1:17, 76; 3:4). The same verb *hetoimazō* ("to prepare" or "to make ready") is now applied to these emissaries. While the messengers do not preach repentance as John did, the sense of anticipation for the arrival of the Messiah is retained.[34]

The Samaritan village refuses to welcome Jesus because "his face was set toward Jerusalem" (9:53; cf. 9:51). The text does not indicate why Jesus' destination is offensive to the Samaritans. Perhaps the rivalry between Jerusalem and Gerazim as the proper place of worship, and more generally the Samaritans' dislike of Jews, are enough reasons to reject Jesus and his entourage.

Even if expected, the insult triggers the ire of James and John, whose suggestion betrays their spiritual dullness and vengeful spirit. Sounding self-righteous, they use Elijah as a sanction to cast judgment. Twice Elijah called down fire from heaven to consume the emissaries of Ahaziah, the king of Samaria, to punish him for his arrogance and impiety (2 Kgs 1:1–16). Not only do James and John want Jesus to follow Elijah's example, they volunteer to call down fire from heaven at Jesus' bidding (9:54). The two brothers want the satisfaction of playing Elijah in pronouncing judgment on this village. They may feel compelled to inflict shame on their enemies to redeem their group's honor, but incinerating a village goes far beyond shaking the dust off one's feet (9:5; 10:10–11)! Jesus' rebuke of his disciples is well deserved indeed (9:55–56).

Self-Denial and Discipleship (9:57–62)

Along the way, three short vignettes underscore the radical nature of what it means to follow Jesus. The people who approach Jesus are serious candidates for discipleship, at least in their own estimation. In the first and the third encounter, Jesus is approached by someone who wants to

---

34. Green 1997: 404; Carroll 2012: 229; Nolland 1993a: 535.

be part of his closer circle of disciples. In the middle encounter, Jesus himself extends the call to follow.

The first person promises to follow Jesus wherever he goes (9:57). While "wherever" simply points to the peripatetic mode of Jesus' ministry, it anticipates the path of suffering ahead, of which this inquirer may or may not even be aware. Jesus' answer addresses the "wandering nature" of his mission. Even wild animals are more secure than he, for foxes have holes and birds have nests in which to lodge, but "the Son of Man[35] has nowhere to lay his head" (9:58). Without the security of place and community, Jesus and his disciples are completely dependent on God's provision and people's hospitality (9:3–5; cf. 10:4–7). While mobile for the work of God's kingdom, itinerancy demands great faith.

Still on the issues of security and belonging, the second and third exchanges involve important social and religious obligations in being part of a family. The second would-be disciple counters Jesus' call to follow with the request, "Lord, first let me go and bury my father" (9:59). This ought to be an eminently legitimate appeal, given the importance of burial in Jesus' culture. Done properly, a burial was a year-long process. Upon a person's death, the corpse was first placed in a sealed tomb. Twelve months later, after the body had completely decomposed, the bones were stored in a box (an ossuary) and placed on a shelf inside the tomb. This secondary burial freed up space inside the family tomb and brought closure to the time of mourning.[36] A proper burial respected the dignity of the deceased, something all would want to do for their relatives and have done for themselves (Gen 23:3–4; Tob 4:3–4; 14:11–13). Even burying a stranger was an act of charity that God would reward. To honor one's father and mother was the fifth commandment of the Decalogue (Exod 20:12; Deut 5:16), the epitome of which was a proper burial, the ultimate act of filial piety (Gen 50:5; Tob 6:14–15; *m. Ketub.* 11:1). Given the privileged status of sons in a family, it would be unthinkable for a man to abandon his duty to bury his father.

Because of the legitimacy of the second would-be disciple's request, Jesus' response is shocking: "Let the dead bury their own dead" (9:60a). We are not privy to the situation that confronts this man. Has his father died recently so that the secondary burial has yet to be completed? Is the father ill or dying and he anticipates the need to fulfill his duty in the near

---

35. See pp. 127–28.
36. McCane 1990: 31–43.

future? Can Jesus' reply be understood in a more charitable way, so that Jesus seems less unfeeling and harsh? Some interpreters add qualifiers to Jesus' saying: "Let the spiritually dead bury their own physically dead."[37] This reading dismisses those family members left behind to fulfill the duty of burial as spiritually dead, which seems uncalled for. Others make use of the practice of secondary burial and consider both instances of "dead" as the physically dead: "Let those already dead in the family tomb rebury their own dead."[38] This interpretation makes no logical sense other than adding more weight to the deadness of the situation. Besides, it asks too much of the readers to be familiar with the details of ancient Palestinian burial customs. Another commentator avoids the specifics altogether: "Let other arrangements be made."[39] This rendering makes Jesus come across somewhat flippant, as though the man had many other means of substituting for his absence.

Perhaps the point is not to dissect the saying just to temper its shock value. Jesus is making a radical point that pits the sacred duty of burying one's father against the proclamation of the kingdom of God (9:60b). Jesus' demand is not meant to be softened. His mission is good news to those who embrace it, but it challenges many of the cultural norms and social expectations of the day. Jesus is not denying the importance of filial obligation (cf. 18:20), but in light of the priority and urgency of the work of God's kingdom, even burying one's father pales in comparison.[40] The focus of the saying has less to do with compassion or duty, but everything to do with Jesus' resolution to fulfill God's mission.

In the third encounter, the would-be disciple requests to bid farewell to one's family, which also seems reasonable (9:61). We assume that the person is not planning for a lengthy leave-taking, and that the intention to rejoin Jesus is sincere. After all, when Elijah threw his mantle on Elisha to continue his work, Elisha went and said goodbye to his family (1 Kgs 19:19–21). Yet once again Jesus turns down the request with another image: "No one who puts a hand to the plow and looks back is fit for the

---

37. Marshall 1978: 411; Carroll 2012: 231; Fitzmyer 1981: 836.
38. Green 1997: 408–9.
39. Nolland 1993a: 542.
40. Bockmuehl (1998: 544–56, 576–77) refutes the interpretations of Martin Hengel and E. P. Sanders that Jesus is launching an attack on the law (e.g., the command to honor one's parents) and requiring disobedience to it. Rather, "let the dead bury their dead" should be understood against Jesus' reframing of family ties around himself and his mission (8:21).

kingdom of God" (9:62). To put one's hand to the plow implies a sense of determination and forward movement. The farmer plows a field to ready it for planting, with the goal of a future harvest. The participle that governs the action of looking (backwards), *blepōn*, is in the present tense, which expresses not a one-time backward glance, but repeated looking, longing for that which has been left behind. Just as Jesus sets his face toward Jerusalem, his followers must set their face the same direction. He denies neither the intrinsic value of a proper burial nor the relational significance of a proper farewell, but the kingdom of God takes precedence over even the good and important things in life. Inasmuch as family and community are gifts from God, they can become "the cares of life" (8:14) that stand in the way of radical discipleship.

Jesus sets the bar high for those who want to follow him. Because the road ahead is difficult, effective workers for God's kingdom need to be unencumbered in every way, from material goods to emotional ties, in order to stay focused. The sacrifice of home and family will be compensated by new kinship ties established by Jesus, made up of those "who hear the word of God and do it" (8:21; 18:28–30). How will these would-be disciples fare? The same invitation and requisite commitment are extended to us today.

Fusing the Horizons: Radical Discipleship

In Christian parlance, the term "radical discipleship" is sometimes used to describe a way of life, spurred by the desire to follow Jesus, that goes beyond what most people in the church are willing to do for the sake of Christ. In this sense, "radical discipleship" often represents not just something good but even heroic. In recent years, however, the adjective "radical" has been associated with Jihadist movements under the label of "radical Islamic extremism" to refer to the so-called Islamic State (ISIS or ISIL), Al Qaida, Boko Haram, and other groups of comparable religious ideologies. Whether positively or negatively, the word "radical" connotes a sense of thoroughgoing, far-reaching, complete commitment over and beyond the norm. Radicalness, though, implies the presence of a gradation—if someone is behaving radically, there are others who are less radical or not radical at all.

When it comes to "radical discipleship," I wonder about a gap between the observable reality of believers' commitment to Christ as reflected in how most Christians live their lives, and the call to cruciform discipleship issued and modeled by Jesus himself. Jesus' call to those who want to follow him does not seem to leave much room for gradations of radicalness. "Let them deny themselves and take up their cross daily and follow me" (9:23). "Let the dead bury their own dead; but as for you, go and proclaim the kingdom of God" (9:60). "Whoever comes to me and does not hate father and mother, wife and children, brothers and sisters, yes, and even life itself, cannot be my disciple" (14:26). "You cannot serve God and wealth" (16:13). "Sell all that you own and distribute the money to the poor; . . . then come, follow me" (18:22). These words of Jesus represent his requirement for *anyone* who wants to be his disciple, not just an elite group of super-followers who present themselves as especially qualified for a "radical discipleship" badge on their spiritual resume. Discipleship entails discarding all encumbrances in this life, even if they pertain to what we perceive as good and worthwhile, in order to carry out the mission of God's kingdom with a single mind, heart, and soul. We hear the high expectations of Jesus and praise God for full-time ministers, missionaries, even martyrs, and others whom we consider as having given it all in answer to their respective call and commission from God. We admire them for reaching that high bar and secretly feel relieved that our assignments seem less radical. Or should it be?

All discipleship is by definition radical discipleship. Following Jesus is not for the faint of heart. Our courage and resolve are not self-generated, because we are so prone to self-preservation, need of comfort, fear of persecution, and weakness of mind. Only the empowering presence of the Holy Spirit can enable us to be responsive and obedient to Jesus' call. The question is not whether our discipleship is radical enough, but whether we dare to invite the Holy Spirit to help us live out our Christian life and witness in true form. The answer to this prayer will be costly in every sense of the word—totally precious and totally demanding.

Luke 10

Sending the Seventy-Two (10:1–16)

In chapter 9, Jesus sent the Twelve into Galilean towns to proclaim the good news of the kingdom of God (9:1–6). Now a larger group of disciples is dispatched in order that they may announce his arrival (10:1), for "the harvest is plentiful but the workers are few" (10:2a). In the OT, harvesting signifies God's eschatological judgment (Mic 4:11–12; Joel 3:12–13) as well as the gathering of his people (Isa 27:12). Given the heightened sense of urgency, the harvest image is apt, as a lot of work is accomplished within a small window of time. Therefore Jesus urges his disciples to ask "the Lord of the harvest to send out laborers into his harvest" (10:2b). It is God's seed, God's sower, and God's harvest (8:5–8). If God recruits his workers, he will provide everything they need to bring in the harvest.

How many workers is Jesus sending—seventy (NRSV, NASB, NKJV) or seventy-two (NIV, NLT, ESV)? The English translations are divided, because the textual evidence does not lean heavily one way or the other.[1] The number seventy lends itself to symbolic interpretation. For example, seventy people born of Jacob went down to Egypt, Israel's exile lasted seventy years, the Sanhedrin was made up of seventy members, and according to legend the Septuagint (the Greek translation of the OT) was translated by seventy scholars. While the number seventy is a significant symbolic number, these allusions are irrelevant to the present context. But if this sending foreshadows the mission of the early church in Acts, then seventy-two is the preferred number. Noah's sons gave rise to seventy-two families, which became the nations of the earth (Gen 10:1–32 LXX).[2] The book of 3 Enoch speaks of seventy-two princes and nations of the world (3 *En.* 17:8; 18:2–3; 30:2). Even though Jesus is only sending the seventy-two ahead of him to the towns of Palestine, the end goal is a mission to the nations (2:30–32; 3:6; Acts 1:8; cf. Gen 12:1–3).

---

1. See Nolland 1993a: 549.
2. The number of nations is seventy in the Hebrew text.

Jesus gives instructions to the seventy-two similar to those he gave to the Twelve, including the power to heal and to exorcise demons, anticipating that they, too, will experience both reception and rejection.[3] Jesus sends his messengers in pairs, for two witnesses are required for credible testimony (Num 35:30; Deut 19:15). Having a travel companion will provide mutual support in the face of opposition (10:3). The practical instructions resemble the ones given to the Twelve. The seventy-two are to travel light with no purse, bag, or sandals, and to trust God for every need (10:4a). Presumably they are not to bring a staff, an extra tunic, bread, or money either (cf. 9:3). The injunction not to greet anyone on the road is to avoid being delayed by social formalities (10:4b). The mission is urgent, and these messengers must devote all time and energy to the task at hand.

As before, God's provision will come through people's hospitality. Jesus' message, *shalom* ("peace"), means more than a regular Jewish greeting but conveys the peace that God's salvation brings (1:79; 2:14; Acts 10:36). If the seventy-two meet someone who welcomes them and their message of peace ("a man of peace"), then the peace remains with that person like a blessing. Otherwise, it is withdrawn.[4] They are to be content with whatever their host provides as God's compensation for their labor. Moving from house to house looking for better food and lodging is distracting and betrays a dissatisfaction with divine care. The town will be more inclined to receive the ministry of guests who carry themselves honorably among them, for the gospel is embodied in what they say and how they act (10:5–9).

If the townspeople are hostile, Jesus instructs his emissaries to issue a strong public warning. Despite their rejection, the truth remains that "the kingdom of God has come near" (10:11b). With the same symbolic action as the Twelve when they were rejected, these messengers are to wipe the dust of the town off their feet as a testimony against them—a gesture normally done to the dirt from gentile land so as not to bring its uncleanness back to Jewish soil (10:10–11a; cf. 9:5). On the day of judgment, harsh as it will be for Sodom because of its wickedness and inhospitality (Gen 18:20; 19:1–29; Ezek 16:49–50), Sodom's punishment will still be more bearable than that which awaits this unbelieving town (10:12).

---

3. Though not explicitly stated, this is implied in 10:9, 17.

4. According to Marshall (1978: 420), taking back the peace is equivalent to a curse, based on the Semitic idea that spoken words possess intrinsic power.

Other towns have already set themselves on the path of destruction because of their hardness of heart (10:13–15). Like a prophet, Jesus pronounces woes on three towns in particular. Chorazin was a village up in the hills north of Capernaum.[5] Bethsaida was where Jesus fed the five thousand (9:10). Capernaum, near Nazareth, was featured prominently in Jesus' early ministry, where he healed, cast out demons, and taught (4:23, 31–44; 7:1–10). Despite the attention Jesus received in these towns, there is little evidence of genuine faith.

For their impenitence, Chorazin and Bethsaida will experience judgment stricter than what Tyre and Sidon will deserve. Many oracles of judgment were pronounced against these gentile cities by the prophets (Isa 23:1–18; Ezek 26:15–21; 28:1–24). That Tyre and Sidon would repent of their sins and sit in sackcloth and ashes[6] long before Chorazin and Bethsaida will is a grievous thing (10:13–14). Even gentiles are easier to reach than God's chosen people! As for Capernaum, Jesus likens its hubris to that of the king of Babylon. Elevating himself to the level of the Most High, the pagan king will be cast down to the realm of the dead (10:15; Isa 14:13–15). The same fate will befall unbelieving Capernaum, whose arrogance will end in humiliating eternal torment.

Why are unbelieving Jewish towns condemned so harshly when they resist the good news of the kingdom? The answer lies in the chain of agency. The disciples are Jesus' emissaries, but Jesus is God's emissary. Whatever treatment the disciples receive is projected back, first onto Jesus and then onto God himself (10:16). If welcoming a lowly little child is like welcoming Jesus and God (9:48), the reverse is true as well. Snubbing a messenger sent by Jesus is tantamount to snubbing God, a serious affront with grave consequences indeed!

Return of the Seventy-Two (10:17–24)

The seventy-two return from their mission brimming with excitement, saying, "Lord, in your name even the demons submit to us!" (10:17). It is the authority of Jesus' name that renders them effective (cf. 9:49–50).[7]

---

5. Green 1997: 416.

6. Sackcloth is a coarse material made from goat's hair. Whether as a sign of repentance or mourning, sackcloth and ashes could either be worn by the mourner, or the mourner could sit in sackcloth and ashes. Cf. Job 2:8; Isa 58:5; Jonah 3:6.

7. The messengers' success prefigures the mission of the early church. In Jesus' name the early Christians will preach (Acts 4:17–18; 5:28, 40; 9:27–28), heal (Acts

Their joy is expected, but their excitement needs refocusing. Jesus does not want them to be obsessed with power but to "rejoice that [their] names are written in heaven" (10:20). The belief that the names of the righteous are recorded in a book in heaven, like a citizens' roll, is well documented in Jewish tradition and in the NT.[8] Spiritual pride is a temptation for those used mightily by God, and even Jesus' emissaries are not immune to it. Their salvation, not their victory over demons, should be the real reason for joy.

The vision that Jesus sees affirms the eschatological significance of the mission of the seventy-two. What does it mean for "Satan [to fall] from heaven like a flash of lightning" (10:18)? Satan is the ruler of all demons and a definable enemy (11:15; 10:19), not simply an amorphous force. The earthly conflict between Satan and his demons on one side, and Jesus and his emissaries on another, is an expression of the conflict between God and Satan in the supernatural sphere. Foundational to Jewish apocalyptic thought is God's final defeat of Satan.[9] In Jesus' vision, the eschatological demise of Satan is depicted as a cataclysmic fall, swift as a flash of lightning. While this cosmic scenario lies yet in the future, the eventuality of Satan's destruction has already been sealed when demons submit themselves to Jesus and his agents.[10] Even though Satan and his minions continue to wreak havoc (11:14; 22:3, 31), there is now a chink in their armor, and their end is inevitable.[11] At present, the authority that Jesus gives his missionaries to "tread on snakes and scorpions and over all the power of the enemy" empowers as well as protects them (10:19a). Snakes and scorpions represent everything evil and oppressive that Satan throws at Jesus and his disciples.[12] In anticipation of more vicious battles ahead, how comforting it is to hear Jesus say, "Nothing will hurt you" (10:19b). There will be casualties and even martyrdom, but with their names written in the book of life, these faithful disciples are assured of their eternal salvation.

3:6, 16; 4:10), cast out demons (Acts 16:18) and baptize (Acts 2:3; 8:16; 10:48; 19:15).

8. Isa 4:3; Dan 7:10; 12:1; 1QM XII, 2; 1 *En.* 47:3; 108:3; Phil 4:3; Rev 13:8; 17:8; 20:12; 21:27.

9. 1QM XVII, 5-8; 11QMelch II, 13–14; *T. Mos.* 10:1; *T. Dan* 5:10; *T. Jud.* 25:3; *T. Levi* 18:12; 1 *En.* 54:5–6; *Sib. Or.* 3:796–807.

10. 4:35, 41; 6:18; 8:2, 32–33; 9:42, 49.

11. Sousa 2013: 104–9.

12. See p. 166.

Without missing a beat, Jesus breaks into joyful speech that recapitulates the theme of reversal and makes known the unity of God the Father and Jesus the Son (10:21–22). Although the Holy Spirit's presence has not been explicitly mentioned since Jesus' baptism, temptation, and inaugural sermon in Nazareth (3:22; 4:1, 14, 18), it is understood that Jesus has been empowered by the Spirit in his teachings and healings. Just as it was at Jesus' baptism, the Father, the Son, and the Holy Spirit now appear again in the same co-text, underscoring the theological significance of this revelation.

First and foremost, Jesus acknowledges the sovereignty of God, the "Lord of heaven and earth." According to his gracious will, God reveals as well as conceals (10:21). Contrary to human expectation, God's revelation is awarded to and eagerly received by "infants," who in their profound neediness are open to instruction and grateful for God's beneficence. They stand in contrast to the "wise and intelligent," not because they are dull of mind, but because they are humble in status and self-perception.[13] Thus far in Luke's narrative, Mary the mother of Jesus, the shepherds in the field, the poor, the handicapped, the demon-possessed, the tax collectors and sinners, etc., characterize these "infants." As for those deemed "wise and intelligent" by human standards, God paradoxically withholds his mysteries from them. They are not lacking in mental faculty per se, but their hardness of heart prevents them from discerning the saving purposes of God. Found among them are the Pharisees and the scribes who know so much about the law yet fail to perceive the ways in which Jesus' teachings and healings reveal the heart of the matter.

What has God revealed and concealed? What are "these things" in verse 21 and "all things" in verse 22? The immediate context, in which Jesus interprets the missionaries' exorcisms as a proleptic fulfillment of Satan's defeat, suggests how the future reign of God has already made itself known in the presence and work of Jesus. This is a mystery not immediately apparent to all because it takes eyes and ears of faith to appreciate it. The messianic focus of Jesus' ministry lies not in the elimination of Rome, but in bringing people to physical, spiritual, and communal wholeness.

That Jesus is at the center of God's saving purposes has everything to do with his filial relationship with God. While the readers have been privy to Jesus' divine sonship from the beginning (1:31–35; 3:22; 9:35),

---

13. Chen 2006: 187–96.

most of the disciples of Jesus have not, except perhaps for Peter, James, and John who witnessed the transfiguration (9:28). Here Jesus emphasizes the mutual knowledge between him and his Father, making God's Son the most insightful and qualified communicator of God's character and ways.[14] Yet the true knowledge of God is given only to those worthy of receiving it, and God has given Jesus the authority to make that determination (10:22). It is therefore not insignificant that Jesus addresses God as Father in his prayer (10:21) and freely speaks of God as his Father (10:22; cf. 2:49; 22:29; 24:49). As a form of address, "Father" (*pater*) is the Greek equivalent of "Abba" in Aramaic (Mark 14:36), a term of filial intimacy used by young and adult children alike.[15] In the remainder of the narrative, Jesus will be shown to do the same in all his recorded prayers (11:2; 22:42; 23:34, 46), underscoring the importance of the theme of God's fatherhood and Jesus' divine sonship in Luke's theology.[16]

In case the disciples are still incognizant of their privileged position, Jesus gives them an encouragement as well as an exhortation: "Blessed are the eyes that see what you see!" (10:23). God's future has impinged upon the present, and the day of salvation has arrived. Even prophets and kings from past generations, faithful and important though they were, did not live to see and hear what the disciples now have access to because they are with Jesus. This privilege is also a responsibility, but Jesus' demand of discipleship is well worth the sacrifice.

Doing Mercy (10:25–37)

A Lawyer's Question (10:25–29)

Luke uses the terms "lawyer" (*nomikos*) and "scribe" (*grammateus*) interchangeably to denote a teacher of the Jewish law. Together with the Pharisees, the lawyers and the scribes have been scrutinizing Jesus on his adherence to the law and the oral traditions (5:21, 30; 6:7). On this occasion, a lawyer stands up and asks Jesus what one must do to inherit

---

14. Jesus' close relationship with God qualifies him to communicate God's heavenly secrets to those whom he chooses (Sousa 2013: 109–12). No seer or supernatural guide is needed for the recipient of the revelation, as is often found in Jewish apocalyptic writings.

15. Barr 1988: 28–47.

16. Chen 2006: 153–55.

eternal life (10:25; cf. 18:18). Although he assumes the posture of a student, his attitude is far from that of a sincere learner. The question has nothing to do with earning one's salvation by means of good works. The Jews look forward to eternal life as God's gift to the righteous, an inheritance reserved for his children. He is asking Jesus what it means to be righteous, but behind that seemingly innocuous question is a test to see if Jesus can come up with the correct—and acceptable—answer to be considered a bona fide teacher.

Not giving up any ground, Jesus answers with a question of his own: "What is written in the law? What do you read there?" (10:26). Put on the defense, the lawyer is forced to show his cards. In fact, he gives a perfectly commendable answer, citing the twin commandments of loving God and loving neighbor (Deut 6:5; Lev 19:18b). The two of them are not in disagreement in their reading of the law (10:28); their difference emerges in how the law is lived out in tangible action, as prompted by the lawyer's next question, "Who is my neighbor?" (10:29).

This second question presumes a connection between loving God and loving neighbor. In Lev 19, the justification of one's love of neighbor follows the command itself, "[for] I am the LORD" (19:18c). A person's horizontal relationship with other people grows out of and is indicative of his or her vertical relationship with God. The lawyer does not quibble about loving God, but the issue of loving one's neighbor is ambiguous. The definition of a neighbor presupposes the existence of a non-neighbor, since a boundary simultaneously excludes as well as includes.

The lawyer is keen on justifying himself (10:29). A clear statement of the qualification of neighbor obligates him to love only those who fall within the category. If he can love those deemed lovable, then his adherence to the law will remain exemplary. That said, the definition of neighbor is open for debate. Although the injunctions of Leviticus apply to fellow Israelites and aliens living among them (Lev 19:33–34), by the time of Jesus the term "neighbor" has become more narrowly defined. Gentiles and Samaritans are certainly not neighbors. Among the Jews, the religious elite will not accept as neighbors those who fail to keep the law as scrupulously as they do. The mentality to hate sinners is prevalent. "Place your bread on the grave of the righteous, but give none to sinners" (Tob 4:17). "Give to the devout, but do not help the sinner" (Sir 12:4–5). The lawyer has in mind a particular definition of a neighbor that concurs with his sense of self-righteousness. In response, Jesus tells a parable that turns his question on its head and gets at the crux of the matter.

A Good Samaritan (10:30–37)

In this day and age, we frequently come across entities such as the Good Samaritan Hospital, Church of the Good Samaritan, the Good Samaritan Food Bank, and other organizations with "Good Samaritan" in their names that offer shelter, legal advocacy, disaster relief, and various forms of community service. The phrase has become synonymous with compassion and aid to the poor. But this was not so at the time of Jesus, when "good Samaritan" was a contradiction in terms that spelled disdain rather than appreciation.

The scene takes place on the road that leads from Jerusalem to Jericho. Along its seventeen-mile stretch the elevation drops 3,500 feet, from Jerusalem at 2,700 feet above sea level to Jericho at 820 feet below sea level. Desolate and rocky, the road is known to be treacherous and frequented by rogues and bandits hiding in the rugged terrain.[17] Tragedy strikes as soon as the characters are introduced. Some robbers attack a hapless traveler, take all his possessions, beat him to a pulp, and leave him by the roadside naked and half-dead.

How dead is half-dead? The Greek word *hēmithanē* ("half-dead") occurs only here in the Bible, so the reader is left to imagine the victim's condition. Elsewhere, the verb can imply that a person "looks dead." Is this victim unconscious, so he looks dead even though he is still breathing? Is he near death so that without help he will die fairly soon? Will those who pass by respond differently depending on whether the man is dead or alive? Stripped of his clothes, the man's ethnicity and social status are unidentifiable.[18] He is a "generic" victim, at the mercy of anyone who is willing to stop, whether to help or to bury him.

A glimmer of hope arises with the arrival of a priest, headed "down the same road" in the same direction (10:31). Perhaps he has just completed his duties in Jerusalem and is on his way home.[19] The description of the priest's response is minimalist. Not only does he choose not to stop, he walks as far away from the half-dead man as possible by crossing to the other side of the road and promptly leaves the scene. Next comes a Levite.[20] He, too, sees the victim, gives him a wide berth, and continues

---

17. Hultgren 2000: 95–96.
18. We assume the victim is Jewish, since Luke's normal practice is to identify a gentile, e.g., Luke 17:16; Acts 8:17; 16:1.
19. Nolland 1993a: 593.
20. Levites are assistants to the priests at the temple (Numbers 3–4).

on his way (10:32). The brevity with which the inaction of the priest and the Levite is depicted mirrors the little attention they pay to the need that confronts them.

Since the priest and the Levite are temple personnel, there has been much speculation on the reason for their inaction.[21] Several legal considerations come into play. First, there is the risk of corpse impurity. A Jew becomes ceremonially unclean for seven days for touching a dead body (Num 19:11–13; Ezek 44:25–27). The man on the ground may have already died or may die in the process of being helped. Taking too close a look, even without touching the body, is risky. The shadow of a corpse, and even the air above it, are also unclean. Second, a Jew is obligated to bury a fellow Jew, even a stranger, as in a neglected corpse, but there is no obligation toward a gentile.[22] Third, priests are held to a higher standard because of their sacred office and are strictly prohibited to touch a dead body (Lev 21:1–15; 22:1–9). Fourth, the law may be overridden in an emergency to save a life (*m. Yoma* 8:6; *b. Meg.* 3b). All these legal considerations compete for priority in a complex situation in which it is difficult to decide, from a distance, whether the victim is alive or dead, a Jew or a gentile. On top of all this, there is the concern for personal safety. What if the robbers are lying in wait to ambush the rescuer?

Given the requirements of the law, we can better appreciate the dilemma faced by the priest and the Levite. The point is not to make them appear less callous. Rather, the discernment of what it truly means to love God and neighbor is put to the test. Is showing compassion more important than ritual purity, when acting on one might transgress the other? No decent priest or Levite would voluntarily put himself in danger of contracting uncleanness. If the priest and the Levite made their decision in order to avoid defilement, their motivation would be one of self-preservation. Had they taken a risk and reached out to the victim, they would have cared more about the other person's wellbeing than their own. This is analogous to Jesus' healing on the Sabbath, when the law to restore life trumps the law to observe the Sabbath. Jesus' story, however, does not show the priest or the Levite as laboring over the decision. They see the victim and crosses over to the other side sans hesitation. Especially when they are going from Jerusalem to Jericho, and not the other way around, they are not even headed for service at the temple! The

---

21. See especially Bauckham 1998: 475–89. Also Marshall 1978: 448; Hultgren 2000: 97; Snodgrass 2008: 355; Bailey 2008: 293.

22. Evans 2012: 117–20.

focus of the parable remains on the contrast between the complacency of the priest and the Levite on the one hand, and the initiative of the Samaritan on the other. One word sets the latter apart from the former: *esplanchnisthē* ("he was moved with compassion," 10:33). While Jesus' audience may be surprised by the behavior of the priest and the Levite, it is the hero of the story that raises everyone's eyebrows and drives home the point.

The rule of three in jokes stipulates that the third character carries the punch line. This parable is similar in structure, as the audience awaits the third person to come along who will bring the story to a redemptive denouement. The expected ordering starts with the priests, the Levites, and then all Israel (Ezra 10:5; Neh 11:3, 20). To have a good Jewish commoner outperform two temple officers would make a delightful story, for even though the religious leaders were respected, the gap in wealth, privilege, and status between them and the populace was sometimes a source of envy and resentment.[23]

Much to the chagrin of Jesus' audience, next comes a Samaritan (10:33). Imagine the side glances rippling through the audience: "What good can a Samaritan do? Do we need more defilement in this scenario?" The hatred of Jews for Samaritans is proverbial.[24] Relevant to the scruples of purity in this story is the Samaritan's intrinsic uncleanness in the eyes of the Jews (*m. Nid.* 4:1; *m. Šeb.* 8:10). From the top of religious respectability, Jesus has taken the story down to the bottom of racial disrespectability, heightening the narrative tension.

The priest and the Levite each get one line of description (10:31–32), but Luke allots considerably more space to the Samaritan, whose response, action, and plan are described in great detail (10:33–37). In legal terms, the Samaritan is subject to the same risks of corpse impurity as the priest and the Levite and is challenged by the same stipulations to love God and neighbor. He may as easily be robbed while lending aid. But his compassion stands out. The same verb, *esplanchnisthē*, is used by Luke

---

23. Gourgues 1998: 710–12.

24. Snodgrass 2008: 346–47. See p. 139. The skirmishes range from murders and retaliations to religious disagreements and desecrating of holy places. Other Jewish writings also speak disparagingly of Samaritans, e.g., *T. Levi* 7:2: "Shechem shall be called 'city of the senseless,' because as one might scoff at a fool, so we scoffed at them." Samaritans were treated as gentiles even though they were partly Jewish. The Jerusalem temple will not accept their temple tax (*m. Šeqal.* 1:5); a Jew can kill a Samaritan with impunity (*b. Sanh.* 57a), and a Jew can charge a Samaritan interest on a loan (*y. 'Abod. Zar.* 5:4).

to denote Jesus' compassion for the widow at Nain who is on her way to bury her son (7:13), and the compassion of the father for his prodigal son (15:20). God's pity shines through the Samaritan.

The Samaritan treats the injured man with whatever he has on him—time, energy, and resources (10:34–35). As it turns out, the man is still alive! The fear of defilement on the part of the priest and the Levite would have cost the man his life had the Samaritan not shown up. Using the supplies normally carried by a traveler, the Samaritan disinfects the man's wound with the wine and eases his pain with the oil.[25] He bandages him up, puts him on his animal, and brings him to an inn to be cared for. The danger for the Samaritan extends from the Jericho road to the inn in a Jewish town. A wounded Jew in the care of a Samaritan would raise suspicion, and an innkeeper might not want to take the man in, or he might charge extra to do so. By leaving two denarii, a sum sufficient to cover room and board for a week or two,[26] and promising further reimbursement, the Samaritan is committing himself financially far beyond the call of duty. From the human point of view, the Samaritan has nothing to gain and everything to lose by tending to a half-dead Jewish man.

No sensible person, not even the lawyer who is bent on self-justification, can deny that the Samaritan's response to the crisis comports with the twin commandment of loving God and loving neighbor. So when Jesus changes the question from "Who is my neighbor?" (10:29) to "Which one of these three . . . was a neighbor to the man who fell into the hands of the robbers?" (10:36), there is only one fitting answer: "The one who did mercy" (10:37a). Whether the lawyer is too proud or too prejudiced to name the Samaritan is secondary. What is primary is Jesus' reframing of the issue of neighborliness from object to subject. The commandment to love one's neighbor is not contingent upon the other party's ceremonial purity, worthiness, status, heritage, or religion, but upon the disposition of the heart of the one who claims to love God and thereby serves as a neighbor to all without prescribed boundaries. If a follower of Jesus commits to being a neighbor, then all people, including enemies, are neighbors (6:27–35). In this manner, the children of God take after their heavenly Father by extending mercy and compassion to others.

With the injunction, "Go and do likewise" (10:37b), the parable ends with an implied cliffhanger. Will the lawyer embrace Jesus' vision of

---

25. Hultgren 2000: 99.
26. Snodgrass 2008: 347; Bailey 2008: 295.

neighborliness? Throughout this pericope, doing is emphasized (10:25, 28, 37), because genuine faith is expressed in concrete action, not the mere hearing of the good news (6:46–49; 8:21). The principle is easy to grasp but hard to implement. The hospitals, food banks, and churches that bear the "Good Samaritan" label must uphold the integrity of their name. For the rest of us, the opportunity to be a neighbor presents itself daily, although not always in the form of a dying man by the side of the road. Will we do mercy?[27]

Martha and Mary (10:38–42)

Coming on the heels of the parable of the good Samaritan in which "doing" is emphasized (10:25, 28, 37), the story of Mary and Martha balances the perspective by focusing on the importance of "hearing." Hearing and doing are integral to the life of discipleship (8:21), like two sides of the same coin. Readers of this story often elevate Mary and denigrate Martha. The story has been further extrapolated to pit justification by faith against justification by works, contemplative spirituality against action-oriented spirituality, life in eternity against life in this world, and even Christianity against Judaism or Protestantism against Catholicism.[28] The point is not to choose one at the expense of the other, not to only be Mary and never be Martha, but to recognize that there is a place and time to be both in the authentic expression of one's faith.[29]

Martha is head of this household, since she welcomes Jesus to her home (10:38).[30] In a world where hospitality was highly valued and scripted, Martha is in line with cultural expectations, busying herself with the needs of her guest. We are not told what she is preoccupied with, or if Jesus' disciples are present, hence increasing the size of the party to serve. Imagine Martha coming home from the market, tidying the house, putting out water for cleansing, setting the table, preparing the meal, doing all that is necessary to offer her best form of hospitality to Jesus, while

---

27. Jesus' ethic always moves from theology to concrete action signified by compassion and solidarity with the suffering. Strahan (2016: 82) calls this a "hermeneutic of action."

28. Spencer 2012: 173–77.

29. Alexander 2004: 197–213.

30. They live in Bethany together with their brother Lazarus. All three are close friends of Jesus (John 11:1—12:8).

becoming increasingly frazzled, tired, and resentful of her younger sister Mary, who has not lifted a finger to help her.

Within a home, there are separate male and female spaces. Mary obviously belongs to the kitchen with Martha. To be sitting at the feet of Jesus is to take on the posture of a disciple, a role typically reserved for male students at that time (10:39). From Martha's standpoint, Mary is shirking her female responsibilities and transgressing the boundaries of social space for her gender. Armed with a sense of self-righteous indignation, she comes to Jesus with a complaint laden with "me" language (10:40). Venting her frustration, she charges Mary with leaving her to do all the work, accuses Jesus of not caring about this blatant inequity, and tells him to rectify the situation by ordering Mary back into the kitchen. The irony is that she is calling Jesus "Lord" while spewing her laundry list of demands. By now, Martha is furious with Mary and with Jesus. A joyous occasion is on the verge of turning into an emotional and relational disaster.

Even though Martha may come across as distracted, bossy, and passive aggressive, one cannot help but sympathize with her original intention. She simply wants to honor Jesus' presence to the best of her ability, which is a wonderful gesture of love. It would have been easy for Jesus to capitulate to Martha's agenda, take a pause in his teaching, and have Mary help her with the preparation. The conversation could surely continue over the meal and the conflict would have been forestalled. Yet Jesus' response takes even the reader by surprise.

Gently rebuking Martha, Jesus puts the situation in perspective. The tone of his double address, "Martha, Martha" (10:41a), is not one of ridicule but of tenderness, like a parent comforting a child throwing a tantrum. Instead of performance, Jesus redirects her attention to that of attitude. Martha's anxiety over many things of earthly value—food, chores, tasks, hospitality—is contrasted with Mary's focus on the one necessary thing that is of eternal value, which is to listen to the words of Jesus (10:39, 41–42). Mary's choice is deliberate because she recognizes the uniqueness of the occasion. She is not sitting at the feet of just any rabbi. Her intention is not to give Martha grief. But their guest is Jesus, the one who brings the good news of God's salvation. Hence Jesus commends her for having chosen "the better portion (*meris*)." *Meris* can mean a portion of food (Gen 43:34; Deut 18:8), playing on Martha's preoccupation with the meal, or it can refer to one's lot (Pss 16:5; 119:57). By commending Mary's choice, Jesus is inviting Martha to join her sister in taking hold of the inheritance that lasts into eternity.

Mary breaks convention to sit at the feet of Jesus and Martha follows convention to offer hospitality to Jesus. Both sisters honor Jesus. Between the two, Mary's choice demonstrates a single-minded focus that gets at the heart of what being with Jesus is about. Martha misses the point, ironically, not because of her rejection of Jesus, but because of her fervent desire to please Jesus in her own way.

In view of Jesus' consistent admonition to both hear his words and do them, Mary cannot sit and listen forever, no more than Martha can serve meals only and never sit down to listen. In the parable that precedes this story, the Samaritan's act of mercy on behalf of a wounded stranger presupposes his proper hearing of the word of God in the law. Here, Mary's careful listening to the word of Jesus obligates her to follow through with obedient action. While the priest, the Levite, and Martha are foils for the exemplars in these stories, they remind the readers that even those who strive to honor God are not immune to the trappings of earthly perspectives.

Luke 11

Teachings on Prayer (11:1–13)

Luke depicts Jesus as a man of prayer, signifying a close communion between the Son and the Father, and presenting a model for Jesus' followers to emulate.[1] In response to his disciples' request, Jesus launches into a series of teachings about prayer that addresses the contents of prayer and especially the character of their heavenly Father.

The Lord's Prayer (11:1–4)

Like Mary (10:39), Jesus' disciples are portrayed as active learners who ask Jesus to teach them to pray as John did for his disciples (11:1). The Lukan version of the Lord's Prayer is shorter than its Matthean counterpart (Matt 6:9–13). Found in different settings in the life of Jesus in Matthew and Luke, this prayer could have been taught on multiple occasions. The variations may be attributed to transmission or usage by the early Christians.

Jesus' prayer displays affinities with other ancient Jewish prayers, such as the Amidah (the Eighteen Benedictions) and the Kaddish. In these prayers we find references to the sanctification of God's name and the establishment of God's kingdom, as well as petitions for provision and forgiveness. While the Lord's Prayer is more concise than typical Jewish prayers, the conceptual elements in it reflect Jewish piety and Israel's reverence for God as Father.

In all the other recorded prayers of Jesus in Luke, God is addressed as "Father" (11:2; cf. 10:21–22; 22:42; 23:34, 46). YHWH has always claimed to be Israel's Father, the one who brought Israel into being by election, who throughout the nation's history rescued, sustained, protected, and led his children. He disciplined them when they went astray and forgave them when they repented. There is ample evidence in the OT and

---

1. See 3:21; 5:16; 6:12; 9:18; 9:28–29; 10:21; 11:1; 22:42–45; 23:34, 46.

Second Temple Jewish literature that points to the authority, generosity, care, redemption, and mercy of Israel's Father for his children.[2]

The notion of divine fatherhood, however, was not unique to Judaism and Christianity. In Greco-Roman thought, the high god Zeus was hailed as Father,[3] and the honorific title, "Father of the Fatherland (*Pater Patriae*)," was given to the Roman emperor.[4] These accolades were connected with the tremendous power accorded to human fathers in ancient patriarchal societies. Under the Roman law of *patria potestas*, a father who was head of the household (*paterfamilias*) had unlimited authority over his children, even adult sons and daughters.[5] This background adds another dimension to thinking about YHWH as the Father of Jesus, Israel, and Jesus' followers, whose unchanging benevolence is contrasted with the fickleness evident in pagan gods, emperors, and human fathers of any stripe.

The opening petitions, "Hallowed be (*hagiasthētō*) your name," and "Your kingdom come" (11:2), are closely related. The sanctification of God's name involves the preservation of God's reputation and honor. The passive voice of *hagiasthētō* raises the question, "Who is sanctifying God's name?" According to Isaiah, Israel "will sanctify the Holy One of Jacob, and will stand in awe of the God of Israel" (Isa 29:23). The future tense means, at present, Israel fails to bring honor to God's name because of its rebelliousness. In Ezekiel, God said, "I will sanctify my great name, which has been profaned among the nations; . . . when through you I display my holiness before their eyes" (Ezek 36:23). God will cleanse his people, give them a new heart, and put his Spirit in them, so that they will obey him and live up to their status as God's children (Ezek 36:16-32). Only then can Israel vindicate the reputation of their Father. Putting these concepts together, God sanctifies his own name by enabling his people to sanctify his name. The initiative comes from God.

God's sanctification of his name is complemented by God's ushering in of his kingdom. As a metaphor, the kingdom of God represents the universal reign of God more so than a physical realm or territory (Ps 95:3; Isa 44:6; Zech 14:9). In spite of Rome's political authority, God's

---

2. E.g., Exod 4:22; Isa 63:16; 64:8; Jer 31:20; Hos 11:1-4; *Jub.* 2.19-20; *Pss. Sol.* 13.7-12; 18.1-4; 2 *Bar.* 13.9-10; see Chen 2006: 73-143.

3. E.g., Homer *Il.* 11.544; Homer *Od.* 24.351; Euripides *Herc. fur.* 339-47. See Chen 2006: 59-61.

4. Chen 2006: 34-59.

5. Ibid., 17-34.

sovereignty is by no means compromised. God alone determines when he will bring about the restoration of Israel (Acts 1:6–7). God's people are passive recipients and grateful participants of the kingdom of God. Although the hopes sounded in "Hallowed be your name" and "Your kingdom come" cast the spotlight on an eschatological reality, that future has already impinged upon the present in the person and work of Jesus, and in those whom Jesus has sent to proclaim the gospel (10:9; 11:20; 17:21).

The next three petitions express one's utter dependence on the Father's provision, mercy, and protection in this present life. The request, "Give us each day our daily (*epiousion*) bread" (11:3), has created some debate over the meaning of the Greek word *epiousion*. Is Jesus referring to "bread for the coming day," "bread for this present day," or "essential bread (bread for subsistence)"? Or is the bread to be understood figuratively, as in what it takes to feed one's spiritual life?[6] Without splitting hairs over etymology or over-spiritualizing a mundane need for survival, it is best to understand Jesus' petition as asking God to provide food every day for one's subsistence, as a good father would for his children. The confidence to pray in this manner is grounded in God's unbroken track record of feeding the Israelites in the wilderness (Exod 16:9–21), as well as in the disciples' experience when they were on their mission to preach the good news (9:3; 10:7; cf. 9:16–17; 12:22).

To the extent that God's children need bread for physical survival, they need forgiveness for spiritual survival. The next petition consists of a vertical and a horizontal dimension: "And forgive us our sins, for we ourselves forgive everyone indebted to us" (11:4a). In the parable of the two debtors (7:41–43), forgiveness of sins is likened to the cancellation of debt. This petition speaks against the vicious cycle of the patronage system that allows the powerful to keep exploiting the powerless by increasing the latter's indebtedness every time help is extended. Just as Jesus exhorts his hearers to be merciful as their Father is merciful (6:36), the disciples are to forgive others as God has forgiven them. It is not that God's love is conditional. Rather, this petition encourages a virtuous cycle that God initiates. Because God first forgives, Jesus' disciples are liberated from the burden of their own sins. In turn they are free to forgive others and, in doing so, secure the confidence that God will continue to be merciful to them. If one truly appreciates God's mercy and forgiveness, one will gladly extend the same to others.

6. Hultgren 1990: 41–54.

The final petition is a plea for divine protection. "Do not bring us into temptation/trial (*eis peirasmon*)" (11:4b). The Greek word *peirasmos* means "test" or "temptation." We find ourselves resisting the negative connotation of God as tempter (Jas 1:13–14), but God's testing of Israel is not new (Exod 16:4; 20:20; Deut 8:2; 33:8).[7] Even so, does it make sense to ask God not to put Jesus' disciples to the test at all, given that struggles in life are inevitable and often have the effect of spiritual strengthening? Jesus told his emissaries to expect rejection (9:5; 10:10–16), and he himself confronted Satan in the wilderness (4:1–13). This petition simply cannot mean exemption from all forms of *peirasmos* (cf. 22:40, 46). The phrase that follows the same petition in Matthew, which is missing in Luke, reads, "but rescue us from the evil one" (Matt 6:13b). The plea for deliverance *from evil* suggests that Jesus is referring to diabolic temptation rather than divine testing. Despite the awkward wording prompted by the verb "to lead," this petition is essentially an acknowledgment of human weakness.[8] God's children are entirely dependent on their Father's empowerment to resist the attacks of Satan and uphold the integrity of their faith.

The Lord's Prayer is ultimately not about the petitioner. Carrying a theocentric thrust, the prayer explains what it means to call God "Father." YHWH is the most powerful and authoritative Father there is, but because he is benevolent, wise, and trustworthy, his children can count on him for sustenance, mercy, and deliverance. Their confidence in God's goodness and responsiveness lies at the heart of the upcoming parable and the sayings that follow.

A Friend at Midnight (11:5–8)

The first three verses form one long question that Jesus poses to his disciples, who are to identify themselves with the man in the parable, caught in a bind between two friends. The setting is a small Galilean village, where families live in close proximity with one another. Because Jesus

---

7. In Jewish tradition, God tests his chosen people to see what they are made of and whether they remain faithful in the face of severe challenges (Knowles 2004: 192). See p. 57.

8. While Knowles (2004: 193) prefers to translate *peirasmos* as "testing" rather than "temptation," he still sees this petition as a "profession of humility and a confession of inability . . . to attain the standards required by the covenant relationship."

calls all three characters in the story "friend," to avoid confusion we will refer to them as the traveler, the host, and the householder.

A traveler shows up at the home of a man and his family. While traveling at night avoids the heat of the day, a midnight arrival, especially if unannounced, is unusual. Staying with friends is safer than going to an inn, lest one unsuspectingly find oneself in a brothel. Besides, if this village is not on a thoroughfare, the availability of an alternate lodging or a restaurant is unlikely. The host, nonetheless, attempts to meet the needs of his weary and hungry visitor. But he is short on bread, a key element in a Jewish meal. In a small village, families use a communal oven, so he has an idea who may have extra bread to spare. Going over to his friend's house, the host asks the householder to lend him three loaves so that he can extend proper hospitality to the traveler. To this reasonable, albeit ill-timed, request, the householder responds poorly from within. He is reluctant to wake his sleeping children by unlocking the door.[9] Inconvenience, however, is an insufficient excuse against the priorities of friendship and hospitality in that culture.

The answer to Jesus' question is a resounding, "No one!" The code of friendship obligates the householder to be eager to help regardless of whether he knows the traveler personally or not. In a small community, the responsibility of hospitality does not rest only on the host and his family, but on everybody. Because friendship and hospitality are tied to the social expectation of gaining honor and avoiding shame, the householder's response shames the host and the traveler, and subjects his entire village to the charge of inhospitality. Fortunately, the punch line presents a happy ending, that "[the householder] will get up and give [the host] whatever he needs" (11:8c). That much is clear. What is unclear is the rationale for his change of heart.

Two problems need attention to unravel this exegetical puzzle. The first revolves around the phrase, "even though he will not get up and give him anything *because he is his friend*" (11:8a). The first two personal pronouns refer to the householder not getting up to give the host anything, but whose friend is whom in the second half of the phrase? The general sense is that the obligation of friendship is not enough to motivate the householder into action, even though the host regards him as his friend

---

9. Ancient peasant homes were made up of one room that doubled as living quarters by day and sleeping quarters by night. Parents and children did not have separate bedrooms.

(11:5a). Perhaps the friendship is not reciprocated in this case, and the host is mistaken about his relationship with the householder.

The second problem is more vexing: "yet because of his *anaideia*" (11:8b) the householder will fulfill the request of the host. What is *anaideia* and *whose anaideia* is the determining impulse for the householder's final action? Many English versions translate *anaideia* as "persistence" (NRSV, NASB, NKJV), which is a mistranslation based on both the etymology and the usage of the Greek word at that time.[10] Others use the synonym "importunity" (KJV, RSV, ASV). The strongest argument against "persistence" or "importunity" is lexical. There is a myriad of primary Greek sources in which *anadeia* is used to mean "impudence, insolence, boldness, rudeness, or shamelessness."[11] The notion of persistence does not even belong to this semantic field. Neither is it evident in the parable itself, for the host asks only once and receives the householder's unpleasant response. The popularity of interpreting *anaideia* as "persistence" may stem from an unwarranted assumption that this parable is making an identical point as the one about a persistent widow in 18:1–8. Once that route is taken, it is easy to impose a superficial reading of Jesus' saying about asking, seeking, and knocking onto the host (11:9–10).

Having ascertained that *anaideia* refers to a negative quality, who owns that rudeness, boldness, or shamelessness? In English, describing shame is tricky. Shameless can be used to describe someone as having no sense of shame or doing something shameful. In our story, it is fitting to speak of the host's *anaideia*, for, after all, he wakes up not only a friend's entire household, but also other neighbors within earshot. The host is rude, bold, and shameful, even though he has no other alternative.[12] It is this commitment to hospitality that necessitates a bold request, causing the householder to give him the bread. Other exegetes argue for the householder's *anaideia* as the motivating factor by interpreting *anaideia* as "an avoidance of shame." The rationale is that the householder does

---

10. It is not until centuries later that *anaideia* can arguably be said to carry a sense of persistence (Nolland 1993a: 625).

11. Snodgrass (1997: 505–13) has conducted a thorough word study of *anaideia* in the works of a wide range of Greco-Roman writers and argues that boldness, rather than persistence, is what the parable teaches about prayer. Waetjen (2001: 703–21) draws from the writings of the early church fathers and concludes that even though the word *anaideia* carries a negative sense in general, it takes on a positive kind of shamelessness in Jesus' parable as an expression of the counterfictional attitudes taught by Jesus.

12. Snodgrass 2008: 443–45.

not want to be responsible for giving his entire village the undesirable reputation of inhospitality. He wants to avoid the shame that may come upon him the next day when others find out about his behavior. This translation, however, stretches the meaning of *anaideia* beyond the Greek usage of the word.[13] The challenge of this parable lies in the details and how the social values of friendship and hospitality interact with the overarching concerns of honor and shame. The big picture, nevertheless, is easy to grasp. In spite of his lame excuses, the householder finally acquiesces to the host's request and gives him what he needs.

How does this parable shed light on prayer, the thematic focus of the immediate co-text? The host may be compared to one asking God for help in prayer, sometimes in the most non-ideal situations. But we cannot simply equate God with the so-called friend whose attitude has much to be desired. Obviously God is not like the householder. The Jewish rhetorical technique of arguing from the lesser to the greater is in play here. If even a reluctant person who snubs the virtue of friendship ends up giving the host what he needs, how much more honorably and eagerly will God respond to his children's request? If the entire village is concerned with its collective honor, how much more will God, the one who sanctifies his own name (11:2), act in a way that upholds his divine honor?

While the disciples are encouraged to come to God in bold confidence for what they need, insolence is not a virtue. Neither is this story about cultivating a friendship with God. Over-allegorizing leads to strange interpretations, so the dramatic details of the plot should be kept within their narrative boundary. Prayer testifies to the trust that God's children have for their heavenly Father. Their boldness grows from their experience of his kindness and dependability. This positive cycle deepens with every petition offered and every prayer answered, to the extent that God reserves the best gift for his children, as promised in the next set of sayings.

Sayings on Prayer (11:9–13)

Jesus presents three images as metaphors for prayer: asking, seeking, and knocking (11:9–10). All three infinitives are in the present tense in the Greek, which carries the sense of a continuous action. One is to

---

13. Bailey 1983: 132.

keep on asking (*aiteite*), keep on seeking (*zēteite*), and keep on knocking (*krouete*). Behind each action is a need, be it the granting of a request, the finding of a lost item, or the opening of a closed door. The emphasis rests on the assurance of God's attention and active engagement, in contrast to the householder's opening line, "Do not bother me" (11:7). The continuous asking, seeking, and finding are not invitations to pester God by sheer repetition, but to exercise confidence in who God is.[14] Like a loving father, God desires that his children come to him honestly and freely with their needs.

Children can ask all they want, but fathers determine when and how to grant their requests. Jesus uses the experience of human fathers to illustrate God's fatherly benevolence. He puts forth two unlikely scenarios for consideration: Will any of his disciples give a snake to his son who asks for a fish, or a scorpion when he asks for an egg (11:11–12)? The answer is of course a resounding "No!" A snake may look like an eel, and a scorpion may ball up like an egg, but neither is a wholesome substitute for fish and egg, and either one may harm the child.[15] If no earthly father, imperfect as they are, would do such a thing, how much more oriented to the benefit of his children would God the Father be (11:13a). The descriptor "evil" (*ponēroi*) does not cast a moral judgment on earthly fathers, but acknowledges the degree of their imperfection when compared with the quintessential goodness of God.

What gift will the heavenly Father give to his children then? Nothing can surpass the gift of the Holy Spirit, the Spirit of God himself (11:13b). Up to this point, Jesus is said to be empowered by the Holy Spirit (3:16, 22; 4:1, 14, 18). Other faithful ones, such as John, Elizabeth, Zechariah, and Simeon, have also experienced the Spirit's filling, guidance, or inspiration (1:15, 35, 41, 67; 2:25–27). Jesus now promises an extended conferral of the Holy Spirit to all the true children of God. This promise of the Father is reiterated after the resurrection (24:49; Acts 1:4–5, 8), and will become a reality beginning with the outpouring of the Spirit at Pentecost (Acts 2:1–42).

---

14. Nolland 1993a: 630.
15. Ibid., 631.

Signs of Unbelief (11:14–32)

The promise of the gift of the Holy Spirit is followed by evidence of unbelief and increasing opposition. The vision of the kingdom of God is often interrupted by misguided expectations and forces of this world, thus Jesus' followers are exhorted to stay the course by listening to the word of Jesus and obeying it (11:28; cf. 8:21).

The Beelzebul Controversy (11:14–26)

Following another exorcism in which Jesus casts out a mute demon from a man, a controversy arises concerning the source of his power. Amazement deteriorates into skepticism when some accuse Jesus of being in league with the devil, "[casting] out demons by Beelzebul, the ruler of the demons" (11:14–15). "Beelzebul" may have been a Greek transliteration of two Hebrew words, combining the name "Baal" and a word that means "exalted abode."[16] Baal was the Canaanite fertility god that wayward Israel worshiped (Judg 2:13; 1 Kgs 16:31–32; 2 Kgs 21:1–3). The term "Beelzebul" is thus a fitting reference to Satan, an enemy of those who worship the true God. To accuse Jesus of casting out demons by the prince of demons is blasphemy, for the charge attributes the work of the Holy Spirit to Satan. Other people demand that Jesus proves his divine agency with a sign (11:16). Jesus will have more to say about signs (11:29–32), but first he dismantles the groundless assumption that he is in cahoots with the devil.

Jesus uses the image of a civil war within a kingdom (11:17–18). Exorcism is a declaration of war against Satan, forbidding his demons to wreak havoc in the lives of their victims. To claim that Satan authorizes Jesus to defy Satan is absurd. Why would Satan want to defeat himself? A divided kingdom is more vulnerable than one that is united, and Satan's domain is no different. While "house falls on house" may depict a war-torn scene of a deserted kingdom, it is even more tragic when a house falls on itself.[17] A civil war weakens the regime, not something Satan would find advantageous.

Going on the offensive, Jesus then challenges his detractors with a counter-question, "How do you explain the work of the Jewish exorcists?" (11:19; cf. 9:49; Acts 19:13–14). Jesus himself is a Jewish exorcist, not a

---

16. Bell 2013: 194.
17. Marshall 1978: 474; Nolland 1993a: 638.

pagan magician. If the Jews accuse him of joining forces with demons, for consistency's sake the same must be said of their own exorcists. If they believe that God endorses the work of the Jewish exorcists to bring release to tortured souls, they cannot attribute Jesus' exorcism to diabolic maneuvering. When Jesus and his emissaries expel demons from their hosts, they register the crumbling of Satan's forces (10:17–18). There is no civil war within the kingdom of Beelzebul. Rather, the real war being waged is between the kingdom of Satan and the kingdom of God.[18]

Jesus' interpretation of his own actions makes better sense: "If it is by the finger of God that I cast out the demons, then the kingdom of God has come upon you" (11:20). First, Jesus is under God's charge. During the time of Moses, Pharaoh's magicians failed to replicate Aaron's miracles, and in defeat they acknowledged that it was the finger of God that turned dust to gnats throughout the land of Egypt (Exod 8:19).[19] Whether the anthropomorphism employs the use of God's finger, hand,[20] or arm,[21] they all signify the authority and power of God. Second, Jesus' exorcisms prove that God's reign has begun. The hoped-for kingdom of God has arrived even if its full consummation lies yet in the future. It is not found in the destruction of Roman power, but in the restoration of individuals to physical, spiritual, and communal wholeness through Jesus' teachings, healings, and exorcisms. Third, Jesus likens Satan to a strong man who appears invincible until a stronger one—Jesus—overpowers him and strips him of his armor and possessions (11:21–22). This is a battle, and one must choose a side (11:23a; cf. 9:50). To enlist in Jesus' army means to gather around him (11:23b), an image for God's reconstitution of Israel on the day of salvation.[22]

Liberating as it is, exorcism alone does not guarantee an improved existence, especially when evil has yet to be completely eradicated. According to popular belief in antiquity, demons would roam about in

---

18. Green 1997: 455.

19. Just as God's finger helped Moses perform miracles to free Israel from Pharaoh's clutches, the same divine finger now enables Jesus, a prophet like Moses (cf. Deut 18:15, 18), to free those tormented by demons (Emmrich 2000: 272–73). The image of God's finger challenges Jesus' opponents to recognize God's work through his miracles, something that even Pharaoh's magicians would acknowledge (Perkins 2004: 261–62).

20. Luke 1:66; Exod 9:3, 15; Acts 4:28, 30; 11:21; 13:11.

21. Luke 1:51; Acts 13:17.

22. See Isa 43:5; Jer 31:8; Ezek 34:13. As a shepherd gathers his sheep, God will gather his people from wherever they have been scattered.

desolate places unless they could inhabit a human host.²³ Having been cast out, an unclean spirit searches for another resting place (cf. 8:32). Without success, it returns to its original "house" (the previous human host) and repossesses the person, bringing along seven other more powerful demons to terrorize the victim even more than before (11:24–26). Despite temporary spiritual improvement, as with a house "swept and put in order," the person is still vulnerable to demonic attack if nothing wholesome is put in the place of the departed demon. Positive examples are found in Mary Magdalene and her friends who support Jesus and his disciples with their own means (8:1–3), as well as in the man among the tombs of Gerasa who now bears witness to God's mighty work in him (8:39). These people were plagued by multiple unclean spirits, but their allegiance to the one stronger than the strong man prevents the demons from returning. Even as Jesus offers a new beginning to many former demoniacs by releasing them from the bondage, it is up to them to turn the new opportunity into a new life altogether.

The Sign of Jonah (11:27–32)

The theme of hearing and doing is sounded again as Jesus responds to a comment from a woman in the crowd. Perhaps out of sheer delight in Jesus' words, she exclaims how blessed Jesus' mother is to have a son like him (11:27). There is nothing wrong with her statement, as Elizabeth also blessed Mary and the child in her womb (1:42). Jesus modifies the woman's statement, however, to reiterate the necessity of both hearing God's word and obeying it (11:28; cf. 6:46–49; 8:21). This short exchange is transitional. It prepares the reader for Jesus' indictment of those who try to test him by demanding a sign instead of putting his teachings into action (11:16).²⁴

Jesus calls the unbelievers around him "an evil generation" (11:29a; cf. 7:31; 9:41), yet they are not outsiders but God's own people who display a hard-heartedness reminiscent of Israel's stubbornness in the past (Deut 1:35; 32:5; Ps 78:8). It is one thing for God to send Moses to the Israelites with a sign to legitimize his message (Exod 4:1–9), it is another

---

23. Green 1997: 459; Marshall 1978: 479; cf. Bar 4:35; Rev 18:2.

24. The Jesus-Moses parallel extends to the demand for a sign. Just as the contemporaries of Moses tested God by asking for a sign and refusing to believe even after signs had been given to them (Num 14:11), Jesus' opponents demand signs to justify Jesus' prophetic claims. See Emmrich 2000: 273–75.

for people to solicit a sign from heaven, without which they refuse to believe (11:29b; John 6:30). Jesus will not capitulate to manipulation. No sign will be given—except—for the sign of Jonah.

Jonah did not bring a sign; he was the sign for Nineveh (11:30a). Because the Ninevites heeded Jonah's warning, the city was spared from destruction (11:32b; Jonah 3:3–10). Jesus compares himself to Jonah as a sign to his generation, for he too is sent by God to call Israel to repentance (11:30b; cf. 2:35).[25] To criticize the unbelief of Israel vis-à-vis the receptivity of the gentiles, Jesus cites the Queen of the south, who recognized Solomon's wisdom and acknowledged Israel's God (11:31a; 1 Kgs 10:1–9; 2 Chr 9:1–8). She and the penitent Ninevites put recalcitrant Israel to shame. The people of Jesus' generation are even more culpable because they reject the one who is greater than Jonah and Solomon (11:31b, 32b). At the final judgment, even gentiles will condemn the unbelieving Jews. Faith in Jesus, not Abrahamic ancestry, is their only means of salvation (3:8).

Integrity and Hypocrisy (11:33–54)

In this section, Jesus addresses the importance of integrity. What is inside should match what is on the outside. When there is integrity, individuals and their neighbors benefit. Blinded by self-deception, hypocrites bring harm to everyone around them.

The Lamp of the Body (11:33–36)

In chapter 8, Jesus introduced the image of a lamp that ought to be put on a lampstand and not under a jar or a bed, in order for people to see the light (8:16). An almost identical picture is evoked here, though this time the lamp is not to be placed in a cellar (11:33). In the earlier passage, the light referred to the forthright nature of the gospel message (8:17), but here Jesus speaks of the human eye as a lamp of the body that evaluates the things hidden in the recesses of the heart (11:34a).

Modern science teaches that the eye receives light rays that bounce off an object in its field of vision. When light enters the eye, it passes through the cornea, the iris, and is focused by the lens to reach the photoreceptors of the retina. The signals from the receptors are then

---

25. Matthew explicitly links the three days Jonah spent in the fish (Jonah 1:17) with the three days Jesus will spend in the tomb (Matt 12:40), but not Luke.

transmitted by the optic nerve to the brain, which interprets the image that the eye sees. In this process, the eye is a recipient and processor of an external light source, not a generator of light.

The primitive understanding of human biology in antiquity, however, assumes that the eye generates the light that enables a person to see. The eye functions as a lamp inside the body, illumining everything both inside and outside a person. This understanding lends itself easily to a moral application. If the eye is healthy (*haplous*; "single" or "sound"), the person is honest and aboveboard.[26] He or she can see, because the whole body is full of light (11:34b). But if the eye is unhealthy (*ponēros*; "evil") and produces no light, not only is the person blind, the body is full of darkness as well (11:34c).[27]

Jesus is concerned with the condition inside a person, whether there is light or darkness. That which is originally light must not become darkness by the instigation of Satan (11:35–36). Spiritual and moral darkness is insidious because it is hidden, and inner darkness is analogous to corruption of every kind.[28] This is so with the people of the evil generation (*genea ponēra*) who demand a sign to authenticate Jesus' authority (11:16, 29). Because their eye is sick and evil (*ophthalmos ponēros*), their motives and actions are suspect. Conversely, Jesus' disciples must live in the light to remain beyond reproach.

Woes to Pharisees and Scribes (11:37–54)

Continuing with the theme of light and integrity, Jesus confronts his opponents at a meal in the house of a Pharisee (11:37). Throughout the narrative, the Pharisees have been judging Jesus' legal understanding, praxis, and piety (5:21; 6:2, 7; 14:3–4; 15:1–2). A particular point of contention revolves around the laws of ritual purity. Jesus is found wanting on this occasion when he fails to wash himself properly before the meal, which entails immersing his hands in water or pouring purified water over them (*m. Yad.* 1:1–5). Because impurity is transmitted through touch, unclean

---

26. *Haplous* and its cognates are used in Greek literature to denote actions "done with integrity, purity of motives, [and] no knowledge or intent of evil" (Garrett 1991: 96–100).

27. In ancient Jewish and Greco-Roman culture, people feared the evil eye, believing that it had the power to cast a curse with its stare. Amulets were worn to ward off its evil advances. See Fiensy 1999: 82–88.

28. Ps 82:5; Prov 2:12–15; Jer 23:11–12; Wis 17:2.

hands defile the vessels as well as the food and drink to be consumed. Ingesting unclean foods further contaminates the internal organs, affecting the person physically as well as the ability to pray and study the law.[29] Thus according to the Pharisees failing to wash is far more serious than dirty fingers. The host is appalled at Jesus' violation of something so basic in legal observance (11:38). In response, Jesus launches into a scathing critique against the attitudes and practices of the religious elite.

Jesus uses the cleaning practices of the Pharisees to evoke self-examination. In those days, the two main rabbinic schools advocated different ways of cleaning vessels. The school of Hillel mandated its students to clean the inside first, since impurities would contaminate from the inside to the outside. The school of Shammai only required the cleaning of the outside of a vessel.[30] Even if the Pharisees purified only the outside, they would still be deceiving themselves by Jesus' evaluation. Like their vessels and dishes that look outwardly clean, the Pharisees' clean hands cannot not mask the filth, greed, and wickedness within them (11:39). If they are so meticulous as to clean both the inside and the outside of inanimate objects, how much more should they attend to the condition of their inner disposition? One cannot fool God, the Creator of both the inside and the outside of all human beings (11:40).

To clean out the filth inside one's vessel, especially the sin of avarice, Jesus prescribes almsgiving, one of the three acts of Jewish piety along with prayer and fasting (11:31; cf. 12:33).[31] By giving to the poor, one identifies with the plight of the dispossessed and dismantles the divisiveness of social hierarchy. The Pharisees will realize a genuine inner purity that renders the cleaning of any vessel, dish, or hand superfluous.

Next Jesus pronounces three woes on the Pharisees. While woes are more like laments than curses, they issue serious warnings and indictments. The first woe targets the Pharisees' obsession with trivial displays of piety at the expense of things that truly matter (11:42). Taking the law of tithing[32] to its extreme, the Pharisees tithe "herbs of all kinds," things required by law, such as mint, and others, like rue, that are not.[33] The dis-

29. Garland 2011: 493. See pp. 72–73.
30. Keener 2014: 211.
31. Sir 7:10; 29:12; Tob 4:7–11; 12:8–9.
32. For the law on tithing, see Lev 27:30–33; Num 18:21–32; Deut 14:22–29. A ten percent tithe is stipulated on crops, oil, wine, and animals for the upkeep of the temple and the support of temple personnel and their families (See Bock 1996: 1116).
33. Rue is not tithed (*m. Šeb.* 9:1).

cipline of tithing is not denounced, but neither should it be used as an excuse to neglect the greater commands to love God and do justice (Mic 6:8).

In the second woe, Jesus charges the Pharisees with an inflated sense of self-importance (11:43; cf. 20:46). In a society where amassing honor and clamoring for high status motivate all social discourse, to love the seat of honor in the synagogues and to be lauded with elaborate greetings in the marketplace are not regarded as negative by Jesus' contemporaries. After all, the Pharisees consider themselves as embodying a superior form of piety and praxis, setting an example for the common people of what devotion to the law ought to look like. From their perspective, they deserve the highest esteem in the public sphere. Not only does Jesus' pronouncement point out the self-centeredness of the Pharisees, it also challenges the entrenched social dynamic of seeking honor that perpetuates classism and self-promotion.[34]

The third woe deals with Pharisaic hypocrisy that brings harm to the unsuspecting (11:44). Corpse impurity extends to graves and tombs (Lev 21:1-3; Num 19:11-22). Since this is a serious defilement, tombs are whitewashed so that passers-by will avoid them. Otherwise, people may walk over an unmarked grave and contract uncleanness through no fault of their own. Jesus likens the Pharisees to these hidden hazards, though their contaminants are far worse than seven days of defilement. People look up to the Pharisees because of their meticulous adherence to the law, but they are ignorant of the deadly filth within—greed, wickedness, neglect of justice, and failure to love God (11:39, 42). Ironically, in the name of an uncompromising commitment to pietistic purity, the Pharisees are actually transmitting spiritual uncleanness to their disciples.[35]

One of the lawyers, responding with what he may think of as "righteous indignation," complains that he and the scribes have been implicated by Jesus' indictment against the Pharisees (11:45). His protest invites three more woes from Jesus, directed at him and his colleagues for abusing their privileged position and doing more harm than good.

The first woe charges the lawyers with imposing unreasonable legal obligations on people but offering no help to ease the burden (11:46). Since most people are illiterate and cannot study the minutiae of the law, these lawyers wield a lot of power as interpreters of God's commandments.

---

34. See p. 136.
35. Nolland 1993a: 666; Marshall 1978: 499.

Jesus argues that there are ways to alleviate the tedium of these observances. Yet instead of giving people relief or extending compassion when they fail to keep the law, the lawyers pile requirement upon requirement on them like taskmasters. Exploiting their authority, they have turned obedience into obligation and commitment into coercion.

In the next woe, Jesus points out the culpability of the lawyers in their treatment of God's messengers (11:47–48). Unlike the Pharisees, who are laypeople, these lawyers are associated with the temple and represent the ruling class of Israel. Going back many generations, Israel's leaders rejected God's prophets and killed many of them.[36] The lawyers, too, refuse to listen to John and Jesus, the prophets of their own time. John has already died; and Jesus they will kill.[37] It is bad enough for the leaders of the people to perpetuate the generational sin of rejecting God's prophets, but it is doubly hypocritical when they build tombs to memorialize the very prophets murdered by their ancestors.[38] It is as though they were killing those ancient prophets all over again by their feigned tribute. Like their ancestors, the lawyers of Jesus' generation are as bloodthirsty as ever. Invoking the authority of divine Wisdom, Jesus finds them guilty of the blood of God's messengers, from Abel to Zechariah (11:49–51). Abel was the first man to be murdered because he acted righteously before God (Gen 4:1–12; Heb 11:4). The martyrdom of Zechariah,[39] the son of Jehoiada the priest, was the last one recorded in the Hebrew Scriptures, where he was stoned to death in the temple court (2 Chr 24:20–22).[40] Between the deaths of Abel and Zechariah, Jesus covers all the prophets that God has ever sent to Israel.

In the final woe, Jesus accuses the lawyers of obstructing the way to knowing God (11:52). The knowledge of God, embodied in the law, is like a house with a locked door. Because people need experts to explain God's commandments to them, the lawyers are like doorkeepers,

36. Neh 9:26; 1 Kgs 19:10; Jer 2:30; 26:20–24.

37. 9:22; 19:47; 22:2, 66; 23:10.

38. Green 1997: 474; Keener 2014: 211.

39. In the parallel passage in Matthew, Zechariah the prophet is referred to as the son of Barachiah (Matt 23:35; Zech 1:1). We are unable to verify from Jewish sources that Zechariah the son of Barachiah was murdered, although Zechariah the son of Jehoiada was stoned to death under the order of King Joash (2 Chr 24:20–21). See Green 1997: 475n82 and Nolland 1993a: 668–69.

40. We are unable to confirm from extant Jewish writings that either Zechariah, whether the son of Barachiah or the son of Jehoiada, perished between the sanctuary and the altar.

giving access to knowing God's character, deeds, and expectations. Yet by their rejection of Jesus, the lawyers strip themselves of the opportunity to know God. Furthermore, their criticism of Jesus becomes an obstacle for those who are seeking after God. It is ironic that these experts, who think of themselves as guides to the law, are in reality unenlightened impediments.

Nothing that Jesus has said endears him to the Pharisees and the scribes, yet everything is on point and their hypocrisy is unmasked. Jesus' scathing remarks have also shamed his enemies, hence their hostility and indignation. By this point of the narrative, Jesus is headed for Jerusalem and the stakes are high. His enemies are on the offensive, waiting for an opportunity to incriminate him with his own words (11:53–54; cf. 20:20, 26). Every question is a trap, and every encounter a test. The vicious cycle of unbelief will spiral down to the killing of God's final prophet.

Luke 12

Facing Persecution (12:1-12)

The hostility of the Pharisees and the scribes toward Jesus has escalated in the wake of his scathing condemnation of their self-serving attitudes cloaked in religious piety and authority (11:39-54). Meanwhile, the crowds continue to flock to Jesus in droves (12:1a; cf. 11:29). Luke's description of people trampling on one another is metaphorical rather than literal. The larger the crowd, the more difficult it is to distinguish between committed followers and casual onlookers. Nevertheless, the formation of Jesus' disciples must continue as the journey to Jerusalem presses on with a heightened sense of tension and urgency.

Because the Pharisees are generally respected by the people who see their outward piety but not their inner disposition, Jesus' disciples should be suspicious of, not enamored by, their lavish display of religiosity. Jesus calls their hypocrisy "the leaven of the Pharisees" (12:1b). Yeast is a type of leaven, a raising agent that causes dough to rise during fermentation. Before the days of dry yeast that can be activated with warm water and sugar, a piece of dough would be broken off to serve as the starter dough for the next batch. When the old and the new batches of dough were kneaded together, the yeast would work its way into the combined dough so that fermentation could continue. The entire starter dough was called leaven, though the term later became synonymous with yeast, the raising agent within the dough itself. Leaven can go bad and ruin a dough as easily as it can cause it to rise. As such, it is a vivid image for something invisible but highly influential.[1] The negative influences of the Pharisees, like spoiled leaven, can misguide the gullible without their being aware of it.[2] Whatever secret motives they conceal now will come to light at the final judgment (12:2). The disciples must not fall into the same pattern

---

1. Nolland 1993a: 677.
2. Garland 2011: 503. Paul also uses the image negatively: "the leaven of malice and evil" (1 Cor 5:8).

of hypocrisy and self-deception. Anything said in the dark and behind closed doors will be subject to exposure one day (12:3).

The opponents of Jesus will sooner or later come after those who pledge their loyalty to him. Although the thought of persecution seems ominous, Jesus puts the disciples' fear in proper perspective. The most an enemy can do is to kill them, but the enemy has no power over their eternal destiny (12:4). The ability to terminate human life, while frightening, is nothing compared to God's authority over salvation and judgment (12:5). The Greek word, *gehenna*, translated as "hell," refers to the Valley of Hinnom, a site near Jerusalem where child sacrifice was once practiced (Jer 7:31–32). It was later turned into a rubbish dump where trash was burned continuously.[3] In Jewish literature, *gehenna* is used as a metaphor for God's eschatological judgment, where the wicked will burn in unquenchable fire (e.g., 1 *En.* 54:6). Surely this eternal death is infinitely more dreadful than martyrdom. Standing before their enemies, Jesus' disciples must not succumb to intimidation and renounce their allegiance to Jesus to save their own skin. So what if they manage to have their lives temporarily spared? If they deny Jesus in front of their persecutors in this life, the Son of Man will not acknowledge them before the heavenly court of angels at the final judgment (12:8–9). The disciples must not exchange their permanent salvation for a temporary reprieve. The promise of eternal life will vindicate a martyr's death, but a coward's escape will be met by the fiery furnace of hell.

One side of fear stems from the power differential between the disciples and the ultimate Judge of all people, but another side of fear is grounded in reverence and relationship. The fear of God is qualitatively different from the terror and panic one experiences before a menacing foe. Using two beautiful illustrations, Jesus reminds his disciples of God's presence in all circumstances, especially in times of persecution. If God remembers every single sparrow, which is but a common little bird worth a negligible one-eighth of a denarius,[4] how much more will he be mindful of his child, for whom there is no price tag (12:6; cf. 12:24)? God's attentiveness is comprehensive, extending to the minutest detail, even the number of hairs on the disciples' heads (12:7). Nothing escapes God's purview, which brings great comfort in persecution and life-threatening

---

3. Green 1997: 482; Nolland 1993a: 676; Carroll 2012: 264.

4. An *assarion* is the smallest denomination of a Roman copper coin, worth a tenth of a drachma or one sixteenth of a denarius. A laborer could earn a denarius in a day.

danger. Because God is benevolent, divine preservation is guaranteed, and the disciples need not be intimidated by their enemies.

It is in this context of trust and faithfulness in the face of persecution that Jesus' saying on the unforgivable sin is to be understood (12:10). Blasphemy generally refers to sacrilegious speech or action against that which is holy. Jesus makes a distinction between "[speaking] a word against the Son of Man," which is forgivable, and "[blaspheming] against the Holy Spirit," which is not. Among those who have seen Jesus and heard his preaching of the good news, many remain hardened with unbelief. They challenge him, jeer at him, and accuse him of casting out demons by the power of Beelzebul (11:15–16; 20:2; 23:35). Should these people have a change of heart, the words spoken against the Son of Man would be forgiven (cf. Acts 3:14–15, 17–19). Strictly speaking, only those who have already become believers can blaspheme against the Holy Spirit, since the Spirit is a gift from God only to those who belong to him (11:13; 24:49). Blasphemy against the Holy Spirit is therefore tantamount to apostasy, when a believer buckles under pressure and denounces his or her allegiance to Jesus. The apostate repudiates the power of the Holy Spirit in the life of the believer, as though one had never been a believer. Lapses of judgment in moments of spiritual weakness may be forgiven, but not a persistent hardening of heart so that one's faith deteriorates from belief to unbelief (cf. Heb 10:26–31, 35–39). The sin of apostasy will not be forgiven, making a disciple's commitment to Jesus an undertaking with life-and-death ramifications.[5]

The warning against apostasy is immediately followed by the promise of divine help, so that Jesus' disciples are not left to their own devices to combat the hostile forces of unbelief. Even if they are dragged before the powers that be, the Holy Spirit will give them the appropriate words for their defense (12:11–12). In Acts, many of the apostles are shown to face such situations,[6] and their boldness in bearing witness surprises even the authorities (Acts 4:13). Only trust, not compromise, will help Jesus' disciples weather the storm.

---

5. Nolland 1993a: 679; Green 1997: 484.

6. Acts 4:1–12 (Peter); Acts 6:8—7:60 (Stephen); Acts 13:13–52 and 21:27—24:22 (Paul).

Wealth and Worries (12:13–34)

For people living at or below subsistence level, survival is a constant source of anxiety. Subscribing to the principle of limited goods, they assume that one's gain is another's loss. Avarice and envy rear their ugly heads in an attitude of scarcity, that there is never enough to go around. In God's economy, this competitive mindset should not characterize Jesus' disciples, because their divine benefactor never runs out of resources. He who notices even worthless sparrows will take heed of their situation (12:6–7). Here Jesus expounds on the danger of greed and the futility of anxious striving. Either tendency breeds a selfish preoccupation that neither honors God nor allows one to freely participate in the program of life laid out by Jesus. While money is neutral in and of itself, its use is not. A person's view of wealth is a barometer of a believer's understanding of, relationship with, and trust in God, even though it does not say everything there is to say about his or her spiritual and moral conditions.

A Rich Fool (12:13–21)

The telling of the parable of the rich fool is provoked by a man who asks Jesus to adjudicate between him and his brother on a dispute over inheritance (12:13). Not knowing the exact nature of the disagreement, we surmise that the two brothers have jointly received some inheritance. According to Jewish law, the firstborn son receives a double portion and has the right to determine when the inheritance is to be divided (Deut 21:1–17).[7] Since a larger plot of land has the potential for a greater yield, one can imagine the older brother's reluctance to subdivide it. This man, presumably the younger brother, is eager to claim his share and is frustrated with his older brother's refusal to give it to him. It is not uncommon in small villages to ask a respected teacher to settle arguments. The man's tone of voice is telling; he simply wants Jesus to endorse his agenda and order his brother to release his share of the inheritance (12:13; cf. 10:40). We are not privy to the family dynamics or any ulterior motive on the part of either brother, but we trust Jesus' diagnosis of the situation. Refusing to be manipulated into playing judge (12:14), Jesus identifies greed as the man's underlying motivation and promptly turns that into a teaching moment for the crowd (12:15a).

---

7. Bailey 2008: 300.

In the ancient Greco-Roman and Jewish worlds, greed was condemned as the epitome of human depravity and the root of evil by philosophers, moralists, and sages alike.[8] Jesus' view is similar. He speaks of the totality of earthly existence, its quality, and its meaning. The guiding principle is that "life does not consist of the abundance of possessions" (12:15b). As we shall see, this is what the rich man in the parable fails to recognize. Even with a stockpile of goods to last a lifetime of merriment, life in its fullness still eludes him.

The parable begins with a rich man who has become even richer, thanks to a bumper crop (12:16). His position is enviable to Jesus' audience, most of whom are poor peasants who would love to have even a fraction of his good fortune. Is the abundant harvest a reward from God? No matter what, the windfall is not of the rich man's doing. He is confronted with the happy problem of dealing with the surplus. Listening in on his soliloquy, the inner disposition of the man's heart is exposed.[9] Missing from his self-talk is any expression of gratitude to God, consultation with family or neighbor, or concern for the poor. His use of the first person possessive pronoun is pervasive—my crops, my barns, my grain, my goods, my soul—claiming everything to be his alone. Running out of space in his barn, he opts to build bigger barns to hoard everything instead of sharing his resources with others (12:17–18). His is a lonely world of one.

Some interpreters try to find excuses for the rich man while others want to turn him into a villain. Perhaps the rich man is simply displaying good financial acumen, increasing his storage capacity so the grain will not go to waste. What if withholding the excess puts him in the position of price gouging when supply dips? Where is the line between prudence in agribusiness and moral indiscretion in price fixing?[10] Although these are interesting questions, Jesus' overarching point has to do with the rich man's view of life, not his business savvy (12:18).[11] He assumes that the

---

8. Job 20:19–20; Prov 1:19; 15:27; Sir 14:9; Eph 5:3; Col 3:5; Dio Chrysostom *Or.* 4.83–96; 17.1–11; 67.7.

9. Soliloquy or interior monologue is a rhetorical feature that reveals the true intentions of a character, whether fictive or real. E.g., the scribes and the Pharisees (5:21–22); Simon (7:39); the disciples (9:46–47); the unfaithful servant (12:45); the prodigal son (15:17–19), the shrewd manager (16:3–4), the unjust judge (18:4–5), and the owner of the vineyard (20:13). See Sellew 1992: 239–53 and Dinkler 2015: 380–84.

10. Green 1997: 489–91; Garland 2011: 514–15.

11. Snodgrass (2008: 397–98) and Hultgren (2000: 108) remind the reader of what the text does not say, so that extrapolations, however historically informed and

stockpile is the answer to a secure future of relaxation and bliss (12:19). All good gifts come from God (Eccl 2:24; 3:13), but the idiom, "eat, drink, and be merry," signifies short-sightedness and self-satisfaction (cf. Isa 22:13; Sir 11:19). To the rich man, an abundance of possessions equals a fulfilling life—for himself. Even though he appears to be minding his own business and not causing anyone overt harm, his inaction toward the poor makes him culpable of injustice and impiety. Lacking self-awareness and blinded by greed, the rich man is in for a rude awakening.

God's indictment is sharp: "You fool (*aphrōn*)![12] This very night they are demanding your soul from you![13] And the things you have prepared, whose will they be?" (12:20). Jewish wisdom speaks of death as "returning the souls that were borrowed" (Wis 15:8). The rich man is a fool but not because he is unintelligent; he knows to increase the storage capacity at his farm and plan for his future. But the future can change at the blink of an eye even for the most prepared (Seneca *Ep.* 104.4–5). His folly lies in the failure to acknowledge God (Ps 14:1; Jer 4:22). God owns everything and God has prerogative over life and death. A godless reliance on material wealth as the determinant of a fulfilling life is both idolatrous and delusional. All the rich man's scheming comes to naught in the ephemerality of his fleeting earthly existence.

Given the fragility of life and the uncertainty of the future, Jesus steers his audience from things of this earth to things of God. Sharing wealth makes one "rich toward God" (12:21). Almsgiving is a mark of Jewish piety, a note repeatedly sounded in Luke (11:41; 12:33; 16:19–31).[14] Rather than storing up treasure for oneself, Jesus' counsel resonates with that of Ben Sira, a Jewish sage: "Store up almsgiving in your treasury, and it will rescue you from every disaster" (Sir 29:12).

The rich fool may not need to hoard his surplus since he already has plenty, but what about those with nothing to spare or to share, like the poor peasants in the crowd? For them Jesus has a word of encouragement.

---

probable, cannot carry the weight of the interpretation.

12. In Greek the vocative for "fool" is *aphrōn*, which sounds like *euphrōn*, a person who is merry. The joke is on the merry fool who will die before he gets to enjoy the sweet life he has paved for himself.

13. This is a literal rendering of the Greek to reflect the present tense and active voice of the verb *apaitousin*. The third person plural subject "they" is a circumlocution for God (or the angels of death) calling in the soul that is on loan to the rich man. Many English versions use a divine passive instead, e.g., "This very night your life is being demanded of you" (NRSV; cf. NIV, NASB, NKJV).

14. See also Tob 4:8–11; 12:8–9; Sir 3:30; 17:22; 40:17, 24.

Building on the assurance that in God's eyes they are "of more value than many sparrows" (12:7), he urges them to let go of anxious striving and cultivate trusting dependence on their Father in heaven.

Freedom from Anxiety (12:22–34)

To the poor and needy who cannot get past their preoccupation with the basic necessities of life, Jesus offers the same advice on the God-honoring view of life: "Do not worry about your life, what you will eat, or about your body, what you will wear. For life is more than food, and the body more than clothing" (12:22–23). Food and clothing constitute only part of the totality of life that encompasses the internal and the external, the spiritual and the physical, the earthly and the eternal. Attention to these things must be put in perspective. Not worrying is a lesson of trust in God's provision, and being free from anxiety releases one to be more fully engaged in the mission of Jesus. Earlier, when Jesus sent his emissaries out to preach the good news, they relied on God's provision through other people's hospitality (9:1–6; 10:1–9). At Bethsaida, God fed thousands by multiplying fish and loaves (9:12–17). When Jesus taught his disciples how to pray, he assured them of God's eagerness to supply the needs of his children (11:2–13). Yet old habits die hard. The lesson has to be repeated, this time with emphasis on the uselessness of obsessive worrying.

Jesus' exhortation on not to worry about food and clothing echoes his teachings on dealing with persecution. He has just told his disciples not to worry about what to say when brought before the authorities (12:11–12), and not to fear the enemies who have no authority over their eternal destiny (12:4). Whether one struggles with mundane sustenance or faces life-threatening persecution, the same principle applies. For those who trust in God's goodness and fatherly care, anxiety and fear will give way to freedom and heavenly treasures.

Three pictures are given to illustrate the futility of worry: the first one on food, the third one on clothing, and in between them, one on life in general. Jesus begins with an argument from the lesser to the greater. Ravens are unclean birds of prey that are of little use to anyone (Lev 11:13–15). They survive by scavenging among dead animals and trash. Yet God feeds them, in that they always manage to find something to eat. If God sees to it that such birds get fed, how much more will he ensure that Jesus' disciples, who are infinitely more valuable to God than ravens and sparrows, will not go hungry (12:24; cf. 12:7; Ps 147:9; Job 38:41)?

Second, in contrast to what God can do, the disciples are reminded of how little they can to do assuage their anxiety. Like the rich fool who has no control over how long he will live, the disciples cannot by worrying lengthen their life span by even a moment (12:25–26). The Greek word *pēchys* is a measure of either time or distance. While reading Jesus' image as increasing one's height by a cubit (or eighteen inches) is lexically acceptable, the temporal sense fits better with the next illustration that speaks of the fleeting nature of wildflowers and field grasses. Not only is worrying ineffective in making one live longer, it can backfire and lead to premature death (Sir 30:24)!

Third, in concert with the idea of God feeding the ravens that neither sow nor reap, Jesus points out that God clothes the lilies of the field that neither toil nor spin. In fact, the beauty of the lilies dwarves the splendor of King Solomon's robes that showcase his wealth and grandeur (12:27; cf. 1 Kgs 10:4–5, 21–23). Grasses, like wild lilies, symbolize transience. They bloom, wither, and die all within a short period of time (Pss 37:2; 103:15–16). God clothes them even if they are alive today and are burned as fuel tomorrow. Since God adorns even insignificant plants that appear ever so briefly, how much more can God be counted on to clothe Jesus' disciples (12:28a)?

This set of reasoning asserts God's pervasive care for all his creation in its finitude. Jesus gently chides his disciples, "You of little faith" (12:28b), to encourage them to grow in trusting God. The proper response is not to be anxious, but to assume a posture of restfulness commensurate with their status as God's children. Otherwise, what sets them apart from the pagans who strive and worry incessantly (12:29–30)? As the disciples give priority to seeking after God's kingdom, they are taking a bold step of faith and activating a virtuous cycle. Their needs are met, they stop worrying, they immerse themselves in the mission of Jesus, their knowledge of God's character is affirmed, and their faith deepens (12:31).

Jesus concludes this segment by reiterating several themes that connect back to the parable of the rich fool. Unlike the greedy man who wants his share of his inheritance (12:13), Jesus assures his "little flock" that God delights in giving them his kingdom (12:32). As God is the quintessential Father and the disciples are his children, so God is the Shepherd and they are his sheep.[15] Children and sheep are well cared for; they do not need to strive or covet, but simply receive in trust and

---

15. Shepherd and sheep are common images found the OT to describe the relationship between God and God's people. See Ezek 34; Ps 23; Jer 31:10; Zech 10:3.

gratitude. Because God's provision is abundant, there is no need to hoard like the rich fool (12:18-19). Free from worry and confident that God will take care of their needs, the disciples are to sell their possessions and give alms (12:33a). Unencumbered by earthly belongings, their generosity will know no bounds as they accumulate treasures in heaven. In God's economy, nothing will be lost or subject to devaluation. Heavenly treasures are out of reach for thieves and moths cannot ruin the purses that contain them (12:33b). Jesus' disciples can start making eternal deposits by aligning themselves with God's saving purpose and doing justice toward that end.

In the end, one's treasure leads to one's heart (12:34). A person whose heart is oriented toward matters of eternal significance will act in ways that store up lasting treasures in heaven. But one like the rich fool, whose focus is solely on earthly pleasures, will go only as far as accumulating earthly possessions, which are, in the final accounting, temporary and devoid of satisfaction.

Fusing the Horizons: Wealth and Security

Although Jesus' teachings on not to worry about the basic necessities of life encouraged a crowd made up of poor peasants for whom living at a subsistence level presented a daily challenge, his telling of the parable of the rich fool was not irrelevant to them either. Greed in the human heart and one's need for security are no respecter of persons. In the Broadway musical, *Fiddler on the Roof*, the main character, Tevye, a Jewish milkman, muses before breaking into song with *"If I Were a Rich Man"*: "Dear God, you made many, many poor people. I realize, of course, that it's no shame to be poor. But it's no great honor either! So, what would have been so terrible if I had a small fortune?" As with human nature, those who have are drawn to amass more for themselves; the richer they grow the less generous they become. Those who do not have are tempted to feel envious of those who have, worrying that there is never enough to go around.

Behind the desire for wealth, whether a little or a lot, is the belief that possessions form the basis of enjoyment in life, security, and the longevity of the family legacy. The ethos of frugality was instilled in me early in my upbringing, as my grandparents moved from China to Hong Kong, and my generation subsequently emigrated to the United States. From a young age

I knew the drill. Be practical in your spending. Save for the rainy day. Do not live beyond your means. Pay off your credit card balance every month. Plan for retirement. Leave something for the next generation. While these reminders have served me well, it is easy to rely on the balance on my bank account as my sole gauge of security. If I did not have a single penny to my name, I would have no choice but to trust God for my next meal, but what do trust and obedience mean when I am not living in dire straits? Many of us reading this commentary probably land somewhere between the extremes in socio-economic terms. While money may be tight, we can find a meal, a change of clothes, or a roof over our heads. Neither are we—or so it seems to us—culpable like the rich fool in Jesus' parable, since we acknowledge that all we have belongs to God and are willing to share at least some of our surplus. That said, we hesitate to sell everything to give to the poor, lest we find ourselves in abject poverty as a result of our radical discipleship!

What soliloquy goes on in our minds? "Renunciation of wealth is a special calling, and mine is not that drastic." "If I invest in the wealth I have, I will have more for charitable giving down the road. I will wait until I have more to give more." "Giving till it hurts is not for everybody, especially when others depend on my income and resources." "Is tithing ten percent good enough, and if so, is that pre-tax or after-tax?" The pragmatic planner in me continues to struggle with the extent to which I am living out Jesus' injunctions based on my attitude toward money and its use. I suspect I am not alone. Perhaps the place to begin is not in our heads—the number crunching, the weighing of pros and cons—but in our hearts, which only God can change, soften, and challenge. May God reframe where we derive our sense of security, from the fleeting possessions that we have to the One who owns all and is generous beyond measure. As Jesus comforted the peasants around him, so he comforts us, "Fear not, little flock, for it is your Father's good pleasure to give you the kingdom."

Watchfulness in Uncertain Times (12:35–59)

The inauguration of God's kingdom has already begun in Jesus' coming, but final consummation lies yet in the future. In the meantime, the good news of God's salvation encounters both reception and rejection. Preparing his disciples for this eschatological crisis, Jesus exhorts them not to be afraid of persecution and not to worry over daily needs, but to trust in their benevolent and all-seeing Father in heaven. Next Jesus teaches the importance of vigilance because of the temporal uncertainties of this cosmic battle that is being waged on the human stage.

Be Vigilant (12:35–48)

For Jesus' followers, courage and trust are appropriate responses to the "what," that is, the nature of the eschatological crisis and the challenges that come with it (12:1–34). Alertness and diligence, however, address the "when," the timing of the onslaught of opposition both now and in the future. Jesus uses three illustrations to underscore the importance of active waiting.

First, a master is about to return, having been away at a wedding banquet. Since banquets go on for days, there is no telling when the master will come home. Vigilant slaves must always be at the ready for their master's appearance at any time, day or night. The idiom, "gird their loins" (12:35a), implies anticipation and alertness.[16] The same phrase is used to describe the manner in which the Israelites ate their very first Passover meal before they left Egypt, with their long robes tucked into their belts at the waist, so that their feet could be freed up for swift and uninhibited movement at a moment's notice (Exod 12:11). Now as the slaves keep watch throughout the night, the lamps must be kept lit, so that as soon as they hear the master's knock, they can open the door and illumine his path (12:35b–36). The master should not have to wait for the lamps to be trimmed even if he comes home in the second or third watch of the night (12:38a).[17] For the slaves who fulfill their duty, Jesus twice declares them blessed (12:37a, 38b). These vigilant slaves will be rewarded with an act of role reversal by their master, something unimaginable in a culture governed by hierarchy and honor. Because the slaves have been faithful in the master's absence, the master will invite them to sit at the table and he will serve them instead (12:37b). The final twist of this parable points forward to the eschatological future, when the faithful servants of

---

16. The translation in the NRSV, "Be dressed for action," weakens the visual image and misses the use of the same verb in verse 37. The point is not what is worn but how the clothing is worn in such a way to allow for rapid movement such as running (1 Kgs 18:46; 2 Kgs 4:29; 9:1; Nah 2:1).

17. 10 pm to 2 am constitutes the second watch, and the master may return between 2 am and 6 am, the third watch.

God will find themselves seated at the messianic banquet, served by none other than Jesus, their master![18]

The second image further emphasizes the certainty of the parousia and the unpredictability of its timing (12:39-40; cf. 9:26). A thief preys on people who are unprepared. A conscientious homeowner would take necessary precautions that involve constant watchfulness. Similarly, the second coming of the Son of Man is likened to the unexpectedness of a thief's intrusion. When a house is burglarized, one suffers material loss at best. But if a disciple is not ready for Jesus' return, he or she will face dire consequences. Those committed to following Jesus must always carry an eschatological mindset, because the future reign of God has already impinged upon the present.

Peter's interjection in verse 41 reiterates the necessity for all who are with Jesus, not just the Twelve, to heed these words. In the third and final image, Jesus employs the master-slave dynamic again (12:42-46). In this household there is a slave who is also a manager that supervises other slaves. The manager can either perform his responsibilities as assigned, feed the slaves under his charge often and regularly, or he can take advantage of his master's delay in returning, defy his orders, gorge himself with food and drink, and mistreat his fellow slaves. A faithful manager will have nothing to fear, but a lazy and disobedient one will be caught red-handed when his master unexpectedly returns. In the end, the master will reward industriousness and faithfulness with even more acknowledgment and responsibility, but will harshly punish sloth and unfaithfulness. The verb, *dichotomēsei*, means "will cut in two" (12:46). While it is hard to imagine the master literally ripping the disobedient manager to shreds, the gruesome picture makes for a vivid hyperbole for a dreadful fate.

Just when we assume the parable is coming to a close, Jesus adds a nuanced touch, distinguishing between two levels of culpability. By definition, a slave is to do his or her master's bidding. Any disobedient slave deserves a beating, the severity of which depends on his or her awareness of the master's expectations (12:47-48a). Defiance is much worse than unwitting transgression. Put positively, responsibility comes with the privilege of knowledge: "From everyone to whom much has been given, much will be required; and from the one to whom much has been entrusted, even more will be demanded" (12:48b). Jesus teaches

---

18. Green 1997: 501. While not every meal scene in Luke contains an allusion to the messianic banquet, the reference to the parousia in 12:40 is suggestive.

the crowd but entrusts the secrets of the kingdom of God to his disciples (8:9; 10:23–24). They must put what they have learned into practice for ignorance is no excuse.

Recognizing Crisis (12:49-59)

In the final section of this chapter Jesus reveals the effects of his coming. In spite of his popular reception among the crowds, Jesus expects his words and deeds to cause tremendous strife, and neutrality is not an option. The power of the gospel lies in its ability to provoke a response. To receive Jesus is to receive God, and to reject Jesus is to reject the one who sent him (9:48; 10:16; cf. 2:34–35).

Fire is a common metaphor for divine judgment in the OT, destroying all that is godless (Isa 66:15–16; Ezek 38:22; Amos 1:4, 7, 10, 14). As God's agent of salvation, Jesus brings a fire of judgment that is tied to the baptism with which he has to be baptized (12:49–50). Jesus is speaking neither of his baptism by John nor the rite of Christian baptism in the book of Acts, but the baptism of his impending death.[19] Baptism pictures a deluge of water overwhelming its object with calamitous suffering, almost like drowning (2 Sam 22:5; Ps 69:1–2). No wonder Jesus' tone betrays a desire to be on the other side of the dreadful fate that awaits him. Put together, the images of fire and baptism warn that Jesus' death will pronounce a judgment upon those who do not believe (3:16–17). Israel is already divided on account of Jesus and his message. That division will continue to escalate, so much so that even families will be torn apart, breaking kindred ties on all levels (12:51–52).[20] Although the angels declared that the birth of Jesus would bring "peace among those whom [God] favors" (2:14; cf. Isa 9:6–7; Zech 9:9–10), that peace will only come to fruition at the cost of tension, conflict, and the death of Israel's Messiah.

In light of the increasing hostility and ominous division that arise as Jesus' mission moves toward its climactic end, it is all the more important for the disciples to develop a heightened sense of awareness. One must know how to interpret the significance of what one sees in order to respond appropriately. When storm clouds rise up in the west, they pick up

---

19. Nolland 1993a: 708; Marshall 1978: 547.

20. It is not that Jesus is against families, but in the event that family commitments compete with the demands of God's kingdom, then Jesus takes priority. See 8:19–21; 9:57–62; 14:26; 18:28–30.

moisture from the Mediterranean and bring rain to the inland (12:54). And when winds come from the south, they carry the scorching heat from the desert of Negev (12:55).[21] If the people are proficient in looking for signs in the sky to predict weather patterns, why can't they read Jesus' message and actions rightly (12:56)? Is it a matter of incompetence or hardness of heart? By calling the people "hypocrites," Jesus likens them to the unfaithful slaves in the last parable who deserve a severe beating (12:47). They know what God, their master, requires of them. Jesus has spoken the word of salvation, but if they refuse to believe, those very words of life will become words of judgment.

The opportunity to accept Jesus' invitation of salvation will not always be there. It is up to Jesus' listeners to exercise wise discernment while there is still time (12:57). Jesus paints one more picture that is not uncommon in village life, in which a debtor is called upon by the creditor to settle a debt. If the debt is not repaid, the creditor will drag the debtor to court. The judge will rule in favor of the creditor and hand the debtor over to the officers who will then throw him or her into prison where conditions are much worse.[22] There the debtor will stay until the entire sum, down to every last penny,[23] is repaid. Given this dreadful eventuality, prudence dictates that the debtor make amends with the creditor even before reaching the magistrate, when there is still room for negotiation (12:58–59). With this analogy, Jesus urges the crowd not to exhaust God's patience, but to turn back while the door of forgiveness is still open.[24]

---

21. Green 1997: 511.

22. According to Hellenistic law, inability or unwillingness to pay back a loan leads to unpleasant consequences. First, punitive interest will be imposed. Next, the debtor's possessions can be confiscated. Third and worst, the debtor will be seized and imprisoned. See Kinman 1999a: 418–19.

23. A *lepton* is worth 1/128 of a denarius. It is the lowest denomination of all the coins circulated in ancient Palestine.

24. Kinman (1999a: 421) stresses Israel's obligation to God, that this parable calls for the Jews to repent not just as individuals but as a nation.

Luke 13

Call to Repentance (13:1-9)

Jesus' warning about the eschatological crisis and impending judgment at the end of chapter 12 continues into chapter 13 as one unit of thought. The parable concerning an unproductive fig tree (13:6-9) forms an *inclusio* with the earlier parable about the debtor who is about to be dragged before the magistrate (12:57-59). Both call for immediate action to avert a disastrous fate. Between them is the focal point of that action, which is repentance (13:1-5).

All Must Repent (13:1-5)

Two incidents are mentioned by Jesus for which no attestation can be found in extant ancient sources. This does not mean they did not occur. We assume that the murder by Pontius Pilate of some Galileans who died while making sacrifices and the crushing of eighteen people as a result of the collapse of a tower at Siloam were historical events (13:1, 4). The pertinent question is not what happened exactly, but the attitude of those who told Jesus about the incidents and Jesus' pointed response to them.

Pilate's cruelty was amply documented by Josephus, the first-century Jewish historian (13:1). On one occasion Pilate had a great number of unarmed Jews slain because they protested his use of funds from the temple treasury to build an aqueduct.[1] On another he sent soldiers to kill a large group of Samaritans on their way to Mount Gerazim, their holy mountain.[2] It is not hard to believe that Pilate executed an unknown number of Galilean pilgrims during Passover, perhaps for fear of an uprising, since that was the only feast where laypeople were permitted to

---

1. Josephus *J.W.* 2.175-77; Josephus *Ant.* 4.60-62. Pilate threatened another group of Jews with violence when they reacted negatively to his bringing images of Caesar into Jerusalem (Josephus *J.W.* 2.169-74; Josephus *Ant.* 4.55-59).

2. Josephus *Ant.* 4.85-87.

kill their own sacrificial animals (13:1).³ Whether Pilate's mixing of the blood of the victims with that of the animals is meant to be taken literally or not, the account still conveys the atrocity of the procurator's behavior and his insensitivity to Jewish scruples.

The second reported incident appears to be caused by natural forces (13:4a). Siloam was a reservoir situated near the southeastern corner of the wall of Jerusalem.⁴ The tower that collapsed could have been a defensive structure on the wall. Whatever its function, when it came down, eighteen innocent lives were lost.

The people who bring these events to Jesus' attention seem to have attributed the demise of those who perished to divine judgment. This mindset that people deserved what they got was prevalent in the ancient world, as expressed in the view that people owed their handicap or misfortune to divine retribution (Job 4:7-9; John 9:2). After all, God did strike people with illness and even death as a form of punishment.⁵ The informants' attitude betrays a sense of moral superiority, as though they and other Galileans or Jerusalemites were spared because their sins were less egregious.

Responding to both accounts, Jesus moves the focus away from the degree of sinfulness of the victims to the universal culpability of human beings (13:2, 4b). There is neither greater glory in being lesser sinners nor greater shame in being worse offenders. The magnitude of one's sins is irrelevant on the day of judgment, for everyone is guilty before God. Everyone is in need of forgiveness lest he or she be consigned to eternal destruction. There is neither room for boasting nor a sense of impunity. Jesus' call for repentance cannot be emphasized more: "Unless you repent, you will all perish as they did" (13:3, 5).

A Fruitless Fig Tree (13:6-9)

To repeat the same point, Jesus speaks of a fig tree in a vineyard (13:6a). The fig and the vine are common Jewish symbols of blessing, peace, and security.⁶ Fig trees are found in abundance around the Mediterranean. A thriving fig tree bears fruit twice a year; early figs arrive in May and June

---

3. Marshall 1978: 553.
4. Ibid.: 554. Cf. John 9:7, 11.
5. Lev 10:1-2; Num 16:1-35; 21:4-6; Acts 5:1-10.
6. 1 Kgs 4:25; 2 Kgs 18:31; Mic 4:4; Zech 3:10.

and late figs between August and October.⁷ The owner's expectation to find fruit on his fig tree is entirely reasonable, especially when a mature tree is in view.

For three years in a row the fig tree has not produced any fruit (13:6b–7). The chance of its returning to fecundity diminishes with every year of barrenness, so much so that the owner is ready to cut it down. An unproductive tree takes up space and drains nutrients that could have gone to healthier plants. But thanks to the gardener's pleading, the tree receives one final chance. He offers to tend the tree, fertilize the soil around it, and give it one more growing season to produce fruit (13:8). And if the last-ditch effort fails, the gardener will let it be removed (13:9).

Given themes of repentance and eschatological crisis that permeate this section, the parable is easy to decipher. God is the owner of the vineyard, Jesus is the gardener, and the languishing fig tree is recalcitrant Israel. The one year of reprieve represents the short time before the day of judgment. In the OT, the ravaging of a fig tree symbolizes divine punishment (Hos 2:12; Amos 4:9). Likewise, John warned those who came out to hear him: "Bear fruit worthy of repentance, . . . even now the ax is lying at the root of the trees; every tree therefore that does not bear good fruit is cut down and thrown into the fire" (3:8–9).

A leafy but fruitless fig tree may have the appearance of life but in reality is good for nothing. Jesus has appealed to divine forbearance on behalf of the impenitent and bought them some extra time, but it is up to them whether to heed the warnings of the last days and turn from their wicked ways. In the end, productivity and judgment are the only options. Will the people choose life and repent, or will they seal their own fate by stubborn unbelief?

Healing a Bent Woman (13:10–17)

Once again, Luke presents a story of Jesus healing on the Sabbath. This account is the first part of a female-male diptych, followed by the healing of a man with dropsy at the beginning of the next chapter (14:1–6). This gendered pairing is reflective of the author's penchant of introducing stories about a man and a woman in close literary proximity.⁸

---

7. Snodgrass 2008: 259.
8. See p. 66, n. 12.

To meticulously observant Jews at the time of Jesus, like the scribes and the Pharisees, Sabbath and purity laws function jointly as important identity markers that separate the Jews from the gentiles, the pious from the impious. The problem with Jesus' opponents is not their desire to subsume all of life under God's jurisdiction, but that in doing so they lose sight of the bigger picture of God's grace and benevolence. Their motive becomes warped and their attitude toward others demanding and judgmental. That which was intended for good ends up being used for evil, earning the Pharisees and the scribes the charge of hypocrisy from Jesus (11:37–52; 12:1; 13:15).[9]

On this particular Sabbath, Jesus is teaching at a synagogue, where he encounters a woman with a bent back (13:10). For eighteen long years she has had a stooped posture. She may be suffering from some form of inflammation of the spine that leads to the fusion of her vertebrae, which over time renders her incapable of straightening up.[10] Jesus and the author, however, attribute her medical condition to demonic oppression. Luke describes her as having "a spirit of weakness"[11] (13:11), and Jesus calls her healing as being "set free from bondage" (13:12b, 16). Although Jesus does not physically cast a demon out of this woman, he attributes her condition to some form of diabolic oppression (cf. 9:38–43).

The woman's presence in the synagogue is likely to be frowned upon by the religious elite. They probably have little sympathy for her, given the connection they make between divine retribution and physical abnormality.[12] She is unclean, an outcast by virtue of her ailment, and her status is as low as the position of her head.

Instead of leaving the woman hidden at the back of the synagogue, Jesus summons her forward. If her shameful condition is publicly condemned, then her restoration must be publicly witnessed (13:12a; cf. 6:8; 8:46–48; 19:5). His pronouncement, "Woman, you have been released (*apolelysai*) from your weakness (*astheneias*)" (13:12b), deals directly with the oppressive spirit that plagues her (13:11). As is often the case with Jesus' words of healing, the passive voice of the verb *apolelysai* acknowledges that God is the subject of the action, the one effecting the

---

9. See p. 81.

10. Green (1997: 521) suggests *spondylitis ankylopoietica*, the inflammation of spinal joints.

11. The Greek word *astheneia* means weakness. Other more descriptive translations include "a spirit of infirmity" (KJV) and "a spirit that had crippled her" (NRSV).

12. See p. 76, n. 9.

liberation (7:14; cf. 5:20; 7:48). The perfect tense also denotes the completeness of the healing. Once cured, she continues to stay cured. When she finally straightens her back and stands tall, she appropriately praises God (13:13). She is restored not only in her body but also in her right to participate in communal life.

As the woman's words of praise linger in the air, the critical spirit of the synagogue ruler ruins the holy moment. Repeatedly he complains to all those who have just witnessed the miracle that the Sabbath law has been violated, and blames the woman for showing up on the Sabbath rather than any other day for healing (13:14). In his view, by laying hands on an unclean woman unrelated to himself, Jesus has transgressed purity and Sabbath laws. After eighteen years of infirmity, one more day of stooping would not have made a difference. Jesus could have waited till after the Sabbath to cure her.

Jesus defends his action with two rhetorical questions that unmasks the hypocrisy of his opponents. First, he cites loopholes within the law that people use to take care of their livestock on the Sabbath (13:15). Supposedly, the Sabbath law applies to human beings, including slaves and resident aliens, as well as livestock, oxen, and donkeys (Deut 5:13–14). Strictly speaking, the Jews are forbidden to untie their ox or donkey on the Sabbath to lead it to water, as untying constitutes work. Practical concern for the wellbeing of the animals necessitates an interpretation of the law that would allow certain processes not to be defined as work. For example, if the animal is not carrying a load, it may be taken out on the Sabbath (*m. Šabb.* 5:1–4). Even though tying a knot—needed after the animal returns from a drink—is considered work, one that prevents it from wandering off is allowed (*m. Šabb.* 15:1–2). Another accommodation is to consider public wells as part of one's private domain, so that animals can drink from it without exceeding the distance they are allowed to travel outside the home on the Sabbath (*m. 'Erub.* 2:1–4). Even the most scrupulous Jews do not want their cattle to die of thirst on the Sabbath, so they are willing to bend the rules to honor the law.

Second, Jesus challenges his opponents' logic and sensibility. If they are willing to adjust the application of the Sabbath prohibitions for the sake of farm animals and lowly beasts of burden, how much more should they show compassion to this woman who has suffered for a long time (13:16)? An ox or a donkey is bound for a few hours, but this woman has been bound by Satan for eighteen long years. One more day of bondage is one more day too long! To the synagogue ruler and his elitist supporters, she may be unclean and unworthy. But to Jesus, she is a daughter of Abraham as much as they are sons of Abraham. Her intrinsic value in God's eyes and place among God's people should not be denied. It is all the more appropriate for God to set her free on the Sabbath, a day of rest created for the rejuvenation for God's people. Even if her healing involves violating the detailed stipulations of purity and Sabbath laws, in the grand scheme of things, her physical, social, and spiritual restoration represents the most authentic expression of honoring the Sabbath. By the end of Jesus' water-tight defense of his action, his opponents are shamed into silence (13:17). Against wholeness there can be no refutation.

The Kingdom of God (13:18-30)

In Luke, phrases such as "the good news of the kingdom of God" (4:43; 8:1), "yours is the kingdom of God" (6:20), "the secrets of the kingdom of God" (8:10), "to proclaim the kingdom of God" (9:2, 60; cf. 9:11), "to see the kingdom of God" (9:27), "to be fit for the kingdom of God" (9:60), and "the kingdom of God has come near" (10:9, 11; cf. 11:2, 20), hardly describe a physical territory with geographical boundary, citizenry, and a governing political structure. Rather, to belong to the kingdom of God is to receive the gift of salvation and come under the reign of God.[13] Although God's rule, as proclaimed and mediated by Jesus, has not come by way of displacing the Romans and reconstituting Israel in the militaristic and political sense, it is no less tangible and perceptible through the ears and eyes of faith. Jesus' teachings and miracles, his mission of liberation and restoration, and his impending death and resurrection are concrete manifestations of God's kingdom and kingship to those who believe.

Images from daily life provide effective descriptions of the characteristics of God's kingdom. First, Jesus likens its expansive potential to the growth of a small seed into a large plant (13:18-19). The mustard seed is proverbially small, yet it can grow into a bush about four feet high.[14] Calling the bush a "tree" may be a bit of an exaggeration, but the point is obvious, that a small seed can yield a sizable plant. In the OT, Assyria and Babylon were depicted as a tall tree with birds nesting in its branches (Ezek 31:5-6; Dan 4:10-12, 20-27). But no matter how prosperous

---

13. The concept of God's kingship is well established in the OT, e.g., Pss 95:3; 145:1; Isa 43:15; Zech 14:9, 16-17; Mal 1:14.

14. The mustard seed is not the tiniest seed in the plant kingdom, but Jesus is using an example familiar to his audience and not teaching botany. See Marshall 1978: 561.

and impressive these nations have become, in the end God rules over all, planting his own tree that grows tall and broad, enough to provide a home for the birds (Ezek 17:22–24). God's kingdom, despite a humble beginning with Jesus and his small band of disciples, will supersede the most powerful of earthly domains.[15] For Jesus' audience, Rome is their Assyria and their Babylon. Will the people be impressed by the mighty power of Caesar, whom they hate but fear, or will they trust that Jesus will deliver them from the clutches of evil and death?

Next, Jesus compares the pervasive influence of the kingdom of God with leaven used in baking (13:20–21). He pictures a woman kneading an old fermented "starter dough" into a new dough. The leaven works its way into the combined batch and causes the bread to rise.[16] Three measures of flour are enough to produce forty large loaves to feed a hundred and fifty people.[17] The Greek verb *ekrypsen*, rendered as "mixed in" (13:21 NRSV), literally means "hid." As the woman kneads the dough, she "hides" the leaven inside the batch. Earlier on, when Jesus warned his disciples of the leaven of the Pharisees, he was exposing their negative influence on the people (12:1–2). In this picture, the leaven represents a positive influence. As the hypocrisy of the Pharisees is hidden and not easily detectable, so is the positive impact of the kingdom of God.[18] Like the tiny mustard seed that grows into a big bush, the beginning of God's kingdom is hardly perceptible from an earthly point of view, with no army and territory to speak of, yet its impact will be unstoppable in due time.

Continuing on with his journey toward Jerusalem, Jesus offers a third image to warn his hearers against presumptuousness concerning their place in God's kingdom (13:22–30). Someone in the crowd asks, "Lord, will only a few be saved?" (13:23), which is the same as asking, "Lord, will only a few enter the kingdom of God?" In response, Jesus focuses not so much on who will be saved, but who will not be.

---

15. Carroll 2012: 287.

16. Hultgren 2000: 406. Given favorable conditions of water, sugar, and warmth, the leavening agent (yeast) will generate carbon dioxide throughout the dough, causing it to rise.

17. Three measures of flour make 144 cups, which weigh about 40 to 50 pounds (Snodgrass 2008: 232).

18. Images are susceptible to extrapolations. Reid (2002: 286) identifies the leaven as the sinners who are "worked into" by Jesus into being vital members of God's kingdom.

The kingdom of God is pictured as a house with a narrow door (13:24). Although God's invitation to enter his "house" is extended to all, it is not as though one could saunter through a wide open gap effortlessly and carelessly. In fact, the imperative, *agonizesthe* ("strive"), is an athletic metaphor, in which a competitor struggles to contend for a prize. The present tense denotes a continuous action. Those who want to enter the narrow door must keep on striving and making the effort to do so. Recalling Jesus' teachings on the cost of discipleship, participation in God's kingdom is not for the faint of heart (9:57–62; 14:25–33). Even though large crowds flock to Jesus, only the truly committed ones can get through that narrow door (cf. 8:5–15).

Although the door is narrow, it is still open. There will come a time when the owner will shut the door, barring further attempts to enter (13:25). The dialogue between the owner and those who find themselves on the outside, pleading to be let in, is sobering. These are not people who openly oppose Jesus; rather, they are false disciples whose self-deception has led them to believe that they are genuine disciples. Are they the ones who began with enthusiasm but whose commitment does not stand the test of time and circumstances (cf. 8:13–14)? Twice the owner of the house declares that he does not know where they come from (13:25, 27a). There is neither recognition nor relationship. All that is left to do is to send them away (13:27b; cf. Ps 6:8). It is distressing that these evildoers claim that they have shared table with Jesus and heard his teachings (13:26). They think they have done enough to earn a place in God's kingdom, but much to their dismay the outcome is not what they have envisioned. In the end, they find themselves excluded from the fine company of the patriarchs, the prophets, and those who truly belong to God, with nothing to do but weep and gnash their teeth in anger and hatred (13:28).[19]

The parable closes with the beautiful scene of the messianic banquet in God's kingdom, a symbol of eternal abundance, joy, and fellowship (13:29; cf. Isa 25:6–9; Ezek 39:17–20). Around that table, God's people come from all corners of the earth. While the OT prophets envisioned God gathering the faithful among Israel who were scattered in all directions (Isa 11:11–16; 43:5–6; Zech 8:6–9), the eschatological gathering will include gentile believers as well.[20]

---

19. Pss 35:16; 37:12; 112:10; Lam 2:16.
20. See Bird 2006: 448–57.

The punch line, "Indeed, some are last who will be first, and some are first who will be last" (13:30), expresses the radical inversion brought about by the values and ethos of God's kingdom, upsetting conventional determinations of status and eligibility. The rich and powerful who revel in human honor and recognition will be shocked to find themselves trailing behind those whom they perceive as worthless and shameful. Yet that is the humble state that makes entry through the narrow door of salvation possible. All are invited, but not all will enter in. The narrow door will not stay open forever. Let those who have yet to show themselves worthy of God's kingdom tarry no more, for the time of repentance is now.

The City that Kills the Prophets (13:31–35)

Herod Antipas arrested and beheaded John (3:19–20; 9:7–9), and now he wants to kill Jesus (13:31). The motive of the Pharisees is not stated. Are they genuine in warning Jesus of potential danger and urging him to get away from Herod's jurisdiction, because they, too, despise Herod's pro-Roman stance and choose to be on Jesus' side?[21] Or are they trying to use Herod's threat as a pretext for getting rid of Jesus, since Jesus has not been endearing himself to them (11:37–12:1)?[22] The Pharisees are not necessarily a homogeneous group. It is one thing for Luke to portray them as Jesus' opponents, it is another to assume that Jesus is dealing with the same Pharisees at every encounter, which would not be the case given his itinerant ministry. Perhaps the Pharisees' warning simply acts as a catalyst for Jesus to affirm his determination to finish his work, regardless of Herod's threat or the grim fate that awaits him in Jerusalem.

In response, Jesus compares Herod, a provincial puppet king, to a fox, a small and cunning animal that can do limited harm (13:32). The phrase, "today, tomorrow, and the next (or third) day," conveys a sense of mission, focused and deliberate. Much more threatening than Herod is Jerusalem, the center of Jewish piety, politics, and power. With its temple and institution, it carries the full weight of Jewish identity and history. Hence it is all the more ironic for Jesus, counting himself among the prophets of old, to identify Jerusalem as "the city that kills the prophets and stones those who are sent to it" (13:34a). Indeed, the Jews had a checkered history of rejecting God's emissaries. King Joash killed

---

21. Green 1997: 537; Nolland 1993a: 740.
22. Carroll 2012: 293; Marshall 1978: 571.

Zechariah son of the priest Jehoiada (2 Chr 24:20–22), Jehoiakim killed Uriah son of Shemaiah (Jer 26:20–23), and Zedekiah's officials threw Jeremiah into a muddy cistern and left him for dead (Jer 38:1–6). Even though the law calls for the stoning of false prophets (Deut 13:1–5), recalcitrant Israel listened to false prophets and murdered the genuine ones instead (11:49). Now the religious leaders are following the same pattern of rejecting God's messengers, first John and then Jesus (7:24–30). Before long, the conflict will reach a climax when they succeed in putting Jesus to death. Like his predecessors, it will also be "impossible for [God's eschatological prophet] to be killed outside of Jerusalem" (13:33b).[23]

With deep pathos Jesus' assessment of Jerusalem moves from indictment to lament. He compares himself to a mother hen, gathering her chicks under her wings to protect them from harm, doing exactly what YHWH did for Israel (13:34b).[24] Yet the more Jesus reaches out to Jerusalem, the more it hardens and sets itself on the path of destruction.

The phrase, "your house is left to you" (13:35a), sounds cryptic. Jeremiah issued a warning to the king of Judah and to Jerusalem, saying that if Israel failed to do justice and insisted on being disobedient, "this house shall become a desolation.. . . I will make you a desert, an uninhabited city" (Jer 22:5–6). Both then and now, the house refers to Jerusalem. It is unnecessary to draw too fine a point on the destruction of the temple vis-à-vis that of the city. Jerusalem and its temple are functionally synonymous. The city will be destroyed on account of its rejection of God's prophets, especially Jesus, who is both Messiah and God's eschatological prophet (19:43–44; 21:5–6, 20–24). History testifies that Jesus' prophecy came to pass when the Romans leveled Jerusalem in 70 CE. Even so, this tragedy will pale in light of the final judgment on the last day.

The discourse closes with a pronouncement and a citation from the OT: "You will not see me until the time comes when you say, 'Blessed is the one who comes in the name of the Lord'" (13:35b). This verse foreshadows Jesus' entry into Jerusalem, when his disciples will apply the welcome extended to the pilgrims to Jesus (19:38; Ps 118:26). Those with the eyes of faith recognize Jesus' identity and mission. But for those who remain skeptical, even Jerusalem's destruction will do little to cure their spiritual blindness. The day will come when the Son of Man will be

---

23. Hays (2015: 462–73) highlights Luke's identification of Jesus, the rejected eschatological prophet, with Jeremiah through the use of indirect allusions, catchwords, and parallels with the prophet's life of suffering and persecution.

24. Deut 32:11; Ruth 2:12; Pss 17:8; 36:7; 63:7; 91:4.

revealed in all his glory. At that time, Jesus' enemies will have no choice but to acknowledge his true status.

Luke 14

Healing a Man with Dropsy (14:1-6)

There are striking similarities between the account of this healing and that of the woman with a bent back in chapter 13. Both stories take place on the Sabbath (13:10; 14:1a), with Jesus operating under the watchful eye of the religious elite (13:14; 14:1b). Both the woman and the man have an illness that is not life-threatening (13:11; 14:2) and are said to be released by Jesus (13:12, 16; 14:4). In defense of his actions, Jesus employs an analogy in both cases that involves the treatment of an ox (13:15; 14:5). While Luke presents these healings as a doublet for emphasis, each story carries a distinctive connection with its immediate context. The account of the bent woman is followed by sayings about the kingdom of God. Her humble status represents those who will gain entry into God's kingdom, long before those who presume they have a place around the messianic table (13:18-30). The man with dropsy is also looked down upon by the able-bodied and law-abiding, his lowliness standing in stark contrast to their status-seeking behavior. Yet it is the likes of him who will be invited to God's eternal feast (14:7-24).

One Sabbath, Jesus is invited to dine at the house[1] of the leader of the Pharisees (14:1a). A meal on the Sabbath requires a heightened sense of boundary-keeping over and above regular observance of purity laws. Also present are, presumably, fellow Pharisees and worthy dignitaries. They are watching Jesus closely in case he does or says anything objectionable on legal grounds (14:1b; cf. 6:7; 11:53-54). More unusual is the presence of a man with dropsy (14:2). We do not know if he is a guest, an intruder, or a trap planted by Jesus' opponents, but his condition smears the high standard of purity scrupulously maintained for this setting.

---

1. The NRSV reads, "when [Jesus] was going to the house" (14:1), implying that the healing took place before the meal. This translation avoids the question as to why an unclean invalid would be found inside a Pharisee's house, but it also removes the cause of tension in the scene (cf. 7:37-39).

Also known as edema, dropsy refers to the swelling of the body caused by water retention. It is symptomatic of more serious health problems, such as congestive heart failure, liver and kidney diseases. A person with dropsy is frequently thirsty, but drinking water causes more bloating and makes matters worse.[2] Because of the swelling, dropsy is hard to conceal. Given the ancient connection between physical illness and divine punishment (cf. John 9:2), the sufferer is likely ostracized by the community and branded a sinner as well.

Greco-Roman writers use dropsy as a metaphor for insatiable greediness. The craving for water is likened to a greedy person wanting more of everything—money, power, status, honor, and the like.[3] The vicious cycle of thirst and swelling, incidentally, mimics the Pharisees' behavior. The more honor and wealth they seek, the more bloated with pride and self-satisfaction they become, and the more oblivious they are to the deadly "spiritual disease" that runs through their veins (11:37–44; 14:7–11; 16:14–15).[4]

On this occasion, Jesus asks the learned elites concerning the legality of healing on the Sabbath (14:3; cf. 6:9). In silence they wait for Jesus to incriminate himself with his response to the man with dropsy (14:4a). As expected, Jesus heals the man and sends him away. The Greek verb *apelysen* means "he sent him away" or "he released him." The double entendre brings out the deeper significance of Jesus' healing, that he sets him free from both physical and diabolic bondage associated with his symptoms (14:4b). Every healing on the earthly stage marks a victory over Satan in the cosmic realm (cf. 10:17–18).

Jesus then reasons with his detractors. If one of them had a son or an ox that fell into a well on a Sabbath, what would the owner or father do? Surely he would do everything to save his son or ox from drowning, even if it meant doing work, such as lifting and pulling, on the Sabbath (14:5). The law permits the violation of the Sabbath law to save a life (*m. Yoma* 8:6; *b. Meg.* 3b), and the possibility of drowning would qualify as a life-and-death emergency. According to the rabbis, a lenient ruling would seek to pull the person or animal out of the pit even if work was involved, and a harsh ruling would allow the provision of food to keep the person or animal alive through the Sabbath, after which rescue efforts

2. Green 1997: 546–47.

3. See Braun 1995: 30–38 and Hartsock 2013: 347–52. Cf. Stobaeus *Flor.* 3.10.45; 4.33.31; Ovid *Fast.* 1.215–16; Polybius 13.2.2.

4. Hartsock 2013: 352–53.

could begin (*m. B. Qam.* 5:6; *b. Šabb.* 128b). Jesus' argument is framed from the lesser to the greater: if his opponents would violate the Sabbath to save a child or a farm animal, how much more should they value the life of a grown man and member of God's household? To the Pharisees, the man with dropsy is not dying and Jesus should have waited till the Sabbath is over. To Jesus, anyone subject to the oppression of Satan is in danger of spiritual death and must be rescued without delay.

Again the Pharisees have no rebuttal (14:6). Jesus has answered his own question by his action. It is lawful to cure on the Sabbath even if the illness is not unto death. Restoring people to physical, social, and spiritual wholeness is saving life and honoring the Sabbath. True rest is more than the cessation of work but wholeness before God.

Fusing the Horizons: Honoring the Sabbath

One of the recurring criticisms the Pharisees and the scribes launched against Jesus was his healing on the Sabbath that violated the fourth commandment. Luke includes four such accounts in his narrative, in which Jesus cast out an unclean spirit from a man (4:31–36), healed another with a withered hand (6:6–11), later a woman with a bent back (13:10–17), and then a man with dropsy (14:1–6)—all on different Sabbaths. Surely Luke is not making the point that Jesus deliberately looked for opportunities to violate the Sabbath to irritate his opponents. Rather, each healing was an object lesson to embody the true meaning of Sabbath rest.

Honoring the Sabbath with the cessation of work was God's gift as well as his command to Israel. The true purpose of Sabbath rest had to do with restoration, bringing God's people to wholeness physically, spiritually, and communally. Jesus could have performed each of these four healings the day after the Sabbath, since other than demon possession none of the other ailments was immediately life-threatening to the victims. Waiting a few more hours would have satisfied the scruples of his opponents who, after all, were not against healing or exorcism per se, but the breaking of the Sabbath law. That Jesus healed those people right then and there on the Sabbath was in fact necessary to drive home his point. For God's rest to be a true gift, there should never be any delay in bringing people to wholeness and full restoration, regardless of what day it was, Sabbath or not. Jesus was not against the commandment, but if he had to choose between Sabbath observance and an opportunity to offer immediate release to the oppressed, he would give priority to the latter because the healing in and of itself was a perfect example of honoring the Sabbath. By setting the logistics of Sabbath observance above God's original good purpose for that very law, the Pharisees and the scribes had lost sight of the forest for the trees.

God's command to honor the Sabbath continues to be a challenge for Jesus' followers today, though not necessarily because of some comprehensive list of prescribed prohibitions. Even before worrying about what is or is not considered to be work, Christians already struggle with taking one day a week for Sabbath observance. Given the tempo of modern living, the blurring of the boundary between work and leisure, the connectivity afforded by technology that allows us to work around the clock and on vacations, and the many professional and social obligations that bleed from weekdays to weekends, we buy into the notion that the more we work, the more we can accomplish, and (perhaps) the more money we can make. We are not unaware of the slew of physical, relational, and psychological pitfalls when we insist on staying on the incessant treadmill of work, yet we seem to have difficulty trusting God for Spirit-empowered productivity when we commit ourselves to keeping the Sabbath. The benefits of obedience can only be appreciated from experience, so what are your plans for this weekend?

Honor in God's Kingdom (14:7–24)

Returning to the meal at the Pharisee's house to which Jesus has been invited (14:1), the behavior of Jesus' meal companions undergoes evaluation. Jesus exposes their arrogance and self-promotion (14:7–11), calls for action that challenges the obligatory burden of reciprocity (14:12–14), and tells a parable of God's grace and judgment at the end of time (14:15–24).

At the time of Jesus, meals meant much more than good food and company. From who was invited and where the meal took place, to how the seating was arranged and what was discussed around the table, the banquet setting was a social enterprise. It served as a forum for establishing one's place, status, reputation, association, and sphere of influence. The principle of balanced reciprocity required that acceptance of an invitation be followed by a reciprocal invitation to maintain the delicate dance between host and guest, who would try to outdo each another in honor and hospitality. People shared table with relatives, friends, and associates of like status. One might aspire to be invited to dine with someone of a higher rank, but nobody had use for anyone of a lower rank. All this maneuvering took time, resources, and strategizing, and not everyone was in the position to keep up with the unending cycle of give and take, obligation and expectation. Yet the inability to do so would cause great shame, something the ancients would avoid at all costs.[5]

Honor and Humility (14:7–11)

At a formal banquet, the most honorable seat was the one next to the host. The best seats were either at the end of the table or in the middle if the seating was arranged in a U-shape. The remaining seats were filled in decreasing ranking in social status, so that the social location of each guest was apparent to all.[6] Place, role, and status were orchestrated in accordance with the accepted norms of hierarchy and social decorum. Fighting for places of honor was normal behavior in Jesus' world (14:7), where humility was suspect and seeking recognition was commended. A boost to an individual's honor would enhance the collective honor of one's family, so any opportunity that could result in an increase of honor and a reduction of shame was seized. The end justified the means.

Challenging his hearers' values, Jesus presents a hypothetical wedding banquet, where important guests tend to arrive late.[7] Those who arrive early are better off not to make presumptions on seating based on their self-assessed rank and file, especially when they are not privy to the guest list and hence the status of other invitees. Rather than risking public ridicule when the host downgrades the self-promoter to a lower spot to make room for a guest of greater honor, one should occupy the lowliest position so that the only direction to go from there is up (14:8–11; cf. Prov 25:6–7). The principle is easy to grasp: "All who exalt themselves will be humbled, and those who humble themselves will be exalted" (14:11). Both humbling and exalting are determined by God who knows all and judges all.

---

5. Neyrey 1991: 361–87.
6. See *b. Ber.* 46b; Josephus *Ant.* 15.21; 1QSa II, 16–21.
7. Marshall 1978: 581.

Undermining Balanced Reciprocity (14:12–14)

In the system of balanced reciprocity, a guest is obligated to return the favor with a future dinner invitation. While Jesus' words are directed toward his host (14:12a), they are just as applicable to the other guests. Concerning the people to invite for a banquet, Jesus envisions two very different guest lists. On the first list are the usual suspects: one's friends, relatives, and rich neighbors (14:12b). On the second are folks that people would loathe to have at their table: "the poor, the crippled, the lame, and the blind" (14:13).

What is the criterion of selection for each list? In the cultural context of Jesus and his contemporaries, social events were inherently utilitarian. The presence of rich neighbors in one's home signified honor by association and the potential of receiving equal or better treatment when the invitation was reciprocated. This kind of social discourse encouraged manipulation and focused on short-term gain.

Jesus exhorts his audience not to keep inviting the people to reap a comparable payback. Rather, he proposes that they invite the poor, the crippled, the lame, and the blind, people who have no wherewithal to enter the arena of balanced reciprocity. Their uncleanness is an affront to the high standard of ritual purity meticulously maintained by the law-abiding Pharisees. Their low status is unattractive and they have no means to return the favor. How audacious of Jesus to expect the head Pharisee to share his table with these unsavory characters!

Jesus is advocating for the long view. If the Pharisees invited their in-group on the first list, their reward and repayment would come from the same source. By inviting those who stand no chance of reciprocating, they are living out the values of God's kingdom. True blessedness is not limited to temporary human accolades and material returns but anticipates an eternal reward given by God at "the resurrection of the just" (14:14; cf. 12:21, 33). The eyes of faith will see beyond the dealings of this world to alignment with God's program and its ethos. In doing so, the endless cycle of obligation, patronage, and balanced reciprocity will be disrupted, releasing God's people to do good out of mercy and wholehearted generosity, rather than a calculating expectation of repayment (cf. 6:32–36).

Are the two lists mutually exclusive? For the Pharisees whose boundaries are impermeable, the people on each list will never recline at the same table. But Jesus himself has shared meals with people across the spectrum (5:29–30; 7:36; 10:38; 24:30). Jesus is not saying that they must exclude their family and friends and only eat with the poor, the crippled, the lame, and the blind, but he is saying the latter group is equally worthy of an invitation.[8] The challenge is to broaden the guest list so that more people can benefit from true inclusive hospitality.

A Great Banquet (14:15–24)

One of the dinner guests exclaims, "Blessed is anyone who will eat bread in the kingdom of God" (14:15). The comment is self-congratulatory and probably receives approving nods from his fellow Pharisees. The speaker assumes that he and his associates are among the blessed, confident that their adherence to the law will earn them a place around God's messianic banquet. Previously, Jesus spoke of those who consider themselves eligible for God's kingdom yet find themselves barred from entry at the very end (13:23–30). The parable of the great banquet makes a similar point that the window of opportunity to embrace the gospel will not be forever available.

The banquet is a popular metaphor to signify the unlimited joy, abundance, and bliss enjoyed by those who are saved.[9] At first glance, the parable identifies God as the host, the meal as the messianic banquet, and the slaves as divine messengers of the gospel. But not every detail of this parable warrants an allegorical reading.[10] The story starts off with a rather common scenario and then makes an unexpected turn toward a surprising ending.

A wealthy and influential man in the community is throwing a dinner at his big house (14:16). Imagine the buzz that surrounds the lengthy guest list, made up of all the well-known figures who match the host in status and recognition. Jesus' audience may already have numbered themselves among the dignitaries for such a prestigious gathering.[11] It was customary to give invitations in two stages. The first invitation, extended with plenty of lead time, would secure an acceptance to attend.

---

8. Garland 2011: 577.

9. Isa 25:6; 2 *En.* 42:5; *m. 'Abot* 4:16.

10. For examples of allegorical readings that are somewhat strained, see Marshall 1978: 586; Hultgren 2000: 338; Snodgrass 2008: 308–9.

11. Green 1997: 558.

When the dinner was ready, a reminder would be sent, at which point those who agreed to come were expected to show up.[12]

Following the same protocol, the host sends his servants to inform those who accepted the invitation that the dinner is ready (14:17). Here the story takes an unhappy turn. Every one of the original invitees no longer wants to come (14:18a). The three excuses presented are but a sampling of what the servants hear. They all pertain to some economic or domestic issue that requires attention. The first person claims that he must go see a parcel of land that he has recently purchased (14:18b). Now who inspects a piece of land after the sale and not before? The second person has bought five yoke of oxen and claims that he has to try them out (14:19). Again, this is a sizable purchase. What prudent farmer would pay a hefty sum for farm animals without knowing if they were strong and able? The third guest does not even bother to send his regrets. He simply says he has taken a wife and is unavailable (14:20). All three reasons seem legitimate on the surface, but under scrutiny they are not as urgent as they appear. Large purchases and getting married tend not to be last-minute decisions. Given that they have plenty of advanced notice for the dinner, these guests, as well as all the others who said they would come but now refuse to show up, do not have a legitimate excuse. They have deeply insulted the host and jeopardized his standing in the community. By shaming the host, these unreliable guests shame themselves as well.

Angered by this sweeping affront, that which the host chooses to do next is highly unconventional. He orders his slave to bring in from the town "the poor, the crippled, the blind, and the lame," the same list of people that Jesus has challenged the head Pharisee to consider inviting (14:21; cf. 14:13). When the slave has done that and there is still room, the master tells him to widen the search even more, beyond the boundary of his town to the roadways and hedges, to compel[13] people to come fill his banqueting table (14:22–23). The owner is determined to show his largesse. By their refusal to come, the original invitees have forfeited their privileged seats and others will enjoy the banquet in their stead (14:24).

---

12. In this parable Jesus describes the rituals of a formal dinner invitation, which reflect the social contract of honor and shame in ancient society. See Braun 1995: 100–106.

13. The less the invitees know the host, the more persuasion is needed to get them to come to the table.

God is a generous host whose banqueting table has plenty of seats. He is no respecter of human standards and status symbols. Neither does he care for lip service paid in the name of religious piety. His benefits are gifts to be shared with those willing to join him. But one must not mock God, as did the original guests who were derailed by other preoccupations. Commitment is for the long haul, and only those who remain faithful to the end will receive their eternal reward.

Cost of Discipleship (14:25–35)

In spite of the heightened tension between Jesus and his adversaries, the size of the crowd around Jesus has not diminished (14:25). Many are drawn to Jesus but few will endure to the end (13:24). Discipleship is a serious undertaking that requires courage and, in some cases, heart-wrenching separation from people and things most treasured, should they become a hindrance to the urgent work of God's kingdom.

In laying out the cost of discipleship, Jesus minces no words. He does not ask of his followers anything that he himself is not willing to go through or give up. Aside from giving up one's life, the relinquishing of possessions and family ties for the sake of the gospel is perhaps the next most formidable challenge for those who aspire to follow Jesus (14:26, 33). While not everyone dies a martyr's death, martyrdom is a real possibility for Jesus' disciples. To carry one's cross means to bear the shame that culminates in a painful, humiliating death, should persecution takes its most grievous course (14:27; cf. 9:23–24).[14] Whether it is death by crucifixion, stoning, beheading, or other torturous means, genuine discipleship demands total sacrifice (cf. 9:9; Acts 7:59–60; 12:1–2).

Putting Jesus above family and possessions is a form of dying to self. The language Jesus uses, that his followers have to "hate father and mother, wife and children, brothers and sisters, and even life itself" (14:26), is jarring. The Greek verb *misei* not only means "hate," but in the present tense it means "hate continually," which sounds even more hard-hearted. How does this "hatred" reconcile with Jesus' teaching on loving one's enemies (6:35)? Isn't honoring one's parents commanded by God and upheld by Jesus (18:20; Exod 20:12; Deut 5:16)?

Lost in translation is the hyperbolic sense of the Semitic expression behind *miseō* ("to hate"). It does not convey an intense feeling of loathing

---

14. See p. 129 and p. 295.

and resentment toward someone or something. Rather, an idiom for comparable preference is found in the OT: "to love one and hate the other," meaning, "to strongly prefer one over the other" (cf. Deut 21:15–17; Mal 1:2–3). The word "hatred" communicates a sentiment more intense than having a preference, hence its idiomatic use can be very effective in the appropriate context. Jesus is not asking his disciples to become resentful and scornful toward family members whom they honor and love. He is using "hate" in the hyperbolic sense to denote a very strong preference, setting a high standard for committed discipleship. To become Jesus' follower, one's "preference"—loyalty, love, and priority—must reside with Jesus over all people and things one holds dear.

Not every disciple is martyred, and not every disciple is called to leave everything. But Jesus' disciples must have the mindset that family, possessions, even life itself pale in comparison with following him. While not necessarily evil in and of themselves, the good things of life can become distractions that hamper the disciples' dedication to Jesus and his mission (2:43–50; 8:19–20; 9:59–62). To the credit of the Twelve, they have left everything to follow him (5:9–11, 27–28; 18:28–30). Yet self-denial is not a one-time demonstration of religious fervor but a lifetime of daily recommitments.

Will people rise to Jesus' challenge of leaving home, selling all their possessions, and even losing their lives should the mission of God's kingdom necessitate such extreme measures? These decisions call for serious contemplation. Jesus gives two analogies on counting the cost before taking the plunge. He frames both images in the form of a rhetorical question that solicits the same response, "No, no such person who would not 'first sit down and estimate or consider'" (14:28, 31).

First, Jesus asks what it takes to build a tower (14:28–30). It does not matter what type of tower is in view, whether a farm building, a watchtower, or a military structure.[15] Whatever its function, the project requires money and planning. A prudent builder makes careful calculations that yield an accurate estimate of the funds needed. Otherwise, a structure with only a foundation and partially completed walls is both non-functional and an eyesore. The incompetent and irresponsible builder will face ridicule and suffer loss. Likewise, discipleship comes with a set of expectations. If would-be disciples realize that they cannot

---

15. Hultgren 2000: 139; Nolland 1993a: 763.

fulfill Jesus' expectations, they are better off not committing themselves than to become deserters when the going gets tough.

The second analogy involves a king planning for battle (14:31–32). Two armies are approaching each other. The stakes are high because of the potential loss of life for the soldiers on the field. If the enemy has twenty thousand soldiers but the king has only half as many, his men must be better equipped and better trained to compensate for the disadvantage in numbers. If not, he is better off sending a delegation to his opponent to negotiate a peace treaty (cf. Prov 24:5). Even though the king may have to make concessions, it is still a wiser course of action than sending ten thousand troops to the front line knowing that casualty will be great. Similarly, those who want to become Jesus' disciples must anticipate the ramifications of their decisions, especially if other people may be affected by it.

To round out this discussion, Jesus offers one more image to address the effectiveness of discipleship. Salt is one of the most common and indispensable necessities of life, used since ancient times for flavoring and preserving food. Its goodness and usefulness are undisputed (14:34a). Normally, it is impossible for salt, consisting of pure sodium chloride, to lose its flavor. In Palestine, however, salt is obtained from putting the water from the Dead Sea, which has a high salt content, through evaporation. The residue left is not pure salt, but a mixture of salt (sodium chloride), gypsum (calcium sulfate), and carnallite (potassium-magnesium chloride).[16] If the sodium chloride leaches away, leaving only the other impurities, it is as though the salt had lost its saltiness (14:34b). In that case, salt can in fact lose its saltiness, as desalinized salt cannot be made salty again.

Jesus' point is not about re-activating the flavor of salt but its irreversible loss of flavor. Real salt is useful and effective. That which is not real salt, even though it looks like salt, is useless and ineffective. Any partial effectiveness is in the end ineffective, rendering the so-called salt "fit neither for the soil nor for the manure pile," but only to be discarded (14:35a). The contrast between useful and useless salt illustrates the difference between an authentic disciple and someone who showcases the appearance of a disciple but has no inner substance or integrity.

The discourse closes with the exhortation: "Let anyone with ears to hear listen" (14:35b; cf. 8:8), resounding again the theme of hearing and

---

16. Garland 2011: 603–4; Green 1997: 567.

doing Jesus' words (8:18, 21; 10:39, 42). Rather than deceiving self and others, those who merely pretend to be disciples may as well not claim to be disciples, lest their hypocrisy be exposed when they are rejected by Jesus at the last judgment (13:25–30; 14:15–24).

Luke 15

Three Lost Parables (15:1–32)

Criticism and Defense (15:1–3)

The three parables in this chapter constitute Jesus' response to the criticism of the Pharisees and the scribes regarding his table fellowship with tax collectors and sinners (15:1–3).[1] From the point of view of the religious elite, Jesus' association with tax collectors and sinners is a breach of purity laws.[2] He ignores the decorum of conventional boundaries by sharing table with the wrong crowd.[3] This kind of behavior is unbecoming of a respected teacher.

In defense, Jesus tells not one, not two, but three parables to illustrate God's attitude toward the lost. The shepherd, the woman, and the father in these stories represent God, to whom the sheep, the coin, and the sons belong. The lost sheep, the lost coin, and the lost younger son correspond to the tax collectors and sinners whom Jesus welcomes to his table. If the first two parables are not enough to move the Pharisees and the scribes, perhaps they will identify with the older brother of the third parable and catch a glimpse of God's compassion for the lost.

At first glance, these parables appear repetitive; the lost is found and there is great rejoicing. On closer reading, each story occupies a distinctive place in the triptych. There is a progression from losing one sheep out of a hundred, to one coin out of ten, and finally to one son out of two. As the lost "item" constitutes an increasing percentage of the owner's total "holdings," from one to ten to fifty percent, the eagerness to find "it" rises. Yet the same exuberance of joy is expressed across the board. The

---

1. See p. 50, n. 13, Neale 1991: 148–54.
2. See pp. 72–73.
3. See pp. 77–78 and pp. 204–5.

third parable wonders if there is only one lost son. Are there in fact two sons lost in different ways?

One Lost Sheep (15:4–7)

The opening question, "Which one of you . . .," compels the hearers to put themselves in the shoes of the shepherd (15:4a). The shepherd is the owner, not a hired hand, so his concern for the lost sheep is natural (cf. John 10:12–13). No explanation is given as to how the sheep got lost, nor blame assigned to careless shepherding, the antics of thieves, or the wandering off of the sheep itself. Sheep are rather dumb; it is unlikely that this lost sheep can find its way back to the fold. When the owner leaves the ninety-nine to search for the lost sheep, we assume that he has arranged for another shepherd to watch over his flock while he is away.[4] The emphasis is not on whether the owner is a responsible or competent shepherd, but on the proactive measures he takes to find the sheep. His determination is implied in the phrases, "until he finds it" (15:4b) and "when he has found it" (15:5a). He will not stop until he succeeds. One can picture the joy and pride of the shepherd as he carries the sheep home on his shoulders[5] and promptly calls for a celebration with his friends and neighbors (15:5–6). Although throwing a party over the recovery of one sheep may seem over the top, this is where Jesus' message defies normal expectations. If the shepherd treats one seemingly insignificant sheep with such persistent care, the compassion and love he has for the entire flock must know no bounds.

The metaphor of God as shepherd is well attested in the OT (Pss 23:1–4; 77:20; Isa 40:11). Kings and priests were also viewed as shepherds. Unfortunately, many of them turned out to be self-serving shepherds, under whose incompetent watch Israel became like lost sheep without a shepherd (Jer 50:6; Ezek 34:1–10; Zech 10:2). So God declared that he would go look for his own sheep, bring them back, and appoint David as shepherd over his flock (Ezek 34:11–16, 23–24, 30–31). As Davidic Messiah, Jesus now takes on the role as God's shepherd who seeks the lost (19:10).

---

4. Hultgren (2000: 53–54) wonders if the shepherd is deliberately portrayed as risking everything for the sake of a lost sheep by leaving the ninety-nine unattended.

5. Nolland (1993a: 772) suggests that the sheep is probably frightened and needs to be carried.

The joy over the repentance of a sinner is especially gratifying because divine initiative is met with human receptivity. The punch line, that "there will be more joy in heaven over one sinner who repents than over ninety-nine righteous persons who need no repentance" (15:7), does not mean that God and his angels are more partial to the sinner than to the righteous. The religious elite may consider themselves righteous (11:37–52; 16:14–15; cf. 18:11–12), but before God they too are sinners (13:1–5; cf. 5:32). If they repent and see themselves as the lost sheep that has been found, the joy in heaven to celebrate their return will be equally ebullient.

One Lost Coin (15:8–10)

From a wealthy shepherd with a hundred sheep Jesus now turns to a poor woman who has lost one of ten silver coins (15:8a). The silver coin is a Greek drachma, valued roughly about the same as a Roman denarius.[6] Nothing is said of her total assets. If that coin amounts to a day's sustenance and this woman is a peasant, then the loss is a sizable one. Nothing is explicitly said of her carelessness; a sheep may wander off but a coin has no legs.[7] Nevertheless, the focus is on its recovery.

The woman does everything to find the coin. She lights a lamp, sweeps the house, and looks into every nook and cranny (15:8b). Every inch of floor space in her dark peasant home has been combed. She has put in as much effort as has the shepherd in the previous parable, so imagine her joy when she, too, finds her lost coin. From this point onwards, both parables proceed in an identical fashion. The woman, too, celebrates with her friends and neighbors (15:9). To quibble over whether she has the resources to throw a party when she cannot even afford to lose a drachma misses the point. Jesus repeatedly emphasizes the joy that is shared when the lost item is found, and that "there is joy in the presence of the angels of God over one sinner who repents" (15:10).

The parables of the lost sheep and the lost coin, featuring yet another male-female pairing[8] typical of Luke's narrative style, create an effective crescendo toward the third parable, which is longer, more complex, and more nuanced. Not only does Jesus want to reassure the tax collectors and sinners that their repentance brings great joy, he also reaches out

---

6. A laborer could earn a denarius in a day.
7. Bailey 1992: 104.
8. See p. 66, n. 12.

to the Pharisees and the scribes, so that they may also recognize God's compassion for them.

Two Lost Sons (15:11–32)

Beyond the first sentence, "There was a man who had two sons" (15:11), Jesus wastes no time in presenting an unthinkable situation in a Jewish family, in which the younger son asks his living father for his share of the inheritance (15:12a). According to Jewish customs, a man's property was transferred to his heirs only upon death (Num 27:8–11; Sir 33:20–24), at which time the oldest son would receive a double portion of the inheritance (Deut 21:17; *m. B. Bat.* 8:4–5). Before the death of the father, the property remained under his control and could neither be subdivided nor sold. Against these practices, the younger son's demand is preposterous and offensive, tantamount to wishing his father dead. Equally odd is the nonresistance of the father, who "divided his property between them" (15:12b). It is tempting to psychoanalyze the father. Why does he spoil his son by consenting to such a disrespectful demand? The son deserves a good scolding! We are baffled by the father's action. The young man gets his way, and his troubles begin.

The next four verses catalog the downward spiral of the young man. Within days he takes all he has and leaves home for a distant country. Not only has he declared total independence from his father, he has also abandoned his responsibility to care for him in his old age (Exod 20:12; Deut 5:16). In essence he has disowned his family. It does not take him long to squander all his money on an extravagant and immoral life among the gentiles (15:13, 30). When a famine hits, he becomes destitute. To survive he hires himself out to a gentile farmer to feed pigs, a job of unmentionable uncleanness to the Jews (Lev 11:7; Deut 14:8). Mistreated and malnourished, he is so hungry that he would even eat the carob pods fed to the pigs (15:14–16). His state of impurity has reached an all-time high.

Whether self-inflicted or not, the younger son's misfortunes are not inclined to earn him any sympathy from Jesus' hearers. The scoundrel deserves to be in this condition, given how he treated his father and his family. Yet his sorry state is pitiable. To be in pagan territory, having cavorted with pagan prostitutes, and now working for a pagan farmer to feed unclean pigs, is as degrading and shameful a state a Jew can find himself. His status as a landowner's son takes a precipitous plunge. He only dares to think of himself as one of his father's hired hands, whose status is even lower than that of household slaves.[9] Nobody cares whether he lives or dies. Famished and weak, he is not far from the brink of death—and he knows it (15:17).

What does it mean for the younger son to come to his senses? Is he showing signs of remorse, or has he simply devised a game plan to deal with his situation, hedging his bets and rehearsing a speech to manipulate his father into taking him back? Is he so motivated by sheer hunger that his repentance is fueled by survival instincts and not genuine remorse?

Talking to himself,[10] the younger son does not make claim to the privileges he had before. He is aware that his actions have rendered him unworthy to be called a son, and he is ready to admit his guilt before God and before his father. If he could be taken back as a hired hand, he could at least be assured of survival, for none of his father's slaves or day laborers is starving (15:17–19). Neither Jesus nor Luke delves into the motive of the young man. The focus is on his reasoning and plan that prompt him to go home (15:20a). When he comes face to face with his father, he says exactly that which he has prepared to say, never mind the fact that he does not get to finish it (15:21). He confesses his sin and asks to become a hired hand, showing humility and propriety, which is quite a change from his former brashness. The turnaround of the young man signifies the repentance that runs through all three parables.[11]

As the transgressor, the younger man is in no position to effect reconciliation. Only the father can reconcile the son to himself, and he does so in such a public and grand gesture that his attitude toward the returning prodigal is evident to all. Why has the father not followed the pattern of the shepherd and the woman to actively go search for his lost son? How often has he turned his face toward the gate of his estate and looked at the dusty road beyond? The father has been waiting for a long time. The fact that he spots the lad from a distance is indicative of his parental yearning.

Imagine the depth of longing that generates the emotional response of the father, who sees his son, wells up with compassion, runs toward him, throws his arms around him, and kisses him (15:20b).[12] The verb that

---

9. Hultgren 2000: 76.
10. See p. 180, n. 9.
11. Snodgrass 2008: 138.
12. Esau ran to meet Jacob, embraced him, and kissed him (Gen 33:4).

expresses the father's compassion, *esplanchnisthē*, appears three times in Luke. Jesus sees the widow whose son is being carried out on a bier for burial and is filled with compassion (7:13). The Samaritan sees the half-dead man by the roadside and is filled with compassion (10:33). Now the father sees his emaciated son and is filled with compassion. It matters not what the young man did, how much he squandered, or what shame he brought on the family. Normally a dignified man does not run lest his legs be exposed, but this father sprints, as fast as he can, toward his son.[13] The young man may not even be recognizable, but the father knows his son no matter how dirty, smelly, and sickly he is. The son never finishes his confession, for his father is already drowning him out with orders to the servants to bring in the best robe, the ring, and the sandals (15:21–22).[14] These are the fittings of a son, not a hired hand. In addition, the father kills a fatted calf[15] and throws a big celebration for his son to reinstate his honor and status (15:23). The younger son's return is likened to the dead returning to life (15:24). The father's exuberance equals the joy in heaven when a sinner repents (15:7, 10).

The second half of the story is as important as the first, if not more so, for with it Jesus brings into focus the gripes that have long been hidden under the cloak of religious correctness (15:1–2). All this time, the older brother of the prodigal has been unaware of the flurry of activities generated by his younger brother's return (15:25). He finds out from one of the slaves what all the fuss is about (15:26). The slave's response is accurate in relaying the cause of the celebration, that the fatted calf is slaughtered because his father has his brother back safe and sound (15:27). But this is the last thing the older son wants to hear.

Most people can appreciate the older brother's anger, so vividly displayed in the dialogue between him and his father. Because he refuses to join in the celebration, once again the father is shown to initiate reconciliation in this broken relationship (15:28). The older brother is transparent; all his grudges come out in full force in his outburst of anger (15:29–30). First, he thinks of himself as a slave even though he

---

13. Within the cultural norms of the parable, the father would have been viewed as foolish, shameful, indulgent, and weak. Yet this father's grace is not calculated as a zero-sum game. God can afford to be generous, so much so that "divine wisdom [can masquerade] as foolishness." See Eastman 2006: 403–5.

14. Sandals distinguish a son from a slave who wears no shoes.

15. A fatted calf takes months to breed and is reserved for a special occasion, when many guests can be invited to enjoy it together.

is the privileged firstborn son. Second, he considers his years of obedience deserving of reward but receiving no recognition. Third, he charges his father with showing partiality. He has not been given even a goat for his faithful service, and here his father is rewarding recalcitrance with a fatted calf. What if the rascal takes off again when he gets bored? What guarantee is there that he will never do it again? Will his father be such a fool, not once but twice? One can "hear" the escalation of his pitch and volume as he rails himself into a frenzy.

Throughout the argument, the older son never calls his father "Father," and he refers to his younger brother as "this son of yours" (15:30). He is so angry that he will not have anything to do with either his father or his brother. By contrast, even in the depth of his misery, the younger son never loses sight of his intrinsic sonship. He would have been happy with the role of a hired hand, but in his thinking and his speech, he still thinks like a son: "my father's hired hands" (15:27), "I will . . . go to my father" (15:18a), "Father, I have sinned against heaven and before you" (15:18b, 21). It is the sense of sonship that gives the younger brother, even if subconsciously, the courage to come home. How profoundly ironic it is for the older brother, obsessed with duty and obedience, to have lost sight of his core identity as his father's firstborn!

But the father has not stopped being a father. He does not rebuke his disgruntled son to reclaim his paternal honor but is equally compassionate toward him. Even though the older son refuses to call him "Father," the first word that comes from the father's mouth is "Son," followed by a twin affirmation of their filial relationship: "You are always with me, and all that is mine is yours" (15:31). The older son has never been shortchanged; his father's estate is there for him to use, enjoy, and inherit. Yet he sees everything as earnings from backbreaking labor. Gift, grace, and mercy are missing from his construal of his relationship with his father, which is manifested in his unwillingness to forgive his younger brother. If only the older son could see himself as a true son, and his father a true father, he would appreciate his father's outrageous response to his brother's homecoming. Hence the father redirects his older son to the blood ties between the three of them, changing "this son of yours" to "this brother of yours" when referring to the prodigal (15:32). The necessity of the celebration has nothing to do with condoning the younger son's behavior, but everything to do with the joy of his return, without which he would have been forever lost and as good as dead.

The parable ends with a cliffhanger. Will the older son join in the celebration or will he continue to seethe in anger? It is ironic that the son who cut all filial ties is now reinstated, whereas the son who never strayed is standing outside the door. The prodigal who did not act like a son retains his sense of identity as his father's son. To the contrary, the older son, whose status as son is embodied as joyless duty, has taken on the identity of a slave without noticing it.

The father has two lost sons. The younger son's lostness, evident in ritual impurity and immorality, is easy to point out. That of the older son is subtler. Common to both is their alienation from their father, which leads to separation from the rest of the family. The beauty of the filial metaphor lies in its inalienability. A father is always a father and a son always a son. Even if father and son separate, they are still father and son. It is most fitting to speak of God as Israel's father and Israel as God's son. Despite Israel's long and checkered history of rebellion against God, God is still the faithful, compassionate Father whose mercy for his children knows no limits.[16]

The Pharisees and the scribes must realize that Jesus is identifying them with the older brother, the tax collectors and sinners with the younger brother, and God with the compassionate father, on whose behalf Jesus accepts both sons. God's grace is risky, and Jesus willingly risks his reputation to reach out to sinners even before they have completely cleaned up their act and fulfilled all the requirements of the law. Like the shepherd, the woman, and the father, Jesus searches and saves. The tax collectors and sinners have been found, but what about the Pharisees and the scribes?

---

16. Exod 4:22–23; Deut 14:1–2; 32:6, 15, 18; Isa 43:6–7; 63:15–16; 64:8–9; Jer 3:14, 19; 31:8–9, 20. See Chen 2006: 73–143.

Luke 16

A Dishonest Manager (16:1–13)

Wealth is one of the biggest hindrances to a life of committed discipleship, regardless of one's position on the economic spectrum. The rich hoard what they have, and the poor covet what they have not. No one is exempt from the lure of possession, be the motivation greed or insecurity. Although money in itself is neutral, the potential power and pitfalls of one's dealings with wealth make it a revealing barometer of one's true attitude toward God, life on earth, and life beyond.

The parable of the dishonest manager is difficult to interpret because it contains many gaps. The plot line is sparse and Jesus' point is not immediately apparent. A manager employed by a rich man finds himself out of a job, having been found guilty of mismanaging his employer's affairs. Taking advantage of a small window of time he has between exposure and dismissal, he uses the authority his master's debtors think he still has to lower their debt burdens. He thus ingratiates himself with them, so that someday when he needs their help, they will be obliged to return the favor. The surprising twist at the end of the parable is the master's positive appraisal of his manager's action, which seems downright dishonest.

Puzzled interpreters have raised questions about the social identity of the manager, the structure of the debts, the legitimacy of the manager's action, and the reason for his commendation. Details have been embellished, historical options suggested, and characters psychoanalyzed, leading to a plethora of reconstructions of the scenario. Depictions of the manager range from cunning and self-serving to merciful and sacrificial. Some see the rich master as a clueless absentee landlord; others cast him as a greedy creditor.[1] We need a historically sensible way to read the story as believable without drowning out the main point with the details.

---

1. For a variety of proposals see Snodgrass 2008: 406–10; some are more convincing than others.

Rich people receive a negative assessment in Luke not because it is sinful to have money but because of the propensity to misuse it (12:16–21; 16:19–31; 18:18–25). Yet Jesus does not introduce the master as a wicked rich man. The sizable debts owed to him speak more of his wealth than the ethics of his lending practice. There is no hint that an exorbitant interest rate has been charged. Without the principal amounts of the loans, such calculations cannot be made. An a priori conclusion that the master is exploitative is unsustainable.[2] The master is a passive character until his comment at the end. Had any unethical lending practice been important for the interpretation, some clue would have been dropped.

The manager is likely to be an employee rather than a high-level household slave.[3] If he were a slave, the owner might have demoted him and relegated him to menial labor rather than fired him. The manager acts as an agent on behalf of his employer. Unlike real estate agents and insurance agents in modern life, who function as go-betweens and sales representatives, an agent in ancient times had substantial authority: "A man's agent is as himself" (*b. B. Meṣ.* 96a; *b. B. Qam.* 113b; *b. Qidd.* 41b–42a). Dealing with the agent was equal to dealing with the sender, so any negotiation conducted by the agent was binding on the sender (cf. Gen 24). The rich man has no recourse for whatever financial losses the manager has incurred. That the manager offers no defense may be indicative of his guilt. Incompetence or irresponsibility does not imply criminality.[4] Nevertheless, trust has been breached. The rich man fires the manager and asks for a final accounting of the books (16:1–2).

The manager's soliloquy reveals his inner motives.[5] Losing the job means losing the roof above his head. In a society governed by the values of honor and shame, digging and begging would land him in the class of expendables and wipe out his standing in the community. Whether he is really too weak to do hard labor or too lazy is a moot point. Given his

---

2. Garland (2011: 642) sees the master as a wicked rich man who gets rich on the back of the poor, but a foolish one to have hired a crooked manager. This interpretation adds a lot of detail absent from Jesus' basic storyline.

3. In the ancient world, not all slaves did menial labor. Some fortunate ones were assigned important responsibility over the owner's estate. Udoh (2009: 315–24) views the *oikonomos* as a "managerial slave." See Kim 1998: 131–35; and p. 93.

4. Lygre (2002: 21–28) suggests that the manager's infraction is not necessarily immoral, but that his performance is so poor that his service is no longer needed.

5. See p. 180, n. 9.

scheming nature, he can concoct a better escape route than resorting to such lowly means of survival (16:3–4).

A brilliant idea soon presents itself, which the manager swiftly puts into action. Since he has yet to return the accounting records to his employer, there is a sliver of time before his dismissal becomes finalized and public. Before people get wind of his expulsion from his employer's estate, they are still under the impression that his financial dealings are sanctioned and legitimate.

The plan is ingenious, even elegant. The manager will reduce the debtors' financial obligations to his master, making himself their benefactor. The numbers represent sizable loans, even if they include both principal and interest. A hundred liquid measures of olive oil, or nine-hundred gallons, are equivalent to three years of a worker's wages. A hundred measures of wheat have an even higher value, equivalent to over a thousand bushels or seven and a half years of wages. These debtors are not poor peasants but business associates or tenant farmers.[6] To any debtor, the reduction of a loan by fifty, or even twenty, percent, is substantial (16:6–7).[7] The debtors have no reason to doubt the authority of the manager, so they are eager to do as told, rewrite the loan voucher, and sign it. It is a win-win situation for both manager and debtor. No one raises the uncomfortable question as to why the paperwork is being doctored, and the rich man will be none the wiser when the manager hands over the books.[8] The dishonest manager has shown his true colors. He has cheated before and he is cheating again. His motive is one of self-preservation, taking advantage of the obligatory rule of reciprocity in social engagement.[9]

---

6. Garland 2011: 645.

7. Goodrich (2012: 547–66) surmises that the reduction of debt reflects the practice of lease adjustment in antiquity, especially in relation to land tenancy, where landowners would give tenants a break to encourage them to stay and in the long run repay what they owed.

8. The suggestion that the manager is foregoing the commission he collects from setting up these loans is untenable. Had the manager been pocketing commission, he would not be worrying about being destitute upon leaving the rich man's house. See Snodgrass 2008: 410; Nolland 1993a: 798–99.

9. deSilva (1993: 255–68) thinks that the manager is incompetent and ineffective but not dishonest. The reduction of debt amounts to waiving the high interest charged by the rich man, making his action one of justice for the benefit of the debtors rather than injustice done to his employer.

Where exactly the parable ends hinges upon the referent of the Greek word *kyrios*. The flow of the narrative is smoother when we attribute the commendation as coming from the rich man ("the lord") and not from Jesus ("the Lord").[10] Verse 8a bridges the transition from the story world to Jesus' exhortation. Having found out that he has been duped twice by his dishonest manager, the rich man praises the rogue, not for his deceitfulness but for his clever strategizing. To maintain his honor, the rich man has to absorb the losses from the reduction of debt,[11] for the debtors cannot be faulted for not knowing that the manager has been terminated. While the employer's commendation does not express approval, it contains a hint of concession. The rich man has been outmaneuvered by his dishonest but shrewd manager.

In some sense verse 8a also begins Jesus' commentary. As "Lord," Jesus commends the manager for his savvy and quick thinking, like the children of this age. The point of emulation is not the manager's dishonesty but his ability to assess the situation, anticipate his prospects, and execute a workable plan. Jesus' disciples, the children of light, must learn to do the same (16:8). Being nimble and decisive in a moment of crisis is a useful skill for navigating the dangers ahead.

As to the arena in which the disciples' shrewdness is to be exercised, Jesus specifies in the next verse, "Make friends for yourselves by means of dishonest wealth, so that when it is gone, they may welcome you into the eternal homes" (16:9). At first glance, befriending dishonesty sounds contradictory to the ethics of Jesus. But that is not what Jesus means. The phrase, "dishonest wealth," is idiomatic, like "ill-gotten gains." It does not imply that every use of wealth is morally suspect, but it highlights the propensity of wealth to be bound up in dishonest dealings. Properly administered, money is a useful resource for furthering God's purposes. Using money to generate more money to give to the poor or to support those who minister to the needy is befriending "dishonest" wealth. Jesus has repeatedly urged his followers to divest themselves of earthly possessions, give alms, and accumulate treasure in heaven (12:33–34; 14:33; 18:22–25). Earthly wealth will not last, but proper use of wealth that embodies God's values and salvific aims will yield eternal dividends.

10. As do many English translations, e.g., NRSV, NIV, NASB, NLT, ESV, etc.

11. Landry and May (2000: 298–305) suggest that the manager's mismanagement has brought shame to the rich man. Since the manager's scheme of debt reduction serves to make his employer appear generous, the latter is willing to take the additional monetary hit to gain back his honor.

Recalling the dishonest manager's hope that his employer's debtors will receive him into their homes when he is in need (16:4), the children of light who befriend wealth and act shrewdly will also be received into God's eternal presence.

In the next three verses, the word "faithful" is repeated four times (16:10, 2x; 11, 12). Still drawing an antithesis between faithfulness and dishonesty, Jesus introduces the concept of scale. A truly faithful person can be trusted in things both small and big. By the same token, someone who cheats in matters with small ramifications will become emboldened to cheat in things of greater consequences (16:10). The core trait—faithfulness or dishonesty—manifests itself regardless of the size of the arena or the scope of influence. The key is for Jesus' disciples to be on the side of faithfulness toward God and fellow human beings in all their dealings, especially financial ones. Framed as two rhetorical questions, Jesus refers back to the dishonest manager whose lack of integrity disqualifies him to manage his own, true, heavenly riches. Earthly wealth is ultimately inferior to true riches in heaven. In order for God to put that which is truly valuable in their hands, the disciples must prove themselves to be reliable in every way at all times.

Since faithfulness requires single-mindedness, a disciple cannot have split loyalties. A slave can only serve one master. Likewise, a disciple cannot be simultaneously and authentically devoted to God and to wealth (*mamōnas*, "mammon," 16:13). Loving one means hating the other and devotion to one means scorn for the other. Even though it is possible to "befriend dishonest wealth" in the way that Jesus prescribes, when wealth becomes an object of worship, it will derail a person's devotion to God (cf. 8:14; 18:18–25). Shrewdness enables the disciples to respond wisely and adroitly to human and diabolic threats, and faithfulness is for the long haul, stretching beyond this age to the age to come.

The Place of the Law (16:14–18)

At first glance, the sayings in this section seem carelessly bundled together, moving from Jesus condemning the Pharisees (16:14–15), to the place of the law in light of the kingdom of God (16:16–17), and then to a comment on divorce (16:18). There is in fact thematic cohesion across these five verses. They affirm the value of the law in light of Jesus' teachings, and they set up the next parable, in which a rich man's unhappy ending has to do with his neglect of the law of Moses and the teachings of the prophets (16:19–31).

As "lovers of money," the Pharisees are at odds with Jesus' claim that one cannot serve both God and mammon (16:13). Their negative response is not surprising, as they have been scoffing and sneering at Jesus all along (16:14).[12] The Pharisees claim they serve God, but Jesus exposes their piety as a veneer of outward religiosity. The inner workings of their hearts may fool others, but they will never get past the scrutiny of divine omniscience (cf. 11:37–44). God knows the hearts of human beings all too well, even when self-deception clouds their judgment.[13] Things prized by human beings, such as the amassing of possessions, love of status, arrogance of fame, lure of influence, wielding of power, neglect of the poor, and the exploitation of the powerless, are abhorrent in God's eyes (16:15).

It is this incongruence exhibited by the Pharisees and their vehement objection to Jesus that raise the question of the place of the law and the prophets in light of the gospel message. Has Jesus dismissed the boundaries and regulations that God gave Israel and replaced them with some radical new rules? No, he has not. As Jesus says in Matthew, "Do not think that I have come to abolish the law or the prophets; I have come not to abolish but to fulfill" (Matt 5:17). The two sayings in 16:16–17 say as much.

Since the time of Moses, Israel has always been governed by the law and the prophets as God's words of instruction, warning, and hope for his people. The ministry of John marks a new era in God's plan of salvation (16:16a). The proclamation of the kingdom of God maintains continuity with the law and the prophets, yet injects something new, hopeful, and exciting. The vision of the good news breaks the existing paradigm, triggering a serious reevaluation of how God saves, when God saves, and whom God saves.

The phrase, "everyone tries to enter it by force" (16:16b), sounds as though the kingdom of God was being attacked. The Greek verb *biazetai* means "to force" or "to strongly urge." Grammatically, the verb form can take on either a middle voice or a passive voice. The difference is whether everyone is forcing his or her way into the kingdom, or that everyone is strongly urged to enter the kingdom. On the one hand, to speak of

---

12. See 5:21, 30, 33; 6:7; 7:39; 11:37–38; 14:1–3; 15:1–2.
13. Deut 8:2; 1 Sam 16:7; 1 Kgs 8:39; Prov 21:2; Jer 11:20; 17:10.

people forcing their way into God's kingdom may refer to the eager response of the poor, the outcasts, and the sinners to John and Jesus. On the other hand, to say that people are strongly urged to enter God's kingdom reflects the insistence of John's and Jesus' proclamations. It is not as though people were dragged into God's kingdom against their will, but the invitation is earnest and urgent. The general sense is that the gospel continues what God has started with the law and the prophets, and the divine will is for people to participate in, rather than to reject, the good news of salvation.

As the law is affirmed, it is also relativized in light of Jesus' preaching (16:17). A stroke of a letter refers to an ornamental mark that scribes put on a letter to distinguish between two similar looking letters. Even these tiny notations will outlast heaven and earth, putting to rest the question of the law's permanence. The complaints of Jesus' critics reflect their misunderstanding of the heart of the law. They focus on the letter of the law but not the spirit of it. Instead of discarding the law, Jesus has revived its foundational meaning and embodied its authentic practice.

The next saying serves as an example of how the law can be manipulated, so that observing the letter of the law does not always mean abidance by the spirit of the law (16:18). The law presupposes that divorces already happened in ancient Israel. When a man gave his wife a certificate of divorce, he relinquished his ownership of her. No longer his possession, she was released to marry another, lest she become destitute. Should the second husband die or send her away again, the first husband could not reclaim her as his possession (Deut 24:1–4). The provision of the certificate of divorce grants the rejected wife a chance of remarrying, and in some cases, that is her sole means of survival. The law also underscores the dignity of marriage, and its dissolution must not be treated lightly.

In this short saying, Jesus singles out a type of frivolous attitude toward marriage and divorce prevalent in his day. Some men seek to dissolve a marriage based on what they consider as objectionable (Deut 24:1). These grounds of divorce, however, range from a charge of unchastity to disliking the wife's appearance. The casual breaking of the marriage vow for reasons other than infidelity is, in Jesus' view, no different from committing adultery. It is a violation of the first marriage regardless of its legal dissolution. This is a pointed illustration of how observing the letter of the law—issuing a certificate of divorce—does not necessarily indicate a respect for the spirit of the law. In the ethics and economy of

God's kingdom, the law and the prophets are not dismissed but held in the highest esteem.[14]

A Rich Man and a Poor Beggar (16:19-31)

The parable of the rich man and Lazarus illustrates the key theme of reversal in Luke, where the rich will be brought low and the poor will be lifted up.[15] Not that it is sinful to be rich, but wealth is a constant snare in the life of faith (8:14; 16:13). In this story, Jesus addresses the attitude toward riches and the issue of social responsibility. The powerless will find hope, and the powerful are forewarned.

The contrast between the two main characters cannot be starker. The rich man is over-the-top rich, as indicated by his dress, lifestyle, and estate (16:19). Purple dye and fine linen were the color and fabric of royalty and those of comparable wealth and status (Sir 40:3-4). Anyone wearing a deep purple cloak over a bright white linen undergarment would turn heads. Every day this rich man is at his own banqueting table. There is neither shortage of food nor of relatives and clients jostling to be at the receiving end of his patronage. A house with a gate suggests a sizable property (16:20a). The gate, however, is more than a symbol of opulence. It is a boundary, barring from his domain anyone whose existence the rich man does not care to acknowledge.

Lazarus belongs to the invisible class of expendables. Poor, covered in sores, and probably lame, Lazarus has been put (*ebeblēto*) at the gate of the rich man's estate (16:20). The Greek verb *ballō* means to put, throw, or cast, and *ebeblēto* is its pluperfect form in the passive voice. It paints a vivid image of a sick beggar being tossed like a piece of trash at the door of a rich man, in the faint hope that someone will throw him some scraps from the rich man's table. But no one pays attention to Lazarus, except for the scavenger dogs that lick his painful blisters (16:21).

How might Jesus' audience assess these two characters? Would they envy the rich man and pity Lazarus? If wealth was interpreted as divine blessing and poverty as divine curse, the rich man might not even be seen as a villain. Some might wonder what grievous sin Lazarus had

---

14. Bates (2013: 83-92) proposes that 16:16-17 is a coded critique of Herod Antipas, whose execution of John and murderous intent toward Jesus constitute a violent attack on God's kingdom. Additionally, 16:18 is an insinuation of Herod's divorce and subsequent marriage to Herodias, his brother's wife.

15. See 1:52-53; 6:20-21, 24-25; 13:23-30; 14:7-11; 17:33; 18:9-14.

committed to deserve this punishment from God. Yet in the story Lazarus has a name and hence a distinctive identity. Lazarus is the diminutive form of Eleazar, meaning "God helps." God's heart is inclined toward the poor and the needy,[16] and Lazarus is not forgotten. By contrast, the rich man remains nameless throughout.

Things change when both men die. Lazarus, starving and sickly, is the first to go. Without a proper burial, would his corpse be left for vultures to pick through? That unimaginable prospect would be the epitome of shame (Jer 16:4; Ezek 29:5). Instead, Lazarus is carried (*apenechthēnai*)[17] to the bosom of Abraham by angels (16:22a); he is in fact not cursed but blessed. No mention is made of Lazarus's faith. As Abraham explains to the rich man, Lazarus has had his share of suffering in his earthly life, so now his comfort will last into eternity (16:25). The poor are lifted up, not momentarily but forever (1:52–53; 6:20–21).

The rest of the story is an extended conversation between the rich man, now dead, and Abraham. The rich man's burial, presumably elaborate, has not bought him eternal bliss. He finds himself in torment in Hades (16:22b–23). Hades is the Greek god of the underworld, whose name has been taken to refer to the realm of the dead. It is sometimes thought to be a temporary abode for the dead to await God's final judgment (Rev 20:11–15). If the rich man can look up and see Abraham and Lazarus, what is the spatial setting of the scene? Are all three men in different parts of Hades, so that they can see each other but cannot cross over to the other side? If the rich man is looking up, is he looking across a divide or is there a vertical distance between him and the other two? If the rich man is in agony in some fiery furnace, but Abraham and Lazarus are in a state of bliss, has some form of punishment already been meted out? It is tempting to speculate on the afterlife, but these questions are unanswerable. The story simply documents the grand reversal of conditions that befalls the rich man and Lazarus.

Death has not changed the rich man; he makes two requests of Abraham, both of which are self-centered and dismissive of Lazarus. The first is a cry of mercy to alleviate his suffering. It is ironic that the rich man addresses Israel's patriarch as "Father" because he does not display

---

16. See 1 Sam 2:8; Pss 40:17; 113:7; 140:12; Isa 41:17; Sir 21:5.

17. Horst (2006: 142–44) argues that the verb connotes more than transporting Lazarus from one realm to another, but the angels are taking him specifically to where he belongs (cf. 6:20).

Abraham's trait of hospitality (Gen 18:1-8).[18] The rich man is still ordering people around: "Send Lazarus to dip the tip of his finger in water and cool my tongue, for I am in agony in these flames" (16:24). If he can call Lazarus by name, he knew of the beggar's presence outside his gate when they were still alive. He never bothered to lift a finger to help him, and now he is telling Lazarus to dip his finger in water to cool his parched tongue!

Abraham cannot grant the rich man's plea for the principle of reversal is at work (16:25). The rich man had his share of good things and Lazarus of evil things when they were alive. The reversal is a direct consequence of the rich man's lack of compassionate and just action toward Lazarus. When it comes to the poor, inaction is not neutral but harmful. The rich man could have given alms and stored up treasures in heaven (12:33), but he squandered those opportunities. His earthly indifference has eternal consequences. Besides, a big chasm, fixed by God, separates the rich man from Abraham and Lazarus (16:26). The unbridgeable distance spells finality. Even if Lazarus wanted to, he could not help. It is too late.

Failing to save himself, the rich man intercedes for his five brothers, hoping that there is still time. His second request also carries a dismissive attitude toward Lazarus, asking Abraham to send the latter to warn his brothers so they will not end up where he is (16:27-28). While the rich man is finally thinking about people other than himself, his purview of concern remains narrowly confined to his family. Their hardheartedness, he feels, is so severe that nothing but a visit from the realm of the dead would shock them into repentance (16:30). But Abraham will have nothing to do with sensational appearances of the dead as a means of persuasion. What is expected of the rich man and his five brothers is not new. The law and the prophets are clear in their teachings on generosity, compassion, and justice for the poor (16:29, 31).[19] Recalling John's teaching on sharing clothing and food with the destitute (3:8, 11), the rich man, in his purple cloak, white linen, and daily fine dining, never gave Lazarus anything to cover his sores or feed his hungry frame. If those five brothers are anything like the rich man, they too cannot plead ignorance. The law and the prophets will be their judge.

---

18. Philo *Abraham* 107-10, 209-11; Josephus *Ant.* 1.196-97.
19. E.g., Lev 23:22; Isa 1:17; Jer 22:3; Mic 6:8.

Luke 17

Leaders of the People, Servants of God (17:1–10)

This short section consists of three sayings (17:1–2, 3–4, 5–6) and a parable (17:7–10). Jesus is speaking of life in the faith community, how the disciples should attend to those who are weak in faith and keep their own attitudes in check.

First, Jesus reminds his disciples of their responsibility to those who are under their care (17:1–2). Metaphorically, stumbling refers to a person faltering in spiritual or moral infraction as a result of doubt, sin, or apostasy. Granted that failure is a normal part of the learning curve in the journey of faith, woe to the disciples should they, by their bad example or misguided teaching, discourage or lead the little ones among them astray. These little ones are not just young in age but also young in faith. They are the lowly, the weak, the poor, the despised, and the vulnerable who have drawn near to Jesus. To stress the seriousness of the offense should the disciples cause another to stumble, Jesus employs an image that borders on the absurd. Imagine taking the heavy top stone used to grind flour in a rotary mill, hanging it around the offender's neck, and hurling both man and stone into the sea.[1] The man will surely drown. Yet Jesus says he would rather see this done to a leader than for the leader to cause a little one to stumble. Jesus values the most vulnerable member of the family of faith, and his disciples must never be callous or careless about their moral and spiritual oversight.

Second, Jesus expects his disciples to show mercy to the penitent (17:3–4). If a fellow believer stumbles for whatever reason, as leaders the disciples must take the initiative to effect restoration through honest confrontation, rebuke, and accountability. If there is genuine repentance, forgiveness is a must. Using hyperbole again to underscore his point, Jesus cites an extreme example of a fellow believer who repeatedly commits a personal offense against the disciple up to as many as seven times a day. If

---

1. Marshall 1978: 641; Green 1997: 612.

each time the offender repents, the disciple must forgive from the heart. Obviously, seven is not to be counted as the absolute limit beyond which no more forgiveness is to be extended. Rather, seven signifies the limitlessness of the willingness to forgive. If Jesus' followers truly understand God's forgiveness of them, they will be able to pay it forward and extend the same to others (cf. 6:36; 11:4).

Finding Jesus' demands daunting, the Twelve ask him to "increase [their] faith" (17:5). Here Luke calls them "apostles," hearkening back to the title Jesus gave them (6:13; 9:10; 22:14; 24:10). As apostles, the Twelve are more than followers; they are leaders among Jesus' flock. Their request for an increase in faith presupposes that they already have latent faith to build on. Jesus' reply reorients faith from quantifiable to actionable. The third hyperbole gives a reality check: "If you *had* faith . . . you *could* say [this] . . . and it *would* obey you" (17:6).[2] The contrast is between the tiny mustard seed[3] and the large mulberry[4] tree known for its deep roots. A little bit of faith can accomplish much, even the impossible feat of uprooting a solidly grounded tree and replanting it in the sea, where the sand is constantly sloshed around by the water.[5] The issue is not the quantity of faith the disciples need to fulfill their responsibilities, but the ability to exercise whatever faith they have for God's redemptive purposes.

Jesus tells one more parable to illustrate the correct attitude the disciples must have in serving God (17:7–10). A small farmer owns a slave who works both on the farm and in the house. Even after plowing the land and tending the sheep, the slave still has to cook for the master and serve the meal before attending to his own needs.[6] While a master may choose to treat the slave with unexpected kindness and reward faithful service, the slave does not have the right to expect special treatment for fulfilling his duty. Similarly, the disciples of Jesus are servants and slaves of God.

---

2. Garland 2011: 680–81.

3. The Palestinian species is "about one millimeter in diameter and [weighs] less than 1/700 of a gram" (Scott 2015: 28).

4. Luke uses *sykaminos* here, which most English translation renders as a mulberry. In 19:4, Zacchaeus climbs a different kind of sycamore (*sykomorea*; also known as a fig-mulberry). There seems to be some confusion here, because it is the *sykomorea* that is known for its deep roots. At any rate, the force of the hyperbole is not affected. See Marshall 1978: 644.

5. Scott (2015: 28–29) notes that the mustard seed is known for its ability to grow powerfully. The exhortation is to ask God for the gift of stronger and deeper faith to accomplish the work of the kingdom.

6. Nolland 1993a: 841–42; Hultgren 2000: 248.

Even though God is a supremely kind Master, their obedience in no way puts God under obligation. In verse 10, the translation of *douloi achreioi* as "worthless slaves" in the NRSV is unfortunate, as though Jesus were asking his disciples to view themselves as useless dregs, contradicting his affirmation of their value to God (12:7, 24). A better rendition of *achreioi* is "unworthy" (NIV, NLT, ESV), a less pejorative term to convey modesty and humility, which are the right attitudes that befit the faithful servants of the Most High. While Jesus speaks of God's immense grace and mercy, he cautions his disciples not to take God for granted. Obedience to God is first and foremost a duty because of God's honor and supremacy.

Healing Ten Lepers (17:11–19)

On his way to Jerusalem, Jesus passes through the region between Samaria and Galilee (17:11). Given the deep-seated hostility between Samaritans and Jews,[7] one would rather be in one region or the other. In between is this liminal zone where nobody feels at home and where the rejects of society are found. As a group, these ten lepers are identified not by their ethnicity but by their common ailment. Leprosy is a dreaded, though non-fatal, skin disease (Lev 13:1–59; Num 5:2–3).[8] The religious and social ostracism is worse than the physical suffering. Staying outside both Samaria and Galilee, the lepers are abiding by what is required by the law. They are to avoid contact with people and announce their presence by crying, "Unclean! Unclean!"

As Jesus is about to enter a village, the lepers call out to him from a safe distance, "Jesus, Master, have mercy on us!" (17:12–13). Are they asking for alms? In the Gospels, those who ask Jesus for mercy end up receiving much more than charity (18:35–43; Matt 15:22–28). The lepers address Jesus as "Master," acknowledging the power differential between them, while hoping that Jesus might do something to help them.[9]

In an earlier account, Jesus touched the untouchable leper as he pronounced his healing. Then he sent the cleansed leper to the priest for inspection and told him to offer the requisite sacrifice as commanded by Moses (5:12–14; cf. Lev 14:1–32). This time, Jesus hears and sees the lepers, but without touching them or uttering any word of healing, he

---

7. See p. 139; p. 154, n. 24; and also Hamm 1994: 277–80.
8. See pp. 73–74.
9. Green 1997: 623.

simply orders them to go show themselves to the priests. As they follow his instruction, they find themselves cleansed of leprosy (17:14). The efficacy of Jesus' miracle is contingent upon the lepers' obedience. Had they taken offense of Jesus' seeming inaction, they would not have been healed. The steps the ten lepers take to go to the priest are in every sense of the word steps of faith.

One—and only one—of the ten lepers returns to Jesus. The man sees more than the cleansing of his skin; he sees the action of God through Jesus.[10] Praising God with a loud voice and falling on his knees, he acknowledges Jesus as the agent of God's visitation, and his appreciation flows into reverence (17:15–17a). Only then does the author reveal the ethnicity of this grateful man, that he is a Samaritan (17:17b). How many Jews and how many Samaritans are among the other nine, we do not know. It is unlikely that all ten are Samaritans. But this man, doubly ostracized as a leper and a Samaritan, has the spiritual insight to come back and thank Jesus.

As remarkable as the Samaritan's gratitude is the others' ingratitude. Jesus' threefold questions are pointed (17:17–18). Jesus is not asking for recognition with every healing; there must have been many others who took their healings for granted. But the failure of the nine to give glory to God stands in sharp contrast to the Samaritan, especially when Jews do not expect Samaritans to do the right thing. In fact, the word *allogenēs* ("foreigner," 17:18), is the term used on inscriptions at the Jerusalem temple that bar gentiles from going into areas where only Jews are allowed.[11] The irony is that this outsider—unclean, marginalized, despised because of his questionable ancestry, and thought to be under divine curse by virtue of his infirmity—demonstrates an understanding of God's salvation and an appreciation of his physical, communal, and spiritual restoration far better than the Jews themselves. To him Jesus pronounces the same blessing as he did to the woman who was healed from her hemorrhage, "Your faith has made you well" (8:48; 17:19; cf. 7:50; 18:42).

---

10. Seeing rightly leads to the glorification of God (Hamm 1994: 283). Cf. 2:20; 5:25–26; 18:43; 23:47.

11. The inscription reads: "No man of another nation (or, no foreigner) to enter within the fence and enclosure round the temple. And whoever is caught will have himself to blame that his death ensues" (*OGIS* 598, cited in Barrett 1989: 53).

The Day of the Son of Man (17:20–37)

The Pharisees once ask Jesus when the kingdom of God will come (17:20a). This question pertains not to the substance or meaning of the kingdom of God but the timing of its arrival. In Jewish eschatological expectation, God's reign is a future event. When "this age" ends, God will usher in "the age to come." Implicit in the question of timing is a follow-up question, "How will we know?" Earlier on, Jesus said, "If it is by the finger of God that I cast out the demons, then the kingdom of God has come to you" (11:20). Embodied in the person and mission of Jesus, the kingdom of God has already been inaugurated even though its full consummation lies yet in the future. A paradigm shift is needed from a "future-oriented eschatology" to a "realized eschatology," in order for Jesus' audience to grasp his answer to the Pharisees (17:20b–21) as well as his declaration concerning the day of the Son of Man (17:22–37).

Jesus begins with a warning against sign-seeking tendencies. The kingdom of God is not to be identified with the use of *paratērēsis* ("observation"),[12] as though some supernatural phenomenon would point a flashing arrow, saying, "Look! Here it is! Oh, wait, there it is!" (17:20b–21a). Rather, the true signs of the kingdom can only be perceived with eyes of faith. They are embedded in the miracles of Jesus that bring wholeness and release to people in bondage, in the countercultural teachings of Jesus that bring God's people back to the foundational intentions of the law, and in the repentance of sinners and tax-collectors who are restored by the grace of God's forgiveness.[13]

To reiterate the point that the kingdom of God has already been inaugurated, Jesus finishes off with the declaration, "Behold, the kingdom of God is among (*entos*) you" (17:21b). The sense of the preposition *entos* has been the focus of much discussion.[14] Three grammatically viable options are considered. First, *entos* is rendered "within" (NIV[1984], NKJV). This translation spiritualizes the concept of God's kingdom, implying that it resides within the person as an individual's inner reality. In the immediate context, however, Jesus is answering some Pharisees who oppose the work that God is doing through him. How can the kingdom of God be conceived of as an inner reality within the Pharisees? This op-

---

12. The term *paratērēsis* is found in ancient medical and scientific literature, where observation informs decision and conclusion. See Nolland 1993a: 852.
13. Garland 2011: 697.
14. Marshall 1978: 655–56; Nolland 1993a: 853–54; Garland 2011: 697–98.

tion should therefore be eliminated. Second, *entos* may be read as "within [your] grasp" (ESV [in its footnote to this verse]). This translation suggests that the kingdom of God is near but offers no further insight. It emphasizes human initiative, that the Pharisees can take hold of the kingdom if they so desire. This reading is still somewhat dissatisfying, shying away from the sense that God's reign is powerfully infringing upon the human sphere. The third option, translating *entos* as "among" or "in the midst of," makes the best contextual sense (NRSV, NLT, ESV, CEB, NIV [2011]). The kingdom of God is embodied in Jesus, who has been walking among friend and foe, showing them what God's reign is all about. Whether the Pharisees embrace it or not, the kingdom of God is in their midst, and it will proceed toward its full manifestation in due time. While God's kingdom has already arrived, in the remainder of this chapter, Jesus broaches the subject of his future return in glory. Living in-between Jesus' first and second comings, his disciples must learn the important lessons of faithfulness and vigilance.

To avoid confusion, a distinction must be made between "the days of the Son of Man" (17:22, 26) and "the day of the Son of Man" (17:24, 30). In the plural, the days of the Son of Man refer to the days of Jesus' earthly ministry in his first coming. The attitudes of people in "the days of the Son of Man" will be compared to "the days of Noah" (17:26) and "the days of Lot" (17:28). In the singular, "the day of the Son of Man," or "the day that the Son of Man is revealed," points to the second coming of Jesus, the parousia, when God's final judgment and final salvation will take place. "The day of the Son of Man" parallels "the day of the LORD" in the OT.[15] Keeping "the (present) days of the Son of Man" and "the (future) day of the Son of Man" distinct is crucial for understanding Jesus' exhortation in this section.[16]

Between the two comings of Jesus, the disciples will find themselves in distress. They will look back with longing for "one of the days of the Son of Man," that is, the "good old days" when Jesus was with them, but there is no going back (17:22). Yet they do not know when Jesus will return in glory either. In these moments, the disciples will be most susceptible to false signs, but they are not to run after shadows (17:23). The future day of the Son of Man will be unmistakable, like lightning flashing

---

15. Ezek 30:3; Isa 13:6; Joel 1:15; 2:1; Amos 5:18, 20; Obad 1:15; Zech 1:14; 2:1, 3; Mal 4:5.

16. Green 1997: 633.

from one end of the sky to the other (17:24). The disciples do not have to chase after it; it will come to them.

In his first coming, Jesus is rejected by his contemporaries (17:25; cf. 9:41; 11:29). He likens his generation to those of Noah and Lot (Gen 6:5—8:22; 19:1-26), whose complacency led to their downfall. At the time of Noah and Lot, people were going about the mundane activities of life—feasting, marrying, buying, selling, farming, and building—when God's judgment destroyed them all, first by flood and then by fire (17:26-29). Their laxity and unresponsiveness to Noah's message and Lot's righteousness led to their demise. Likewise, if the present generation continues to turn a deaf ear to the gospel of salvation, the same fate will come upon them on the day of the Son of Man (17:30).

At the parousia, judgment will be fierce and swift. Whether one is resting on a roof or working in the field, when disaster hits there is but one thing to do: Run! There is no time to collect one's possessions or linger (17:31). Whatever the reason for that backward glance during her escape from Sodom, that moment of hesitation cost Lot's wife her life, and she was turned into a pillar of salt (17:32; cf. Gen 19:26). Indeed, human beings have neither ultimate control over their own lives nor the ability to secure it. Survival in God's kingdom is counterintuitive to earthly instinct, for "those who try to make their life secure will lose it, but those who lose their life will keep it" (17:33). Will the disciples trust that following Jesus, even to the point of death, is the pathway to eternal life? Will they subscribe to the eschatological perspective that this physical life and all that is in it are limited, but the future promise of God is limitless?

Jesus' mission is to save, but it also divides and separates (2:34-35; 3:16-17; 12:51-53). The good news of the kingdom of God forces a decision on the hearer. On the day of judgment, those who are saved will be separated from those who are slated for punishment. Whether it is husband and wife in the same bed or two women grinding meal together, the one who is ready will be taken and saved, and the one who is left will be destroyed (17:34-35).[17]

Jesus' warning is clear, but the final exchange between him and the disciples is ambiguous. The disciples ask, "Where, Lord?" to which Jesus replies, "Where the corpse is there the vultures will gather" (17:37). Why

---

17. Merkle (2010: 169-79) inverts the images to argue that those who are taken are judged and those who are left behind, like a remnant, are saved. This does not alter the message of final separation of the delivered from the condemned.

should the disciples worry about where the parousia will take place, since Jesus' glorious return will be as visible as lightning across the whole sky (17:24)? If they are asking where the saved will be taken, Jesus' answer appears to go in the opposite direction. Vultures are birds of prey; their circling above a carcass is an image that anticipates imminent destruction. Perhaps the disciples are not tracking with Jesus. The point is the certainty of destruction, not the location thereof. Those who reject the message of salvation are like dead animals ready to be devoured.

The road ahead will not be easy, but God's final salvation is well worth the present suffering. By giving his disciples a preview of what is to come, Jesus is cultivating in them a long view on this journey of faith. When the disciples get discouraged or despair of their lives, they will remember the big picture that Jesus has painted for them in these words. Elsewhere, Jesus also promised that the Holy Spirit will accompany them to face their accusers (12:4–12). That assurance will sustain them through many trials and persecutions to come.

Luke 18

A Widow and an Unjust Judge (18:1-8)

Taken on its own, this parable is sometimes read as an encouragement to pray often and in resolute earnestness in times of difficulty (18:1). The broader context from 17:22 to 18:8, however, suggests a wider interpretive horizon that takes into account the future-oriented mindset that Jesus' disciples need to cultivate.

In the ancient world, short life expectancy left many women as widows. The status of women in a patriarchal society was already lower than that of men, and widowhood further landed them near the bottom of the social ladder. According to Jewish law, a widow was not allowed to inherit from her deceased husband's estate (*m. B. Bat.* 8:1). Three options were available to her. First, she could remarry if she was still young and marriageable (cf. 1 Tim 5:11-14). Second, she could return to her father's house (cf. Ruth 1:1-17). Third, she could remain in her husband's family until his heirs gave her the amount of money designated in the marital agreement, to which she would be entitled if her husband died or divorced her. Beyond this, her husband's family could send her away (*m. Ketub.* 4:12; 5:1; 11:1; 12:3). Even if she were to remain under the roof of her husband's family, she could be ignored, mistreated, victimized, or sold as a slave. Her wellbeing was dependent upon another's goodwill. The numerous injunctions in the OT on caring for widows attest to their vulnerability and oppression.[1] Together with orphans, widows occupied a special place in God's heart for divine protection and provision.[2]

The two characters are a study in contrasts. A judge, a powerful man of notable social standing, comes face to face with a widow, a powerless woman of low status. The judge is probably rich if his injustice involves corruption and bribes.[3] The widow is poor. This "unjust judge," (18:6)

1. Exod 22:22; Deut 24:17; Isa 10:1-3; Jer 22:3; Ezek 22:7; Zech 7:10; Mal 3:5.
2. Deut 10:18; Pss 68:5; 146:9; Prov 15:25. See pp. 95-96.
3. Cotter 2005: 331-32.

who "[has] no fear of God and no respect for anyone" (18:4, cf. 18:2), is a vexing character. By definition, a judge executes justice under the watchful eye of YHWH, the Judge of all judges (Deut 1:16–17; 16:18–20).[4] How will this widow stand a chance before an influential but contemptuous judge?

The specific nature of the widow's grievance is unknown. Perhaps it has to do with property or money withheld from her that she desperately needs for survival.[5] She demands a just verdict so that her opponent will do what is right. Normally, a woman is accompanied by a male figure in the public sphere. But this widow has neither husband, father, son, nor kinsman redeemer to advocate on her behalf. She has no choice but to go to court herself, which in a man's world exposes her to ridicule and stonewalling.[6] If the unjust judge accepts bribes to grant favors or expedite cases, she has no resources to gain a hearing via that channel. Her only recourse is to show up day after day at the city court and make her plea loudly, clearly, and repeatedly: "Grant me justice against my adversary" (18:3).

For the judge to refuse to grant the widow justice is more than pretending that she does not exist (18:4). Is he acting out of spite, that he has the power to help but chooses not to? If so, he shows no decency of human kindness, and his contempt for God and for people is all the more heinous. Yet, over time, even the tough exterior begins to crack when the widow's incessant cries for justice outlast the judge's resistance.

The judge's soliloquy reveals his inner reasoning, which displays no real change of heart.[7] He finds the widow bothersome, and his decision to acquiesce is completely self-serving: "I will grant her justice, so that she may not wear me (*hypōpiazē*) out by continually coming" (18:5 NRSV). This translation puts it too mildly. In the Greek, the verb literally means to strike in the face or give someone a black eye. In the present tense, *hypōpiazē* denotes continuous action. It is comical to imagine the poor widow giving the unjust judge a shiner by hitting him repeatedly. The image is metaphorical; the judge is concerned that if this continues she

---

4. Spencer (2012: 277) thinks that this judge is a Roman magistrate, who has no fear of YHWH and no respect for the Jews. But if this were the case, the character's ethnicity would likely be specified (cf. Luke 7:2; 10:33, 17:6; Acts 8:27; 10:1).

5. Hultgren 2000: 254–55.

6. According to Cotter (2005: 333–35), the widow's frequent appearance in a public male space would cast a negative light on her as deliberately attracting male attention.

7. See p. 180, n. 9.

may shame him and damage his reputation.[8] A judge who has no respect for people still cares about what other people think of him, particularly in a society where retaining honor is a high priority. In the end, the widow receives justice in spite of the judge's impure motives.

At first glance, Jesus' closing comment appears to identify the widow with God's elect and the unjust judge with God (18:6–8a). The first identification is reasonable, but the second is problematic. Rather than simply equating God and the unjust judge, a better reading of the story weaves a contrast into an argument from the lesser to the greater. If even an incredibly nasty and untrustworthy judge relents and acts on the side of justice, how much more will God be willing to vindicate his chosen ones from the injustices imposed upon them? The answer to Jesus' rhetorical questions in verse 7 is, "Of course he will, swiftly and definitively!" Because God is sovereign, God's just action is based on his merciful character. Seen from this perspective, the widow's tactic of hounding the judge repeatedly is not exactly a fitting model for prayer. God cannot be harassed into answering prayers, and persistence does not mean unrelenting pressure until God caves. What different kind of persistence is in view then, since this parable is supposed to address the disciples' need "to pray always and not to lose heart" (18:1)? At the very end of verse 8b, Jesus asks, "And yet, when the Son of Man comes, will he find faith on earth?" This question brings us back to Jesus' teaching at the end of chapter 17.

In 17:22–37, Jesus warns of the inevitable separation on the day of judgment between those who are saved and those condemned to destruction. For those who pay no attention to the day of reckoning, the time for repentance will expire. Meanwhile, Jesus' disciples must persevere in the face of suffering. If they keep faith to the very end, the return of the Son of Man will be their moment of vindication and glory.

Against this backdrop of Jesus' eschatological discourse, the parable of the widow and the unjust judge takes on another layer of meaning. To encourage the disciples who may be fearful of the trials and tribulations before the return of the Son of Man, Jesus reassures them that God is not like the unjust judge. He will not drag his feet but deliver his chosen ones without delay. Their need to "pray always and not to lose heart" is part of the long view of persevering discipleship that focuses on God's promised future. On this side of eternity, Jesus' return may seem long

---

8. Cotter 2005: 338–42.

delayed. But on the eternal timeline, God is swift in granting justice to his chosen ones. While the exhortation to pray and not give up is helpful in dealing with the daily vicissitudes of life, it is ultimately the hope of eternal salvation that enables the disciples to remain committed to Jesus, so that "when the Son of Man comes, [he will indeed] find faith—and faithfulness—on earth" (18:8).[9]

A Pharisee and a Tax Collector (18:9–17)

The parable of the Pharisee and the tax collector (18:9–14) is often linked with the preceding parable of the widow and the unjust judge (18:1–8), because both stories are about prayer. In the literary context, the parable of the widow and the unjust judge actually connects better with the latter half of chapter 17, whereas the parable of the Pharisee and the tax collector flows more naturally into the pericope that follows (18:15–17).

Throughout the narrative, Jesus has been criticized by the Pharisees for his association with tax collectors (5:27–32; 7:29–30, 34; 15:1–2). So when Jesus tells a story about a Pharisee and a tax collector, Luke's readers are predisposed to view the Pharisee with suspicion and the tax collector with empathy. The author says as much in his introduction, implying that the Pharisee represents the self-righteous religious elites who look down on others (18:9), and the tax collector the targets of their disdain. Without Luke's framing, Jesus' first-century audiences would have had the exact opposite attitudes, hence the shock value of the parable as it unfolds.

The Pharisee and the tax collector are caricatures who represent contrasting self-understandings and dispositions toward God. The setting seems normal enough, that "two men went up to the temple to pray" (18:10),[10] until the characters are introduced. The pious Pharisee is a welcomed fixture at the temple. He embodies Jewish piety at its best with his comprehensive knowledge and meticulous observance of the law.[11] The tax collector's presence, however, is jarring. Tax collectors were despised by all ranks of society. They were considered ritually unclean because they worked with and for the Romans, and morally suspect because they made a living from exploiting their fellow Jews, overcharging them on

---

9. Mappes 2010: 300–306.

10. Probably at a Tamid service of burnt offering and prayer (see p. 16, n. 12). See Hamm 2003: 223–24.

11. See pp. 72–73.

tariffs and taxes.[12] So what is this tax collector doing at the temple? He is out of place and nobody wants him there.

The Pharisee is probably standing in the Court of Israel, where he can observe the sacrifice and pray while the priest offers incense in the sanctuary (cf. 1:10). Normally, Jews stand up and pray out loud (1 Sam 1:26; 1 Kgs 8:22). Verse 11a may be translated from the Greek as "the Pharisee, standing by himself, was praying thus" (NRSV, ESV, cf. NLT) or "the Pharisee stood up and prayed about himself" (NIV). Both renderings are grammatically and contextually viable, but they carry different emphases. "Standing by himself" underscores the Pharisee's separatist attitude. Even when praying, he stands apart from other worshipers to avoid defilement from a casual brush of garment.[13] The other translation, with him praying "about himself," anticipates the content of a prayer peppered with first person pronouns.

The Pharisee's prayer comes across self-righteous and prideful, at least to Luke's readers. Aside from the perfunctory "thank you" to God in the opening phrase, the rest is about him. Yet this prayer may in fact be inspiring to other Jews around him and to Jesus' audience. First, dissociation from "thieves, rogues, and adulterers," is commendable (18:11b). Even the singling out of the tax collector is not judged as mean-spirited, because the latter deserves to be numbered among the worst offenders of society. Second, the twice-weekly fasts the Pharisee observes far exceed the requirement of the law (18:12a). In the OT, Israel fasted in times of crisis, mourning, and repentance,[14] and there was no mandated regular fast except on the Day of Atonement (Lev 16:29–34; 23:27–32). This Pharisee routinely goes beyond the call of duty. Third, a ten percent tithe on all his income is excessive (18:12b). Tithing is required by the law (Lev 27:30–33; Deut 14:22–27), but specifically what needs to be tithed was stipulated in the oral traditions of the rabbis. Earlier on, Jesus complained that the Pharisees "[tithed] mint, rue, and herbs of all kinds [but neglected] justice and the love of God" (11:42). Rue is in fact not on the list of things to tithe. By tithing all his income, the Pharisee includes things that are required and things that are not to ensure that he is beyond reproach. In spite of his exemplary piety, at least outwardly, his self-congratulatory attitude and derision of the tax collector are not lost

---

12. See p. 50.
13. Bailey 2008: 347.
14. E.g., Judg 20:26; 1 Sam 31:13; Ezra 8:21; Esth 4:16; Jer 36:9.

to Luke's readers, who are reminded of the Pharisees who oppose Jesus in real life (11:37–44).

For the second caricature, Jesus gives a lengthier description of the tax collector's body language but registers a briefer prayer (18:13). The man is said to be "standing far off," but where is he? Ritually unclean, he is barred from the inner courts of the temple. Perhaps he is standing in the Court of Gentiles, where he cannot see the sacrifice being offered and the nearby commercial activities of buying and selling are distracting. It is curious that the Pharisee is aware of the tax collector's presence if they are standing in separate parts of the temple. Be that as it may, not only is this tax collector shunned by his fellow Jews, his body language also conveys his sense of unworthiness. He is too ashamed to look up to heaven to pray (cf. Ezra 9:6), and he beats his breast in deep anguish (23:27, 48; cf. Nah 2:7), saying, "God, be merciful to me (*hilasthēti moi*), a sinner" (18:13). The Greek noun *hilastērion*, which means "the place of propitiation" or "the means of expiation," refers to the mercy seat, the cover of the ark of the covenant in the holy of holies (Exod 25:17–22). In a Tamid service, if this is the setting Jesus has in mind, a sacrificial animal is offered to atone for the sins of Israel. The tax collector thus prays that the atoning efficacy of the burnt offering will cover his sins, grave as they are.[15] This sinner is not asking for mercy as in pity (*eleēson me* or *eleēson hēmas*; cf. 16:24; 17:13; 18:38–39); he is pleading for forgiveness.

Jesus' assessment of the two is more shocking to his audience than to Luke's readers. It is not the respected Pharisee, but the scorned tax collector, whom Jesus declares to be right with God (18:14a). The one who thinks he is righteous is blinded by his self-absorption, whereas the one whom everyone regards as unrighteous is cognizant of his spiritual poverty. God's response to both attitudes is that the tax collector returns home forgiven and justified, while the Pharisee remains guilty and unjustified. The principle of reversal is operative, that "all who exalt themselves will be humbled, but all who humble themselves will be exalted" (18:14b; cf. 2:51–52; 14:11).

Next Jesus draws attention to little children, whose humility and lowliness, like the tax collector in the parable, will gain them entry into God's kingdom. Bringing infants to be touched by Jesus for blessing, protection, or healing is a wonderful thing (18:15). Acting as self-appointed gatekeepers, the disciples rebuke the parents and dismiss these infants

---

15. Snodgrass 2008: 473.

as unworthy of even a moment of Jesus' time and attention. Given the high infant mortality rate in antiquity, children had low status for they had little utilitarian value.[16] It is understandable why the disciples become annoyed at the parents. Their indignation, however, leads to their own chastisement when Jesus insists on letting the infants be brought to him (18:16; cf. 9:46-48). He points out that the kingdom of God belongs to these little ones, who remain open, trusting, grateful, unpretentious, and uncalculating. Only if the disciples truly receive the good news of the kingdom as a pure gift themselves can they welcome others without prejudice.

A Rich Ruler (18:18-30)

At the start of the travel narrative, a lawyer asked Jesus what he must do to inherit eternal life (10:25). The same question is now posed by a rich ruler toward the end of the travel narrative (18:18). Inheriting eternal life is the same as entering the kingdom of God. In both conversations, Jesus' response moves the questioner from knowing the law (10:26-28; 18:20-21) to living it out in acts of justice and mercy (10:29-37; 18:22).

The ruler (*archōn*) is a man of influence. The same Greek term *archōn* is used of the leaders of the people who join forces with the chief priests to have Jesus condemned (23:13, 35; 24:20). If this ruler also possesses some religious and political clout, he may well be a member of the ruling council or a leader of the local synagogue. Why he calls Jesus "good Teacher" is ambiguous (18:18). In Luke, those who are not Jesus' disciples address him as "Teacher,"[17] but this is the only place where "good Teacher" is used. Whether it is meant to flatter or not, Jesus finds the descriptor inappropriate and attributes goodness to God alone (18:19).[18]

Having put the ruler in his place, Jesus asks him about the law. Out of the Ten Commandments (Exod 20:1-17; Deut 5:6-21), Jesus cites only five (18:20). This does not mean that he expects the ruler to abide by only half of the commandments, but he specifically confronts him with the ones concerning relationships within one's family and community—the command to honor one's parents, and the prohibitions against adultery, murder, theft, and bearing false witness. Imagine the tone in the ruler's

16. See pp. 136-37.
17. 7:40; 8:49; 9:38; 10:25; 11:45; 12:13; 19:39; 20:21, 28, 39.
18. "For he is good; for his steadfast love endures forever" is a common refrain of praise for God, e.g., 1 Chr 16:34; 2 Chr 5:13; Ezra 3:11; Pss 106:1; 135:3.

reply that he has kept all these commandments since his youth (18:21). Is he proud of himself? Does he expect Jesus to praise him and assure him of his inheritance?

To the ruler's dismay, Jesus points out his sin of omission. It is not enough to abide by the prohibitions of the law; he also needs to live out the ethos of God's kingdom in active means, starting with caring for the poor.[19] Jesus challenges him to relinquish his possessions, sell all that he owns, cross social boundaries, level the playing field, and share the proceeds with the poor (18:22; cf. 14:33). The richer the ruler, the tighter the grip wealth has on him, and the more unwilling he is to let go of it all. His depth of sadness is directly proportionate to the size of his wealth. Where would such a radical step leave him in social and financial standing? Would he not lose all honor, power, and influence if he was no longer rich? If earthly possessions is more alluring to him than heavenly treasures, then the ruler has not yet grasped the true meaning of inheriting eternal life (18:23; cf. 12:33–34; 16:13).

The ruler's failure to respond to Jesus' demand bespeaks the irresistible pull of wealth and its attendant attitudes and worldviews. The absurdity of squeezing a camel through the eye of a needle illustrates the impossibility for a rich person to enter God's kingdom by his or her own volition (18:24–25).[20] The bystanders' question, "Then who can be saved?" (18:26), is legitimate, especially when a direct link between wealth and divine approval is assumed. Nevertheless, Jesus assures them that "what is impossible for mortals is possible for God" (18:27). Only God's movement in the human heart can bring freedom from the clutches of riches, as demonstrated by the early Christians who sell their possessions and share the proceeds with the poor (Acts 5:32–37).

Speaking of giving it all up, Peter reminds Jesus that he and his fellow disciples have left everything—family, possessions, security—to follow him (18:28; cf. 5:11, 28). Despite their proximity to Jesus, they do not always embrace the values of the kingdom (9:46; 18:15; 22:24). Their learning curve is steep. The road ahead is strewn with persecution and difficulties, and the disciples can use all the encouragement they can get. Without a hint of chastisement, Jesus gives them what they need to hear, that they will be compensated—in kingdom terms—in this life as well as in the life to come (18:29–30).

19. E.g., Deut 24:14; Prov 14:21; 19:17; Isa 58:7.

20. The speculation that a narrow gate in Jerusalem called the Needle's Eye forms the backdrop of Jesus' hyperbole is unfounded.

Obtuseness and Insight (18:31-43)

In Lukan parlance, the term "disciples" includes a larger group of followers. When the author wants to refer specifically to the inner circle of Jesus, he uses the designation "the Twelve" or "the apostles."[21] What Jesus is about to say is for the ears of the Twelve only (18:31a). This is the last of several passion predictions found in this Gospel since Peter's identification of Jesus as the Messiah (9:20), and it is the one with the most detail.

The previous passion predictions spoke of Jesus' suffering, rejection, betrayal, death, and resurrection on the third day (cf. 9:22, 44; 17:25). In this final prediction, two significant elements are added. First is the theme of fulfillment. As ominous as the fate of the Son of Man sounds, it comes as no surprise because it has already been anticipated in the OT (18:31b). Jesus is not a victim; his mission is to fulfill God's final salvation for Israel and the nations, as promised by the prophets of old.[22] Through death this mission will lead to life.

Second, Israel's Messiah "will be handed over (*paradothēsetai*)" by his own people to be killed in the hands of the gentiles (18:32-33a). The verb *paradidōmi* means "to betray" or "to hand over." As the passion narrative unfolds, Judas, one of the Twelve, will make an arrangement with the chief priests and the temple officers "to betray (*paradounai*) [Jesus] to them" (22:3-6). The Jewish authorities will bring Jesus to Pilate, who in turn will hand Jesus over (*paredōken*) for crucifixion (23:25). The same root verb *paradidōmi* connects all these actions, that Jesus is first betrayed by the Jews and then handed over to the gentiles. The mockery, the insult, the spitting, and the flogging are but depictions of the utter humiliation of the Son of Man in a culture where shame is worse than death. Yet the enemies of Jesus, whether Jew or gentile, will not have the last word, for the passion prediction ends with a note of vindication and triumph: "And on the third day he will rise again" (18:33b).

From the postresurrection perspective of Luke's readers, Jesus' prediction may seem overly obvious, for every detail will soon be fulfilled in Jerusalem. Yet the Twelve who are closest to Jesus remain slow to understand. They did not grasp the meaning of Jesus' talk of his suffering before they embarked on the journey (9:45a), they still do not at this point (18:34a). The disciples' dullness, though, is not because of human

---

21. See 8:1; 9:1, 12; 22:3, 47 for "the Twelve" and 6:13; 9:10; 17:5; 22:14; 24:10 for "the apostles."

22. E.g., Isa 43:1—44:8; 51:1—52:10; 62:1-12; Ezek 36:22—37:28.

failure, but God has hidden the meaning from them (9:45b; 18:34b). Behind divine concealment is divine mystery. Despite the obtuseness of the Twelve, Luke injects a glimmer of hope with one last healing before the passion narrative, where Jesus restores the sight of a blind man. This miracle functions as an apt metaphor for the disciples' spiritual journey. Their vision is presently obscured, but they will be able to see clearly when God lifts the veil (cf. 24:25-27; 44-46).

Jericho was located sixteen miles to the east of Jerusalem. On the road approaching the city sits a blind beggar who has heard that Jesus is about to come his way (18:35-37).[23] In Judea, Jesus is called "the Nazorean" (18:37; 4:34; 24:19). But instead of calling him "Jesus of Nazareth" the blind man shouts, "Jesus, Son of David, have mercy on me!" (18:38). Luke's readers know that the title, "Son of David," carries strong messianic and royal overtones (1:32; 3:31; cf. 20:41).[24] The blind beggar's identification of "Jesus of Nazareth" as "Son of David" is striking. Who would expect this man, useless in the eyes of the world, to possess insight into Jesus' identity? He is the poster child of Jesus' earlier prayer, in which he thanked God for hiding the mysteries of the kingdom from the wise and the intelligent and revealing them to infants (10:21). Like an infant, this blind beggar has neither status nor utilitarian value (18:15-17), yet he has knowledge that comes by divine revelation.

In spite of strong rebuke from the people around Jesus, the blind beggar is not deterred and his shouts become louder and more insistent: "Son of David, have mercy on me (*eleēson me*)!" (18:39). His plea is reminiscent of the cry of the ten lepers, "Jesus, Master, have mercy on us (*eleēson hēmas*)" (17:13). Although the beggar may be asking for alms, his reference to Jesus as the Son of David suggests otherwise. When Jesus asks what he wants, the blind man expresses his desire to be made whole, "Lord, let me see again" (18:40-41). In his present state, he is relegated to the fringes of society, looked down upon as ritually unclean and morally suspect.[25] He has no means to make a living, and he is excluded from the communal and religious life of his people. He wants more than charity; he desires complete restoration physically, spiritually, and socially. While

---

23. In Mark, Jesus heals blind Bartimaeus while leaving Jericho (Mark 10:46). Luke moves up the timing and location of Jesus' encounter with the blind man, in order to locate the ensuing story about Zacchaeus inside the city (19:1-10).

24. See p. 21, n. 20 and Collins 2010: 24-32.

25. See pp. 72-73.

blindness is considered to be impossible to heal,[26] the man believes that the Davidic Messiah can and will bestow a divine blessing and do for him what is impossible for human beings.

Jesus restores the man's sight and commends him for his faith (18:42). The newly healed man finds himself in good company alongside a woman with a sinful past, another who hemorrhaged for twelve years, and a Samaritan leper (7:40; 8:48; 17:19). All of them have a new lease on life on account of their trust in the saving power of God through Jesus. The man now lives into this new commitment as a follower of Jesus. No longer an outcast, he joins the crowd in attributing all praise and glory to God (18:43).

---

26. Garland 2011: 742.

Luke 19

Zacchaeus the Tax Collector (19:1-10)

The story of Zacchaeus is probably known to every child who has spent time in Sunday school. While the thought of a short grown man climbing a tree may be delightful to children, ancient Jews would have frowned on the spectacle as absurd and totally lacking in decorum. Yet to the onlookers that day, Jesus' acceptance of the chief tax collector is even more ridiculous than the latter's violation of socially accepted behavior. In chapter 18, Jesus noted the impossibility for a rich person, held captive by the lure of possessions, to enter God's kingdom (18:24). The disciples asked, "Who then can be saved?" (18:26). Zacchaeus's transformation concretizes Jesus' reply, "What is impossible for mortals is possible for God" (18:27).

This is the last appearance of tax collectors in the Lukan narrative. Even though the author has frequently spoken of tax collectors responding positively to John and Jesus,[1] the story of Zacchaeus is the most detailed. Located sixteen miles to the east of Jerusalem and just west of the Jordan, Jericho was a popular stopping point for travelers coming down the Jordan Valley before going up to Jerusalem.[2] It was a gateway city, a prime location for the Romans to tax goods brought into Judea from Perea. Imagine Zacchaeus and his colleagues running a vibrant trade in this city. As chief tax collector he functions like a district manager (19:1-2).[3] Their business success is achieved by charging people more taxes than what the Romans actually require, lining their own pockets by dishonest means.[4] Zacchaeus's wealth earns him neither respect nor status. His infamy may be summed up by his traitorous collusion with the gentile overlords and shameless exploitation of his own people.

1. See 3:12; 5:27-29; 7:29, 34; 15:1.
2. Walker 2006: 101.
3. Green 1997: 668.
4. See p. 50.

The text does not indicate why Zacchaeus wants to see Jesus, or if he has heard of or met Jesus before. Luke simply emphasizes his eagerness, that he will figure out a way to see Jesus even at the expense of his personal dignity. Being "of small stature (*hēlikia mikros*)," Zacchaeus's view is blocked by the crowd around Jesus (19:3). Perhaps the obstruction is deliberate. Given his notoriety, Zacchaeus is easily spotted. Dressed in expensive garb, the little man is now scuttling among the people, trying to get to Jesus. Unlike Jairus the synagogue ruler (8:41) or the rich ruler (18:18), the crowd finds no reason to step aside and grant him passage. Undeterred by the human barrier, he runs up the road and scales a sycamore tree[5] for a better view (19:4). Although the Greek noun *hēlikia* can refer to a measure of either time (12:25) or length (2:52), in this context it has to be his shortness, rather than his youth, that explains the need to find a good perch on a high branch.[6] A sycamore fig, with its broad branches and abundant foliage, provides a secure and discreet observation deck. Zacchaeus's choice location notwithstanding, it is undignified for an adult male to climb a tree, especially when he has to lift his robe and expose his legs (cf. 15:20b).

Had Jesus not blown Zacchaeus's cover, he could have remained unnoticed and slithered down the tree when everyone has left. Catching a glimpse of Jesus may be all that he has hoped to achieve, but Jesus has better ideas. The repetition of the participle, "hurrying" (*speusas*; 19:5–6), signifies both the urgency of Jesus' summons and the immediacy of Zacchaeus's obedience. Jesus' self-invitation to stay at Zacchaeus's home is met with joyful hospitality. It is a visit that Jesus is compelled to do (*dei*). In Luke, the verb *dei*, when found on the lips of Jesus and translated as "it is necessary" or "I must," points to God as the instigator of that salvific necessity.[7]

Normally, the coming together of guest and host symbolizes the best of social discourse, where kinship, hospitality, and mutual honor are suitably expressed by parties of common status and shared values. Jesus' proposal, however, grates on all who are present. Zacchaeus is a sinner, unworthy to play host to Jesus (19:7). Staying at that house is tantamount

---

5. See p. 232, n. 4.

6. Parsons (2001: 50–57) notes that the explicit mention of Zacchaeus's shortness is also derogatory. Calling someone short is an invective strategy found in Greco-Roman literature to imply a negative character assessment. Cf. the positive description of Saul as standing head and shoulders above everyone else (1 Sam 9:2).

7. See p. 45, n. 30.

to condoning all that is ritually impure and morally despicable about its owner. Whose side is Jesus on?

The crowd underestimates Jesus' power to effect transformation. Coming down from the tree, whether nimbly or clumsily, Zacchaeus does not care how he looks in front of all these people. The first thing that comes out of his mouth is a plan that "[bears] fruits worthy of repentance" (3:8). Acknowledging Jesus as "Lord," Zacchaeus resolves to give half his possessions to the poor and to pay a fourfold restitution to anyone whom he has cheated (19:8). The compensation is more than adequate and fair, for the law only obligates him to add an extra twenty percent to the amount of money stolen from others (Lev 6:1–5).[8] His penitence is expressed in acts of justice, which will result in a change in profession and a drop in economic status. Zacchaeus's relinquishment of his possessions for his salvation stands in stark contrast to the rich ruler who forfeits eternal life by refusing to let go of his wealth (18:22–24).

Jesus' response is not only for Zacchaeus but for all to hear. He declares the tax collector and his entire household saved, that is, forgiven and accepted (19:9a).[9] In Luke, the Greek word "today" (*sēmeron*) signifies more than the day of an event, but the immediacy of God's salvation as a present reality.[10] Today is the day of salvation, even for the chief tax collector, the outcast of outcasts. The rejection of Zacchaeus by his fellow Jews is so complete that they no longer view him as kin with a shared ancestry. But Jesus reinstates his place in the family of Israel, affirming that "he, too, is a son of Abraham" (19:9b; cf. 14:16). With this, Zacchaeus is restored to spiritual and communal wholeness.

Jesus' closing comment, "for the Son of Man came to seek out and to save the lost" (19:10), is a fitting summary of his mission. For every Zacchaeus who is found, there are many scribes and Pharisees who do not even acknowledge their lostness. No rupture of the divine-human relationship is so irreparable that the call to repentance and offer of forgiveness are withdrawn, yet it takes both gracious divine initiative and humble human response for reconciliation to occur.

---

8. A repayment of four or five times is required if cattle is stolen and the animal has already been sold or slaughtered (Exod 22:1; 2 Sam 12:6).

9. Cf. Acts 11:14; 16:15, 31; 18:8.

10. See p. 62.

The Slaves and Their Minas (19:11-27)

Leaving Jericho, Jesus has only about sixteen miles to reach Jerusalem, the end of a long journey that occupies almost ten chapters in Luke (9:51–19:28). Anticipation fills the air. The disciples have heard Jesus' warnings of conflict and persecution on the one hand (12:4-12; 17:22-37) and his calls to vigilance and faithfulness on the other (12:35-48; 18:1-8). Given the import of Jerusalem and the presence of the temple as the center of Israel's national identity, religious history, and eschatological hope, it is understandable for some to wonder if the confrontation that Jesus is about to face in Jerusalem will immediately usher in the kingdom of God in its full consummation (19:11). Some may even imagine a rebellion against the Romans, when the Messiah will deal a decisive blow to Israel's enemies. In light of the Jews' messianic fervor heading into Passover, these aspirations are misguided. The parable of the ten minas encourages the obedient to stay faithful and warns the recalcitrant of impending judgment.

The flow of the parable of the minas is somewhat awkward, as two plotlines that can easily be developed on their own are woven into a single tale. For the sake of clarity, the two subplots will be addressed separately in the following discussion.

The story features a nobleman traveling to a far country to claim royal power and then returning to rule as king (19:12). In the Roman Empire, vassal kings had to seek formal approval from the emperor before assuming jurisdiction over a territory, which lends verisimilitude to the story.[11] Summoning ten of his slaves and giving each of them a mina, the nobleman instructs them to do business with the money until he returns (19:13). A mina was equivalent to about a hundred denarii, three or four months' worth of wages for a day laborer.[12] While not a large sum, it is sizable enough for an industrious slave to make something of it. In those days, slaves were not necessarily relegated to menial tasks; some could have been given responsibilities to act as managers and agents to conduct transactions on behalf of their masters.[13] Since it will be a while

---

11. Herod the Great, Antipas, Archelaus, Phillip, and Agrippa I all had to make this journey to Rome to validate their authority. See Josephus *Ant.* 14.370-85; 17.206-49, 299-320; Josephus *J.W.* 2.1-38, 80-111.

12. Hultgren 2000: 285.

13. Green 1997: 678.

before the nobleman reaches the far country and then journeys home, the slaves will have enough time to work with the sum entrusted to them.

Upon his return as king, the nobleman calls his slaves into account (19:15). While there are ten slaves, only three reports are given as a representative sample. The first two exhibit the same productive pattern. According to their abilities, they present their king with a tenfold and fivefold increase, respectively. Both are commended for their trustworthiness and rewarded proportionately with authority over ten and five cities (19:16–19). Their faithfulness in a modest assignment gives the king confidence to increase their scope of responsibility, trusting that having been faithful in little they will be faithful in much (16:10a).

The third slave's performance is disappointing. He has nothing to show for but the original mina wrapped up in a piece of cloth. He attributes his unproductivity to his fear of the master, whom he regards as exploitative and unreasonable (19:20–21). Reading between the lines, the wicked slave probably did not want to fail in a business venture and then be forced to cover the losses, so he did not even try. Whether his portrayal of the master is accurate or not, his excuse becomes the standard by which he is judged. Inaction is negative action. The slave did not even bother to dig a hole and bury the money in the ground. Even if he did not want to take any risk, he could have put the money in the bank to earn interest, however little it might yield (19:22–23). He displays neither effort nor savvy.

In his indignation, the king confiscates the wicked slave's mina and gives it to the first slave (19:24). At first, the bystanders' challenge of the fairness of giving even more to someone who already has a lot seems justifiable, until the king reveals his rationale: "To all those who have, more will be given; but from those who have nothing, even what they have will be taken away" (19:25–26). The issue is not partiality, but faithful obedience is contrasted with unfaithful disobedience. To the extent that sloth and irresponsibility deteriorate into a vicious cycle of loss and destruction, faithfulness and obedience fuel a virtuous cycle of ever increasing growth and opportunity.

The second subplot of the parable is less developed. It concerns a conspiracy against the nobleman about his claim of royal authority. Some citizens of the country who hate him send a delegation to the distant overlord to voice their objection of his rule over them (19:14). This happened to Herod Archelaus when he went to Caesar Augustus after the death of his father Herod the Great. Because Archelaus was a cruel man, the Jews sent their own representatives to Rome and succeeded in persuading the emperor to reduce Archelaus's territory to half of Herod's kingdom (Josephus *Ant.* 17.299–320). Archelaus was also given the lesser title of ethnarch. In the parable, we do not know why the citizens disapprove of the nobleman. The attempt is presumed to have failed because the nobleman returns with royal power nonetheless (19:15a). This substory ends abruptly with the gruesome slaughter of the rebellious citizens on account of treason (19:27).

It is prudent not to over-allegorize every detail. Simply put, Jesus is identified with the nobleman, the disciples with the slaves, and the hateful citizens with the enemies of Jesus. The broad picture connects faithfulness with reward and rebellion with judgment, a message already sounded in other teachings of Jesus. That said, what is the point of the time lag necessitated by the nobleman's travel to a distant country and his return as king who then has the power to evaluate his slaves and execute his enemies? Jesus' teaching on the future return of the Son of Man is instructive here (9:26; 17:22–36; cf. 21:25–28). The nobleman's journey and return signify the departure of the Son of Man and his second coming.[14] For the original hearers of the parable, the postresurrection ascension of the Son of Man lies yet in their future (24:51). But Luke's readers have a more complete picture. Like the productive slaves, their reward awaits them at the parousia if they do well with the "spiritual minas," the good news of the kingdom of God, entrusted to them. There will always be others who remain hard-hearted to the very end. Like the citizens who oppose the king, their judgment is imminent.

Entry into Jerusalem (19:28–40)

Ten chapters ago, Luke marked the point at which Jesus concluded his Galilean ministry and began his journey toward Jerusalem (9:51). Along the way, references to Jesus' destination are inserted here and there to maintain a sense of movement (13:22; 17:11; 18:31; 19:11). The beginning of this pericope situates Jesus coming up toward Jerusalem from Jericho, pausing at Bethany and Bethphage, just about two miles to the east of Jerusalem on the slope of the Mount of Olives (19:28–29). Both Bethany and Bethphage were small hamlets, where pilgrims would stop

---

14. Marshall 1978: 288–89; Snodgrass 2008: 539.

for a quick rest to replenish supplies on their way to and from the great city.

Jesus sends two disciples to retrieve a colt from the village. If anyone asks them why they are untying the animal, they should reply that the Lord has need of it (19:30-31). It is unclear who are sent and whether the colt is in Bethany or Bethphage, but the details of the account suggest more than finding transportation. First, Jesus and his entourage are on the Mount of Olives, the location where God is said to fight against the nations to deliver Israel (Zech 14:4). Second, everything encountered by the two disciples is exactly as Jesus has described (19:32-34), emphasizing his prescience and intentionality. Although Luke does not mention that Jesus has made any prior arrangement, this is probable since his close friends Mary, Martha, and Lazarus live in Bethany (John 11:1; 12:1). Third, Jesus' self-designation as "Lord" is a claim to authority uncontested by the owner of the animal (19:31). Fourth, that Jesus specifies the colt as one that has never been ridden before reflects his self-understanding as a kingly figure. According to the Mishnah, "None may ride on [a king's] horse and none may sit on his throne" (*m. Sanh.* 2:5).

Jesus' mode of entry into Jerusalem reenacts the words of Zechariah concerning God's return on the day of salvation: "Rejoice greatly, O daughter Zion, Shout aloud, O daughter Jerusalem! Lo, your king comes to you, triumphant and victorious is he, humble and riding on a donkey, on a colt, the foal of a donkey" (Zech 9:9). Jesus the humble king on a borrowed colt stands in sharp contrast to earthly kings on stallions and war horses (Ps 33:1; Prov 21:31; Zech 9:10). He is representing YHWH returning to Zion. To those who believe that Jesus is the Son of God and Israel's Messiah, this symbolic action is appropriate. But to unbelieving eyes this gesture is tantamount to blasphemy.

Fueled by their own messianic fervor, the disciples seize the moment to acclaim Jesus as king. They may catch the allusion to Zechariah in Jesus' action but have yet to understand the significance of his humility. After throwing their garments on the colt as a makeshift saddle, the disciples put Jesus on it (19:35). They pave the way by spreading more garments on the road while paying homage to their king (19:36; cf. 2 Kgs 9:13).[15] Riding on a colt that does not even belong to him, Jesus looks nothing like a king ready to lead a military campaign against the Romans. The disciples, however, do not seem to be bothered by the seeming un-

---

15. Marshall 1978: 714; Green 1997: 685.

realism of it all. If Jesus can calm the seas, feed the multitudes, cast out demons, cleanse lepers, cure infirmities, and even raise the dead, can he not defeat the Romans?

When Jesus reaches the place on the Mount of Olives where Jerusalem finally comes into full view, the crowd bursts into loud praises for God and the powerful deeds he has empowered Jesus to perform among them (19:37). With joyous affirmation the disciples sing, "Blessed is the king who comes in the name of the Lord!" (19:38a; Ps 118:26). Psalm 118 is usually sung to welcome pilgrims to Jerusalem. Here the disciples have replaced "the one who comes" with "the king who comes." This slight alteration returns the psalm to its pre-exilic usage, when it was used to greet Israel's king at his coronation ceremony or when he came to worship at the temple.[16] The messianic overtone is unmistakable. The earlier musings on the identity of the Messiah, "the one who is to come" (3:15–16; 7:18–22), is now answered by the disciples, who hail Jesus as "the king who comes"—not just in the name of the Lord but who *is* the Lord himself![17]

The second half of the disciples' praise, "Peace in heaven, and glory in the highest heaven!" (19:38b), resonates with the song of the angelic hosts at Jesus' birth: "Glory to God in the highest heaven, and on earth peace among those whom he favors" (2:14). All glory belongs to God, for only God's reconciliatory power can bring peace both in heaven and on earth through the mission of the Messiah.

The significance of Zech 9 and Ps 118 is not lost to the Pharisees in the crowd. They recognize the royal and messianic implications in the scene before them. Because they reject Jesus' messianic identity, they demand that he order his disciples to be quiet (19:39). It is possible that they worry about the Romans mistaking this spontaneous procession for a brewing Jewish rebellion, which may result in bloodshed, desecration of the temple, and disruption of the feast of Passover.[18] But Jesus is not about to acquiesce to the Pharisees' religious and political agenda. This is the moment of celebration and affirmation of his kingship. Even if Jesus were to silence his disciples, "the stones would shout out" (19:40). How ironic

---

16. This scene is reminiscent of how Greco-Roman cities would welcome the arrival of a royal dignitary. See Kinman 1999b: 279–94.

17. According to Denaux (2002: 55–57), the themes of Jesus' kingship and the indictment of those who do not recognize it (19:28–48) echo those of the parable of the ten minas (19:11–27). These two pericopes are mutually interpretive.

18. Marshall 1978: 716.

it is that even inanimate objects would have a better sense of the purpose of God than the learned among Israel!

Indictment of Jerusalem and Its Temple (19:41-48)

Coming to Jerusalem, Jesus' sentiments mirror those of the prophet Jeremiah, who wept for the great city on account of the impenitence of its people and the calamity that was about to befall them (19:41; cf. Jer 9:1; 13:17; 14:17). Jesus' indictment of Jerusalem forms a chiasm in the next three verses (19:42-44). At both ends of the A-B-A' structure, Jesus charges Israel for failing to recognize the connection between God's promise of salvation and his own mission. "The things that make for peace" (19:42a; cf. 2:14) denote "the time of visitation from God" (19:44b; cf. 1:68; 7:16). Everything that Jesus does is a divine visitation, since he is God's agent of salvation. Noteworthy is the reason Jesus gives for Jerusalem's dullness, that God has hidden this insight from recalcitrant Israel (19:42b; cf. 9:45; 18:34). Human resistance is punished by divine concealment, setting up a vicious cycle, so that those who reject Jesus and his message become increasingly unable to perceive the truth (8:10; 10:21; Isa 6:9-10).

In between Jesus' double-indictment is a horrifying scene of destruction reminiscent of Israel's past. Jerusalem's enemies will lay siege to the city, crush its inhabitants both young and old, and level all its structures (19:43-44a; cf. 13:34-35; 21:6). Not one stone will be left on top of another. In the past, the Babylonians were allowed to raze and ravage the holy city as God's judgment of Israel's disobedience (Jer 52:4-5). If God used foreign oppressors to punish his people (Isa 29:3; Jer 6:6; Ezek 4:1-3; 21:22), what stops him from meting out the same on this generation?

The theme of judgment continues when Jesus enters the temple and promptly drives out the merchants who are doing vibrant business there (19:45). At the time of Jesus, there were commercial activities in the Court of Gentiles, where pilgrims bought sacrificial animals and exchanged money for temple currency. These practical considerations were necessary, as many worshipers traveled long distances to attend these special feasts and could not be expected to carry, for instance, their unblemished lamb the entire way. It is unlikely that Jesus is outlawing buying and selling altogether, but commercial activities in the Court of Gentiles are a distraction to the foreigners who are here to worship Israel's God. Who would benefit from the trades within the temple precincts?

The merchants maybe, but above all, the temple authorities.[19] Corruption at the top trickles down to corruption below.

The first half of Jesus' declaration is taken from Isaiah: "My house shall be called a house of prayer for all the peoples" (Isa 56:7). Jesus' omission of "for all the peoples" further underscores the disrespect shown to the foreign pilgrims (19:46a). The only section of the temple to which they have access has been turned into a marketplace.[20] The second half recalls Jeremiah's famous discourse against the temple. At the time of Jeremiah, Israel's leaders assumed that if the temple was standing, the people would be guaranteed God's protection regardless of how they behaved. Jeremiah, however, warned of such complacency. YHWH could choose to reside in the temple or remove his presence from it. Through the prophet, God posed a rhetorical question to the corrupt temple leadership, "Has this house, which is called by my name, become a den of robbers in your sight?" (Jer 7:11). The robbers were the greedy leaders of the temple who gave Israel a false sense of security, peace, and hope. Now Jesus charges the same rank and file for lining their pockets and turning the house of God into their robber's den (19:46b). As history repeats itself, the Romans will do to Herod's temple what the Babylonians did to Solomon's temple.

Jesus' action is symbolic in the sense that it is not intended to be a sweeping reform of the temple and its practices. Jesus makes a point and issues a warning, but the following day it will be business as usual. There is no mention of the authorities coming to arrest Jesus, which speaks to the small scale of the disturbance vis-a-vis the size of the temple precincts as a whole. Nevertheless, Jesus' indictment is not lost to the temple leadership. As Jesus teaches in Jerusalem, the rift between him and the Jewish leaders widens. With every ensuing conflict, the latter strengthen their resolve to do away with him (19:47–48).

---

19. Green 1997: 692–93.
20. Marshall 1978: 721.

Luke 20

Challenge and Riposte (20:1—20:44)

Jesus' indictment of the Jerusalem temple is followed by a series of challenge and riposte between him and the temple elites. Who is authorized by God to lead and teach God's people? As each story unfolds, the hypocrisy of the Jewish leaders is exposed. The creativity of human self-justification is limitless when self-interest rejects the purpose of God.

Jesus now teaches at the temple, the revered center of Jewish cultural, political, economic, and religious identity. Jerusalem is Jesus' destination where suffering and death await him (18:31–33; cf. 9:22, 44; 17:25). Unlike in Galilee where he was opposed by the Pharisees, synagogue leaders, and local teachers of the law, here he encounters the upper echelon of Jewish leadership, the power brokers between the Jewish populace and their Roman overlords. Then there is the Passover, a feast that fuels the Jews' indignation of foreign occupation and revives their hope for divine intervention. Any claim on authority and divine legitimation must carry religious and political connotations. No longer is Jesus the twelve-year-old who engaged the legal experts and asked intelligent questions of them (2:46–47). Now the tables are turned; Jesus assumes the role of teacher, responding to one question after another, redirecting his audience to the crux of the matter.

Jesus' Authority (20:1–8)

In Jerusalem, Jesus continues to preach the good news and is immediately met with resistance from the gatekeepers of Jewish religious life. A representative group from the Sanhedrin, made up of chief priests, scribes, and elders, demands to know the source of Jesus' authority (20:1–2). These three groups are the exact same ones identified by Jesus as those who will reject and kill him (9:22), and their murderous intent is reiterated after the temple incident in the previous chapter (19:47).

"By what authority are you doing these things?" (20:2). It is the responsibility of the members of the Sanhedrin to discredit anyone who does not possess the right training to teach the people. Jesus is an anomaly, an outsider from the backwaters of Galilee who does not meet their standards. They are prepared to ridicule him regardless of the answer he gives. A claim to divine authorization would lead to a charge of blasphemy, and an appeal to human authority would be discredited by his lack of qualifications.[1] By shaming Jesus in public, the leaders can buttress their own standing, reminding the people to listen to them and not to Jesus.[2] Besides, they have not forgotten how Jesus disrupted the commercial activities at the temple and accused them of turning the temple from a house of prayer into a den of thieves (19:45–46).

Answering a question with a counter-question is a common strategy in a dispute (12:3). By putting the spotlight on John and his baptism (20:4), Jesus is aligning himself in solidarity with John. A correct assessment of John's authority will shed light on the question about Jesus himself (3:15–16; 7:24–35). There can only be two answers to the origin of John's authority—divine or human. Jesus and his opponents can agree on these two options, but will they reach the same conclusion?

The temple leaders weigh the pros and cons of each option to see which one benefits them more. On the one hand, they are unwilling to attribute a heavenly origin to John's authority. Why would God send a prophet to proclaim "a baptism of repentance for the forgiveness of sins" (3:3) that undermines the temple cult and all its provisions? Besides, it would be useless to endorse John now because no one would believe them (20:5; cf. 7:30–33). On the other hand, they themselves think that John's authority is of human origin, but that would set them at odds with the people. If a false prophet is subject to stoning (Deut 13:1–10), then the failure to acknowledge a true prophet is as culpable. To attribute John's authority to human origin may put the leaders themselves in danger of being stoned, for John's prophetic status is widely accepted by the people (20:6; cf. 7:26–29). Either way, Jesus has them pinned to the wall. Emerging from their unholy huddle, the temple leaders give a non-answer that claims ignorance (20:7). Self-protection overrides integrity. The pericope ends abruptly with Jesus bringing the discussion to a close. If they do not answer his question, he is not obligated to answer theirs (20:8). But Luke

1. Garland 2011: 784.
2. Green 1997: 699.

has already divulged the answer to his readers, that John and Jesus both have divine authorization (7:24–35), a truth appropriated only through the eyes of faith.

Some Wicked Tenants (20:9–19)

To further underscore the legitimacy of his divine agency, Jesus tells a parable that exposes the audacity of the temple leadership in trying to supplant God's authority. An absentee landlord leases his vineyard to tenant farmers. A contractual agreement is formalized, that the rent be paid in the form of produce from the land at a mutually agreed upon interval of time. Whatever surplus the land produces the tenants may keep for themselves.[3] The time comes to collect the share of the yield from the tenants. Things go awry when thrice the landowner sends a slave and each time the slave returns empty-handed, beaten, and insulted. Changing strategy, the landowner sends his son, in the hope that the son will garner the respect of these tenants and be given what is due him. Emboldened by their brazen attacks on the owner's slaves, the tenants plot the unthinkable. They kill the heir to make themselves owners of the vineyard, assuming—wrongly—that either the owner has died or has transferred the ownership of the vineyard to his son.[4] Their plan backfires; the owner returns, destroys the wicked tenants, and assigns others to tend his vineyard (20:9–16).

Taken at face value, the landowner's decision to send his son and heir to a group of thugs seems terribly naïve. What makes him think that the tenants will have a change of heart if they have clearly developed a pattern of dishonoring their contract and inflicting bodily harm on his emissaries? Jesus' parables often speak truths that defy human reasoning. Once the interpretive connections have been made, the message becomes clear.

The vineyard is a metaphor for Israel with God as its owner.[5] This image is especially visible at the temple, for "under the cornice spread a golden vine with grape-clusters hanging from it, a marvel of size and artistry to all who saw" (Josephus *Ant*. 15.395 LCL). The emphasis falls on the accountability of the tenants, here identified with the leaders of

3. Marshall 1978: 728; Green 1997: 705.
4. Nolland 1993b: 952.
5. Ps 80:8–16; Isa 5:1–7; 27:2–5; Jer 2:21; Ezek 19:10–14; Hos 10:1.

the Jews, charged to oversee and nurture God's people. The three slaves represent the prophets that God sent to Israel, whom Israel rejected time and again.[6] Jesus wept over Jerusalem and called it "the city that kills the prophets and stones those who are sent to it" (13:34; 11:47–51; cf. Acts 7:52). The description of the owner's son as "my beloved son" (*ton huion mou ton agapēton*, 20:13a) refers to an only son, the sole heir of the estate. This beloved son is Jesus, at whose baptism the voice from heaven asserts his divine sonship: "You are my Son, the beloved" (*su ei ho huios mou ho agapētos*, 3:22; cf. 9:35).[7] The son should garner higher respect than a slave, though a note of uncertainty is present in the owner's soliloquy, "*perhaps* they will respect him" (20:13b). True to form, the wicked tenants throw the son out of the vineyard and kill him as their climactic act of violence. The plot of the parable foreshadows the death of Jesus at Golgotha, located outside the city walls (23:33; cf. Heb 13:12). As for the wicked tenants, they will be judged for their heinous act, an ominous note that presages the destruction of Jerusalem and its temple (19:43–44; 21:5–6). New tenants will tend the vineyard. God is not destroying Israel, but entrusting Israel to other faithful leaders. One might surmise that the apostles will play a leadership role among the reconstituted people of God, a renewed Israel that will include both Jewish and gentile followers of Jesus (cf. 22:28–30).

"May it never be!" (20:16), exclaims Jesus' audience. Are they horrified at the tenants' behavior or at the owner's response to the slaying of his son? Jesus explains further with a citation of Ps 118:22: "The stone that the builders rejected has become the cornerstone (*kephalēn gōnias*)" (20:17). The builders are the Jewish leaders who discard Jesus like a useless piece of stone, not knowing that this particular piece is in fact the most important stone in the building. Literally translated, the Greek reads, "head of the corner" (*kephalēn gōnias*), the first perfectly squared piece of stone laid at the building's foundation. Against this piece all other stones on the two walls that meet at that corner are aligned. This cornerstone has the power to destroy anyone who falls on it or is crushed under it (20:18; cf. 2:34). Identifying himself as the cornerstone, Jesus is the central figure through whom God will accomplish his plan of salvation for Israel and the world. Acceptance of Jesus as the embodiment of God's kingdom and

---

6. See 1 Kgs 22:19–28; 2 Chr 6:7–10; Neh 9:26; Jer 2:30; 38:1–6.

7. A secondary allusion to Isaac as Abraham's beloved son may be present (Gen 22:2).

kingship will lead to salvation, and rejection will result in destruction, as it is with the wicked tenants.

This is no small attack on the most powerful leaders of Jerusalem, and the chief priests and the scribes know it. With the crowd rallying around Jesus, they cannot arrest him yet (20:19). Any disturbance will send negative signals to the Romans, and they cannot afford any unwanted military action especially at Passover. The wait for an opportune time continues.

Paying Taxes to Caesar (20:20–26)

To avoid further public shaming by Jesus, the Jewish leaders keep Jesus under surveillance and send spies instead to trap him (20:20). While their opposition to Jesus may be religious in nature, for pragmatic reasons a political charge is needed to take advantage of the authority of the Romans to execute dissidents. They need Jesus to say something self-incriminating, so that Pilate will have no choice but to hear their case and condemn him.

Feigning humility, the leaders' spies address Jesus as "Teacher" (20:21a), a title used in Luke primarily by unbelievers.[8] After some flattering but insincere comments about Jesus being truthful and authoritative in his teachings, they set the trap with this question: "Is it lawful for us to pay tribute (*phoros*) to Caesar, or not?" (20:21–22). Mark uses the word *kēnsos* (Mark 12:14), which refers to the poll tax levied on an adult. Luke's term, *phoros*, is more general, meaning either tribute or tax. The poll tax is only one denarius per year, equivalent to one day's wage for a field laborer.[9] Though the tax itself is not a big sum, paying tribute symbolizes a forced admission of loyalty. It brings shame to the Jews and insult to YHWH. To add salt to the wound, the Jewish ruling council is tasked to collect the tribute. But as long as the Sanhedrin ensures that money is deposited into the Roman treasury, the Roman governor will permit the temple cult to operate with minimal intervention. Any hint of uprising will invite the Romans to use force, something to be avoided at all costs.[10]

---

8. See 7:40; 8:49; 9:38; 10:25; 11:45; 12:13; 18:18; 19:39; 20:28, 39; 21:7.

9. If the tribute included a land tax, it would entail about three weeks' worth of wages (Green 1997: 711).

10. Green 1997: 711–12.

The trick question is about legality, whether Mosaic law overrides Roman law (20:22a). If Jesus said, "Yes, pay tribute to Caesar," he would be branded as pro-Roman and the people would turn against him. If he said, "No, do not pay tribute to Caesar," the Jewish leaders could charge him for sedition. The spirit behind this question is similar to the one about the source of Jesus' authority (20:2). Both are intended to either get Jesus to lose favor with the populace or to say something that is religiously or politically reprehensible and self-incriminating.

Jesus asks for a denarius, which the spies readily produce (20:23–24a). They have no business carrying coinage that has the image of the emperor's head engraved on it inside the bounds of the temple. Furthermore, Jesus highlights the politics of the coin by drawing attention to the head and the titles on the coin (20:24b). In the Roman Empire, every emperor minted his own coins, which were circulated as effective means of political and religious propaganda.[11] At the time of Jesus, a denarius had the side portrait of Tiberius's head on one side, together with his accolades: "Tiberius Caesar, son of the divine Augustus." On the other side was Livia, his mother, and the inscription "Pontifex Maximus," meaning "Chief Priest." Because the tax must be paid with Tiberius's denarius, paying tribute becomes an acknowledgment of the divine sonship and high priesthood of the emperor, which is blasphemous to the Jews.[12]

The question about paying taxes is ultimately not about money but sovereignty. Should the Jews obey Caesar or YHWH? Sidestepping the trap, Jesus forges a nuanced answer: "Give back to the emperor the things that are the emperor's, and to God the things that are God's" (20:25). Implicit in the verb *apodidōmi* ("render" or "give back") is a sense of obligation and duty. The claims of Caesar are always subsumed under the fundamental claims of God, but one's allegiance to God does not preclude submission to Caesar's political authority. Instead of pitting God against Caesar, Jesus advocates a hierarchy of authority, with God's above Caesar's. The payment of tribute is not a capitulation to an ungodly regime and rebellion against YHWH, but the honoring of an earthly ruler that God has allowed to have jurisdiction over his people at this time. Loyalty to God is not compromised by paying tribute to Tiberius. What is not said, but implied, is if civic obedience competes with obedience to God,

---

11. Evans 2005: 324–25.
12. Marshall 1978: 735–36.

then God's authority overrides that of Caesar. Paying taxes to Caesar, in Jesus' estimation, is not one of those situations.

The spies are stunned into silence (20:26). Even the vast power of the Roman emperor cannot be wielded irrespective of God's supremacy. In the next two sets of interchange, the focus will shift to Jesus' authority, both in his interpretation of scripture and in what scripture says about his status.

Interpreting Moses on Resurrection (20:27–40)

For anyone claiming divine authorization, the litmus test is the ability to interpret scripture accurately. Behind the next question posed by the Sadducees on the resurrection lies the skepticism as to whether Jesus truly understands Moses and his teachings. They call him "Teacher" (20:27, 39), but is he worthy of that title?

The Sadducees were members of a religious sect within Judaism at the time of Jesus.[13] Coming from aristocratic families, they colluded with the high priests and the Romans to protect mutual interests, wealth, status, and influence. They held the Pentateuch in high regard but did not believe in the resurrection of the dead (20:27; Acts 4:1–3).

Jesus is tested with a hypothetical situation that is concerned with Moses' provision of levirate marriage and the reality of resurrection. According to Deuteronomy, if a man dies childless, his brother may marry the widow and have a child to carry his late brother's name and inherit his property (20:28; Deut 25:5–10).[14] The scenario involves a family with eight sons. When the first dies childless, another brother marries his widow to produce an heir for his dead brother. But this second brother also dies, and the third brother marries her, and so on. After a total of seven consecutive levirate marriages not a single heir is produced. Finally the woman dies. The Sadducees ask Jesus whose wife she will be at the resurrection, since she can only be the wife of one man (20:29–33).

Since the Sadducees do not believe in the resurrection, whatever answer Jesus gives has no real significance for them. The sole purpose of the question is to discredit Jesus. If he claims that she is the wife of all eight brothers, they could charge him for condoning polyandry. If he says

---

13. Josephus *Ant.* 13.297–98; 18.16–17; Josephus *J.W.* 2.164–66.

14. The brother may cede the right to a near relative, which is how Boaz, the kinsman redeemer, came to marry Ruth under the stipulations of a levirate marriage (Ruth 3:9—4:12).

she is the wife of only one brother, he would be guilty of revoking Moses' law of levirate marriage.

Jesus debunks the Sadducees' assumption that life operates identically in this age and in the age to come (20:34–36). Marriage is necessary for procreation on this earth. People die and children are born to perpetuate a family's name, possessions, culture, and race. But those who live with God in the age to come will be like angels who live forever. Without death, procreation is unnecessary and all marriages are rendered obsolete, levirate or otherwise. Asking whose wife this eight-timed widow will be in the age of resurrection betrays the Sadducees' ignorance about life in eternity.

To strengthen his argument with these opponents who privilege the Pentateuch, Jesus must show that even Moses believed in the resurrection (20:37–38). At the burning bush, God said to Moses, "I am the God of your father, the God of Abraham, the God of Isaac, and the God of Jacob" (Exod 3:6; cf. 3:15–16). By the time of Moses, the patriarchs were long gone, yet God used the present tense, "I am," when referring to himself as Abraham's, Isaac's, and Jacob's God. Jesus argues that these men, while dead by human reckoning, are alive to God, the God of the living and not of the dead.[15] Therefore, God must have kept Abraham, Isaac, and Jacob alive by way of the resurrection, since God can raise the dead. Theologically, the Sadducees' disbelief in the resurrection is an untenable position to hold.

Jesus' opponents have no rejoinder. Some scribes even compliment Jesus for his explanation (20:39–40). That nobody dares to ask any more trick questions opens up an opportunity for Jesus to launch a counterattack and assert his authority once and for all.

David's Son as David's Lord (20:41–44)

Still on the topic of scriptural interpretation, Jesus returns fire with his own challenge to his detractors. He appeals to the common expectation of a kingly Messiah from the line of David (2 Sam 7:12–16; Ps 89:20–37), based on the messianic readings of many OT passages. For example, Isaiah spoke of an "endless peace for the throne of David and his kingdom" (Isa 9:2–7) and "a shoot [that] will come out from the stump of Jesse" (Isa 11:1–9). Jeremiah prophesied that God would "raise up for

---

15. Nolland 1993b: 967.

David a righteous Branch, and he shall reign as king and deal wisely" (Jer 23:5; 33:14-18). And in Ezekiel God promised to "set up over [Israel] one shepherd, [his] servant David" (Ezek 34:23-31). Jesus' query in verse 41 is not to denounce the Davidic descent of the Messiah. Rather, he is asking his audience to reconcile this conviction with what David himself wrote: "The Lord said to my Lord, 'Sit at my right hand, until I make your enemies your footstool.'" (20:42-43, citing Ps 110:1). Since David wrote the psalm, he was speaking of YHWH ("the Lord") exalting the Messiah ("my Lord") to an honorific position at the right hand of God over all his enemies. The riddle raised by Jesus is how the Messiah can at the same time be David's son, who is below David in status, and be David's Lord, who is above David in status? If the father is greater than the son, why is David calling his son "Lord" (20:44)?

In order for the Messiah to be both David's son and David's Lord, the normal expectation of an endless string of kings, one after another in dynastic succession, is inadequate. According to Ps 110, the Messiah sits at the right hand of God, a position far higher than any human ruler. Only one person can uniquely fill this role as David's son and Lord, and that is the exalted Christ. God will raise Jesus from the dead and give him the seat of honor in heaven. Jesus' riddle anticipates the climax of Luke's story and provides the confessional language of the early Christians to hail Jesus as Lord and Messiah (Acts 2:34-36; 7:56). But without a post-resurrection perspective, it would be hard for Jesus' audience to crack the riddle.

Jesus has outwitted all his opponents. Far from signaling consent, their silence displays a posture of self-protection, bafflement, and hard-heartedness. The deeper they venture into their evil conspiracies, the less their chance of a course reversal.

Warnings against the Scribes (20:45—21:4)

After a series of successful rebuttal against a string of challenges from his enemies, Jesus warns his disciples and those around them about the scribes and their antics (20:45). The first three descriptors point to the scribes' penchant for recognition and status (20:46). Parading around in expensive long robes signifies their elite status over the commoners in simple garb (cf. 7:25; 16:19). Having attracted attention with their attire, they also love to be lauded in public with lofty titles. Whenever there is "value-added" seating, whether in the synagogue or at a banquet, they expect to be given the choicest seats commensurate with the honor that comes with them. The picture that Jesus paints is one of over-the-top ostentation, a complete antithesis of the lowliness and humility that characterize the ethos of God's kingdom (11:43; 14:7–11).

Indulgence in self-importance is bad enough, but Jesus continues to rail against the scribes for exploiting widows, some of the weakest and the poorest in society.[16] They are said to "devour widows' houses and for the sake of appearance say long prayers" (20:47a). Are the scribes charging widows exorbitant sums for legal aid to settle their late husbands' estates? Are they taking advantage of some widows' hospitality? Are they defrauding widows and shamelessly causing them to become destitute? And are the long prayers a fake display of piety to deceive widows into believing that they are men of integrity?[17] Whatever the scribes do to the widows, their reprehensible behavior will not escape the watchful eyes of God. Punishment that fit the crime will surely be meted out (20:47b).

---

16. See p. 239 and Snodgrass 2008: 453.
17. Marshall 1978: 750; Nolland 1993b: 976; Green 1997: 727.

Luke 21

Warnings against the Scribes (20:45—21:4), cont.

With the thought of scribal showiness and the widows' plight still in the air, Luke includes one final vignette to illustrate authentic devotion that is pleasing to God. In Jerusalem, worshipers would bring gifts and tithes to the temple to fulfill a vow, give alms, or help maintain the temple and its facilities. The officiating priest would be told the amount and purpose of the gifts before the sums were deposited into the receptacles in the treasury.[1] Here Jesus stands watching as rich people bring in their gifts (21:1). No value judgment is made of their motive or mannerism. Along comes a poor woman, identified as a widow by her clothing, who puts in *lepta duo* ("two small copper coins"; 21:2). A *leptos* was the coin with the least value in circulation in Palestine at that time. It amounted to 1/132 of a denarius, or 1/132 of the daily wage of a field laborer. To say that the poor widow has two of those coins means she has nothing. Existing far below subsistence level, she puts the two coins, hardly of any purchasing value, into the offering receptacle. She has essentially given God everything she owns.

The widow slips in, and she slips out. She is not even aware of Jesus' gaze. She does not need a lesson on devotion and sacrifice; her action speaks for itself. It is to everyone else around that Jesus directs his comment, that the widow's offering is greater than all the other gifts from the rich people (21:3-4). Jesus' criterion is proportionality. None other than this poor widow has given a hundred percent to God. Now she is completely dependent on God for survival. In her experience, piety and trust make up two sides of the same coin. Her humble qualities, not the self-aggrandizement of the scribes, will call forth divine commendation and compassion.[2]

1. Garland 2011: 817; Marshall 1978: 751.
2. Green (1997: 728) suggests that the widow's predicament illustrates how the system of temple taxes, which offers the poor no relief of tax burden, is devouring

Apocalyptic Discourse (21:5-38)

As God's Messiah, Jesus has the foreknowledge of a true prophet to speak about the impending fall of Jerusalem and the return of the Son of Man at the end of the present age. By the time of the writing of the Gospel of Luke, the fall of Jerusalem and the destruction of the temple had already taken place in 70 CE. Another two thousand years have since gone by and the end has yet to come, yet both the fall of Jerusalem and Jesus' second coming are happenings that characterize the last days. The emphasis of Jesus' discourse is not on charting a timeline, but on knowing the signs and portents that will better prepare Jesus' followers to face persecutions with perseverance however and whenever the end comes.

Fall of Jerusalem (21:5-24)

The temple in Jerusalem was the pride and joy of the Jews. In 20/19 BCE, Herod the Great embarked on a massive building and renovation project to elevate the splendor of the second temple[3] and its precincts. The people contributed and the king spared no expense. The temple, henceforth called Herod's temple, exhibited the best of craftsmanship, turning costly materials, massive stones, marble columns, and golden decorations into a sight to behold.[4]

Jesus and his disciples are at the temple. Some people comment admiringly on how devoted the Jews were to God by giving lavishly to the temple's adornment and upkeep (21:5). Standing next to the grand structures that exude an air of invincibility, Jesus gives an unbelievable response: "The days will come when not one stone will be left upon another; all will be thrown down" (21:6). This is the second time in a matter of days that he has painted an ominous picture concerning the fate of the great city and its famous temple (19:44). Divine judgment will come upon Jerusalem because of the unfaithfulness of its leadership and the rejection of God's agents (13:33-35; 19:45-46; 20:9-19, 45-47).

---

widows' houses in the name of God's command.

3. The first temple, built by Solomon, was destroyed by the Babylonians in 586 BCE. Rebuilding efforts began after the Jews were allowed to return to Jerusalem at the time of Cyrus the Great, the Persian king. The second temple was completed during the reign of Darius.

4 For detailed descriptions, see Josephus *J.W.* 1.401; 5.190-214; Josephus *Ant.* 15.391-402. Its fame was not lost to Roman historians, e.g., Pliny *Nat.* 5.15.70; Tacitus *Hist.* 5.8.

"When will this happen? Will there be a sign?" (21:7). These questions miss the point entirely. More important than knowing when and what to expect is how to remain faithful in order to be saved, for the fall of Jerusalem is but the beginning of an escalation of tribulations that will culminate in the end of the age.

First of all, discernment is of prime importance. In troubled and confusing times, false claimants will surface and pretend to be the messiah. It is tempting, in a moment of desperation, to chase after promises of deliverance that call for allegiance to fight one's enemies (21:8; cf. 17:23). These empty pursuits will amount to nothing.[5] Jesus' disciples follow Jesus alone; they must not be fooled by lies that purport to know that "the time is near."

Second, Jesus' disciples are not to be afraid. Terrifying and chaotic though they are, these events "must (*dei*)[6] take place" (21:9); they are a divine necessity in God's salvific agenda. They include uprisings and wars between nations, natural disasters such as earthquakes, famines, and plagues, as well as celestial omens (21:10–11). These phenomena are frequently cited in prophetic and apocalyptic literature as signs of divine judgment.[7] They will become increasingly rampant and severe as the current age moves toward the end, and the fall of Jerusalem is but a foretaste of things to come.

Third, the disciples must persevere. Opposition and betrayal will come from all quarters, from the Jewish synagogue to the gentile courts, from family, friends, and foes (12:12, 16–17). The apostles will find themselves arrested and tried before governing authorities, and some will face death. Yet their ordeal is an opportunity to further testify about Jesus, and they will be empowered to speak irrefutable words of wisdom (21:13–15; cf. 12:11–12).[8] While they will not be granted immunity to suffering, the promise that "not a hair of [their] head will perish"[9] assures them of God's

---

5. Theudas (Acts 5:36), Judas the Galilean (Acts 5:37), "the Egyptian" (Acts 21:38). Cf. Josephus *J.W.* 2.286–87.

6. See p. 45, n. 30.

7. Ezek 38:18–23; Joel 2:30–32; Zech 14:4–5; Rev 6:8, 12–14.

8. On the apostles' arrests, trials, and imprisonments, see Acts 4:1–21; 5:17–40; 8:3; 9:22–25; 12:1–6; 18:12–16; 22:4; 23:33—26:32. Some died, such as Stephen and James (7:60; 12:1–2).

9. An idiom that signifies physical safety, so 1 Sam 14:45; 2 Sam 14:11; 1 Kgs 1:52; Acts 27:34.

rescue, if not in this life then in the life to come (21:18-19; cf. 9:22-26; 12:4-7; 17:33).

Having exhorted his disciples to be discerning and courageous in the face of impending calamities, Jesus proceeds to describe the way in which Jerusalem will be destroyed (21:20-24). When gentile armies lay siege on Jerusalem, these will be "the days of vengeance" (21:22a),[10] signaling the beginning of the end. Those who have a chance to flee must take refuge in the mountains of Judea. Those thinking of entering the city must turn back and stay away. Fenced in by the enemies, no supplies can be delivered to feed the people and no one can escape. In time the resistance of the besieged people will be weakened as hope fades and famine sets in. When the city is finally razed, "Jerusalem will be trampled on by the gentiles" (21:24a). The Romans will pillage, kill, and take people captive. The innocent will suffer alongside the wicked, including pregnant women and nursing mothers. Yet Jesus insists that these atrocities against Jerusalem constitute the fulfillment of prophecy (21:22b; Dan 8:10, 13; Zech 12:3), thereby opening the way to the mission to the gentiles (21:24b; 24:47; Acts 1:8; 28:28).

The Parousia of the Son of Man (21:25-38)

With hardly any transition, Jesus moves from talking about the imminent demise of Jerusalem to his return at the end of time. The second coming of the Son of Man will be preceded by various supernatural phenomena (21:25-26). The celestial bodies, the raging seas, and the shaking of the heavens bring to mind images in the OT that have to do with God's wrath. For example, on the day of judgment, the sun, moon, and stars will not give light (Isa 13:9-11; Ezek 32:7-8), "the earth quakes, ... the heavens tremble (Joel 2:10), "the moon [shall be turned] to blood" (Joel 2:30-31), and "[the nations] roar like the roaring of mighty waters" (Isa 17:12). What a dreadful sight that must be! No wonder the world will be thrown into confusion. Yet the sense of foreboding is limited to the enemies of God, whose final annihilation is near. Then Jesus will return "coming in a cloud with power and great glory" (21:27; cf. 9:26; 17:22-30), in the same way as his ascension into heaven in a cloud (Acts 1:9). When the end draws near, the followers of Jesus will interpret all these supernatural events as good news. Rather than cowering in fear, they will stand tall,

---

10. "The day of vengeance" refers to God's judgment on his enemies, though it is also the time of God's vindication of the saved. See Deut 32:35; Isa 34:8; 61:2; Jer 51:6.

hold their heads up high, confident of their final redemption (21:28). In the meantime, they must remain alert spiritually and learn to read the times correctly. A simple illustration of the fig tree gets the point across. Fig trees lose their leaves in the winter, so when they sprout new leaves in the spring, one can tell that summer is about to arrive (21:29–30). By the same token, the final consummation of God's kingdom comes with identifiable signs, to which Jesus' disciples must pay attention and prepare themselves accordingly (21:31).

Jesus says, "This generation will not pass away until all things have taken place" (21:32). All those living between the first ("the already") and second ("the not yet") comings of Jesus will encounter wars, disasters, even heavenly signs. Whether it is the fall of Jerusalem or the final judgment, these prophetic warnings will come to pass for certain, outlasting the present heaven and earth (21:33). Through vigilance and perseverance, Jesus' disciples will persist to the end. One can lapse into spiritual stupor by living an undisciplined life of dissipation and drunkenness. A preoccupied life, dragged down by daily worries and concerns, is not enlightening either. Both extremes blur one's vision of what God is doing in the world (21:34a). When the final days catch unbelievers off guard like a trap (21:34b–35), prayer is the only way to build a hedge of protection against apostasy. Only those left standing before the Son of Man when he returns will be saved (21:36).

With this, Luke concludes his accounts of Jesus' teachings at the temple. Jesus' nightly departure to the Mount of Olives will provide an opportunity for the temple leaders to arrest him away from the public eye (21:37; 22:39). For the time being, the crowds are eager to hear his teachings (21:38), but their curiosity is short-lived as attraction will soon turn into hostility.

Luke 22

Betrayal of Jesus (22:1-6)

Passover and Unleavened Bread are important feasts for the Jews (22:1). Passover, celebrated on Nisan 14, commemorates the night of the tenth plague when God spared all the firstborn of the households of Israel whose doorposts and lintels were marked with the blood of the Passover lamb (Exod 12:21-27). Unleavened Bread, which begins on Nisan 15 and lasts seven days until Nisan 21, also hearkens back to the exodus. When the Israelites departed from Egypt in a hurry, the dough in their kneading bowls had no time to be leavened (Exod 12:33-34). While each feast recalls a distinctive element in the historic event, together they represent God's liberation of his people from slavery. Their celebration is mandated in the OT as a perpetual ordinance.[1] By the time of Jesus, the nomenclatures "Passover" and "Unleavened Bread" are used interchangeably. As the Jews attend the festivities under the watchful eyes of the Romans, nationalistic sentiments run high and the yearning for deliverance is felt all the more deeply.

The Jewish leaders are waiting for the right opportunity and co-conspirator to do away with Jesus (22:2). Their machinations are part of the cosmic battle between God and Satan that is being waged on the human stage (10:18; 22:31). Before Jesus started his public ministry, he had a faceoff with the devil, after which Satan "departed from him until an opportune time" (4:13). That opportune time has finally arrived. To begin the final confrontation, Satan first penetrates Jesus' inner circle by entering Judas Iscariot, one of the Twelve (22:3, 47; cf. 6:16). Judas is not demon-possessed in the normal sense of the word (cf. 4:33-34, 41), but he has come under Satan's control in will and action. The negotiations between Judas and the temple authorities reflect the workings of a conniving mind. The active verbs, "he went away," "he conferred," and "he consented," hardly exonerate Judas from his complicity with the

1. Exod 12:1-20; Lev 23:4-8; Num 28:16-17; Deut 16:1-8.

chief priests and the temple police (22:4-6). By offering them a service that they need and eagerly accept, Judas shares Satan's agency in handing Jesus over (*paradounai*) to the power of darkness (22:53). With this transaction, Jesus' first passion prediction, that "The Son of Man is going to be betrayed (*paradidosthai*) into human hands" (9:44), is fulfilled.

Jesus Hosts the Passover Meal (22:7-23)

Given that Passover is on Nisan 14 whereas the feast of Unleavened Bread begins on Nisan 15 and continues for seven days, Luke's timestamp lacks precision. The lamb is sacrificed on the afternoon before Passover begins at sundown. Strictly speaking, since Passover precedes Unleavened Bread by a full day, the day on which the lambs are killed should not be called "the day of Unleavened Bread" (22:7). But by the time of Jesus, these two feasts have essentially been combined into one, and the terms are interchangeable. That said, Luke is very clear in noting that the last meal that Jesus shares with his disciples is a Passover meal (22:8, 11, 13, 15).

Preparation for the Meal (22:7-13)

This is the last opportunity for Jesus to celebrate the Passover with his disciples, a fitting occasion for him to explain the connection between his death and God's covenant with Israel. The law stipulates that the Passover meal must be eaten within the city limits of Jerusalem. With the city packed with pilgrims, space is at a premium. Being visitors themselves, Jesus and his group will need to rent a gathering place; hence, it is prudent to make prearrangements (cf. 18:28-34).

The choice of sending Peter and John (22:8-9), two trusted disciples from his inner circle (8:51; 9:28), may imply that Jesus knows he is a marked man. Caution is taken not to disclose any name or address. Instructions are given for Peter and John to recognize the people with whom arrangements have been made (22:10-12). When the two enter Jerusalem, a man carrying a jar of water will meet them. Water jars are normally carried by women, so a man doing so will be easy to spot. He will lead them to the house where the meal is to be held. A further confirmation will come from the owner of the house. He will refer to Jesus as the teacher who plans to eat the Passover with his disciples. Even the large upper room, where they will meet, is an uncommon feature in homes in ancient Palestine.² With all these signs, it will not be difficult for Peter and John to find the place. Reserving a furnished room, however, is only the first step. They will also have to buy an unblemished lamb, stand in line at the temple to wait for the animal to be slaughtered and sacrificed, and then bring it back to be roasted. Other foods, wine, and herbs have to be procured to complete the meal.³ Since making preparations is the humble work of servants, the errand that these two are sent to run will stand in sharp contrast to the disciples' behavior at the meal, when they compete with one another for greatness (22:24–27).

With near-identical wording—*heuron kathōs eirēkei autois* ("they found it as he had said to them," 22:13) and *heuron kathōs eipen autois* ("they found it as he said to them," 19:32)—Luke concludes here, as in his account of Jesus sending two disciples to borrow the colt, that every word of Jesus must come to pass. Even though the reappearance of Satan may trigger a sense of foreboding for the readers (22:3), the author is quick to assure them that Jesus remains in control despite the prospect of death.

The Last Supper (22:14–23)

Ancient Passover meals contained a number of ritualistic elements. The head of household pronounced the blessing over the cup to begin the meal. Throughout the meal, four cups of wine were shared. The family consumed the Passover lamb, dipped bitter herbs in sauce, and ate unleavened bread. The symbolism behind the food was explained. A question-and-answer ritual between the youngest son and the father would prompt the retelling of the exodus story. In addition, the participants sang the Hallel (Pss 113–118). Full of meaning, the commemorative meal allowed God's people to express their gratitude for past deliverance and renew their hope of future salvation.⁴

The "hour" in verse 14 means more than the time when the meal is to begin. With the ominous shadow of the diabolic hour of darkness lurking around the edges (22:53), this is the hour of Jesus' battle with Satan. The hour of darkness is temporary, but the hour of salvation will last forever. As head of the household, Jesus presides over the Passover

---

2. Ancient Palestinian homes had only one story. An upper room could be built on the flat rooftop and accessed by a stairwell that ran along a wall outside the house (Marshall 1978: 792).

3. Garland 2011: 852–53.

4. Green 1997: 758; Nolland 1993b: 1048.

meal for his fictive family. His deep desire to eat this meal with his closest associates before his suffering is not a matter of sentimentalism (22:15). Rather, this meal carries eschatological significance. When Jesus says, "I will not eat it until it is fulfilled in the kingdom of God" (22:16), he hints at a denouement beyond his death. If the Passover commemorates God's historic salvation of his people, the next celebration will be at the messianic banquet, when the final salvation of God has been accomplished. With a backward glance at the first exodus, Jesus pronounces hope and confidence in the second and ultimate exodus.

Using the cup and the bread as symbolic elements, Jesus explains how God's covenant is ratified by his death. In Matthew and Mark, there is only one bread saying and one cup saying (Matt 26:26–29; Mark 14:22–25). In Luke, the bread saying (22:18–19) is sandwiched between two cup sayings (22:17, 20). It is possible for the two cup sayings to be associated with two of the four cups taken at different points of the meal. In Luke's account, the second cup saying after supper might correspond to the third cup of a traditional Passover meal (22:20). But if Matthew and Mark only record one cup saying, Luke may have split the content of Jesus' original statement into two. The part about his not drinking the fruit of the vine until the coming of the kingdom of God (22:18) is moved up to before the bread saying (22:19). This way verses 16 and 18 reinforce Jesus' confidence about his death as a major propelling force toward fulfilling the kingdom of God. Meanwhile, the bread saying and the second cup saying are paired up to emphasize the self-giving nature of Jesus death that reaffirms God's commitment to his people (22:19, 20).

Normally, each person drinks from his or her own cup at a Passover meal. On this occasion, Jesus holds up one loaf of bread and one cup of wine to be shared by all (22:17b, 19a). Partaking of a single loaf and drinking from a common cup are gestures of unity and solidarity, tightening the kinship ties and mutual commitment already resident at that table.

Taking the loaf of bread, Jesus gives thanks, breaks it, and gives it to his disciples (22:19a). This recalls the feeding of the multitudes, when Jesus took the loaves and fish, "blessed and broke them, and gave them to the disciples" (9:16). That miracle reminds people of God's provision for Israel in the wilderness. It is soon followed by Peter's declaration that Jesus is God's Messiah (9:20) and Jesus' prediction of his suffering and death (9:22). That God will bring deliverance through the death of his Messiah, already hinted at in chapter 9, is now made explicit in the bread saying: "This is my body, which is given for you" (22:19b). The bread represents Jesus' body. The phrase, "for you (*hyper hymōn*)," carries a substitutionary sense, as in, "on your behalf." Giving his life for the sake of his disciples, Jesus dies in order that they may live, and he does so voluntarily as an act of self-sacrifice.

The theme of self-giving carries over to the second cup saying: "This cup that is poured out for you (*hyper hymōn*) is the new covenant in my blood" (22:20). The symbolic shift from the wine in the cup to the blood that is poured out is provocative. Pouring out blood is a graphic image for a violent death. It also brings to mind the covenant renewal ceremony in Exod 24, in which Moses took some of the blood from the sacrificial animals and dashed it on the people, saying, "See the blood of the covenant that the LORD has made with you in accordance with all these words" (Exod 24:8). This ceremony formalized the covenant between God and Israel. But when Israel repeatedly broke this original covenant, God sent Jeremiah with the promise of a new covenant, in which God will forgive the people's sins and inscribe his law on their hearts (Jer 31:31–34). In Jesus' blood, by his violent yet sacrificial death, this renewed covenant is sealed. In other words, through Jesus' death reconciliation between God and God's people is guaranteed.

Not only does Jesus want his disciples to understand the significance of his death, he also wants them to pass it on as they continue to share meals of fellowship with other believers. Hence, he exhorts them, "Do this in remembrance of me" (22:19b). By means of the elements of the bread and the cup, the disciples are to remember the non-negotiable role of Jesus in reconciling them to God. Subsequently, they must also lead a life of self-giving and servanthood.

As if Jesus' talk of violent death is not horrific enough, Jesus now declares that a betrayer is in their midst (22:21). The thought of a traitor is a jarring intrusion to the sorrowful yet intimate scene. Like the righteous sufferer in the psalm, Jesus' "bosom friend in whom [he] trusted, who ate of [his] bread, has lifted the heel against him" (Ps 41:9). Even though this does not come as a surprise to the Son of Man, Judas will bear the consequence of his actions (22:22; cf. Acts 1:18–19). While the precise meeting point between God's sovereignty and human treachery will remain a mystery, God's purposes will not be thwarted. It is not with fear but with a sense of warning that Jesus announces his betrayal. Seeking to expose the unnamed traitor (22:23), the disciples are probably saying to one another, "Who is the rotten scoundrel? Surely not I!" Before long, each and every one of them will betray and desert Jesus. It is not a matter of when, but how.

Servanthood, Faithfulness, Preparedness (22:24-38)

It is as though the disciples never heard a word Jesus said about self-sacrifice in giving his body and pouring out his blood for them (22:19-20). They are too preoccupied, first with trying to ferret out the identity of the traitor (22:23), then with quarreling over the identity of the greatest among them (22:24).

As unbecoming as the disciples' behavior seems to us modern readers who consider humility a virtue, their clamoring for greatness was in fact the honorable thing to do among men in the ancient world. If the goal in life was to amass honor and minimize shame, fighting to be first was par for the course. In a graceless system where human relationships were monitored in terms of debits and credits, even the noble-sounding ideal of benefaction was turned into a means of oppression. A benefactor with resources and influence might perform a favor for a client. The law of balanced reciprocity would obligate the client to publicly lavish the benefactor with praise, elevating the latter's status to a higher level. This system made the powerful more powerful and the powerless more powerless. At every stratum of the social ladder, a habit of competitiveness prevailed. The disciples are caught up in this relentless pursuit of honor and recognition, making it difficult to internalize Jesus' teachings on servanthood and humility.

Jesus' observation on gentile kings and benefactors speaks to this social contract that perpetuates an ethos of manipulation (22:25). His chastisement aligns with what he has always taught his disciples, that the least is the greatest (9:48). The same radical reversal is operative in the two examples Jesus gives to define greatness: the greatest must become like the youngest and the leader like the servant (22:26). Benefaction must transcend the calculating measures of this world, so that one gives without expecting anything in return (cf. 6:30-36; 14:12-14). Likewise, leadership is best expressed through service and servanthood. Sitting at the bottom of the social pyramid, neither a young child nor a servant is of much worth in the eyes of this world. But in God's kingdom, those who perform the lowliest task will receive the highest honor. The disciples are to seek divine approval, not human acclaim. Now gathered around the Passover table, the illustration of the server serving the served is especially apt (22:27). Jesus, the host of the meal, ought to be served, yet he identifies himself as the one who serves his disciples, to the extent of giving his life for them (cf. Mark 10:45).

Fusing the Horizons: Countercultural Greatness

When we read the Gospel of Luke, we wonder if the twelve apostles-in-training would ever learn the important lesson of humility taught and modeled by Jesus. Twice they were caught arguing over who the greatest among them was (9:46; 22:24). They complained that a stranger was casting out demons in Jesus' name as though they were the only ones empowered to do so (9:49). Then when parents brought their infants to Jesus to be blessed, they reprimanded them as though their little ones were not worthy of Jesus' attention (18:15). These close companions of Jesus seemed to have difficulty shaking a sense of self-importance, so engrained in their culture of amassing honor and shunning shame. Whether it was showcasing one-upmanship or claiming authority, the disciples behaved in a way that stood in sharp contrast to Jesus' teachings and modus operandi. Jesus had always taught a countercultural and counterintuitive way of being: "Some are last who will be first, and some are first who will be last" (13:30). "All who exalt themselves will be humbled, and those who humble themselves will be exalted" (14:11; 18:14). They were to receive the kingdom of God with the lowliness and receptivity of a child.

Likewise, this relentless pursuit of greatness pervades the world in which we live. Our culture's version reads: "The first will be first, and the last will be last." It reflects our sense of order, fairness, and industry. Those who put in the effort and get there first, they earn the prize fair and square. We use idioms like "The early bird gets the worm," "First come, first served," and "You snooze, you lose." The first *should* be first, and the last *should* be last, so goes the mantra of upward mobility. Companies want to be first; educational institutions want to be first; individuals want to be first; countries want to be first. Those who are first are seen as smarter, faster, bigger, and better. On the contrary, coming in last implies slower, dumber, missing out, and falling behind.

Is it always better to be first—at what cost? I am not suggesting that we should replace excellence with mediocrity, work ethic with laziness, or innovation with complacency. After all, I am a teacher and a Chinese

American immigrant. While I am no "Tiger Mom," I encourage my students to try hard, do the best they can, and be lifelong learners with integrity. Yet the move from "trying and doing one's best" to "getting ahead at someone else's expense" can be subtle. We would expect this sort of behavior to be less overt in church and academia than in the political arena and the corporate marketplace, but no institution, religious or secular, escapes this indictment because of our fallen nature. Everywhere, from our external environment to the deep recesses of our hearts and private thoughts, the lure of greatness poses a constant temptation and threat to authentic discipleship.

At the institution where I teach, there used to be a tradition during its Commencement exercises where faculty processed down the aisle in order of academic ranking. Over time, there were shifts in the line-up as professors were promoted and received tenure. The graduates and their families were none the wiser as they watched the colorful array of regalia pass by. But faculty did not always walk behind or in front of the same person each year. The ordering in the queue was not lost to those whose titles reflected their academic ranking. The procession thus became an annual reminder of each faculty member's progress up the ladder with respect to his or her peers. If seniority was measured by length of service, productivity, and achievement, how was each factor assessed? There was the question as to which carried more weight—tenure, promotion, or years of service. One could imagine how rapidly these calculations deteriorated into a veiled form of competition, all in the name of assigning honor where honor was due.

Even though students did not notice what was going on, every year I pondered the implication of this practice as my name was called to take my place in line. Without fail, I succumbed to the temptation of assessing the "place of honor"—to use Jesus' term—that I had earned to date, and whether I was standing in the right spot. Also without fail, I felt the rebuke of the Holy Spirit for thinking that thought. What were we telling our graduates who had just spent years preparing to be servant leaders of the church and the community? Did that status-conscious queue really reflect how this faculty operated as colleagues in committees and task forces? If the answer was a resounding "No," why were we complicit in promoting comparisons that put one colleague above another?

I am pleased to report that this tradition was discontinued several years ago, and in retrospect I am amused by the silliness of it all. But isn't this precisely the point, that clamoring for greatness is a silly display of human pride and insecurity? Paul's admonition to the church in Rome was relevant then and still is today: "For by the grace given to me I say to everyone among you not to think of yourself more highly than you ought to think, but to think with sober judgment, each according to the measure of faith that God has assigned" (Rom 12:3). May we not conform to the world's definition of greatness, but be transformed by the humility and sacrifice of our Lord Jesus Christ.

Although the disciples have much to be desired in humility and service, at least they have been faithful. They left home and family to follow this itinerant teacher (5:11, 28; 18:28; cf. 9:57–62). The ridicule and skepticism launched against Jesus would implicate them as well (5:21, 30; 8:53; 11:15). All things considered, they have persevered (22:28). Now, on the eve before his death, Jesus promises that he will share his kingly authority with them in the eschaton (22:29–30).[5] For a citizen to eat at the king's table is the highest honor, but in God's kingdom, a seat at the messianic table is a reward for fidelity. If the disciples stop vying for power, they will be given authority to "sit on thrones" and govern the twelve tribes of Israel.[6] These words of encouragement will enable the disciples to see their way forward when the path between now and the glorious future is strewn with challenges.

A short interchange between Jesus and Simon Peter illustrates the fragility of human confidence and the need of divine help. It must have sent a chill down the spines of the Twelve when Jesus says, "Satan has demanded (*exētēsato*) to sift you all[7] like wheat" (22:31b). The verb *exaiteomai* means "to demand" or "to ask for permission," which recalls the testing of Job, where nothing would happen to him apart from God's consent (Job 1–2). Satan may attempt to destroy the faithful, but his power is not unlimited. Nevertheless, sifting is an image of shaking, separating the useful wheat from the useless chaff. The devil's sifting is designed to cause some to fall away even as others hang on. Satan has already entered Judas (22:3), and he is bent on tearing through the others.

Peter is singled out as the object of Jesus' intercessory prayer. The double designation, "Simon, Simon," communicates a sense of pathos and urgency (22:31a; cf. 10:41). By reverting to Peter's given name prior

5. Nelson 1993: 358–61.
6. Green 1997: 770.
7. In the Greek, *hymas* is plural, hereby "you all."

to his becoming a disciple (4:38; 5:3–10; cf. 6:14), Jesus may be implying that this diabolic assault will be so severe that Peter is in danger of backsliding to "becoming a Simon" again. Peter will indeed stumble, but he will survive the ordeal. The tenacity of his faith is not contingent upon his ability to stay faithful. Supported by Jesus' prayers, after he has turned back he will strengthen his brothers (22:32).

Isn't Peter the leader among the apostles? How can he stumble? Peter does not believe he will either! He claims that he is ready to follow Jesus to prison and to death (22:33). Good intentions notwithstanding, Peter underestimates the ferociousness of the devil's attack and overestimates the strength of his will and courage. On the one hand, Peter will not fulfill his promise to follow Jesus to prison and to death in the short term (23:54–62). On the other hand, he will in fact be thrown into prison for Jesus' sake (Acts 4:1–3; 5:15–18; 12:1–5) and will die a martyr as a witness to the gospel (John 21:18–19).

Jesus is not fazed by Peter's empty promise. He knows Peter is not ready, despite his bravado and naïveté. Rather, Jesus predicts that before the cock will crow Peter will have denied knowing him three times (22:34). The specificity and imminence of this prediction are striking, for in a few hours, Satan's onslaught will come so fast that Peter will buckle under the pressure. Yet thanks to Jesus' prayers, the disciples' faith will not be destroyed.

The last set of instructions pertains to preparedness. Earlier when Jesus sent his disciples out to proclaim the good news, they traveled "without a purse, bag, or sandals," depended on others' hospitality, and lacked nothing (22:35; cf. 9:1–3; 10:4). But now the environment is much more hostile. If Jesus is in danger, so are his disciples. They must assume a posture of vigilance, even self-defense. They will need their own purse and bag, as no one will provide for them. And if they cannot afford to have both, then possessing a sword takes priority over a cloak (22:36). Given Jesus' teachings on loving one's enemies (6:27–36; 22:49–51), it is unlikely that he is advocating retaliation as a solution to rejection. Perhaps, in troubled times, some level of self-protection is appropriate.

Even though evil forces are at work, Jesus insists that all that is about to transpire fulfills God's intentions. He identifies himself with the servant of YHWH, who "was numbered among the lawless" (22:37; Isa 52:13). In his ministry, Jesus reached out to people who fell short of the legal standards of morality or purity. He contracted uncleanness from lepers and corpses (5:13; 7:14–15), healed a paralytic and forgave him of his sins (5:20-25), cast out a legion of evil spirits from a gentile demoniac (8:26-33), and shared table with tax-collectors and sinners (5:27-32; 15:1-2). He brought the gospel to the "lawless," and as a result he is now numbered as one of them.[8]

Still lacking understanding of Jesus' pacifistic approach to violence and of the divine necessity of his suffering, the disciples are preoccupied with carrying a sword. In fact, they produce two, to which Jesus responds with exasperation, "It is enough" (22:38). Before long the disciples will use their weapon to defend Jesus (22:49-50). They continue to struggle with the type of battle that Jesus is waging against Satan. Only after Jesus' death and resurrection will clarity begin to emerge.

Jesus' Arrest and Peter's Denial (22:39-65)

Things deteriorate rapidly after the Passover meal, and the disciples' failure becomes increasingly apparent. First, they are unable to keep watch with Jesus at the garden (22:39-46). Next, when the authorities come to arrest Jesus, they react in panicked aggression (22:47-53). Finally, Peter denies knowing Jesus (22:54-62). Had the Gospel ended here, it would be tragic. Thanks to Jesus' prediction of his disciples' restoration, Luke's readers press on, braving these hours of darkness toward the narrative's victorious conclusion.

Prayer at the Mount of Olives (22:39-46)

Leaving the upper room, Jesus brings his disciples to the Mount of Olives to a place that they frequent, "as was his custom" (22:39; cf. 21:37), which explains Judas's confidence in finding an opportunity for the Jewish leaders to capture Jesus without interference from the crowd (22:6). The text does not specify when Judas took off, but when he reappears it is to betray Jesus (22:47-48). Neither the name "Gethsemane" nor the garden setting is mentioned. For the readers, a sense of premonition hangs in the air.

It is not with sword but with prayer that Jesus and his disciples will prepare for Satan's assault. The command, "Pray that you may not come into trial/temptation (*eis peirasmon*)," begins and ends the pericope (22:40, 46), stressing the effectiveness of prayer by which Jesus himself

8. So Green 1997: 775. Marshall (1978: 826) views this reference as a foreshadowing of Jesus being crucified in between too criminals. This allusion is at best secondary, for it does not fit the immediate context.

receives strength. Recalling the last petition of the Lord's Prayer, "Do not bring us to the time of trial" (11:4), the request for divine protection is especially urgent now as a fierce spiritual battle looms ahead. Since the Greek noun *peirasmos* can be translated as "trial" or "temptation," the situation facing Jesus and his disciples is twofold. While they are tried and tested in their obedience to God, they are at the same time tempted to commit apostasy as Satan attempts to lure them away from God.

Jesus goes off on his own to pray (22:41). Addressing God as "Father," the Son prioritizes God's will above his own, even as he wishes he did not have to drink the cup of suffering and death (22:42a). If the cup of wrath is a metaphor of judgment,[9] what innocent person would want to drink it? Emotional ambivalence aside, the second half of the prayer is emphatically forceful: "Not my will but (*alla*) yours be done" (22:42b). The Greek conjunctive *alla* signifies a strong adversative. Regardless of Jesus' desire God's will must prevail. This struggle represents the ultimate expression of Jesus' divine sonship. His commitment to his heavenly Father means unwavering obedience unto death.

In many English versions, verses 43 and 44 are placed in square brackets because they are missing from the more reliable manuscripts. The later addition may be attributed to a scribe. Be that as it may, Jesus' prayer has been heard. God provides an angel to strengthen and encourage his Son even though the cup is not removed (22:43). The spiritual intensity of this struggle far exceeds the physical torture that Jesus will endure. The reader gets a visceral sense of the depth of Jesus' anguish and the massive amount of energy it takes to fight this battle. He is perspiring so profusely that large beads of sweat drip onto the dirt below like drops of blood (22:44). Jesus will indeed drink the cup of suffering, but God will give strength to see him through.

Jesus emerges from his time of prayer strengthened for what lies ahead. The disciples, meanwhile, have not been praying and have succumbed to sleep because of grief (22:45). If the anticipation of Jesus' death is already too much to bear, how will they stand when the agonizing ordeal finally gets underway? Once again, Jesus commands them to pray for divine help, as they will soon face opposition that will shake them to the core (22:46).

---

9. Isa 51:17; Jer 25:15–17; Lam 4:21–22; Ezek 23:31–33.

The Arrest (22:47–53)

In one crisp verse Luke describes Judas' betrayal. The plan to capture Jesus is executed with purposefulness, precision, and speed. The timestamp, "while he was still speaking" (22:47), identifies the place of arrest as the same unnamed location on the Mount of Olives where Jesus brought his disciples to pray (22:39). Judas's sudden appearance with "the chief priests, the officers of the temple police, and the elders" (22:52) in tow gives no time for anyone to escape. That Judas is repeatedly described as "one of the Twelve" deeply underscores the heinousness of his action (cf. 6:13, 16; 22:3). It was not that long ago that Judas was at table with Jesus, eating the Passover meal in the bond of kinship.

None of Jesus' overtures of hospitality at the meal has effected a course reversal for Judas. With a kiss he singles Jesus out for his captors in the shadows of the night. One might wonder if Judas actually kisses Jesus or if Jesus' question has stopped him in his tracks (22:48).[10] Either way, the enemies know whom to arrest. How audacious of Judas to turn a sign of respect into a violation of trust. The irony is not lost to Jesus, who explicitly names the act of betrayal, thereby bringing the woe that he has earlier pronounced to bear on his betrayer (22:22; cf. 9:44).

No longer groggy, the disciples jump into vigilante mode. Having two swords on them (22:38), they do not hesitate to pull one out of its sheath and ask, "Lord, should we strike with the sword?" (22:49). Not even waiting for a response, one of them takes aim and cuts off the right ear of the high priest's slave (22:50).[11] More violence would ensue had Jesus not ordered his disciples to stop wielding their weapon (22:51). Instead, Jesus heals the man's ear as a sign of non-retaliation. Whether out of panic or a protective sense of justice, the disciples have failed to love their enemies. They must trust that God's plan will prevail even though objective circumstances seem otherwise.

Turning to his captors, Jesus challenges the pathetic tactic with which they have orchestrated his arrest (22:52–53). Despite the power they claim, the Jewish leaders are cowards. They are afraid that Jesus' supporters will start a commotion that attracts negative attention from the Romans (19:47–48; 20:19; 22:2), so they arrest him by stealth. They are also afraid of Jesus, whose power is incomprehensible to them, so they send temple police officers armed with swords and clubs. If they

10. Nolland 1993b: 1088.
11. It is Peter who cuts off Malchus's ear according to John 18:10.

cannot tell the difference between a teacher and a bandit, where is their moral compass? Rather than arresting Jesus in public, they resort to dubious tactics, contracting the services of a traitor and displaying a disproportionate amount of force. Such is the power of darkness—cunning, underhanded, and miscalculated. The sad irony is that the temple elites, who are supposed to be the religious guardians of the people, have been conscripted by the diabolic power to do its bidding. Judas is not the only one into whom Satan has entered (22:3)!

Peter's Denial (22:54–65)

Jesus is taken to the house of Caiaphas the high priest, with Peter trailing apprehensively at a safe distance (22:54). At first glance, Peter is making good on his word to follow Jesus to prison (22:33). Nothing is said of the whereabouts of the other disciples. While Peter lingers in Caiaphas's domain, he is alone in a hostile environment. Someone has lit a fire in the middle of the courtyard to keep warm, so Peter joins the servants to warm himself, perhaps also to appear less conspicuous (22:55).

But not for long. Three consecutive queries expose Peter's association with Jesus despite his vehement denial. A servant-girl notices him against the light of the fire and claims that she has seen him with Jesus (22:56). Another man identifies him as one among the group around Jesus (22:58a). An hour later, a third person insists that Peter is Jesus' companion because of his Galilean origin (22:59). Perhaps Peter's attire or his accent has given him away. To all three challenges, Peter gives the same answer: "No, I do not know this man!" (22:57, 58b, 60a).

Several things are striking about Peter's denials. First, even if the first comment from the servant-girl catches Peter by surprise, the second and the third should not. Between each query, Peter has time to think. But with each successive denial, his tone gets more desperate and emphatic. It is as though he were talking himself into believing that he really did not know Jesus. Yet the more he denies it, the more unconvincing he sounds. Second, Peter's nervousness works against his effort to blend into the background. The servant-girl is not even talking to Peter; she is making a comment about him to other bystanders (22:56). But he interrupts her to say he does not know Jesus, and in doing so invites a direct challenge from someone else (22:58). Third, Peter severs his ties not only with Jesus but also with his fellow disciples. While the first and third comments pertain to Peter's relationship with Jesus, the middle one places him as one who belongs to a group. Fourth, Peter cannot plead ignorance because Jesus has already warned his disciples that those who deny him before others will themselves be denied at the final judgment (9:26; 12:8-9).

If Peter cannot stand up to the scrutiny of a servant-girl, how will he fare before those in power? The words of the third denial are still hanging in the air when the cock crows (22:60b). In a heartbreaking moment, Jesus turns toward Peter and their eyes meet (22:61). What kind of a look is it? Given that Jesus is fully aware of Peter's weakness (22:31-32), one cannot imagine a searing look of anger. Even a look of disappointment would be difficult for Peter to bear. Perhaps it is a look of sorrow, mingled with compassion and forgiveness. Whatever that look may be, it jogs Peter's memory. Jesus' prediction of his denial now rings loud and clear, down to its minutest detail (22:34). But it is too late to take back his answers. The prophecy has been fulfilled, and Peter has failed his Lord.

Peter's failure, while monumental, is not irredeemable, for Jesus has prayed for the protection of his faith (22:32a). Even so, regret hits Peter at the core, leaving him weeping bitterly (22:61). As shameful as this moment is in Peter's history, it marks the beginning of his turning. Not only will Jesus' prayer effect his repentance, it will empower him to strengthen his fellow disciples (22:32b). Peter will be found among his fellow disciples on the day of the resurrection and will have an opportunity to face Jesus again (24:12, 34).

The rest of the night Jesus spends in the custody of Caiaphas's guards, who pass the time abusing and beating him (22:63, 65). Mocking Jesus as a prophet, the guards play a game in which they blindfold him, hit him, and make him identify his assailant (22:64). The following day Herod and his soldiers, and then the Jewish leaders, will mock Jesus as a king (23:11, 36). In the end the joke will be on his enemies, for Jesus is truly prophet and truly king. For now, the power of darkness holds sway (22:53).

Before the Sanhedrin (22:66-71)

Although the accounts of the trials of Jesus in the Gospels vary in order and in detail, all four record that Jesus faces Jewish as well as Roman authorities. Rather than harmonizing four portraits into a composite picture, which is impossible to do anyway, it is more instructive to let each evangelist tell his story in a way that communicates his theological emphasis.

In Luke's treatment, the tension between Pontius Pilate and the Jews is palpable. Both sides engage in a tussle of domination, even though politically and militarily Rome has the upper hand. The Jewish leaders and Herod cannot put Jesus to death for lack of juridical authority in Jerusalem. They need to enlist the cooperation of the Roman governor, however unwitting and unwilling Pontius Pilate may be. The Jewish authorities put forth a religious argument that a false prophet must die, justifying their murderous action with legal sanction. Herod views Jesus as a mere curiosity and acts out of spite when he does not get what he wants from him. Pilate resolves to political expediency and takes the path of least resistance. The crowd is consumed by nationalistic fervor. All these players, with their own agenda to push and ax to grind, turn a blind eye to justice and condemn an innocent man to death on the Roman cross.

In the morning on the day of preparation for the Sabbath, Jesus is taken from the house of Caiaphas the high priest to the meeting place of the Sanhedrin (22:66). The Sanhedrin is the ruling council, made up of the upper echelon of powerbrokers in the Jewish world—the chief priests, the elders, the scribes, and other wealthy aristocrats such as the Sadducees.[12] Since Jerusalem is under the jurisdiction of Pontius Pilate, the Sanhedrin does not have the authority to enforce capital punishment. Technically, Jesus is not on trial but at a hearing, being interrogated by those who hope to build a strong enough case against him to take to Pilate.[13]

The Sanhedrin's line of questioning carries political and religious overtones. The opening bid, "If you are the Messiah, tell us" (22:67a), is a trap. The Jewish leaders have already decided that Jesus cannot be the Messiah. They want an affirmative answer to use his words against him.[14] Given that "Messiah" is commonly understood to be the Davidic ruler who will deliver Israel from its enemies, acceptance of this title can be heard as a claim to kingship, which is tantamount to committing treason against the Roman emperor.

---

12. Twelftree 2013: 836–40; Ferguson 2003: 567–70. While garnering religious influence, the Pharisees are not among them because they are laypeople, lacking the political clout that the members of the Sanhedrin have for orchestrating Jesus' death in an arena that involves the Romans.

13. Nolland 1993b: 1106; Garland 2011: 899.

14. Skinner 2010: 76–77.

Without falling for the trap, Jesus points out the futility of engaging the council members in a real dialogue, for their unbelief has already led to a foregone conclusion (22:67b-68; cf. 20:1-8). By saying, "The Son of Man will be seated at the right hand of the power of God" (22:69; cf. Ps 110:1b), Jesus makes a claim that surpasses even their definition of Messiah. In Luke, "Son of Man" language is found in contexts that speak of Jesus' suffering,[15] vindication, and exaltation.[16] By identifying himself with the lord of Ps 110:1 who sits at the right hand of the LORD, Jesus the Son of Man anticipates his enthronement in heaven (Acts 1:11; 2:34-36; cf. 7:55-56). Sensing a potential charge of blasphemy in Jesus' claim to an exalted status, the elders press further, "Are you, then, the Son of God?" (22:70a). The second question is not that different from the first. When God promised David that there will always be a king on Israel's throne, he said, "I will be a father to him, and he shall be a son to me" (2 Sam 7:14; cf. Ps 2:7). If Israel's king is the Son of God, then divine sonship and Davidic messiahship point to the same role. But if the elders want to indict Jesus, the title "Son of God" is more useful than "Messiah" because of its non-Jewish implications. Pagan rulers, such as Caesars and Pharaohs, were often hailed as sons of deities. Pilate would take a claim to be "Son of God" as a challenge to Caesar more readily than a claim to be "Messiah."

To the question of his divine sonship Jesus gives a maddeningly ambiguous response: "You say that I am" (22:70b). He does not refuse the identification but also comes shy of affirming it outright. Grabbing hold of whatever they can get out of this answer, the council members declare that they have the evidence that they need (22:71).[17] The Sanhedrin has done its job even if the hearing is a sham. Off to the governor Jesus will go.

---

15. 9:22, 44, 58; 18:31-33; 22:22, 48; 24:7.

16. 9:26; 12:8, 40; 17:22-30; 18:8; 21:27, 36; 22:69.

17. Luke does not record the false testimonies against Jesus found in two other Gospels (Matt 26:59-63; Mark 14:55-61). But if Jesus' words already give his interrogators enough reason to press charges, other testimonies simply reinforce the same accusation.

Luke 23

Before Pilate and Herod (23:1-12)

Armed with what they consider to be a viable complaint, the members of the Sanhedrin appear as a united front before Pontius Pilate, the Roman governor (23:1). Because of the vast number of celebrants in Jerusalem at Passover, Pilate has come down from Caesarea to keep an eye on the Jews. The temple leaders accuse Jesus of misleading the Jewish people. Under this overarching charge they produce two pieces of evidence: that Jesus forbids the Jews to pay taxes to Caesar and that he claims to be a king (22:2; cf. 23:13).

Ironically, by twisting the facts to fit the charges, the Jewish leaders themselves are guilty of misleading Pilate. When Jesus was asked whether the Jews should pay taxes to Caesar, his answer was not an unequivocal prohibition, but a challenge to honor the demands of God over those of the emperor (20:21-25). Also, Jesus never made an explicit claim to be Messiah or king in response to their interrogation about his identity (22:67-70). At best, they may infer Jesus' entry into Jerusalem, riding on a borrowed colt, an insinuation of kingliness (19:35-40). When the disciples and the crowds chanted, "Blessed is the king who comes in the name of the Lord," the Pharisees criticized what they perceived as misguided praise, for they themselves did not believe that Jesus was a king. But if Jesus made no effort to deny the title or subdue his companions, his silence can be used as evidence of his monarchical pretensions. Then when Jesus spoke of a nobleman who received royal power in the parable of the ten minas (19:11-27), and the Jewish leaders interpreted that as Jesus' self-identification, they could also use that as proof of his kingly aspirations. One can see how with some clever manipulation a case can be made against Jesus to at least pique Pilate's interest.

From a religious point of view, perverting the nation is comparable to impersonating a prophet, a crime punishable by death (Deut 13:1-5). If a false prophet pretends to speak and act on God's behalf without divine authority, he is blaspheming. As a pagan, Pilate will not take the charge of blasphemy seriously. The Sanhedrin will have come up with a political charge to goad him into action. Given Pilate's history of violence against the Jews (13:1) and his overall lack of sensitivity toward Jewish scruples, one would not expect the governor to view the situation before him as much more than a nuisance.[1] Yet Pilate's political prowess may inform him of negative consequences should he mishandle the Sanhedrin's complaint about Jesus. Even though the Jews need Pilate's juridical authority, they loathe the power that the governor has over them. In the end, Pilate's self-interest will determine his course of action, but not without pressure from the Jews.

Pilate's opening question, "Are you the king of the Jews?" seems perfunctory, to which Jesus replies with a noncommittal answer, "You say so" (23:3; cf. 22:70). Pilate's nonchalant attitude comes through in his dismissal of the accusations against Jesus as unsubstantiated (23:4).[2] Luke's account may not have included the entire line of questioning by Pilate, but the sparsity of detail seems to suggest a lack of interest on the part of the governor. Yet the Jewish leaders are persistent. They portray Jesus as a troublemaker who has been stirring up the people all the way from Galilee down to Judea and Jerusalem (23:5). Creating an impression that the entire nation has been led astray by Jesus, they insinuate that this Galilean teacher has a following. If Pilate dismissed the case and the crowd erupted, he would be held responsible for the aftermath, something a provincial official would rather not see under his watch.

The governor's hand is forced. Kicking the can down the road, Pilate sends Jesus to Herod Antipas, the tetrarch of Galilee, who is also in Jerusalem for the festival (23:6–7). The text is silent about the governor's motives. It is unlikely that Pilate would cede his authority to Herod, whom he dislikes (23:12). Might Herod have some insight into Jesus' activities in Galilee?

Herod is delighted to have Jesus brought before him because he has been wanting to see him for a long time (23:7–8; cf. 9:7–9). This by no means suggests that Herod is favorably inclined toward Jesus. After all, he imprisoned John for criticizing his moral indiscretions (3:19–20), then he beheaded John (9:9) and sought to kill Jesus too (13:31). Herod's

1. See p. 48, n. 4 and pp. 190–91.

2. Skinner (2010: 78–79) sees a more manipulative Pilate whose attitude toward Jesus reflects his disdain toward the Jewish leaders, hence his refusal to take their concern seriously.

interest in Jesus is purely self-serving; he wants Jesus to perform some spectacular signs to satisfy his curiosity. Herod belongs to the evil generation that asks Jesus for a sign because of its unbelief (11:16, 29–30). After questioning Jesus at length, Herod receives neither sign nor response (23:9). Jesus' silence differs strikingly from the incessant accusations that the Jewish leaders hurl at him (23:10). The power of Herod is curtailed by Jesus' silence. Unable to render a guilty verdict, the king stoops to the level of his soldiers and joins them in mocking Jesus. They dress him up in a brilliant robe and laugh at his pitiable appearance (23:11). Then Herod returns Jesus to Pilate like a discarded toy. Whatever enmity that existed between the Galilean tetrarch and the Roman governor dissolves that day as they stand on the same side of injustice. The so-called friendship between the two is nothing but an evil alliance (23:12).[3]

Pilate's Verdict (23:13–25)

Jesus' innocence stands in stark contrast to the flagrant breach of justice on the part of all his opponents. According to Moses, at least two witnesses are required to convict a person (Deut 19:15). Unwittingly, Pilate and Herod take on the role of the two witnesses who testify to Jesus' innocence because both fail to find Jesus guilty of any of the charges leveled against him (23:4, 14–15, 22). In fact, Pilate vouches for Jesus' innocence three times, asserting that Jesus "has done nothing to deserve death." Twice he offers to have him flogged as a compromise, hoping to appease the Jewish leaders and the crowd and to put an end to the volatile situation in front of him (23:16, 22). Torturing Jesus does not make Pilate any more just when leniency is but a tool of political expediency.

Before Pilate and Herod, the chief priests, the scribes, and the elders relentlessly press charges against Jesus (23:1–2, 5, 10, 13). By now they have rallied the crowd behind them (23:13). The more Pilate tries to release Jesus, the more resolute the Jews are in calling for Jesus' death. Only a few days ago the crowds were so supportive of Jesus that the chief priests did not dare to arrest him in public (19:37, 48; 20:19; 21:38). What causes the change of heart? Perhaps the people have bought into the accusations against Jesus, spun from half-truths and distorted evidence. Jesus is a teacher from Galilee, interesting but still a stranger to most. Shouldn't they trust their leaders' judgment? Besides, the terms of the conflict have

3. Not only are Pilate and Herod united against Jesus, they are also united against their Jewish subjects as each flexes his political muscles (Skinner 2010: 80).

shifted. Now the battle lines are drawn between the Jews and the Romans. Jewish nationalism rules the day, and the crowd will side with the Sanhedrin. Whatever Pilate wants to do the Jews will oppose. If Pilate offers to release Jesus, they will push back on a united front.[4]

The pressure on Pilate escalates to a breaking point as the Jews keep shouting, "Away with this fellow! Release Barabbas for us!" (23:18). The call for Barabbas's release is based on a local custom in which the Romans would release someone for the Jews at the festival (23:17).[5] Barabbas is a captured criminal, already proven guilty of murder and sedition (23:19, 25). This man is destined to die, most likely by crucifixion, a punishment that fits the crime. The Jews are asking a lot from Pilate. First they want him to kill Jesus, an innocent man, then they demand to keep alive a rebel whom he prefers not to release for obvious reasons. Pilate's repeated efforts to release Jesus only make the crowd more insistent and frenzied as they keep screaming: "Crucify, crucify him!" (23:21, 23).

Crucifixion was a cruel capital punishment that combined immense torture and unbearable shame, reserved for runaway slaves, insurrectionists, and others who challenged the sovereignty of Rome. The victim's arms were tied or nailed to the crossbeam and the body was hoisted up, bloodied and naked, on the vertical beam for the world to see. With or without a small wooden peg to support the weight of the body, the victim sagged and became increasingly unable to breathe. A slow death followed as the person expired by asphyxiation. As if the physical torment were not enough, the victim was humiliated before, during, and after death. Soldiers were known to ridicule the criminals and toyed with different positions of hanging for their own entertainment. Corpses were left on the crosses for scavengers and wild animals to finish off. In the ancient world where honor was valued and shame was shunned, the denial of burial was an extreme affront to one's dignity. Crucifixion was such a horrible punishment that it could not be mentioned in polite company. Cruelty to the body notwithstanding, the power of public shaming made it an effective deterrent to those who resisted the authority of Rome.[6]

---

4. Nolland 1993b: 1127, 1133.

5. Because of questionable textual evidence, verse 17 is omitted from some English versions (NRSV, NIV, ESV). While this custom is not found in available ancient sources outside of the Gospels, the Greeks and Romans were known to show clemency at religious festivals and give amnesty to political prisoners. See Josephus *Ant.* 20.208–10, 215; Nolland 1993b: 1129.

6. Hundreds and thousands were known to be crucified along major thoroughfares

Calling vehemently and vindictively for Jesus' crucifixion, the Jewish leaders and the people are fully engulfed by the power of darkness (22:53). "Their voices prevailed" (23:23), and Pilate loses his grip in this tug of war for power. He acquiesces to the demands of the Jews and grants them both the execution of Jesus and the release of Barabbas (23:24–25a). Luke's reiteration of Barabbas's crimes of insurrection and murder adds pathos to the conviction of Jesus, whose actions and teachings champion nothing but love, peace, and reconciliation.[7]

In the end, Pilate chooses the path of least resistance. He gives up advocating for Jesus' innocence and succumbs to pressure from the Jewish leaders and the riotous crowd. By stating that Pilate "handed Jesus over as they wished" (23:25b), Luke holds all of Jesus' opponents responsible. Although Pilate's soldiers will carry out the execution, the verdict to crucify Jesus is clearly marked as Pilate's decision that reflects the will of the Jews. Pilate has picked his battles. Releasing one rebel is better than having to suppress an uprising from a multitude of angry Jews.

Crucifixion (23:26–43)

On the way to the place of execution, the Roman soldiers grab Simon of Cyrene and make him carry the horizontal beam of Jesus' cross, perhaps because Jesus is too weak after enduring many beatings and floggings (23:26). Simon is likely a Jewish pilgrim who, "coming from the country," is not part of the mob that called for Jesus' death.[8] Carrying the cross and walking behind Jesus, Simon is a visual reminder of Jesus' solemn challenge that those who wish to be his followers must deny themselves and take up their cross (9:23; 14:27). In the Roman Empire, carrying the cross signifies shame and death. Anyone on the path of discipleship must not be naïve about this possibility, which for some will become a reality.

Public executions attract crowds. A large number of onlookers follow the procession of death outside the city to witness the crucifixion.

---

across the Roman Empire. See p. 129 and Hengel 1977: 22–38, 46–63; Josephus *J.W.* 5.450–51.

7. Heil (1991: 175–86) identifies a dozen points of irony within the trial scenes of Jesus before Pilate and Herod, so that "the audience is required to hold together in indissoluble tension the paradoxical tragedy of Israel's responsibility for the death of innocent Jesus with the tragic paradox that Jesus *must* suffer and die in order to accomplish God's salvific plan."

8. A sizable Jewish community resided in Cyrene, a city in North Africa (cf. Acts 2:10).

Presumably, those who insisted that Pilate put Jesus to death are now joined by others in Jerusalem (23:27a). By the roadside, Jesus encounters some women beating their breasts and wailing loudly, expressing deep sorrow (23:27b; cf. 18:13; 23:48). Are they mourning for Jesus' impending demise, or are those tears of regret over the actions of the Jews and their leaders? Regardless of the reason why they seem inconsolable, Jesus tells them that not he, but they and their children, should be the focus of their mourning (23:28). "The days are coming" is a catchphrase to denote a prophetic pronouncement (23:29a; cf. 17:22). With three images Jesus points to future disasters that are far worse than his impending death.

First, the image of childbearing is one with which the women can identify (23:29b). According to ancient societal norms, fecundity was considered a sign of divine blessing and barrenness a sign of divine curse. Jesus declares that a time will come when it is actually blessed to be barren with "wombs that never bore" and "breasts that never nursed," because those women will never see their children suffer. The imminent calamity will be so horrific that they would rather be spared from bringing any offspring into this world.

Second, Jesus predicts that those caught in these difficult times will cry out to the mountains to fall on them and the hills to cover them (23:30; cf. Hos 10:8). God's judgment of Samaria at the time of Hosea was likened to that which Jerusalem will soon experience. The divine wrath unleashed upon the Jerusalemites will be so unbearable that its inhabitants will appeal to nature to put them out of their misery. An earthquake will cause boulders to roll down the slopes to crush them, or tear the ground apart and swallow them in the cracks.[9] To die is better than to live—this is how dire the conditions will be.

The third image of the wood follows the same lines, though the specific picture is opaque. A downward spiral from bad to worse is portrayed as conditions worsen from "when the wood is green" to "when it is dry" (23:31). The progression from moist, green wood to dry wood becomes seriously worrisome when burning is involved, and fire is a common metaphor for divine judgment. A bit enigmatic is what Jesus means by "if they do this"—who are they and what action is in view here? Is Jesus referring to the Jews' mistreatment of him, that they will receive punishment that is far worse? Or is he referring to God's action, that if this is

---

9. Nolland 1993b: 1137.

happening to Jesus, what will God do to recalcitrant Israel?[10] It is hard to capture the precise meaning of this image, but based on the trajectory sketched by the other two images, Jesus' point is well taken. Things will go from bad to worse for those who do not align themselves with the purposes of God (13:34–35; 19:41–44; 21:20–24).

The description of the crucifixion itself is minimal. Jesus and two criminals, one on each side, are crucified at the place called "the Skull" (23:32–33).[11] As the soldiers cast lots to divide his clothing, Jesus prays for the forgiveness of his enemies (23:34). The contrast between the soldiers' actions and Jesus' concern is striking. Although it is customary for the victims' clothes to be given to the soldiers at an execution, this practice adds further insult to an unmentionably undignified way to die—to hang naked on a cross for the world to see. Yet Luke's appeal to the experience of the righteous sufferer in the psalms, "They divide my clothes among them, and for my clothing they cast lots" (Ps 22:18), tempers the exploitation of Jesus. God's salvific purposes will come to fruition despite the atrocities done to his Son.[12]

Shamed and tortured, Jesus prays, "Father, forgive them; for they do not know what they are doing" (23:34a). This prayer is not found in some ancient manuscripts, and its absence lends to a smoother transition from verse 33 to verse 34b. Nonetheless, its content carries great relevance and import. First of all, Jesus walks his talk; he loves his enemies, prays for those who abuse him, and forgives his debtors (6:27–28; 11:4). He intercedes for all who have had a hand in seeking his death, be they the temple authorities, Herod and Pilate, their soldiers, his disciples who betrayed and abandoned him, the crowd who called for his death, and the like. Even though these perpetrators are responsible for their actions, in his prayer Jesus attributes them to ignorance. But ignorance does not imply innocence. Whereas Satan entered Judas, Judas was no mere pawn as he made a deal with the Jewish leaders to hand Jesus over (22:2–6). Neither Pilate nor Herod had a shred of goodwill toward Jesus to exercise justice on his behalf. All knew what they were doing. Their ignorance has to do with spiritual obtuseness, the unbelief and failure to understand the fulfillment of God's salvation in this particular manner. While ignorance

---

10. Garland 2011: 919.

11. Luke omits the Aramaic name "Golgotha" (Mark 15:22) and only retains a reference to its meaning.

12. Green 1997: 820.

thus defined does not exonerate them from guilt, it leaves room for repentance.[13]

The mockery from the Jews continues at an unrelenting pace. With each challenge Jesus' enemies etch a deeper mark in their culpability, yet with each taunt they also unknowingly profess the truth about Jesus' identity. The entire scene is an enactment of what the enemies of the righteous sufferer do to him as depicted in Ps 22: they make faces at him, shake their heads, and tell him to call upon God to rescue him (Ps 22:7–8).

First, the Jewish leaders deride him as an imposter, a messianic pretender who cannot save himself, let alone others (23:35). The titles they sneer at, "the Messiah of God" and "his chosen one," are the very ones that depict the identity of Jesus (9:20, 35). Throughout the Gospel, Jesus' mission is to save people through his healings, exorcisms, and declarations of forgiveness. But the leaders remain hardened in unbelief. To them, Jesus had better demonstrate his ability to save by saving himself first, otherwise he is not worthy to be called "the Messiah of God and his chosen one."

Next, the Roman soldiers are amused by the thought of Jesus saving himself, since they are the ones who nailed him to the cross. With a cruel sense of humor, they give Jesus sour wine to drink, reenacting the insult the righteous sufferer received from his enemies (23:36; Ps 69:21). A king drinks fine wine, but in this parody Jesus only gets the cheap wine that soldiers drink. The title "King of the Jews" signifies rebellion against Caesar. Used earlier by Pilate (23:3), this title is now inscribed on the placard above Jesus' head (23:37–38). Imagine a soldier pointing his finger, first at the sign and then at the figure hanging on the cross, and laughing at what he perceives to be a ridiculous parody of royal dignity.

Third, one of the criminals keeps hurling similar insults at Jesus, "Are you not the Messiah? Save yourself and us!" (23:39). A victim of crucifixion, this man probably carries strong anti-Roman sentiments. He would have expected Israel's Messiah to use violence and lead an uprising against the Romans, but Jesus' passivity is disappointing and useless to him.

Common to all the jeers and jabs is the call for Jesus to save himself and prove his status and power. Even the Messiah will not save himself, for only God saves. The Messiah succumbs to the will of the Father

---

13. Acts 2:37–38; 3:17–21; 13:26–28; 17:30.

(22:42), so that none of his tormentors will get the spectacle they ask for. Most ironic, still, is that all of them have repeatedly confessed Jesus' identity with their lips, even though they do not believe a word of it.

The other criminal chastises his counterpart for irreverence and recalcitrance (23:40–42). Unlike the first criminal who taunted Jesus' messianic identity, this one acknowledges that crucifixion is due punishment for their wrongdoing. Even though they die at the hands of the Romans, their deserved sentence is meted out by God. The second criminal rightly accuses the first criminal of impenitence and being dismissive of God's justice.[14] His request that Jesus remember him when he comes into his kingdom is indicative of his repentance and acknowledgment of Jesus' messianic status (23:42). Remembrance here is more than mental recollection; it is mindfulness that leads to deliverance (cf. 1:72; Judg 16:28; Ps 106:4; Jer 15:15).

Jesus' response is a solemn assurance of the man's salvation: "Truly I tell you, today (sēmeron) you will be with me in paradise (en tō paradeisō)" (23:43). In the Septuagint, the Greek translation of the OT, the noun paradeisos means garden, a reference to Eden (Gen 2:8; 13:10). In Isaiah, the term is used to point forward to God's eschatological restoration, that Zion's wilderness will be made as paradise, a garden (Isa 51:3; cf. Rev 2:7). Paradise is therefore a place of eternal bliss for those who remain faithful to God. The concern here is not where the two will go after they die. What matters is the certainty of the second criminal's salvation. Even in one's dying moments, it is not too late to repent and receive the gospel. "Today" (sēmeron) underscores the immediacy of the criminal's redemption. God's salvation, previously thought to be a hope for the future, has been brought near today in Jesus (2:11; 4:21; 5:26; 19:5, 9).

Death and Burial (23:44–56)

It is unclear how long Jesus has been hanging on the cross, as the narrative clock winds down to the last three hours of his life. No more dialogue is recorded. The reader imagines the three victims waning in strength as time passes. The gravity of the scene is palpable. From about the sixth to the ninth hour (12 noon to 3 PM), darkness covers the land (23:44). The full moon during Passover would preclude a total solar eclipse, so some interpreters attribute the darkness to a dust storm thick enough to block

---

14. Marshall 1978: 872.

out the sun's light (23:45).[15] A supernatural phenomenon is also possible. The specific cause of the darkness is secondary, its symbolic meaning is primary. In these three hours the "power of darkness" (22:53) appears to have reached its height. Seeing Jesus at death's door, evil seems to be winning the eschatological battle. Yet the ominous portent is temporary and evil's power is limited. In the prophetic books of the OT, the darkening of the sun is one of many apocalyptic signs that precede the day of the LORD, on which the righteous will be saved and the wicked will be judged.[16] Although Jesus' death is the result of a breach of justice, it is at the same time a divinely ordained step in the execution of God's final salvation and judgment. This oppressive darkness is in effect a sign that vindication is near.

Within this dark period, God gives another sign of hope, in which the curtain of the temple is torn in two (23:45). Does the rending of the curtain represent another pronouncement of judgment on the corruption of the temple, or the granting of access to God, symbolized by the opening up of the most holy place?[17] This access was hitherto barred to all except the high priest, who entered once a year on the Day of Atonement to atone for his own sins and the sins of Israel (Lev 16:1–34; Heb 9:2–7). In Mark, the tearing of the curtain occurs after the death of Jesus (Mark 15:37–38). By moving this event from after to before the death of Jesus, Luke embeds the tearing of the curtain within the period in which darkness covers the land. This reordering encourages the reading of the two signs as mutually interpretive. If the emphasis is on the evil done to Jesus, then the darkness symbolizes its power and the tearing of the curtain God's condemnation of the temple and all the corruption it represents. A positive train of thought, however, is also conceivable. If the darkening of the sun is a harbinger of the day of the LORD—not merely a day of judgment but also a day of salvation—and the torn curtain at the temple means access to God, then both signs fit well with the salvific efficacy of

---

15. Nolland 1993a: 1156; Marshall 1978: 875.

16. Joel 2:10, 30–31; 3:15; Amos 8:9; Zeph 1:15. In Acts 2:19–20, Peter cites Joel 2:30–31, marking the sending of the Holy Spirit on the day of Pentecost as the fulfillment of Joel's prophecy and the inauguration of the last days.

17. Nolland (1993b: 1157) lists a variety of interpretations. Marshall (1978: 875) argues that the curtain is not the one at the entrance of the holy of holies (Exod 26:33) but the one outside the sanctuary (Exod 38:18), else the torn curtain would not be visible to the public.

Jesus' death. Both readings are instructive, and the double-layered interpretations of these signs should be preserved.

The Son of God whose life is "about [his] father's business" (2:49) remains obedient to the very end. With his last breath Jesus cries, "Father, into your hands I commit my spirit" (23:46). His final words are a near-verbatim citation of Ps 30:6a in the Greek translation of the OT (Ps 31:5a in the Hebrew text). Instead of the future tense, *parathēsomai* ("I will commit"), Jesus uses the present tense, *paratithemai* ("I commit"), since he is dying. Like all his others prayers in Luke, Jesus addresses this last one to God his Father.[18] The rest of that verse reads, "You redeemed me, O Lord, God of truth" (Ps 30:6b LXX). As Jesus surrenders his life to his Father's will (22:42), he also trusts in God's redemption (9:22; 18:33). In faith and faithfulness Jesus draws his last breath and dies.

Following Jesus' death, three sets of responses are listed. The first comes from a Roman centurion. Since he is a gentile commander loyal to the emperor, little sympathy is expected from him. Yet, having seen the mistreatment and taunting of Jesus on the one hand, and Jesus' intercession and compassion for his enemies on the other, the centurion glorifies God and is convinced that Jesus is innocent (*dikaios*; 23:47). Even though the centurion and Pilate came to the same conclusion that Jesus did not deserve to die (23:4, 14, 22), Pilate lacked the insight that God was at work in Jesus. On one level, the centurion construes Jesus' innocence in the legal sense—that he was not guilty. On another level, the Greek word *dikaios* means "righteous," a term that denotes a right standing before God.[19] Luke uses it in a titular sense to refer to Jesus himself as "the Righteous One" (Acts 3:13; 7:52; 22:14). It is indeed ironic that a foreign soldier can discern the truth about Jesus, but those closest to the truth remain obtuse.[20]

Second, the crowds begin to show signs of remorse (23:48). This is an ill-defined group. Some were intrigued by Jesus' teachings, some were among the mob calling for his crucifixion, and others were bystanders who watched the execution out of curiosity. Now some of these folks return to their homes, beating their breasts. Is the mourning for all three

18 10:21–22; 11:2; 22:42; 23:34.

19. Luke uses *dikaios* to describe the likes of Zechariah, Elizabeth, Simeon, Joseph of Arimathea, and Cornelius (1:6; 2:25; 23:50; Acts 10:22).

20. Based on Luke's use of *dikaios* and his identification of Jesus with the Isaianic servant, Easter (2012: 35–51) reads *dikaios* christologically and suggests that the centurion is confessing Jesus as Messiah as well.

victims whose corpses still hang on the cross? Are they regretting their part in calling for Jesus' death? It is unclear what the people are grieving over but its rhetorical effect is poignant. These weeping onlookers, together with the wailing daughters of Jerusalem (23:27–28), form an *inclusio* around the account of Jesus' death, giving the account an overarching sense of pathos surrounding Israel's rejection of its long-awaited Messiah.

The last group consists of acquaintances and followers who know Jesus personally, whom Luke simply describes as watching from a distance (23:49). The author makes special mention of the women who have followed Jesus from Galilee. Among them are Mary Magdalene, Joanna, Mary the mother of James, and perhaps Susanna (24:10; cf. 8:2–3). Have they not come closer for fear of being arrested or implicated? Be that as it may, these eyewitnesses can testify that Jesus really died, a necessary precondition for the resurrection (Acts 2:32; 3:15; 10:39–40).

In the Roman Empire, the shaming of the victims extended beyond their crucifixion to the denial of a burial (Tacitus *Ann.* 6.29). The corpses of the criminals were left on the cross, either to rot or to be picked clean by vultures. Such further indignity would have been suffered by Jesus had Joseph of Arimathea[21] not stepped up to give Jesus a burial—and a burial fit for a king that turns out to be!

As a member of the Sanhedrin, Joseph of Arimathea would have been an unlikely candidate to think and act graciously toward Jesus, especially when the ruling council was presented as operating on a unified front (22:70; 23:1). Yet among the temple elites Joseph is an anomaly, a "good and righteous man . . . waiting expectantly for the kingdom of God" (23:50–51). He does not appear to be a follower of Jesus in any formal sense of the word, though his disagreement with his peers would have caused him to witness the crucifixion with a vastly different set of lenses.

Asking Pilate for Jesus' body is a risky proposition that goes against the Roman policy of non-burial for victims of capital punishment (23:52).[22] Joseph could be taken by the Romans as belonging to Jesus' band of disciples; hence, a potential troublemaker. And if the Sanhedrin found out about this, they might expel him from their ranks, which would greatly affect his reputation and social standing. The text does not say why Joseph wants the body or why Pilate gives it to him. Perhaps

---

21. Arimathea was located twenty miles northwest of Jerusalem.

22. Evans (2012: 128–30) notes that even though Roman policy did not permit crucified criminals to be buried, exceptions were made for Jewish victims.

Joseph is already turning toward Jesus, and his sense of justice compels him to declare Jesus' innocence with a proper burial. A bribe may have been given to Pilate in exchange for the body. Pilate may have been less bound by Roman legalities in the provincial regions of the empire, so that the release of Jesus' body will not get him into trouble with his superiors. Since Joseph is a member of the Sanhedrin and has considerable status and influence among the Jews, Pilate may be able to extract from him a reciprocal favor if he grants him this request.[23] All this, admittedly, is conjecture, but as long as Joseph has the body for burial, Jesus' honor is preserved. From a Jewish perspective, even the dead body of a convicted criminal should be buried in order not to defile the land (Deut 21:22–23), so how much more the body of Jesus, the Messiah of Israel and Son of God?

Joseph has but a few hours left of the day of preparation to remove Jesus' body from the cross and place it in a tomb before Sabbath begins at sundown (23:53–54). With a bit of haste, the dead body is appropriately wrapped in linen cloth. This scene triggers a flashback to the baby Jesus who was also wrapped in cloth (2:7, 12). The king of Israel, who was born in a borrowed shelter, who rode into Jerusalem on a borrowed donkey and spoke of his kingdom in a borrowed room, is now buried in a borrowed tomb. Despite the humble appearance, Jesus is buried in a rich man's tomb carved out of rock. The tomb is brand new and has never been used before (cf. 19:30). These details speak volumes about the high regard Joseph has for Jesus, let alone the tremendous political and social risk he has to assume in giving Jesus this honorable burial.

The male disciples of Jesus are nowhere in sight, but the women who came from Galilee have not left (23:49, 55). They follow Joseph to the tomb to see that Jesus' body is properly situated, placed on one of the ledges against the wall of the burial chamber. Knowing the location of the tomb will allow the women to return after the Sabbath to finish anointing the body with perfumes and spices that they now go home to prepare (23:56). In the meantime, while Joseph and the women observe their Sabbath rest, Jesus lays at rest in the tomb.

---

23. Nolland 1993b: 1164; Garland 2011: 939.

Luke 24

Resurrection (24:1-49)

As we turn the page to the final chapter in Luke's Gospel, Jesus' passion predictions have been "partially" fulfilled. While he was betrayed, mocked, and killed, the climactic element of that prediction—that he will be raised—has yet to come to fruition. The reality of Jesus' resurrection will govern how the first twenty-three chapters of Luke are to be understood. Without this chapter, the suffering and death of Israel's Messiah as integral to God's final salvation will make little sense. As chapter 24 unfolds, although puzzlement and confusion still linger among the disciples, illumination will come from Jesus to restore their joy and faith.

An Empty Tomb (24:1-12)

The women who came with Jesus from Galilee[1] followed Joseph of Arimathea to the tomb before going home to prepare perfumes (23:55-56). Having observed the Sabbath, they return at daybreak on the first day of the week with their spices to anoint Jesus' body (24:1). Given the warm climate in Palestine, fragrances are used to counteract the stench of a decomposing corpse. Their planned action would complete the process of a proper burial.

What a surprise awaits the women when they arrive at the tomb! They find what they do not expect and do not find what they expect. The stone plugging the entrance of the tomb has been rolled to the side, and the body of Jesus is missing (24:2-3). Luke gives no explicit description of the resurrection, simply the result thereof—an empty tomb. Imagine the women's exclamations of perplexity, mingled with sadness, horror, indignation, and anger. Added to the confusion and bewilderment is the sudden appearance of two angels, whose dazzling raiment is comparable

---

1. Mary Magdalene, Joanna, Susanna, among others, were named in 8:2-3. Cf. 24:10.

to Jesus' dazzling white garment at the transfiguration (24:4; cf. 9:29). The women drop to the ground in fear as the angels deliver the message with a question, "Why do you keep seeking (*zēteite*) the living among the dead?" (24:5a). The Greek verb *zēteite* is in the present tense, denoting the futility of looking for Jesus over and over where he may not be found. There appears to be a tinge of chastisement in the angels' tone, as though the women should have known better. "He is not here; but (*alla*) is risen (*ēgerthē*)!" (24:5b). The conjunction *alla* is a strong adversative, stressing the sharp contrast between what is expected and what is. Jesus is gone from the tomb; he alive, not dead, and only by the power of God (cf. 9:7; 24:34).

The resurrection should not have come as a shock had the women remembered what Jesus had said about his suffering and vindication (24:6–7; 9:22, 44; cf. 18:31–33). Realizing that the empty tomb signifies that Jesus has risen from the dead, they take the news to the eleven apostles and those who are with them (24:8–9). These women, Mary Magdalene, Joanna, Mary the mother of James, and others, are eyewitnesses of Jesus' death and burial (23:55; 24:10). Now they have seen the empty tomb and met the angels, yet their testimony is dismissed by the men as nonsense (24:11)! The apostles' skepticism may have stemmed from a widely held bias against women as credible witnesses in the patriarchal society of the time (Josephus *Ant.* 4.219). Even though the disciples have seen Jesus raise the dead (7:14–15; 8:54–55; cf. John 11:43–44), the thought of Jesus himself being raised is preposterous. Perhaps they are too distraught to think outside the box.

Nevertheless, Peter runs to the tomb to verify the women's words (24:12). The tomb is still empty. The rock remains on the side so that he can look inside. All that is left is the linen shroud in which Joseph wrapped Jesus' body. Had the body been stolen, a thief would not have bothered to remove the linen cloth. Jesus' body has vanished, and Peter learns nothing more than that which the women have already told him. He, too, goes home, wondering what has transpired.[2] The word is out that Jesus is risen, but everyone is still in the dark, in need of enlightenment that only Jesus can provide.

---

2. Others also have gone to verify that the tomb is indeed empty (24:24).

To Emmaus and Back (24:13-35)

The story of two disciples' encounter with Jesus on the road to Emmaus moves from obtuseness to recognition, confusion to clarity, and despondency to joy. Later on that same day, Cleopas and his companion are headed for the village of Emmaus, about seven miles from Jerusalem (24:13, 18a).[3] Like the women who reported to the apostles what the angels had said (24:10), these two will soon be returning to Jerusalem to do the same after their encounter with Jesus (24:33, 35). Together they constitute two witnesses, enough to qualify for credible testimony admissible in a Jewish court (Deut 19:15).

Cleopas and his companion are believers. Given the danger of associating with Jesus, only trusted disciples would have been privy to the latest developments, as these two are, including the report from the women that Jesus is alive. The reason for their departure from Jerusalem is not stated. They may be pilgrims or residents, going to Emmaus for the night to rest, since the village is within walking distance from Jerusalem.[4] It is also possible that the recent events have so discouraged Jesus' disciples that these two are leaving Jerusalem without staying for the entire feast.[5] The suggestion that their departure signals a division among the followers of Jesus is hard to substantiate,[6] though Luke describes the two as "looking sad" (24:19). At any rate, here they are, as concerned and confused as the women and the apostles, struggling to construct a coherent picture from the latest events. Even though they find the women's story incredible, their conversation continues to revolve around bits and pieces of information they have gathered (24:14).

Along comes the risen Jesus, who joins them on their journey (24:15). The failure of Cleopas and his companion to identify Jesus by sight reflects their spiritual dullness. The author attributes this blockage to God, so that their eyes "were kept from recognizing [Jesus]" (24:16). This is not unlike God concealing from the Twelve the full comprehension of Jesus' passion predictions (9:45; 18:34). Human reasoning is limited; a true understanding of God's plan can only come by way of revelation.

---

3. The location of Emmaus is debated. Marshall (1978: 892-93) considers three options but each has its flaws. As long as Emmaus is within walking distance from Jerusalem, where it is exactly does not matter as much.
4. Nolland 1993b: 1200.
5. Marshall 1978: 892.
6. Green 1997: 844.

When Jesus asks the two about their deliberations, they are surprised at his ignorance (24:17–18). Cleopas assumes Jesus is a pilgrim and wonders if he is the only stranger who has no inkling of the latest happenings in Jerusalem. How ironic! Not only is Jesus not a stranger to these events, he is the central figure with firsthand experience from beginning to end. He knows the what, why, when, and how of every minute in the last few days, yet Cleopas thinks he knows nothing. Pressed a bit further by Jesus, the two proceed to recount for him what they know, from the trial to the resurrection (24:19–24).

Several themes in Luke are reiterated in the summary of the two disciples. First, Jesus is viewed by many as "a prophet mighty in deed and word," (24:19; cf. 7:16; 9:8, 19). Second, even though crucifixion is a Roman capital punishment, the Jewish leadership is responsible for handing Jesus over to be condemned (24:20). Third, Jesus' followers look to him to redeem Israel (24:21; cf. 9:20; Acts 1:6). It is this messianic hope that suffered a crushing blow when the disciples watched Jesus die on a Roman cross. Fourth, Jesus' disciples struggle to grasp the truth. Even with a message from two angels, they remain fixated on the empty tomb (24:22–24). Whether by their actions or their questions, they miss seeing Jesus' rejection, humiliation, and death as an integral part of God's salvation (9:46, 49, 54; 18:34; 22:24, 38).

Jesus' rebuke is pointed. He attributes the obtuseness of Cleopas and his companion to foolishness. Jesus is not talking about their lack of intellectual capability, but spiritual openness and faith. They are slow to believe with their hearts that which the prophets have already declared—that Israel's Messiah must suffer to enter his glory (24:25–26). If the thought of a suffering Messiah is too much of a contradiction in terms, then the idea of a dead Messiah is even more unfathomable. How can God's Messiah be shamed and killed on a Roman cross when he is expected to deliver Israel from the pagans?

Tracing a line from Moses and the prophets down to himself, Jesus explains how the Scriptures are to be read to bring his coming and the shape of his mission into focus (24:27). If only Luke had included the specific texts in Moses and the prophets to which Jesus referred! Perhaps the author is saving the scriptural expositions for the speeches in his second volume (Acts 2:14–36; 3:12–26; 7:2–53; 13:16–41). Here he merely hints at the connection between the idea of a suffering Messiah and Israel's pattern of rejecting the prophets God sent to them (11:47–51; 20:9–19).

As Messiah, Jesus is more than a prophet, though his royal status does not preclude the destiny of a prophet (13:33-34).

Arriving at Emmaus, the conversation between Cleopas, his companion, and Jesus would have ended had the two not insisted that Jesus stay with them for the evening (24:28-29). Jesus' pretense that he needs to keep going creates an opportunity for the others to extend hospitality to this stranger who has just explained to them that which they thought he knew nothing about! As with other meal scenes in Luke, this one provides a context for fellowship, teaching, and revelation.[7] But there is more. This is also a scene of recognition, when the two disciples finally register that they are in the presence of the risen Lord.[8]

Although invited in as a guest, Jesus reverses the roles and becomes the host at the table. His actions—taking, blessing, breaking, and giving the bread to the two disciples—bring to mind the feeding of the five thousand and the Last Supper (9:16; 22:19; 24:30).[9] The memory of these two events jolts the two out of their spiritual stupor. Their eyes are opened by God and they recognize that it is Jesus who has been accompanying them all along. Then Jesus vanishes (24:31). While Jesus has been raised bodily, he operates in a sphere that transcends physical limitations. Rather than feeling perplexed that Jesus has disappeared, the two reflect on their experience that day, how their hearts burned within them when they were in Jesus' presence (24:32). A burning heart expresses more than a relational warmth of intimacy; it signifies an inner transformation. What seemed disjointed and fragmented before is now an integrated picture. With Jesus' help, the two have connected the dots in their Scriptures and drawn the line from Moses through the prophets to Jesus. They now understand the necessity of the death of the Messiah and the victory of his resurrection.

The two waste no time in returning to Jerusalem (24:33). Seven miles can be covered in about two hours, but what a different journey this is! Gone are the sorrow, confusion, and fear as they burst upon the

---

7. See Luke 5:29-32; 7:36-50; 14:1-24; 15:1-2; 22:14-30.

8. Per Nolland (1993b: 1201) the recognition scene is a crucial point in a Greek drama.

9. Maloney (2013: 77) overstates the case that this meal is the fulfillment of Jesus' promise at the Last Supper that he will not eat another Passover meal and drink of the fruit of the vine until the kingdom of God comes (22:16, 18). Granted that Luke advocates a realized eschatology, the messianic banquet at the final consummation, to which Jesus refers in his sayings, lies yet in the future.

gathering of disciples, huffing and puffing with excitement. Before they get to deliver their news, the others interrupt to tell theirs: "The Lord has really (*ontōs*) risen, and he has appeared to Simon!" (24:34). The adverb, *ontōs*, overturns their earlier skepticism; the Lord has risen *indeed*. Of special mention is the appearance to Simon Peter, who because of his denials is all the more in need of assurance. Jesus' appearance to Peter connotes forgiveness, so that turning back he can encourage and lead the others (22:32). The pericope closes with the two from Emmaus describing their encounter with Jesus, and how the breaking of bread marked the moment of recognition (24:35).

Commissioning the Twelve (24:36–49)

In the midst of the excitement, Jesus appears and says, "Peace be with you" (24:36). In Luke, bringing peace is more than a customary Jewish greeting (Judg 19:20; 1 Sam 25:6); it conveys the peace of salvation.[10] Any turmoil from the crucifixion is relativized and redeemed by the saving peace that comes from believing that Jesus is truly Israel's suffering Messiah, vindicated by God and raised from the dead.

The good news of the resurrection notwithstanding, Jesus' sudden appearance scares his disciples (24:37). Based on the testimonies of Peter and the two disciples from Emmaus, the others believe that Jesus has been raised. Yet what they know in their heads has yet to filter down to their hearts, for the first thought that comes to mind is not the risen Lord but an apparition that is standing in front of them. No wonder Jesus issues a gentle rebuke of their unwarranted fears and doubts (24:38). Accommodating his disciples' nervous state of mind, Jesus shows them his disfigured hands and feet, invites them to touch him, and reassures them that it is really him (24:39–40). A ghost has a disembodied existence, but Jesus stands among them in flesh and bones, scars and all. His bodily resurrection does not negate his violent death as though they never happened. Rather, it verifies that glorification and vindication must come by way of humiliation and death. Slowly but surely, the disciples' joy peeks through their fear, though disbelief and wonderment linger (24:41). What else does it take to convince them? Ghosts do not eat but people do, so Jesus asks for food. They give him some broiled fish and watch him eat it (24:42–43). With that, any residual doubt is erased.

---

10. See 1:79; 2:14; 7:50; 8:48; 10:5; 19:38.

Just as the two disciples who went to Emmaus needed an enlightened way to reread the Scriptures in view of Jesus' story, so do the apostles. Seeing how Scripture attests to Jesus' messianic mission affirms the cohesiveness of God's plan. Jesus reminds them that the whole of Scripture—Moses, the prophets, and the psalms—points to the suffering and vindication of the Messiah (24:44–46; cf. 24:26). First, the Messiah is the Davidic king whose kingdom will last forever (2 Sam 7:12–16; Ps 2:7). Second, the Messiah is the righteous sufferer in the psalms of lament (Pss 22:7–8, 18; 31:5; 69:21). Third, the Messiah is the prophet rejected and killed by his own people (Jer 2:30; 7:25–26; 25:4). And fourth, the Messiah is the servant of YHWH who stays silent before his enemies and is numbered with the transgressors (Isa 52:13—53:12; 61:1–2). All these biblical strands converge in the person and mission of Israel's Messiah, resulting in a divinely authorized tension of shame and glory, injustice and vindication. It is not the promise of salvation that is difficult to accept, but how salvation is accomplished through the death of the Messiah.

With the big picture in view, Jesus' disciples are commissioned to preach repentance for the forgiveness of sins (24:47), similar to John's "baptism of repentance for the forgiveness of sins" (3:3). The apostles' role as witnesses is not to be ethnocentric; they are to start from Jerusalem and reach out (24:48; cf. Acts 1:8), so that from Israel and through Israel "all flesh shall see the salvation of God" (3:6; cf. 2:30–32). In the name of Jesus, they are to bear testimonies about everything they have seen and heard from the first day until now.

Compared to the earlier dispatches of Jesus' disciples into the villages of Galilee (9:1–6; 10:1–12), the commissioning of the apostles at this time bears greater import and presents greater challenges. Now that Israel's Messiah has suffered, died, and been raised from the dead, the message of the kingdom will be even better news for those who receive it by faith, but also all the more offensive for those who do not. The apostles will be empowered by the Holy Spirit (24:49; cf. 11:13; Acts 1:3; 2:33) to carry out their mission, as will subsequent generations of believers.[11] Before jumping into action, Jesus instructs them to remain in Jerusalem and wait, for one more thing needs to happen before the outpouring of the Holy Spirit, which is Jesus' departure to his heavenly glory.

---

11. Acts 2:1–13; 2:38–39; 5:32; 8:14–17; 10:44–47; 19:1–7.

Ascension into Heaven (24:50–53)

The final scene of the Gospel of Luke takes place in Bethany, two miles east of Jerusalem on the slopes of the Mount of Olives (24:50a).[12] This is the starting point of Jesus' entry into Jerusalem riding on a borrowed colt, an action suggestive of his humble kingship to effectuate God's deliverance of Israel from their enemies (19:29–38; cf. Ps 118:26; Zech 9:9; 14:1–4). At that time, the disciples approached Jerusalem with a sense of foreboding on the one hand (9:22–24, 44; 18:31–33) and a heightened confidence in Jesus' messianic status on the other (19:38). Returning to the same location on the far side of the crucifixion and the resurrection, they possess a more complete understanding of how the events of late fit into the trajectory of God's plan of salvation, a trajectory that has been embedded in the Scriptures all along. The last step is the ascension of Jesus, the heavenward exaltation of the Messiah to the right hand of God (Acts 2:32–33; 5:30–31; 7:55–56).

As Jesus is blessing his disciples, he is carried up to heaven (24:50b–51). At the beginning of the travel narratives, Luke writes: "When the days drew near for [Jesus] to be taken up, he set his face to go to Jerusalem" (9:51). At that stage of the narrative, the emphasis fell on the determination with which Jesus embarked on his fateful journey. The Greek in 9:51a can be translated as "when the day of his ascension drew near" (*tas hēmeras tēs analēmpseōs autou*), a foreshadowing of this moment on the Mount of Olives. In the OT, Enoch and Elijah were taken up into heaven without encountering death.[13] Jesus' experience is unique because he did die, then God raised him from the dead before taking him up. The resurrection is Jesus' vindication and the ascension his glorification.

Luke's narrative closes with the disciples worshiping Jesus, returning to Jerusalem with joy, and gathering at the temple blessing God (24:52–53). For the first time in the story, Jesus is presented as the object of worship, most fitting for his glorified status. With praise and gratitude the disciples wait for the Holy Spirit as instructed. Their fear has given way to courage, as evidenced in their continual presence in the temple. Returning to the setting of the Jerusalem temple, Luke's story comes full circle. Jesus' disciples are the next generation of the faithful remnant

---

12. See Acts 1:1–12. The two accounts of Jesus' ascension form the seam that connects Luke to Acts. While some of the details are different, they are not contradictory.

13. For Enoch, see Gen 5:24; Sir 44:16; 49:14; Heb 11:5. For Elijah, see 1 Kgs 2:11; Sir 48:9.

of Israel, following the footsteps of Zechariah, Elizabeth, Mary, Joseph, Simeon, and Anna (Luke 1–2). Transformed and armed with a new sense of confidence and purpose, they will emerge in Luke's second volume, the book of Acts, as bold witnesses, empowered by the Holy Spirit, to carry the good news of the kingdom of God to all near and far.

Bibliography

Adams, Dwayne H. 2008. *The Sinner in Luke*. ETSMS 8. Eugene, OR: Pickwick.
Alexander, Loveday C. 1986. "Luke's Preface in the Context of Greek Preface-Writing." *NovT* 28:48–74.
———. 2004. "Sisters in Adversity: Retelling Martha's Story." In *A Feminist Companion to Luke*, edited by Amy-Jill Levine, 197–213. Feminist Companion to the New Testament and Early Christian Writings 3. London: Sheffield Academic.
Bailey, Kenneth E. 1983. *Poet and Peasant and Through Peasant Eyes: A Literary-Cultural Approach to Parables in Luke*. Combined ed. Grand Rapids: Eerdmans.
———. 1992. *Finding the Lost: Cultural Keys to Luke 15*. St. Louis, MO: Concordia.
———. 2008. *Jesus Through Middle Eastern Eyes: Cultural Studies in the Gospels*. Downers Grove, IL: IVP Academic.
Barr, James. 1988. "*Abba* Isn't 'Daddy.'" *JTS* 39:28–47.
Barrett, C. K. 1989. *The New Testament Background: Selected Documents*. Rev. ed. San Francisco: Harper & Row.
Bates, Matthew W. 2013. "Cryptic Codes and a Violent King: A New Proposal for Matthew 11:12 and Luke 16:16–18." *CBQ* 75:74–93.
Bauckham, Richard. 1998. "The Scrupulous Priest and the Good Samaritan: Jesus' Parabolic Interpretation of the Law of Moses." *NTS* 44:475–89.
———. 2006. *Jesus and the Eyewitnesses: The Gospel as Eyewitness Testimony*. Grand Rapids: Eerdmans.
Bell, Richard H. 2013. "Demon, Devil, Satan." In *Dictionary of Jesus and the Gospels*, edited by Joel B. Green, et al, 193–202. 2nd ed. Downers Grove, IL: IVP Academic.
Billings, Bradly S. 2009. "'At the Age of 12': The Boy Jesus in the Temple (Luke 2:41–52), the Emperor Augustus, and the Social Setting of the Third Gospel." *JTS* 60:70–89.
Bird, Michael F. 2006. "Who Comes from the East and the West?: Luke 13.28–29/Matt 8.11–12 and the Historical Jesus." *NTS* 52:441–57.
Bock, Darrell L. 1991. "The Son of Man in Luke 5:24." *BBR* 1:109–21.
———. 1996. *Luke 9:51–24:53*. BECNT 3B. Grand Rapids: Baker.
———. 2013. "Son of Man." In *Dictionary of Jesus and the Gospels*, edited by Joel B. Green, et al, 894–900. 2nd ed. Downers Grove, IL: IVP Academic.
Bockmuehl, Markus. 1998. "'Let the Dead Bury Their Dead' (Matt 8:22/Luke 9:60): Jesus and the Halakhah." *JTS* 49:553–81.
Bond, Helen K. 2013. "Herodian Dynasty." In *Dictionary of Jesus and the Gospels*, edited by Joel B. Green, et al., 379–82. 2nd ed. Downers Grove, IL: IVP Academic.
Borgman, Paul. 2006. *The Way According to Luke: Hearing the Whole Story of Luke-Acts*. Grand Rapids: Eerdmans.
Braun, Willi. 1995. *Feasting and Social Rhetoric in Luke 14*. SNTSMS 85. Cambridge: Cambridge University Press.
Brown, Raymond E. 1993. *The Birth of the Messiah: A Commentary on the Infancy Narratives in Matthew and Luke*. New updated ed. New York: Doubleday.

Carroll, John T., and Joel B. Green. 1995. *The Death of Jesus in Early Christianity*. Peabody, MA: Hendrickson.

Carroll, John T. 2012. *Luke: A Commentary*. NTL. Louisville: Westminster John Knox.

Charlesworth, James H., ed. 1983. *The Old Testament Pseudepigrapha*. Vol. 1. Garden City, NY: Doubleday.

———, ed. 1985. *The Old Testament Pseudepigrapha*. Vol. 2. Garden City, NY: Doubleday.

Chen, Diane G. 2006. *God as Father in Luke-Acts*. StBibLit 82. New York: Peter Lang.

Collins, John J. 2010. *The Scepter and the Star: Messianism in Light of the Dead Sea Scrolls*. 2nd ed. Grand Rapids: Eerdmans.

Corbin-Reuschling, Wyndy. 2009. "Zacchaeus's Conversion: To Be or Not To Be a Tax Collector (Luke 19:1–10)." *ExAud* 25:67–88.

Cosgrove, Charles H. 2005. "A Woman's Unbound Hair in the Greco-Roman World, with Special Reference to the Story of the 'Sinful Woman' in Luke 7:36–50." *JBL* 124:675–92.

Cotter, Wendy J. 2005. "The Parable of the Feisty Widow and the Threatened Judge (Luke 18.1–8)." *NTS* 51:328–43.

Danby, Herbert, trans. 1933. *The Mishnah*. Oxford: Clarendon.

de Boer, Esther A. 2004. "The Lukan Mary Magdalene and the Other Women Following Jesus." In *A Feminist Companion to Luke*, edited by Amy-Jill Levine, 140–60. Feminist Companion to the New Testament and Early Christian Writings 3. London: Sheffield Academic.

Denaux, Adelbert. 2002. "The Parable of the King-Judge (Lk 19:12–28) and Its Relation to the Entry Story (Lk 19:29–44)." *ZNW* 93:35–57.

deSilva, David A. 1993. "The Parable of the Prudent Steward and Its Lucan Context." *CTR* 6:255–68.

Dinkler, Michal Beth. 2015. "'The Thoughts of Many Hearts Shall Be Revealed': Listening in on Lukan Interior Monologues." *JBL* 133:373–99.

Dunn, James D. G. 1972. "Spirit-and-Fire Baptism." *NovT* 14:81–92.

———. 1996. *Christology in the Making: A New Testament Inquiry into the Origins of the Doctrine of the Incarnation*. 2nd ed. Grand Rapids: Eerdmans.

Easter, Matthew C. 2012. "'Certainly This Man Was Righteous': Highlighting a Messianic Reading of the Centurion's Confession in Luke 23:47." *TynBul* 63:35–51.

Eastman, Susan. 2006. "The Foolish Father and the Economics of Grace." *ExpTim* 117:402–5.

Edwards, James R. 2015. *The Gospel according to Luke*. PNTC. Grand Rapids: Eerdmans.

Emmrich, Martin. 2000. "The Lucan Account of the Beelzebul Controversy." *WTJ* 62:267–79.

Evans, Craig A. 2005. *Ancient Texts for New Testament Studies: A Guide to the Background Literature*. Peabody, MA: Hendrickson.

———. 2012. *Jesus and His World: The Archaeological Evidence*. Louisville: Westminster John Knox.

Ferguson, Everett. *Backgrounds of Early Christianity*. 3rd ed. Grand Rapids: Eerdmans.

Fiensy, David A. 1999. "The Importance of New Testament Background Studies in Biblical Research: The 'Evil Eye' in Luke 11:34 as a Case Study." *Stone-Campbell Journal* 2:75–88.

Fitzmyer, Joseph A. 1981. *The Gospel according to Luke I–IX: Introduction, Translation, and Notes*. AB 28. Garden City, NY: Doubleday.

———. 1985. *The Gospel according to Luke X-XXIV: Introduction, Translation, and Notes*. AB 28A. Garden City, NY: Doubleday.
Ford, J. Massyngbaerde. 1984. *My Enemy Is My Guest: Jesus and Violence in Luke*. Maryknoll, NY: Orbis.
Foster, Ruth Ann, and William D. Shiell. 1997. "The Parable of the Sower and the Seed in Luke 8:1-10." *RevExp* 94:259-67.
Gagnon, Robert A. J. 1994. "Luke's Motives for Redaction in the Account of the Double Delegation in Luke 7:1-10." *NovT* 36:122-45.
García Serrano, Andrés. 2014. "Anna's Characterization in Luke 2:36-38: A Case of Conceptual Allusion?" *CBQ* 76:464-80.
Garland, David E. 2011. *Luke*. Zondervan Exegetical Commentary on the New Testament 3. Grand Rapids: Zondervan.
Garrett, Susan R. 1990. "Exodus from Bondage: Luke 9:31 and Acts 12:1-24." *CBQ* 52:656-80.
———. 1991. "'Lest the Light in You Be Darkness': Luke 11:33-36 and the Question of Commitment." *JBL* 110:93-105.
Gathercole, Simon. 2005. "The Heavenly ἀνατολὴ (Luke 1:78-9)." *JTS* 56:471-88.
Goodrich, John K. 2012. "Voluntary Debt Remission and the Parable of the Unjust Steward (Luke 16:1-13)." *JBL* 131:547-66.
Gourgues, Michel. 1998. "The Priest, the Levite, and the Samaritan Revisited: A Critical Note on Luke 10:31-35." *JBL* 117:709-13.
Grant, Michael. 1975. *The Twelve Caesars*. New York: Charles Scribner's Sons.
Green, Joel B. 1997. *The Gospel of Luke*. NICNT. Grand Rapids: Eerdmans.
Hagner Donald A. 2012. *The New Testament: A Historical and Theological Introduction*. Grand Rapids: Baker Academic.
Hamm, Dennis. 1994. "What the Samaritan Leper Sees: The Narrative Christology of Luke 17:11-19." *CBQ* 56:273-87.
———. 2003. "The Tamid Service in Luke-Acts: The Cultic Background behind Luke's Theology of Worship (Luke 1:5-25; 18:9-14; 24:50-53; Acts 3:1; 10:3, 30." *CBQ* 65:215-31.
Hanson, K. C. 2008. "All in the Family: Kinship in Agrarian Roman Palestine." In *The Social World of the New Testament: Insights and Models*, edited by Jerome H. Neyrey and Eric C. Stewart, 25-46. Peabody, MA: Hendrickson.
Harrill, J. Albert. 2000. "Slavery." In *Dictionary of New Testament Background*, edited by Craig A. Evans and Stanley E. Porter, 1124-27. Downers Grove, IL: InterVarsity.
Harris, Sarah. 2012. "Why Are There Shepherds in the Lukan Birth Narrative?" *Colloq* 44: 17-30.
Hartsock, Chad. 2013. "The Healing of the Man with Dropsy (Luke 14:1-6) and the Lukan Landscape." *BibInt* 21:341-54.
Hays, J. Daniel. 2015. "The Persecuted Prophet and Judgment on Jerusalem: The Use of LXX Jeremiah in the Gospel of Luke." *BBR* 25:453-75.
Heil, John Paul. 1991. "Reader-Response and the Irony of the Trial of Jesus in Luke 23:1-25." *ScEs* 43:175-86.
Hengel, Martin. 1977. *Crucifixion in the Ancient World and the Folly of the Message of the Cross*. Philadelphia: Fortress.
Horst, Pieter W. van der. 2006. "Abraham's Bosom, the Place Where He Belonged: A Short Note on ἀπενεχθῆναι in Luke 16.22." *NTS* 52:142-44.
Hultgren, Arland J. 1990. "The Bread Petition of the Lord's Prayer." *AThR* 11:41-54.

Bibliography

———. 2000. *The Parables of Jesus: A Commentary*. Grand Rapids: Eerdmans.
Jeffers, James S. 1999. *The Greco-Roman World of the New Testament Era: Exploring the Background of Early Christianity*. Downers Grove, IL: InterVarsity.
Keener, Craig S. 2005. "'Brood of Vipers' (Matthew 3.7; 12.34; 23.33)." *JSNT* 28:3–11.
———. 2014. *The IVP Bible Background Commentary*. 2nd ed. Downers Grove, IL: InterVarsity.
Kilgallen, John J. 1998. "Forgiveness of Sins (Luke 7:36–50)." *NovT* 40:105–16.
Kim, Kyoung-Jin. 1998. *Stewardship and Almsgiving in Luke's Theology*. JSNTSup 155. Sheffield: Sheffield Academic.
Kinman, Brent. 1999a. "Debtor's prison and the Future of Israel (Luke 12:57–59)." *JETS* 42:411–25.
———. 1999b. "Parousia, Jesus' 'A-Triumphal' Entry, and the Fate of Jerusalem (Luke 19:28–44)." *JBL* 118:279–94.
Klassen-Wiebe, Sheila. 1994. "Luke 3:15–17, 21–22." *Int* 48: 397–401.
Knowles, Michael P. 2004. "Once more 'Lead Us Not *Eis Peirasmon*.'" *ExpTim* 115: 191–94.
Koester, Helmut. 1992. *Ancient Christian Gospels: Their History and Development*. 2nd ed. Edinburgh: Bloomsbury T. & T. Clark.
Kuhn, Karl A. 2001. "The Point of the Step-Parallelism in Luke 1–2." *NTS* 47: 38–49.
Landry, David T. 1995. "Narrative Logic in the Annunciation to Mary (Luke 1:26–38)." *JBL* 114: 65–79.
Landry, David T., and Ben May. 2000. "Honor Restored: New light on the Parable of the Prudent Steward (Luke 16:1–8a)." *JBL* 119:287–309.
Longenecker, Bruce W. 2012. *Hearing the Silence: Jesus on the Edge and God in the Gap: Luke 4 in Narrative Perspective*. Eugene OR: Cascade.
Lygre, John G. 2002. "Of What Charges?: (Luke 16:1–2)." *BTB* 3:21–28.
Maloney, Francis J. 2013. *The Resurrection of the Messiah: A Narrative Commentary on the Resurrection Accounts in the Four Gospels*. Mahwah, NJ: Paulist.
Mappes, David A. 2010. "What Is the Meaning of 'Faith' in Luke 18:8?" *BSac* 167: 292–306.
Marshall, I. Howard. 1978. *The Gospel of Luke: A Commentary on the Greek Text*. NIGTC 3. Grand Rapids: Eerdmans.
Martin, Thomas W. 2006. "What Makes Glory Glorious?: Reading Luke's Account of the Transfiguration over against Triumphalism." *JSNT* 29:3–26.
Martínez, Florentino García. 1996. *The Dead Sea Scrolls Translated: The Qumran Texts in English*. 2nd ed. Translated by Wilfred G. E. Watson. Leiden: Brill and Grand Rapids: Eerdmans.
Mason, Steve. 2000. "Pharisees." In *Dictionary of New Testament Background*, edited by Craig A. Evans and Stanley E. Porter, 782–87. Downers Grove, IL: InterVarsity.
McCane, Byron R. 1990. "Let the Dead Bury Their Own Dead: Secondary Burial and Matt 8:21–22." *HTR* 83:31–43.
McComiskey, Douglas S. 2008. "Exile and the Purpose of Jesus' Parables (Mark 4:10–12; Matt 13:10–17; Luke 8:9–10)." *JETS* 51:59–85.
Merkle, Benjamin L. 2010. "Who Will Be Left Behind?: Rethinking the Meaning of Matthew 24:40–41 and Luke 17:34–35." *WTJ* 72:169–79.
Miller, David M. 2007. "The Messenger, the Lord, and the Coming Judgment in the Reception History of Malachi 3." *NTS* 53:1–16.

———. 2010. "Seeing the Glory, Hearing the Son: The Function of the Wilderness Theophany Narratives in Luke 9:28-36." *CBQ* 72: 498-517.
Moles, John. 2011. "Luke's Preface: The Greek Decree, Classical Historiography and Christian Redefinitions." *NTS* 57:461-82.
Neale, David A. 1991. *None but the Sinners: Religious Categories in the Gospel of Luke*. JSNTSup 58. Sheffield: JSOT Press.
Nelson, Peter K. 1993. "Luke 22:29-30 and the Time Frame for Dining and Ruling." *TynBul* 44:351-61.
Neyrey, Jerome H. 1991. *The Social World of Luke-Acts: Models for Interpretation*. Peabody, MA: Hendrickson.
Nolland, John. 1989. *Luke 1-9:20*. WBC 35A. Dallas: Word.
———. 1993a. *Luke 9:21—18:34*. WBC 35B. Dallas: Word.
———. 1993b. *Luke 18:35—24:53*. WBC 35C. Dallas: Word.
———. 2013. "Sabbath." In *Dictionary of Jesus and the Gospels*, edited by Joel B. Green, et al, 820-23. 2nd ed. Downers Grove, IL: IVP Academic.
Parsons, Mikeal C. 2001. "'Short in Stature': Luke's Physical Description of Zacchaeus." *NTS* 47: 50-57.
Perkins, Larry. 2004. "Why the 'Finger of God' in Luke 11:20." *ExpTim* 115:261-62.
Phillips, Thomas E. 2008. "'Will the Wise Person Get Drunk?': The Background of the Human Wisdom in Luke 7:35 and Matthew 11:19." *JBL* 127:385-96.
Porter, Stanley E. 2000. "Inscriptions and Papyri: Greco-Roman." In *Dictionary of New Testament Background*, edited by Craig A. Evans and Stanley E. Porter, 529-39. Downers Grove, IL: InterVarsity.
Puig i Tàrrech, Armand. 2012. "The Glory on the Mountain: The Episode of the Transfiguration of Jesus." Translated by John F. Elwolde and Roberto Martinez. *NTS* 58:151-72.
Reid, Barbara E. 2002. "Beyond Petty Pursuits and Wearisome Widows: Three Lukan Parables." *Int* 56:284-94.
Rist, John M. 2005. "Luke 2:2: Making Sense of the Date of Jesus' Birth." *NTS* 56:489-91.
Scott, James W. 2015. "The Misunderstood Mustard Seed: Matt 17:20b; Luke 17:6." *TJ* 36:25-48.
Sellew, Philip. 1992. "Interior Monologues as a Narrative Device in the Parables of Luke." *JBL* 111:239-53.
Skarsaune, Oskar. 2002. *In the Shadow of the Temple: Jewish Influences on Early Christianity*. Downers Grove, IL: InterVarsity.
Skinner, Matthew L. 2010. *The Trial Narratives: Conflict, Power, and Identity in the New Testament*. Louisville: Westminster John Knox.
Snodgrass, Klyne R. 1997. "*Anaideia* and the Friend at Midnight (Luke 11:8)." *JBL* 116:505-13.
———. 2008. *Stories with Intent: A Comprehensive Guide to the Parables of Jesus*. Grand Rapids: Eerdmans.
Soards, Marion L. 1990. "Luke 2:22-40." *Int* 44:400-405.
Sousa, Mathew E. 2013. "The 'Johannine Thunderbolt' in Luke 10:22: Toward an Appreciation of Luke's Narrative Sequence." *Journal of Theological Interpretation* 7:97-113.
Spencer, F. Scott. 2012. *Salty Wives, Spirited Mothers, and Savvy Widows: Capable Women of Purpose and Persistence in Luke's Gospel*. Grand Rapids: Eerdmans.

Strahan, Joshua Marshall. 2016. "Jesus Teaches Theological Interpretation of the Law: Reading the Good Samaritan in Its Literary Context." *Journal of Theological Interpretation* 10:71–86.

Strauss, Mark L. 1995. *The Davidic Messiah in Luke-Acts: The Promise and Its Fulfillment in Lukan Christology*. JSNTSup 110. Sheffield: Sheffield Academic.

Strelan, Rick. 2007. "A Note on ἀσφάλεια (Luke 1:4)." *JSNT* 30:163–71.

Thurston, Bonnie. 2001. "Who Was Anna?: Luke 2:36–38." *PRSt* 28:47–55.

Topel, John. 1998. "The Tarnished Golden Rule (Luke 6:31): The Inescapable Radicalness of Christian Ethics." *TS* 59:475–85.

Twelftree, Graham H. 1993. *Jesus the Exorcist: A Contribution to the Study of the Historical Jesus*. WUNT 2. Reihe 54. Tübingen: Mohr Siebeck.

———. 2013. "Sanhedrin." In *Dictionary of Jesus and the Gospels*, edited by Joel B. Green, et al, 836–40. 2nd ed. Downers Grove, IL: IVP Academic.

Udoh, Fabian E. 2009. "The Tale of an Unrighteous Slave (Luke 16:1–18[13])." *JBL* 128:311–35.

Verbrugge, Verlyn D. 2008. "The Heavenly Army on the Fields of Bethlehem (Luke 2:13–14)." *CTJ* 43:301–11.

Waetjen, Herman C. 2001. "The Subversion of 'World' by the Parable of the Friend of Midnight." *JBL* 120:703–21.

Walker, Peter. 2006. *In the Steps of Jesus: An Illustrated Guide to the Places of the Holy Land*. Grand Rapids: Zondervan.

Webb, Robert L. 1991. "The Activity of John the Baptist's Expected Figure at the Threshing Floor (Matthew 3:12 = Luke 3:17)." *JSNT* 43: 103–11.

Williamson, H.G.M., and Magnar Kartveit. 2013. "Samaritans." In *Dictionary of Jesus and the Gospels*, edited by Joel B. Green, et al., 832–36. 2nd ed. Downers Grove, IL: IVP Academic.

Witherington III, Ben. 1979. "On the Road with Mary Magdalene, Joanna, Susanna, and Other Disciples: Luke 8:1–3." *ZNW* 70:243–48.

SCRIPTURE INDEX

OLD TESTAMENT

Genesis

1:28	15
2:2–3	81
2:8	300
3:1–19	57
4:1–12	174
4:25	26n28
5:1–32	55n27
5:24	312n13
6:5—8:22	237
8:17	15
10:1–32	145
11:10–26	55n27
12:1–3	145
12:1–2	19
12:2–3	28
12:18	44n27
13:10	300
15:6	15n9
15:8	16
17:1	16
17:9–14	26
17:12	38
17:16	16
17:17	16
17:19	16
18:1–8	230
18:11–13	16
18:20	146
19:1–29	146
19:1–26	237
19:26–37	26n28
19:26	237
20:18	15n10
21:2	16
21:4	26
21:5	16
21:17	17n14
22:1–19	57
22:2	54, 263n7
22:9–13	54
22:16–18	28
23:3	141
25:25–26	26
26:12	110n5
29:25	44n27
29:31—30:23	16n11
29:32–35	26n28
32:30–31	41
33:4	217n12
38:4–5	26n28
41:46	55
43:34	157
50:5	141

Exodus

2:24–25	28
3:6	267
3:15–16	267
4:1–9	169
4:22–23	58, 220n16
4:22	21n19, 34, 160n2
6:6	24, 74
7:16	27
8:19	168
9:3	168n20
9:15	168n20
12:1–20	275n1
12:11	186
12:21–27	275
12:33–34	275
13:2	34, 38
3:12	34

Exodus (continued)

3:21-22	132
3:21	29
14:11	44n27
15:1-21	24n24
16	127
16:3	58
16:4	57, 162
16:9-21	161
17:1-7	60
17:2	57
19:2	132
20:1-17	245
20:2-3	59
20:8-11	81
20:12	141, 209, 216
20:20	57, 162
22:1	252n8
22:22	239n1
23:14-17	42
23:20	100
24:1	131
24:8	279
24:9	131
25:17-22	244
26:33	301n17
29:38-42	16n12
30:1-6	16
30:7-8	16n12
31:12-17	81
32:1-8	59n1
33:9-11	133
33:19	90
34:6	90
34:19-20	34
34:29-30	131
34:5-7	132
38:18	301-17
40:35	21
40:36-38	132

Leviticus

5:11	38
6:1-5	252
10:1-2	191n5
10:9	17
11:7	116, 216
11:13-15	182
12:1-8	38
12:2	38
12:3	26, 38
13:1—14:57	74
13:1-59	233
13:45-46	74
14-15	49
14:1-32	233
15:25-27	118
16:1-34	301
16:29-34	243
19:2	72
19:9	82
19:18	151
19:33-34	151
20:21	15n10
21:1-15	153
21:1-3	173
21:14	15
22:1-9	153
23:4-8	275n1
23:5-6	42n22
23:22	230n19
23:27-32	243
24:14-16	76
25:10-17	62
27:30-33	172n32, 243

Numbers

3-4	152
4:3	55
4:23	55
5:2-3	74, 233
6:1-8	17
6:24-26	18
9:18	132
9:22	132
12:1-15	74n6
14:11	169n24
15:38-40	119n20
16:1-35	191n5
18:15-16	38
18:21-32	172n32
19:11-22	173
19:11-16	96

Scripture Index 323

19:11–13	153	21:22–23	304
21:4–6	191n5	22:12	119n20
23:11	44n27	23:25	82
24:17	29	24:1–4	227
27:8–11	216	24:1	227
28:16–17	275n1	24:14	246n19
33:38	132	24:17	239n1
35:30	146	25:5–10	266
		26:12–13	96n11
		28:4	23
		28:15	76n9

Deuteronomy

1:16–17	240	28:27–28	76n9
1:35	169	32:5	169
4:34	24	32:6	220n16
5:6–21	245	32:11	199n24
5:12–15	81	32:15	220n16
5:13–14	194	32:18	220n16
5:16	141, 209, 216	32:35	273n10
6:4–9	61	33:8	162
6:4–5	59		
6:5	151		
6:13–14	59	## Judges	
6:13	59	2:11–13	59n1
6:16	60	2:13	167
8:2	58, 162, 226n13	5:1–31	24n24
8:3	59	6:23	17n14
10:17–18	25n25	11:12	66, 115n13
10:17	20	13:2–24	16n11
10:18	239n2	13:24–25	29
13:1–11	64	15:11	44n27
13:1–10	261	16:28	300
13:1–5	199, 292	19:20	310
14:1–2	220n16	20:26	243n14
14:8	116, 216		
14:22–29	172n32	## Ruth	
14:22–27	243		
16:1–8	275n1	1:1–17	239
16:1–4	42n22	2:2–3	82
16:16	42n22	2:12	199n24
16:18–20	240	3:9—4:12	266n14
18:8	157		
18:15	168n19	## 1 Samuel	
18:18–19	51n16		
18:18	133, 168n19	1:1–20	16n11
19:15	99, 146, 294, 307	1:3	42n23
21:1–17	179	1:7	42n23
21:15–17	34, 210	1:21	42n23
21:17	216	1:24–28	39

1 Samuel *(continued)*

1:26	243
2:1–10	24
2:8	229n16
2:19	42n23
2:26	29
3:19	29
9:2	251n6
14:45	272n9
16:1–13	33
16:7	226n13
16:19	35
17:12	33
17:15	35
17:58	33
21	82n2
21:1–6	82
22:20	82n2
25:6	310
31:13	243n14

2 Samuel

1:12	79n14
5:4	55
5:7	33n8
7:12–16	267, 311
7:14	21, 54, 133, 291
12:6	252n8
14:11	272n9
16:10	66
22:3	27
22:5	188

1 Kings

1:52	272n9
2:11	312n13
4:25	191n6
8:22	243
8:39	226n13
10:1–9	170
10:4–5	183
10:21–23	183
13:1–6	83
16:13–21	167
17–18	41
17:8–24	64, 92, 97
17:23	97
18:46	186n16
19:10	174n36
19:19–21	142
22:19–28	263n6

2 Kings

1:1–16	140
2:10–11	139n31
4:18–37	97
4:29	186n16
4:42–44	126
5:1–14	64, 92, 94
5:6	95
5:20–27	74n6
9:1	186n16
9:13	256
15:5	74n6
17:24–41	139
18:31	191n6
21:1–3	167

1 Chronicles

1:1–42	55n27
16:7–36	24n24
16:34	245n18
24:6–19	15n8

2 Chronicles

5:2	33n8
5:13	245n18
6:7–10	263n6
9:1–8	170
24:20–22	174, 199
24:20–21	174n39
28:1–4	59n1
35:21	115n13

Ezra

3:11	245n18
8:21	79n14, 243n14
9:6	244
10:5	154

Nehemiah

9:21	58
9:26	174n36, 263n6
10:35–36	38
11:3	154
11:20	154
12:1–7	15n8

Esther

4:16	79n14, 243n14

Job

1–2	283
2:8	147n6
4:7–9	191
20:16	49n6
20:19–20	180n8
33:4	22
38:41	182

Psalms

1:1–3	50n9
2:7–8	21
2:7	54, 59, 133, 291, 311
2:8	59
3:5	113
4:8	113
6:8	197
10:17–18	87
11:1	6n8
11:4	44
14:1	181
16:5	157
17:8	199n24
17:15	15n9
18:2	27
22	128n12
22:7–8	299, 311
22:18	298, 311
23	183n15
23:1–4	214
23:1	35
27:1	29, 112
30:6 (LXX)	302
31	128n12
31:5	302, 311
33:1	256
35:16	197n19
36:7	199n24
37:2	183
37:12	197n19
40:17	229n16
41:9	279
41:13	27
51:5	49
63:7	199n24
65:7	114n10
68:5–6	87
68:5	239n2
69	128n12
69:1–2	188
69:21	299, 311
72:18	27
74:13	114n10
77:15	24
77:16	114n10
77:20	214
78:8	169
78:19–20	127
78:70–71	35
80:1	35
80:8–16	262n5
82:5	171n28
89:9	114n10
89:19–20	133
89:20–37	267
89:26–29	21
91:4	199n24
91:11–12	59
95:2	6n8
95:3	160, 195n13
95:8–10	57
103:15–16	183
104:30	22
105:8–9	28
106:1	245n18
106:4	300
106:23	133
107:17	76n9
107:28–29	113
110	268
110:1	268, 291
112:10	197n19

Scripture Index   325

Psalms (continued)

113–118	277
113:7	229n16
118:22	263
118:26	98, 199, 257, 312
119:57	157
130:7–8	28
132:17–18	27
135:3	245n18
137:5	83
140:12	229n16
145:1	195n13
146:9	239n2
147:9	182

Proverbs

1:19	180n8
2:12–15	171n28
3:34	25n25
8:1—9:6	102
14:21	246n19
15:25	239n2
15:27	180n8
19:17	246n19
20:8	52n22
20:26	52n22
21:2	226n13
21:31	256
24:5	211
25:6–7	205

Ecclesiastes

2:24	181
3:13	181
11:5	22

Isaiah

1:1	14n5
1:16–17	49
1:17	96n11, 230n19
1:25	52n19
2:11–12	25n25
4:3	148n8
4:4	52n20
5:1–7	262n5
6:5	69
6:9–10	110, 258
8:14–15	40
9:2–7	267
9:2	29, 112
9:6–7	21n20, 29, 188
10:1–3	239n1
10:33–34	50n10
11:1–10	21n20
11:1–9	267
11:1–4	43
11:1	29
11:10	29
11:11–16	197
13:6	236n15
13:9–11	273
14:13–15	147
14:29	49n6
17:12	273
22:13	181
23:1–18	147
25:6–9	197
25:6	207n9
27:2–5	262n5
27:12	145
29:3	258
29:5–6	52
29:18	99
29:23	160
31:6	28, 49n5
32:15	52n18
32:17	15n9
34:8	273n10
35:5	99
35:6	99
35:10	87
40:3	28, 48
40:4–5	48
40:9	36
40:11	214
41:16	52n22
41:17	229n16
42:1–4	133
42:1	54, 55, 133
42:6–7	40
42:7	29
42:18	99
43:1—44:8	247n22

Scripture Index 327

43:5–6	197	3:14	49, 220n16
43:5	168n22	3:19	220n16
43:6–7	220n16	4:22	181
43:8	99	5:12–13	88
43:15	195n13	6:6	258
44:1–5	133	7:5–7	96n11
44:3	52n18	7:11	259
44:6	160	7:25–26	311
46:13	40	7:31–32	177
49:2	6n8	9:1	258
49:6	40	9:13–14	59n1
49:7	133	11:20	226n13
49:10	87	13:17	258
51:1—52:10	237n22	14:17	258
51:3	300	15:7	52n22
51:5–8	39	15:15	300
51:17	286n9	15:19	49n5
52–53	128, 133	16:4	229
52:7	6n8, 36	17:7–8	50n9
52:9	39	17:10	226n13
52:10	39	18:11	28
52:13	284	22:3	230n19, 239n1
56:1	39	22:5–6	199
56:7	259	23:2	35
58:5	147n6	23:5	21n20, 29, 268
58:6	61	23:11–12	171n28
58:7	50n11, 246n19	23:16–18	88
59:5	49n6	25:4	311
59:8	29	25:15–17	286n9
60:1	29	26:20–24	174n36
60:20	87	26:20–23	199
61:1–2	36, 61, 311	31:8–9	220n16
61:1	62	31:8	168n22
61:2	61, 273n10	31:9	34
62:1–12	247n22	31:10	183n15
63:15–16	220n16	31:12	87
63:16	21n19, 160n2	31:13	87
64:8–9	220n16	31:20	21n19, 160n2, 220n16
64:8	21n19, 160n2	31:31–34	279
66:13	39	33:14–18	268
66:15–16	188	33:15	21n20
		36:9	243n14
		38:1–6	199, 263n6
Jeremiah		50:6	214
1:1–3	47n1	51:2	52n22
1:2	14n5	51:6	273n10
2:21	262n5	52:4–5	258
2:30	174n36, 263n6, 311		

Lamentations

2:16	197n19
4:21–22	286n9

Ezekiel

1:1–3	47n1
1:1	54n26
4:1–3	258
14:6	49n5
16:49–50	146
17:22–24	196
18:7	50n11
18:30	49n5
19:10–14	262n5
21:22	258
22:7	239n1
23:31–33	286n9
26:15–21	147
28:1–24	147
29:5	229
30:3	236n15
31:5–6	195
31:10–12	50n10
32:7–8	273
34	183n15
34:1–10	214
34:8	35
34:11–16	214
34:12–16	35
34:13	168n22
34:16	87
34:23–31	268
34:23–24	21n20, 214
34:23	35
34:29	87
34:30–31	214
36:16–32	160
36:17	118
36:22—37:28	247n22
36:23	160
36:25	49
36:27	52n18
36:33	49
37:14	52n18
37:24–25	21n20
37:24	35
38:18–23	272n7
38:22	188
39:17–20	197
44:25–27	96, 153

Daniel

4:10–12	195
4:14	50n10
4:20–27	195
7	128
7:10	148n8
7:13–14	127, 130
7:13	98
8:10	273
8:13	273
12:1	148n8
12:2	120n22

Hosea

2:12	192
10:1	262n5
10:8	297
11:1–4	160n2
11:1–2	59n1
11:1	58

Joel

1:14	79n14
1:15	236n15
2:1	236n15
2:10	273, 301n16
2:28–29	52n18
2:30–32	272n7
2:20–31	273, 301
3:5	6n8
3:12–13	145
3:15	301n16

Amos

1:1	14n5
1:4	188
1:7	188
1:10	188
1:14	188
2:10	58
4:9	192

Scripture Index 329

5:18	236n15	2:3	236n15
5:20	236n15	3:8	29
8:9	301n16	3:10	191n6
9:11	21n20	6:12–13	21n20
		6:12	29
		7:10	96n11, 239n1

Obadiah

		8:6–9	199
1:15	236n15	9:9–10	21n20, 188
		9:9	98, 256, 312

Jonah

		9:10	256
		10:2	214
1:17	170n25	10:3	183n15
3:3–10	170	11:17	83
3:5	79n14	12:3	273
3:6	147n6	13:9	52n19
		14:1–4	312

Micah

		14:4–5	272n7
		14:4	256
1:1	47n1	14:9	160, 195n13
4:4	191n6	14:16–17	195n13
4:11–12	145		
5:2	10, 21n20, 33		
6:8	173, 230		

Malachi

7:14	35	1:2–3	210
		1:14	195n13

Nahum

		3:1–3	51n16
		3:1–2	124n4
2:1	186n16	3:1	17, 28, 100
2:7	244	3:2–3	49n8, 52n19
		3:5	239n1

Habakkuk

		4:2	28
		4:5–6	17, 28, 51n16, 100, 124n4
2:20	44	4:5	236n15

Zephaniah

New Testament

1:14–15	49n8		
1:15	301n16		
2:1–2	49n8		

Matthew

		1:1–17	55
		1:6	33, 56

Haggai

		1:16	56
1:1	47n1	1:18	20n18
		3:3	48

Zechariah

		3:13–15	53n25
		4:13	65
1:1	47n1, 174n39	4:23	6n9
1:14	236n15	5:1—7:29	86
2:1	236n15	5:17	226

Matthew (continued)

5:39	89
6:9–13	159
6:13	162
7:24–27	91
8:28	114
9:9	86
10:1–4	85
10:3	86
10:4	86n11
12:40	170n25
13:57	63
14:3–12	124
15:22–28	233
16:15–17	127
16:18	85n8
23:35	174n39
26:1–13	102n18
26:14	85n7
26:20	85n7
26:26–29	278
26:59–63	291n17
27:3	86n11

Mark

1:3	48
1:6	17, 101
1:14—3:19	6n11
1:14	6n9
1:16–20	65, 68
1:21–39	65
1:35	67
2:1	65, 75n7
2:14	86
2:26	82n2
3:13–19	85
3:14	85
3:19	86n11
4:10	85n7
5:1	114
5:13	116
6:2–3	63
6:4	63
6:17–29	53, 124
10:45	281
10:46	248n23
11:10	23n22

11:27—13:32	6n11
12:14	264
14:3–9	102n18
14:17	85n7
14:22–25	278
14:36	150
14:55–61	291n17
15:22	298n11
15:37–38	301
16:5	131

Luke

1–2	313
1:1	7, 12
1:2	3, 13
1:3	1, 4, 13, 14
1:4	7, 13
1:5	14, 30
1:6	15, 36n12, 302n19
1:7	15
1:9	36n12
1:10	243
1:11	36n12
1:12–13	35
1:12	17
1:13–14	30
1:13	17, 22, 25, 26, 69
1:14–17	17
1:14	20, 25
1:15–16	36n12
1:15	17, 20, 23, 101, 166
1:16–17	17, 100, 124n4
1:16	28
1:17	28, 36n12, 37, 140
1:18	15, 18, 21, 22
1:19	18, 22
1:20	18, 22, 27, 76n9
1:21–22	18
1:23	18
1:24	18, 23
1:25	18, 36n12, 37
1:26	22
1:27	19, 33
1:28	20, 36n12
1:29–30	35
1:30	17n14, 20, 22, 69
1:31–35	133, 149

Scripture Index 331

1:31–33	20	1:69–71	27, 36
1:32–35	54	1:69	36, 36n12
1:32–33	36, 51	1:72–73	28
1:32	20, 33, 36n12, 248	1:72	300
1:34	19, 21, 22	1:74–75	27
1:35–37	20	1:76	28, 36n12, 140
1:35	20, 21, 22, 39, 60, 66, 166	1:77	28, 37
1:36–37	22	1:78–79	28, 35, 112
1:36	19, 22, 37	1:78	28, 29n30, 96
1:37	22	1:79	28, 29, 36, 146, 310n10
1:38	22, 36n12, 41	1:80	29, 48
1:39–45	10	2:1–21	52
1:39–40	23	2:1–7	10
1:39	37	2:1–5	31
1:41	23, 166	2:1–2	33
1:42	23, 23n22, 169	2:1	30, 33
1:43	23, 36n12	2:2	32
1:44	20, 23, 26	2:4	19, 33, 41
1:45–46	36n12	2:5–6	33
1:45	21, 23, 23n22	2:6	34
1:46–49	24	2:7	34, 304
1:47	20, 36n12	2:8	35
1:48	20, 24, 35, 37	2:9	30, 35
1:49	24	2:10–11	51
1:50–55	24	2:10	17n14, 20, 23, 26, 35, 36, 40, 69, 79
1:50–53	100		
1:51–54	24	2:11	9, 31, 33, 36, 36n12, 62, 300
1:51–53	61, 87	2:12	34, 36, 37, 304
1:51–52	25, 36	2:13	36
1:51	24, 168n21	2:14	36, 37, 76, 146, 188, 257, 258, 310n10
1:52–53	228n15, 229		
1:52	35	2:15	37
1:53	126	2:16	34, 37
1:54–55	24	2:17	37
1:56	25	2:19–20	37
1:57–58	25	2:19	40
1:57	25	2:20	234n10
1:58	20, 23, 26, 36n12	2:21	38
1:59	26, 38	2:22–24	38
1:60	26	2:22–23	61
1:61	26	2:22	41
1:63	26	2:23	34, 39, 41
1:64	27	2:24	41
1:65	27, 30	22:25–28	39
1:66	27, 168n20	22:25–27	39, 166
1:67–79	30	2:25	15, 18, 39, 302n19
1:67	27, 166	2:26	29, 29n17
1:68	27, 36n12, 97, 258	2:27	39, 41

Luke (continued)

2:28–29	39
2:29	39
2:30–32	36, 145, 311
2:30	39
2:31–32	48
2:31	40
2:32	8, 40, 133
2:33	40
2:34–35	45, 60, 188, 237
2:34	40, 52, 263
2:35	40, 170
2:36–37	41
2:36	39
2:37–38	18
2:37	39
2:38	39, 41
2:39	41, 61
2:40	42, 43
2:41–42	42
2:41	61
2:43–50	210
2:43–46	43
2:44	43
2:46–47	260
2:46	43
2:48	44
2:49	44, 58, 150, 302
2:50–51	40
2:50	45
2:51–52	244
2:51	45
2:52	42, 45, 63, 251
3:1–2	47
3:2	48
3:3	28, 48, 76, 261, 311
3:4–6	8
3:4	28, 48, 140
3:5–6	48
3:6	36, 40, 145, 311
3:7–9	52, 62, 98
3:7	49
3:8–9	192
3:8	49, 50, 112, 170, 230, 252
3:9	50, 52
3:10	50
3:11	50, 230
3:12–13	51, 100
3:12	50, 250
3:14	50, 51
3:15–17	98
3:15–16	257, 261
3:15	51
3:16–17	51, 188, 237
3:16	51, 94, 98, 166
3:17	40, 52
3:19–20	53, 98, 124, 198, 293
3:19	47
3:21—4:3	57
3:21–22	58, 131
3:21	53, 127, 159n1
3:22	54, 59, 62, 133, 149, 166, 263
3:23	20, 33, 55, 56, 60, 63
3:31	33, 56, 248
3:34	56
3:38	56
4:1–13	111, 162
4:1	54, 58, 60, 62, 149, 166
4:2	58
4:3	58
4:4	58
4:5	59
4:6–7	59
4:8	59
4:9	58, 59
4:12	60
4:13	60, 275
4:14—6:16	6n11
4:14–15	10, 60, 67
4:14	54, 60, 62, 149, 166
4:16–20	61
4:16	61
4:18–19	9, 61, 75, 87
4:18	54, 61, 65, 77, 149, 166
4:20–21	62
4:21	9, 62, 77, 99, 300
4:22	20, 56, 62, 63
4:23	63, 65, 69, 92, 147
4:24–27	92, 124
4:24–26	18n15, 131
4:24	63
4:25–27	63
4:25–26	124n4
4:26	97
4:27	95

Scripture Index 333

4:28–29	69, 99	5:12	73, 74, 75
4:28	62, 64	5:13	74, 99, 119, 284
4:29	64	5:14	74, 107
4:30	64, 64n7, 115	5:15	74
4:31–44	147	5:16	75, 159n1
4:31–39	65	5:17–26	9n13, 62
4:31–37	65	5:17	72, 75
4:31–36	203	5:19	75
4:31	65, 92	5:20–25	285
4:32	65	5:20	75, 194
4:33–37	60n2	5:21–22	180n9
4:33–36	114	5:21	72, 76, 98, 99, 107, 150, 171, 226n12, 283
4:33–35	9n13		
4:33–34	275	5:22	76
4:33	65	5:23	76, 78
4:34	65, 66n10, 115, 115n13, 248	5:24–26	84
4:35	54n10, 66, 113, 135n26, 148n10	5:24	76, 97, 98, 128n9
		5:25–26	234n10
4:36–37	66	5:25	99
4:37	66, 74	5:26	62, 77, 135, 300
4:38–39	69	5:27–32	242, 285
4:38	66, 284	5:27–30	50n13
4:39	66, 113	5:27–29	250n1
4:40–41	65, 66	5:27–28	210
4:40	74	5:27	77, 86
4:41	66, 113, 115, 135n26, 148n10, 275	5:28	77, 110, 246, 283
		5:29–35	101
4:42–44	65	5:29–32	9n13, 25, 309n7
4:42–43	67, 69	5:29–31	93
4:42	67, 75	5:29–30	207
4:43–44	10	5:30	78, 99, 150, 226n12, 283
4:43	45n30, 65n7, 195	5:31–32	9, 78, 100
4:44	67	5:32	215
5:1–11	65, 71, 85	5:33	79, 226n12
5:1	68	5:34	79
5:2	68	5:35	79
5:3–10	284	5:36–38	100
5:3–4	68	5:36	79
5:4	69	5:37	80
5:5	68, 69	5:38	80
5:6–7	69	5:39	80, 100, 102
5:7	68	5:44	136
5:8–10	114	6:1–2	84
5:8	23n23, 69, 74	6:1	82
5:9–11	210	6:2	99, 171
5:10	68, 69	6:3–4	82
5:11	70, 77, 110, 246, 283	6:4	84
5:12–14	233	6:5	82, 128n9

Luke (continued)

Reference	Pages
6:6–11	203
6:6	83
6:7	72, 83, 99, 150, 171, 201, 226n12
6:8	83, 193
6:9	83, 202
6:10	84
6:11	84, 99
6:12–16	85, 123
6:12	53, 85, 127, 159n1
6:13	84, 137, 232, 247n21, 287
6:14	69n2, 85, 284
6:16	86n11, 275, 287
6:17–49	71
6:17	67n14, 87
6:18–19	87
6:18	148n10
6:19	119
6:20–26	62
6:20–25	25
6:20–21	87, 228n15, 229
6:20	99, 195, 229n17
6:21	96, 126
6:22–26	100
6:22–23	88
6:24–26	88
6:24–25	228n15
6:27–36	87, 284
6:27–35	155
6:27–28	298
6:27	88
6:29	89
6:30–36	280
6:30	89
6:31	89
6:32–36	206
6:32–34	89
6:35	90, 209
6:36	90, 161, 232
6:38	90
6:39	90
6:40	90
6:41–42	90
6:43–45	91, 112
6:43–44	50n9
6:46–49	156, 169
6:46	91
6:47–48	91
6:49	91, 111
7:1–17	118
7:1–10	97, 147
7:1	65
7:2	93, 240n4
7:3–5	118
7:4	93
7:5	92, 93
7:6–8	93
7:6	23n23, 94
7:7–8	94
7:9	94, 107, 108
7:10	94
7:11–17	18n15, 114, 124n4
7:11–15	9n13
7:11	85, 95
7:12	95, 118
7:13	28, 96, 155, 218
7:14–15	131, 284, 306
7:14	96, 119, 121, 194
7:15	97, 99, 135
7:16	97, 124, 135, 258, 308
7:17	67n14, 98
7:18–22	257
7:18	98
7:19	98
7:20	98
7:21–22	62
7:21	99
7:22	9, 99
7:23	99
7:24–35	125, 261, 262
7:24–30	199
7:24–28	17
7:24–27	124n4
7:24–26	99
7:25	268
7:26–29	261
7:26–27	100
7:27	28
7:28	100
7:29	50n13, 100, 102, 250n1
7:29–30	242
7:30–33	261
7:30	72, 100, 101
7:31–32	101
7:31	101, 169

Scripture Index   335

7:33	101	8:17	112, 170
7:34	50n13, 78, 101, 242, 250n1	8:18	112, 212
7:35	101	8:19–21	188n20
7:36–50	9n13, 62, 102n18, 109, 309n7	8:19–20	112, 210
7:36	102, 207	8:21	91, 112, 119, 142n40, 143, 156, 167, 169, 212
7:37–39	201n1	8:22–56	108
7:37	103, 103n21	8:22	84, 113, 114
7:38	104	8:23	113
7:39–40	136	8:24	113
7:39	103, 105, 180n9, 226n12	8:25	113, 114
7:40	103, 105, 245n17, 249, 264n8	8:26–33	285
		8:26	114
7:41–43	9, 161	8:27–29	115
7:41	105	8:28–30	60n2
7:42	105	8:28–29	115
7:43	105	8:28	115
7:44–46	105	8:31–32	116
7:47–48	106	8:32–33	116, 148n10
7:47	106	8:32	169
7:48	106, 194	8:34–35	116
7:49	107	8:35	116
7:50	107, 108, 119, 119n21, 234, 310n10	8:36	116
		8:37	116
8	85	8:39	117, 169
8:1–3	169	8:40–42	117
8:1	85, 85n7, 108, 195, 247n21	8:40–41	134
8:2–3	108, 303, 305	8:40	118
8:2	148n10	8:41–56	123n1
8:3	124	8:41–42	118
8:4–21	108	8:41	251
8:4	109	8:43–48	117
8:5–15	197	8:43	118
8:5–8	145	8:44	119
8:5	109	8:45	119
8:6	109	8:46–48	193
8:7	109	8:47	119
8:8	110, 110n5, 135, 211	8:48	107, 119, 119n21, 120, 234, 249, 310n10
8:9–10	110, 136	8:49–55	117
8:9	84, 136, 188	8:49	105n27, 120, 245n17, 264n8
8:10	110, 110n7, 195, 258	8:50	120
8:11	111	8:51	85, 120, 131, 276
8:12	111	8:52–53	120
8:13–14	197	8:53	283
8:13	111	8:54–55	306
8:14	111, 143, 225, 228	8:54	121
8:15	111	8:55	99, 121
8:16	112, 170		

Scripture Index

Luke (continued)

Reference	Pages
8:56	121
9:1–6	10, 85, 123, 125, 145, 182, 311
9:1–3	284
9:1–2	123
9:1	85, 135, 247n21
9:2	195
9:3–5	141
9:3	123, 146, 161
9:4	124
9:5	124, 140, 146, 162
9:6	124, 135
9:7–9	123, 198, 293
9:7–8	124, 127, 131
9:7	306
9:8	127, 308
9:9	125, 127, 209, 293
9:10–11	125
9:10	84, 85, 123, 124, 125, 147, 232, 247n21
9:11	195
9:12–17	182
9:12	85, 125, 134n23, 247n21
9:13–14	125
9:13	125
9:14–15	126
9:14	84
9:16–17	161
9:16	126, 126n5, 278, 309
9:17	126
9:18	127, 131, 159n1
9:19	127, 308
9:20	127, 131, 133, 247, 299, 308
9:21	127, 134
9:22–26	273
9:22–24	312
9:22	45n30, 127, 128, 135, 136, 139, 174n37, 247, 260, 278, 291n15, 302, 306
9:23–24	209
9:23	129, 144, 296
9:24	129
9:25	130
9:26	128n9, 130, 132, 187, 255, 273, 289, 291n16
9:27	130, 195
9:28–36	127
9:28–29	159n1
9:28	53, 85, 131, 150, 276
9:29	131, 306
9:30	132
9:31	132, 138, 139
9:32	132
9:33	132, 134n23
9:34	132
9:35	131, 133, 149, 263, 299
9:36	134
9:37–38	134
9:38–43	193
9:38–42	60n2
9:38	105n27, 118, 245n17, 264n8
9:39–40	135
9:40	84, 137
9:41	135, 169, 237
9:42	135, 148n10
9:43	135
9:44	127, 128n9, 135, 247, 260, 276, 287, 291n15, 306, 312
9:45	136, 247, 248, 258, 307
9:46–48	245
9:46–47	180n9
9:46	136, 246, 281, 308
9:47	136, 137
9:48	137, 147, 188, 280
9:49–50	147
9:49	137, 148n10, 167, 281, 308
9:50	137, 168
9:51—19:28	253
9:51—19:27	138
9:51	64n7, 123, 138, 139, 140, 255, 312
9:52–56	139, 139n31
9:52–55	18n15
9:52	140
9:53	140
9:54	23n23, 131, 140, 308
9:55–56	140
9:57–62	188n20, 197, 283
9:57	64n7, 141
9:58	141, 291n15
9:59–62	210
9:59	141
9:60	141, 142, 144, 195
9:61	142
9:62	143

10:1–12	10, 311	10:39	157, 159, 212
10:1–9	182	10:40	23n23, 157, 179
10:1	145	10:41–42	157
10:2	138, 145	10:41	157, 283
10:3	146	10:42	212
10:4–7	141	11:1	23n23, 84, 159, 159n1
10:4	146, 284	11:2–13	182
10:5–9	146	11:2	130, 150, 159, 160, 165, 195, 302n18
10:5	310n10		
10:7	161	11:3	59, 161
10:9	130, 146n3, 161, 195	11:4	90, 161, 162, 232, 286, 298
10:10–16	162	11:5	164
10:10–11	140, 146	11:7	166
10:10	254	11:8	163, 164
10:11	146, 195	11:9–10	164, 165
10:12	146	11:11–12	166
10:13–15	147	11:13	52, 166, 178, 311
10:13–14	125, 147	11:14–23	60n2
10:15	147	11:14–15	167
10:16	147, 188	11:14	148
10:17–19	60n2	11:15–16	178
10:17–18	168, 202	11:15	148, 283
10:17	23n23, 146n3, 147	11:16	167, 169, 171, 294
10:18	36, 148, 275	11:17–18	167
10:19	148	11:19	167
10:20	148	11:20	130, 161, 168, 195, 235
10:21–22	149, 159, 302n18	11:21–22	168
10:21	149, 150, 159n1, 248, 258	11:23	168
10:22	149, 150	11:24–26	116, 169
10:23–24	188	11:27	169
10:23	150	11:28	167, 169
10:25–37	9, 139	11:29–32	167
10:25	105n27, 151, 156, 245n17, 245, 264n8	11:29–30	294
		11:29	169, 170, 171, 176, 237
10:26–38	245	11:30	170
10:26	151	11:31	170, 172
10:28	151, 156	11:32	170
10:29–37	245	11:33	170
10:29	151, 155	11:34	170
10:31–32	154	11:35–36	171
10:31	152	11:37—12:1	198
10:32	153	11:37–52	193, 215
10:33–37	154	11:37–44	202, 226, 244
10:33	28, 96n12, 154, 218, 240n4	11:37–38	226n12
10:34–35	34, 155	11:37	102, 171
10:36	155	11:38	172
10:37	155, 156	11:39–54	176
10:38	64n7, 156, 207	11:39	172, 173

Luke (continued)

11:40	172
11:41	181
11:42	9, 172, 173, 243
11:43	173, 269
11:44	174
11:45	105n27, 173, 245n17, 264n8
11:46	173
11:47–51	263, 308
11:47–50	63
11:47–48	174
11:49–51	174
11:49	199
11:52	174
11:53–54	175, 201
12:1–34	186
12:1–2	196
12:1	176, 193
12:2	176
12:3	177, 261
12:4–12	238, 253
12:4–7	273
12:4	177, 182
12:5	177
12:6–7	179
12:6	177
12:7	177, 182, 233
12:8–9	177, 289
12:8	128n9, 291n16
12:10	178
12:11–12	178, 182, 272
12:12	272
12:13	105n27, 179, 183, 245n17, 264n8
12:14	179
12:15–21	88
12:15	179, 180
12:16–21	222
12:16–17	272
12:16	180
12:17–18	180
12:18–19	184
12:18	180
12:19	181
12:20	181
12:21	181, 206
12:22–31	111
12:22–24	59
12:22–23	182
12:22	161
12:24	177, 182, 233
12:25–26	183
12:25	45n31, 251
12:27	183
12:28	183
12:29–30	183
12:31	183
12:32	183
12:33–34	224, 246
12:33	172, 181, 184, 206, 230
12:34	184
12:35–48	253
12:35–36	186
12:35	186
12:37	186, 186n16
12:38	186
12:39–40	187
12:40	187n18, 291n16
12:41	23n23, 187
12:42–46	187
12:45	180n9
12:46	187
12:47–48	187
12:47	189
12:48	187
12:49–53	52
12:49–50	188
12:51–53	237
12:51–52	188
12:54	189
12:55	189
12:56	189
12:57–59	190
12:57	189
12:58–59	189
13:1–5	215
13:1	190, 191, 293
13:2	191
13:3	191
13:4	190, 191
13:5	191
13:6–9	190
13:6–7	192
13:6	191
13:8	192
13:9	192

Scripture Index 339

13:10–17	203	14:11	205, 244, 281
13:10	201	14:12–14	204, 280
13:11–16	60n2	14:12	206
13:11	193, 201	14:13	206, 208
13:12	193, 201	14:14	206
13:13	194	14:15–24	204, 212
13:14	194, 201	14:15	207
13:15	193, 194, 201	14:16	207, 252
13:16	193, 194, 201	14:17	208
13:17	195	14:18	208
13:18–30	201	14:19	208
13:18–19	195	14:20	208
13:20–21	196	14:21	208
13:21	196	14:22–23	208
13:22–30	196	14:24	208
13:22	255	14:25–33	197
13:23–30	207, 228n15	14:25	209
13:23	23n23, 196	14:26–27	84
13:24	197, 209	14:26	144, 188n20, 209
13:25–30	212	14:27	209, 296
13:25	197	14:28–30	210
13:26	197	14:28	210
13:27	197	14:31–32	211
13:28	197	14:31	210
13:29	130, 197	14:33	209, 224, 246
13:30	198, 281	14:34	211
13:31	125, 198, 293	14:35	135, 211
13:32	47n3, 198	15:1–3	213
13:33–35	271	15:1–2	89, 171, 218, 226n12, 242, 285, 309n7
13:33–34	63, 309		
13:33	45n30, 64n7, 128, 199	15:1	51n13, 250n1
13:34–35	258, 298	15:2	72
13:34	198, 263	15:4	214
13:35	98, 199	15:5–6	214
14:1–24	309n7	15:5	214
14:1–6	192, 203	15:7	215, 218
14:1–3	226n12	15:8	215
14:1	102, 201, 201n1, 204	15:9	215
14:2	201	15:10	215, 218
14:3–4	171	15:11–32	9
14:3	72, 202	15:11	216
14:4	201, 202	15:12	216
14:5	201, 202	15:13	216
14:6	203	15:14–16	216
14:7–24	201	15:17–19	180n9, 217
14:7–11	202, 204, 228n15, 269	15:17	217
14:7	205	15:18	219
14:8–11	205	15:20	28, 96n12, 155, 217, 251

Luke (continued)

15:21–22	218
15:21	217, 219
15:23	218
15:24	218
15:25	218
15:26	218
15:27	218, 219
15:28	218
15:29–30	218
15:30	216, 219
15:31	219
15:32	219
16:1–2	222
16:3–4	180n9, 223
16:4	225
16:6–7	223
16:8	224
16:9	224
16:10	225
16:11	225
16:12	225
16:13	111, 144, 225, 226, 228, 246
16:14–15	202, 215, 225
16:14	226
16:15	226
16:16–17	225, 228n14
16:16	226
16:17	227
16:18	225, 227
16:19–31	9, 62, 88, 181, 222
16:19	228, 268
16:20	228
16:21	228
16:22–23	229
16:22	229
16:24	230, 244
16:25	229, 230
16:26	230
16:27–28	230
16:30	230
16:31	230
17:1–2	231
17:3–4	231
17:5–6	231
17:5	84, 232, 247n21
17:6	232, 240n4
17:7–10	231, 232
17:11–19	9n13, 139
17:11	64n7, 233, 255
17:12–13	233
17:13	244, 248
17:14	99, 107, 234
17:15–17	234
17:16	152n18
17:17–18	234
17:17	234
17:18	234
17:19	234, 249
17:20–21	235
17:20	235
17:21	130, 161, 235
17:22—18:8	239
17:22–37	235, 241, 253
17:22–36	255
17:22–30	273, 291n16
17:22	236, 297
17:23	236, 272
17:24	236, 237, 238
17:25	45n30, 127, 128, 237, 247, 260
17:26–29	237
17:26	236
17:30	128n9, 236, 237
17:31	237
17:32	237
17:33	228n15, 237, 273
17:34–35	237
17:37	237
18:1–8	9, 164, 242, 253
18:1	239, 241
18:2	240
18:3	240
18:4–5	180n9
18:4	240
18:5	240
18:6–8	241
18:6	239
18:7	241
18:8	241, 242, 291n16
18:9–14	9, 25, 228n15, 242
18:9	242
18:10–14	51n13
18:10	242
18:11–12	215
18:11	243

Scripture Index 341

18:12	79, 243	19:10	214, 252
18:13	244, 297	19:11–27	257n17, 292
18:14	22, 244, 281	19:11	253, 255
18:15–17	9n13, 242, 248	19:12	253
18:15	244, 246, 281	19:13	253
18:16	245	19:14	254
18:18–25	222, 225	19:15	254, 255
18:18	151, 245, 251, 264n8	19:16–19	254
18:19	245	19:19–31	226
18:20–21	245	19:20–21	254
18:20	142, 209, 245	19:22–23	254
18:21	246	19:24	254
18:22–25	224	19:25–26	254
18:22–24	252	19:27	123, 255
18:22	144, 245, 246	19:28–48	257n17
18:23	246	19:28–29	255
18:24–25	246	19:28	64n7
18:24	250	19:29–38	312
18:26	246, 250	19:29	230
18:27	246, 250	19:30–31	256
18:28–34	276	19:30	304
18:28–30	143, 188n20, 210	19:31	256
18:28	70, 110, 246, 283	19:32–34	256
18:29–30	111, 247	19:32	277
18:31–33	127, 260, 291n15, 306, 312	19:35–40	292
18:31	85, 85n7, 247, 255	19:35	256
18:32–33	247	19:36	64n7, 256
18:33	247, 302	19:37	257, 294
18:34	247, 248, 258, 307, 308	19:38	98, 199, 257, 310n10, 312
18:35–43	9n13, 233	19:39	105n27, 245n17, 257, 264
18:35–37	248	19:40	257
18:37	248	19:41–44	298
18:38–39	244	19:41	258
18:38	248	19:42–44	258
18:39	248	19:42	258
18:40–41	248	19:43–44	5, 199, 258, 263
18:41	23n23	19:44	97, 258, 271
18:42	99, 107, 234, 249	19:45–46	261, 271
18:43	135, 234n10, 249	19:45	258
19:1–10	51n13, 248n23	19:46	259
19:1–2	250	19:47—21:38	44
19:3	45n31, 251	19:47–48	259, 287
19:4	232n4, 251	19:47	174n37, 260
19:5–6	251	19:48	294
19:5	45n30, 193, 300	20:1—21:33	6n11
19:7	251	20:1–8	291
19:8	252	20:1–2	260
19:9	9, 62, 252, 300	20:1	128

Luke *(continued)*

20:2	178, 261, 265
20:4	261
20:5	261
20:6	261
20:7	261
20:8	261
20:9–19	63, 271, 308
20:9–16	262
20:13	180n9, 263
20:16	263
20:17	263
20:18	263
20:19	264, 287, 294
20:20	175, 264
20:21–25	292
20:21–22	264
20:21	105n27, 245n17, 264
20:22	265
20:23–24	265
20:24	265
20:25	265
20:26	175, 266
20:27	266
20:28	245n17, 264, 266
20:29–33	266
20:34–36	267
20:37–38	267
20:39–40	267
20:39	105n27, 245n17, 264n8, 266
20:41–44	82
20:41	248, 268
20:42–43	268
20:44	268
20:45–47	271
20:45	268
20:46	173, 268
20:47	269
21:1	270
21:2	270
21:3–4	270
21:5–6	199, 263
21:5	271
21:6	258, 271
21:7	264n8, 272
21:8	272
21:9	45n30, 272
21:10–11	272
21:13–15	272
21:18–19	273
21:20–44	5
21:20–24	199, 273, 298
21:22	273
21:24	273
21:25–28	255
21:25–26	273
21:27	273, 291
21:28	274
21:29–30	274
21:31	274
21:32	274
21:33	274
21:34–35	274
21:34	274
21:36	274, 291n16
21:37	274, 285
21:38	274, 294
22:1	275
22:2–6	298
22:2	174n37, 275, 287, 292
22:3–6	247
22:3	60, 85, 148, 247n21, 275, 277, 283, 287, 288
22:4–6	276
22:6	285
22:7	276
22:8–9	276
22:8	276
22:10–12	276
22:11	34, 85, 276
22:13	276, 277
22:14–30	309n7
22:14	84, 232, 247n21
22:15	276, 278
22:16	130, 278, 309n9
22:17	278
22:18–19	278
22:18	130, 278, 309n9
22:19–20	280
22:19	126, 126n5, 278, 279, 309
22:20	278, 279
22:21	279
22:22	135, 279, 287, 291n15
22:23	279, 280
22:24–27	277
22:24	246, 280, 281, 308

Scripture Index   343

22:25	280	22:60	288, 289
22:26	280	22:61	289
22:27	281	22:63	289
22:28–30	111, 263	22:64	289
22:28	283	22:65	289
22:29–30	283	22:66	128, 174n37, 290
22:29	150	22:67–70	292
22:30	85	22:67–68	291
22:31–34	111	22:67	290
22:31–32	289	22:69	128n9, 291, 291n16
22:31	60, 148, 275, 283	22:70	291, 293, 303
22:32	284, 289	22:71	291
22:33	23n23, 284, 288	23:1–2	294
22:34	284, 289	23:1	292, 303
22:35	284	23:3	293, 299
22:36	284	23:4	293, 294, 302
22:37	45n30, 284	23:5	293, 294
22:38	23n23, 285, 287, 308	23:6–7	293
22:39–46	285	23:7–11	125
22:39	274, 285, 287	23:7–8	293
22:40	111, 162, 285	23:9	294
22:41–42	53	23:10	174n37, 294
22:41	286	23:11	289, 294
22:42–45	159n1	23:12	293, 294
22:42	150, 159, 286, 300, 302, 302n18	23:13	245, 292, 294
		23:14–15	294
22:43	286	23:14	302
22:44	286	23:16	294
22:45	286	23:17	295, 295n5
22:46	111, 162, 285, 286	23:18	295
22:47–53	285	23:19	295
22:47–48	85, 285	23:21	295
22:47	247n21, 275, 287	23:22	294, 302
22:48	135, 287, 291n15	23:23	295, 296
22:49–51	284	23:24–25	296
22:49–50	285	23:25	247, 295, 296
22:49	23n23, 287	23:26	296
22:50	287	23:27–28	303
22:51	287	23:27	79, 244, 297
22:52–53	287	23:28	297
22:52	287	23:29	297
22:53	60, 276, 277, 289, 296, 301	23:30	297
22:54–62	285	23:31	297
22:54	288	23:32–33	298
22:55	288	23:33	263
22:56	288	23:34	54, 90, 150, 159, 159n1, 298, 302n18
22:58	288		
22:59	288	23:35	133, 178, 245, 299

Luke (continued)

23:36	289, 299
23:37–38	299
23:39	299
23:40–42	300
23:42	400
23:43	9, 62, 300
23:44–46	60
23:44	300
23:45	301
23:46	54, 150, 159, 159n1, 302
23:47	15, 234n10, 302
23:48	79, 244, 297, 302
23:49	303, 304
23:50–51	303
23:50	302n19
23:51	39
23:52	303
23:53–54	304
23:54–62	284
23:55–56	305
23:55	108, 304, 306
23:56	304
24:1	305
24:2–3	305
24:4	306
24:5	306
24:6–7	306
24:7	45n30, 128, 128n9, 291n15
24:8–9	306
24:10	84, 108, 232, 247n21, 303, 305n1, 306, 307
24:11	306
24:12	289, 306
24:13–33	10
24:13	307
24:14	307
24:15	307
24:16	307
24:17–18	308
24:18	307
24:19–24	308
24:19	248, 307, 308
24:20	245, 308
24:21	308
24:22–24	308
24:24	306n2
24:25–27	248
24:25–26	308
24:26	311
24:27	132, 308
24:28–29	309
24:30	126, 126n5, 207, 309
24:31	309
24:32	309, 310
24:33	307, 309
24:34	289, 306, 310
24:35	307, 310
24:36	310
24:37	310
24:38	310
24:39–40	310
24:41	310
24:42–43	310
24:44–46	248, 311
24:44	45n30, 132
24:47	273, 311
24:48	311
24:49	52, 150, 166, 178, 311
24:50–51	312
24:50	312
24:51	132, 255
24:52–53	312

John

1:45–49	85n6
1:46	19n17
5:14	76n9
6:30	170
6:67	85n7
6:71	86n11
8:33–39	50
9:2	76n9, 191, 202
9:7	191n4
9:11	191n4
10:12–13	214
11:1—12:8	156n30
11:1	256
11:43–44	306
12:1–8	102n18
12:1	256
12:4	86n11
12:7	102n19
18:2	86n11
18:5	86n11

Scripture Index   345

18:10	287n11	3:22–23	133
20:24	85n7	4:1–21	272n8
21:2	85n6	4:1–12	178n6
21:18–19	284	4:1–3	266, 284
		4:4	13, 70
		4:6	48

Acts

		4:10	148n7
1:1–12	312n12	4:13	178
1:1	1, 5	4:17–18	147n7
1:2	85n5, 138n30	4:28	168n20
1:3	311	4:30	168n20
1:4–5	166	4:33	85n5
1:5	52	4:34–35	50n11
1:6–7	161	4:38	9
1:6	128, 308	5:1–10	191n5
1:8	9, 36, 40, 48, 95, 139, 145,	5:15–18	284
	166, 273, 311	5:17–40	272n8
1:9	273	5:28	147n7
1:10	131	5:30–31	312
1:11	138n30, 291	5:32–37	246
1:13	85	5:32	311n11
1:18–19	279	5:36	272n5
1:22	138n30	5:37	272n5
2:1–42	166	5:40	147n7
2:1–13	311n11	6:2	85n5
2:1–4	52n20	6:8—7:60	178n6
2:3	148n7	7:2–53	308
2:10	296n8	7:8	26
2:14–36	308	7:37	133
2:19–20	301n16	7:52	263, 302
2:23–24	128	7:55–56	291, 312
2:23	9	7:56	54n26, 268
2:32–33	312	7:59–60	209
3:32	303	7:60	272n8
2:33	311	8:3	272n8
2:34–36	268, 291	8:4	13
2:37–38	299n13	8:5–25	139
2:37	85n5	8:14–27	311n11
2:38–39	311n11	8:16	148n7
2:41	70	8:17	152n18
3:6	148n7	8:27	240n4
3:12–26	308	9:2	10n15
3:13	302	9:15	40
3:14–15	128, 178	9:22–25	272n8
3:15	303	9:27–28	147n7
3:16	148n7	10	95
3:17–19	178	10:1	240n4
3:17–21	299n13	10:11	54n26

Acts (continued)

10:22	15, 302n19
10:35	3
10:36	146
10:37	67n14
10:38	54
10:39–40	303
10:44–47	311n11
10:45	40
10:48	148n7
11:14	252n9
11:18	40
11:21	168n20
12:1–6	272n8
12:1–5	284
12:1–2	209, 272n8
13:11	168n20
13:13–52	178n6
13:16–41	308
13:6	3
13:17	168n21
13:26–28	299n13
13:26	3
13:36	120n22
13:47	112
15:7	6n9
16:1	152n18
16:10–17	2
16:15	252n9
16:18	148n7
16:31	252n9
17:30	299n13
18:8	252n9
18:12–16	272n8
18:25–26	10n15
19:1–7	311n11
19:9	10n15
19:13–14	167
19:15	148n7
19:23	10n15
20:5–15	2
20:24	6n9
21:1–18	2
21:20	85
21:27—24:22	178n6
21:38	272n5
22:3	85
22:4	10n15, 272n8
22:14	302
23:33—26:32	272n6
24:3	14
24:14	10n15
24:22	10n15
26:20	67n14
26:25	14
27:1—28:16	2
27:34	272n9
28:28	95, 273

Romans

1:1	6n9
12:3	283

1 Corinthians

5:8	176n2
11:30	120n22

Ephesians

5:3	180n8

Philippians

4:3	148n8

Colossians

3:5	180n8
4:11	3
4:14	2, 3

1 Timothy

5:11–14	239

2 Timothy

4:11	2

Philemon

24	2

Hebrews

9:2–7	301
10:26–31	178
10:35–39	178
11:4	174
11:5	312n13
11:22	132
13:12	263

James

1:13–14	162

2 Peter

1:15	132

Revelation

2:7	300
4:4	131
6:8	272n7
6:12–14	272n7
7:9	131
11:7	116n16
13:8	148n8
14:6	6n9
17:8	116n16, 148n8
18:2	169n23
20:1–3	116n16
20:11–15	229
20:12	148n8
21:27	148n8
22:16	29

ANCIENT SOURCES INDEX

Jewish Sources

Apocrypha

Baruch

4:35	169n23

Sirach/Ecclesiasticus

1:1–30	102
3:30	181n14
7:10	172n31
11:19	181
12:4–5	151
14:9	180n8
17:22	181n14
21:5	229n16
24:1–34	102
29:12	172n31, 181
30:24	183
33: 20–24	216
36:17	34
40:3–4	228
40:17	181n14
40:24	181n14
44:16	312n13
48:9	312n13
48:10	17
49:14	312n13

Tobit

1:17	50n11
4:3–4	141
4:7–11	172n31
4:8–11	181n14
4:17	151
6:14–15	141
12:8–9	172n31, 181n14
14:11–13	141

Wisdom of Solomon

2:10–20	128n12
3:1–9	128n12
3:2	132
7:4	34
7:6	132
15:8	181
17:2	171n28

Dead Sea Scrolls

1QM (War Scroll)

XII, 2	148n8
XVII, 5–8	148n9

1QSa (Rule of the Congregation, appendix a to 1QS)

II, 16–21	205n6

4Q174 (Eschatological Midrash)

3 I, 11	21n20

4Q252 (Commentary on Genesis A)

V, 3–4	21n20

4Q285 (Sefer Hamilḥamah)

V, 2–4	21n20

4Q521 (Messianic Apocalypse)

2 II, 5–8	62n5

1QMelch (Melchizedek)

II, 13–14	148n9

Josephus

Against Apion

1.1–5	12n1
1.53–56	13n2

Jewish Antiquities

1.196–197	230n18
4.55–59	190n1
4.60–62	190n1
4.85–87	190n2
4.219	306
5.348	42
7.363–366	15n8
10.50	42
13.297–298	266n13
14.10	26n27
14.370–385	253.11
15.21	205n6
15.391–402	271n4
15.395	262
17.206–249	253n11
17.299–320	253n11, 255
18.16–17	266n13
18.29–30	139n33
18.35	48n4
18.36–38	47n3
18.55–62	48n4
18.85–89	48n4
18.116–119	47
18.118	53n24
20.118–136	139n33
20.197	26n27
20.208–210	295n5
20.215	295n5

Jewish War

1.401	271n4
2.1–38	253n11
2.80–111	253n11
2.164–166	266n13
2.169–174	190n1
2.175–177	190n1
2.232–246	139n33
2.286–287	272n5
5.190–214	271n4
5.450–451	296n6
5.451	129n13
5.534	26n27

The Life

65–66	47n3

Philo of Alexandria

On the Life of Abraham

107–110	230n18
209–211	230n18

On the Embassy to Gaius

299–305	48n4

On the Life of Moses

2.291	139n31

Pseudepigrapha

2 Baruch (Syriac Apocalypse)

13:9–10	160n2

1 Enoch (Ethiopic Apocalypse)

10:4–6	116n16
18:11–16	116n16
20:1–7	18n16
40:1–10	18n16
47:3	148n8
49:1–4	43n26
54:5–6	148n9
54:6	177
108:3	148n8

2 Enoch (Slavonic Apocalypse)

42:5	207n9

3 Enoch (Hebrew Apocalypse)

17:8	145
18:2–3	145

30:2	145	*Bava Qamma*	
		5:6	203
4 Ezra		8:6	89
12:32	21n20		
		Eruvin	
Jubilees		2:1–4	194
2:19–20	160n2	*Hagigah*	
5:6–11	116n16	1:1	43n25
11:15	26n27	1:8	81
Psalms of Solomon		*Ketubbot*	
13:7–12	160n2	4:5	20n18
17–18	21n20	4:12	239
17:37	43n26	5:1	239
18:1–4	160n2	11:1	141, 239
		12:3	239
Sibylline Oracles		*Niddah*	
3:796–807	148n9	4:1	154
Testament of Dan		*Sanhedrin*	
5:10	148n9	2:5	256
Testament of Judah		*Shabbat*	
25:3	148n9	5:1–4	194
		7:2	81
Testament of Levi		15:1–2	194
3:5–8	18n16	18:3	83
7:2	154n24	19:2	83
18:12	148n9	*Shevi'it*	
		8:10	154
Testament of Moses		9:1	172n33
10:1	148n9		
		Sheqalim	
		1:5	154n24

Rabbinic Literature

Mishnah

Tamid
5:1—7:3   16n12

Avot
1:1   72
4:16   207n9

Yadayim
1:1–5   171

Bava Batra
8:1   239
8:4–5   216

Yoma
8:6   83, 153, 202

Ancient Sources Index   351

352 Ancient Sources Index

Babylonian Talmud

Bava Metzi'a
96a   222

Bava Qamma
113b   222

Berakhot
46b   205n6

Megillah
3b   153, 202

Qiddushin
22b   51
41b–42a   222

Sanhedrin
57a   154n24

Shabbat
128b   203

Jerusalem Talmud

Avodah Zarah
5:4   154n24

EARLY CHRISTIAN SOURCES

Clement of Alexandria

Miscellanies
5.12   2n2

Eusebius

Ecclesiastical History
3.4.6   2n2
3.39   13n2

Irenaeus

Against Heresies
3.1.1   2n2

3.14.1   2n2

Jerome

De viris illustribus
7.1   2n2

Tertullian

Against Marcion
4.2.2   2n2
4.2.5   2n2
4.5.3   2n2

OTHER GRECO-ROMAN SOURCES

Orientis Graeci Inscriptiones Selectae

458   37n15
598   234n11

Anti-Marcionite Prologues 2n3

Dio Chrysostom

Orations
4.83–96   180n8
17:1–11   180n8
67:7   180n8

Diodorus Siculus

1.3   12n1

Diogenes Laertius

10.14   42n21

Euripides

Madness of Hercules
339–347   160n3

Ancient Sources Index

Herodotus
Histories

1.114–116	42n21

Homer
Iliad

11.544	160n3

Odyssey

24.351	160n3

Ovid
Fasti

1.215–216	202n3

Philostratus
Vita Apollonii

1.7	42n21
4.45	97n14

Pliny the Elder
Natural History

5.15.70	271n4

Plutarch
Alexander

4.4–5.5	42n21

Polybius

2.37	12n1
13.2.2	202n3

Seneca
Epistulae morales

104.4–5	181

Ad Marciam de consolatione

20.3	129n13

Stobaeus
Florilegium

3.10.45	202n3
4.33.31	202n3

Tacitus
Annales

6.29	303
15.44	48n4

Historiae

5.8	271n4

AUTHOR INDEX

Adams, D. H., 78n13
Alexander, L. C., 12n1, 156n29

Bailey, K. E., 105n28, 153n21, 155n26, 165n13, 179n7, 215n7, 243n13
Barr, J., 150n15
Barrett, C. K., 234n11
Bates, M. W., 228n14
Bauckham, R., 13n2, 85n6, 153n21
Bell, R. H., 167n16
Billings, B. S., 42n21
Bird, M. F., 198n20
Bock, D. L., 76n10, 128n8, 172n32
Bockmuehl, M., 142n40
Bond, H. K., 15n7
Borgman, P., 134n23
Braun, W., 202n3, 208n12
Brown, R. E., 20n18, 32n6, 56n29

Carroll, J. T., 5n7, 6n10, 84n4, 95n9, 118n19, 121n23, 129n13, 140n34, 142n37, 177n3, 196n15, 199n22
Chen, D. G., 149n13, 150n16, 160nn3-5, 220n16
Collins, J. J., 51n16, 128n8, 248n24
Corbin-Reuschling, W., 50n12
Cosgrove, C. H., 103n21, 104nn23-24
Cotter, W. J., 239n3, 240n6, 241n8

de Boer, E. A., 108n3
Denaux, A., 257n17
deSilva, D. A., 223n9
Dinkler, M. B., 180n9
Dunn, J. D. G., 128n8

Easter, M. C., 302n20
Eastman, S., 218n13
Edwards, J. R., 3n4, 4n5, 5n6, 51n13
Emmrich, M., 168n19, 169n24

Evans, C. A., 37n15, 95n10, 153n22, 265n11, 303n22

Ferguson, E., 30n3, 42n22, 137n28, 290n12
Fiensy, D. A., 171n27
Fitzmyer, J. A., 17n13, 101n16, 142n37
Ford, J. M., 14n6
Foster, R. A., 110n6

Gagnon, R. A. J., 93n4, 94n7, 95n8
García Serrano, A., 41nn18-19
Garland, D. E., 33n7, 47n2, 60n3, 65n8, 66n11, 68n1, 70n4, 75n8, 92n1, 103n20, 118n18, 135n25, 172n29, 176n2, 180n10, 207n8, 211n16, 222n2, 223n6, 232n2, 235nn13-14, 249n26, 261n1, 270n1, 277n3, 290n13, 298n10, 304n23
Garrett, S. R., 132n19, 171n26
Gathercole, S., 29n30
Goodrich, J. K., 223n7
Gourgues, M., 154n23
Grant, M., 31n4, 47n2
Green, J. B., 6n10, 14n4, 31n5, 34n9, 70n4, 93n5, 95n10, 101n15, 103n20, 104n23, 117n17, 118n19, 121n23, 124n3, 126n6, 129n13, 130n15, 132n18, 134n24, 138n29, 139n33, 140n34, 142n38, 147n5, 168n18, 169n23, 174nn38-39, 177n3, 178n5, 180n10, 187n18, 189n21, 193n10, 199n21, 202n2, 207n11, 211n16, 231n1, 233n9, 236n16, 250n3, 253n13, 256n15, 259n19, 261n2, 262n3, 264nn9-10, 269n17, 270n1, 277n4, 283n6, 285n8, 298n12, 307n6

Hagner, D. A., 3n4
Hamm, D., 16n12, 233n7, 234n10, 242n10
Hanson, K. C., 20n18
Harrill, J. A., 93n3
Harris, S., 35nn10–11
Hartsock, C., 202nn3–4
Hays, J. D., 199n23
Heil, J. P., 296n7
Hengel, M., 129n13, 296n6
Horst, P. W. van der, 229n17
Hultgren, A. J., 152n17, 153n21, 155n25, 161n6, 180n11, 196n16, 207n10, 210n15, 214n4, 217n9, 232n6, 240n5, 253n12

Jeffers, J. J., 93n3, 137n28

Kartveit, M., 139n32
Keener, C. S., 43n24, 49n7, 51n14, 172n30, 174n38
Kilgallen, J. J., 103n22, 106n29
Kim, K., 222n3
Kinman, B., 189n22, 257n16
Klassen-Wiebe, S., 52n20
Knowles, M. P., 162nn7–8
Koester, H., 2n3
Kuhn, K. A., 30n2

Landry, D. T., 21n21, 224n11
Longenecker, B. W., 64n7
Lygre, J. G., 222n4

Maloney, F. J., 309n9
Mappes, D. A., 242n9
Marshall, I. H., 4n5, 5n6, 34n9, 51n14, 61n4, 82n3, 84n4, 86n10, 92n1, 103n21, 104n25, 108n2, 114n11, 118n19, 123n2, 132n18, 142n37, 146n4, 153n21, 167n17, 169n23, 173n35, 188n19, 191nn3–4, 195n14, 199n22, 205n7, 207n10, 231n1, 232n4, 235n14, 255n14, 256n15, 257n18, 259n20, 262n3, 265n12, 269n17, 270n1, 277n2, 285n8, 300n14, 301n15, 301n17, 307n3, 307n5
Martin, T. W., 134n22

Mason, S., 72n5
May, B., 224n11
McCane, B. R., 141n36
McComiskey, D. S., 111n8
Merkle, B. L., 237n17
Miller, D. M., 18n15, 131n17, 133n21
Moles, J., 12n1

Neale, D. A., 101n16, 213n1
Nelson, P. K., 283n5
Neyrey, J. H., 205n5
Nolland, J., 26n26, 51n14, 61n4, 82n1, 88n13, 101n16, 103n21, 104n25, 114n11, 123n2, 128n10, 132n18, 134n24, 139n33, 140n34, 142n39, 145n1, 152n19, 164n10, 166nn14–15, 167n17, 173n35, 174n39, 176n1, 177n3, 178n5, 188n19, 199n21, 210n15, 214n5, 223n8, 232n6, 235n12, 235n14, 262n4, 267n15, 269n17, 277n4, 287n10, 290n13, 295nn4–5, 297n9, 301n15, 301n17, 304n23, 307n4, 309n8

Parsons, M. C., 251n6
Perkins, L., 168n19
Phillips, T. E., 102n17
Porter, S. E., 37n15
Puig i Tàrrech, A., 131n16

Reid, B. E., 196n18
Rist, J. M., 32n6

Scott, J. W., 232n3, 232n5
Sellew, P., 180n9
Shiell, W. D., 110n6
Skarsaune, O., 86n9
Skinner, M. L., 290n14, 293n2, 294n3
Snodgrass, K. R., 96n11, 109n4, 110n5, 153n21, 154n24, 155n26, 164nn11–12, 180n11, 192n7, 196n17, 207n10, 217n11, 221n1, 223n8, 244n15, 255n14, 269n16
Soards, M. L., 39n17
Sousa, M. E., 148n11, 150n14
Spencer, F. S., 156n28, 240n4
Strahan, J. M., 156n27

Strauss, M. L., 29n31
Strelan, R., 13n3

Thurston, B., 41n18, 41n20
Topel, J., 89n14
Twelftree, G. H., 115n15, 290n12

Udoh, F. E., 222n3

Verbrugge, V. D., 36n13

Waetjen, J. C., 164n11
Walker, P., 60n3, 113n9, 250n2
Webb, R. L., 53n23
Williamson, H. G. M., 139n32
Witherington III, B., 108n1